THE WEST

A TREASURY OF
ART AND LITERATURE

THE WEST

A TREASURY OF
ART AND LITERATURE

Edited by T.H. Watkins
and Joan Watkins

BEAUX
ARTS
EDITIONS

"The Birth of Dawn" (Pawnee). Reprinted with the permission of The Ohio University Press/Swallow Press, Athens.

Creation Myth (Lakota Sioux). From *The Portable North American Indian Reader* edited by Frederick W. Turner III. Copyright © 1973, 1974 by The Viking Press, Inc. Used by permission of Viking Penguin, a division of Penguin Books USA Inc.

"Rain Song" (Sia). From *American Indian Prose and Poetry,* by Margot Astrov. Copyright © 1946 by Margot Astrov. Copyright renewed. Reprinted by permission of HarperCollins Publishers, Inc.

"A Prayer of the Night Chant" (Navajo). From *American Indian Prose and Poetry,* by Margot Astrov. Copyright © 1946 by Margot Astrov. Copyright renewed. Reprinted by permission of HarperCollins Publishers, Inc.

Barry Lopez. "The Stone Horse." Reprinted by permission of Sterling Lord Literistic, Inc. Copyright © 1988.

Frederic Remington. From "A Sergeant of the Orphan Troop." *Harper's Monthly Magazine,* August, 1897.

Elizabeth B. Custer. From *Following the Guidon.* Copyright © 1966 by the University of Oklahoma Press.

Wooden Leg. "Young Men, Go Out and Fight Them," from *Wooden Leg: A Warrior Who Fought Custer,* interpreted by Thomas B. Marquis. Lincoln: University of Nebraska Press, 1962.

John G. Neihardt. From *A Cycle of the West.* Copyright 1943, 1946, 1953, John G. Neihardt. Published by the University of Nebraska Press, Lincoln and London.

Erskine Wood. "An Officer's Son with Chief Joseph." Reprinted by permission of *American Heritage* magazine, a division of Forbes, Inc., 1976.

John (Fire) Lame Deer. From *Lame Deer: Seeker of Visions.* Copyright © 1972 by John (Fire) Lame Deer and Richard Erdoes. Reprinted by permission of Simon & Schuster, Inc.

N. Scott Momaday. From "An American Land Ethic." Reprinted with permission of Sierra Club Books.

James Welch. "Thanksgiving at Snake Butte." Copyright © James Welch.

Leslie Marmon Silko. From *Almanac of the Dead.* Copyright © 1991 by Leslie Marmon Silko. Reprinted by permission of Simon & Schuster, Inc.

Paul Horgan. "The River of Palms," from *Book Two: The Spanish Rio Grande,* from *Great River,* by Paul Horgan. Copyright © 1964; © renewed 1982 by Paul Horgan. Reprinted by permission of Farrar, Straus & Giroux, Inc.

Willa Cather. From *Death Comes for the Archbishop,* by Willa Cather. Copyright 1927 by Willa Cather; © renewed 1955 by the Executors of the Estate of Willa Cather. Reprinted by permission of Alfred A. Knopf, Inc.

Harvey Fergusson. From *Followers of the Sun.* Copyright © 1927 by Alfred A. Knopf, Inc.; © renewed 1955 by Harvey Fergusson. By permission of William Morrow & Company, Inc.

Rita Magdaleno. "Hermanita." © Rita Maria Magdaleno.

Meriwether Lewis and William Clark. From *The Journals of Lewis and Clark,* published by the Penguin Group.

Francis Parkman. From *The Oregon Trail,* published by the Penguin Group.

Bernard DeVoto. From *Across the Wide Missouri,* by Bernard DeVoto. Copyright © 1947 by Houghton Mifflin Company; © renewed 1975 by Avis DeVoto and Joseph R. Porter. Reprinted by permission of Houghton Mifflin Company. All rights reserved.

A.B. Guthrie, Jr. From *The Way West,* by A.B. Guthrie, Jr. Copyright 1949; © renewed 1976 by A.B. Guthrie, Jr. Reprinted by permission of Houghton Mifflin Company. All rights reserved.

Horace L. Greeley. From *An Overland Journey,* by Horace Greeley, edited with notes by Charles T. Duncan. Copyright © 1963 by Alfred Knopf, Inc. Reprinted by permission of Alfred A. Knopf, Inc.

Mrs. Frank Leslie. "Thirty-three Hundred Miles in a Pullman Hotel Car." Edited by Richard Reinhardt.

Robert Louis Stevenson. From *Across the Plains.* Copyright 1911 by Charles Scribner's Sons.

Harry French. From "The Rowdy Brakeman." Adapted by Richard Reinhardt from Chauncey Del French's *Railroadman* (1938). Copyright 1970 by Richard Reinhardt.

Vicente Pérez Rosales. From *We Were '49ers!* Copyright © 1976 by Edwin A. Beilharz and Carlos U. López.

William Swain. From *The World Rushed In.* Copyright © 1981 by J.S. Holiday. Reprinted by permission of Simon & Schuster, Inc.

Anonymous. "Culture on Bitter Creek," from *The Mining Frontier: Contemporary Accounts from the American West in the Nineteenth Century,* edited by Marvin Lewis. Copyright © 1967 by the University of Oklahoma Press.

Gene Fowler. From *Timber Line,* by Gene Fowler. Copyright 1933 by Gene Fowler; © renewed 1960 by A. Fowler. Reprinted by permission of the heirs of Gene Fowler.

John Taylor Waldorf. From *A Kid on the Comstock.* Used by permission of the Friends of the Bancroft Library.

Isabella L. Bird. From *A Lady's Life in the Rocky Mountains,* by Isabella L. Bird. New edition copyright © 1960 by the University of Oklahoma Press.

Frank A. Crampton. From *Deep Enough: A Working Stiff in the Western Mine Camps,* by Frank A. Crampton. New edition copyright © 1982 by the University of Oklahoma Press.

Will James. From *Lone Cowboy: My Life Story.* Reproduction permission granted by The Will James Art Company, 2237 Rosewyn Lane, Billings, MT 59102.

"The High Loping Cowboy." © Copyright 1970, American West Publishing Company.

"Boomer Johnson," from *Songs of the Lost Frontier,* by Henry Herbert Knibbs. Copyright 1930 by Henry Herbert Knibbs; © renewed 1958 by Ida Julia Knibbs. Reprinted by permission of Houghton Mifflin Company All rights reserved.

"The Wrangler Kid." Copyright © 1948 by Stella M. Hendren.

"Git Along Little Dogies." © Copyright 1970, American West Publishing Company.

J. Frank Dobie. Reprinted from *Coronado's Children: Tales of Lost Mines and Buried Treasures of the Southwest,* by J. Frank Dobie. Copyright © 1930 by the Southwest Press; © 1958 by J. Frank Dobie; © 1978 by the University of Texas Press. By permission of the University of Texas Press.

Robert M. Utley. Reprinted from *Billy the Kid: A Short and Violent Life,* by Robert M. Utley. By permission of the University of Nebraska Press. Copyright © 1989 by the University of Nebraska Press.

Zane Grey. From *Riders of the Purple Sage,* by Zane Grey. Published by the Penguin Group.

Larry McMurtry. From *Lonesome Dove.* © 1985 by Larry McMurtry. Reprinted with the permission of Wylie, Aitken & Stone, Inc.

Don Russell. "Cody, Kings, and Coronets," from Don W. Russell, *The Wild West: A History of the Wild West Shows,* (Fort Worth: Amon Carter Museum of Western Art, 1970); extract first printed in *The American West* 7 (July, 1970), pp. 4–10, 62.

Emma Mitchell New. "Years Came Along One After the Other..." from *Pioneer Women: Voices from the Kansas Frontier,* by Joanna L. Stratton. Copyright © 1981 by Joanna L. Stratton.

Mari Sandoz. From *Old Jules.* Copyright © 1935, 1963. Reprinted by permission of McIntosh and Otis, Inc.

Milton Shatraw. From *Thrashin' Time.* © Copyright 1970, American West Publishing Company.

Helen Ellsberg. "Meanie: The Life and Good Times of A Roman-Nosed Mare." © Copyright 1969, American West Publishing Company.

Wallace Stegner. From *Wolf Willow,* by Wallace Stegner. Copyright © 1955, 1957, 1958, 1959, 1962 by Wallace Stegner. Reprinted by permission of Brandt & Brandt Literary Agents, Inc.

Ivan Doig. Excerpt from *This House of Sky, Landscapes of a Western Mind.* Copyright © 1978 by Ivan Doig. Reprinted by permission of Harcourt Brace & Company.

Frank Waters. From *The Colorado.* Copyright © Frank Waters.

Stanley Vestal. From *Short Grass Country.* Copyright © Stanley Vestal.

Josephine Johnson. From *Now in November.* Published by The Feminist Press at the City University of New York. Copyright © 1934, 1962 by Josephine Johnson. All rights reserved.

Woody Guthrie. "The Telegram that Never Came," from *Bound for Glory,* by Woody Guthrie. Copyright 1943 by E. P. Dutton; © renewed 1971 by Marjorie M. Guthrie. Used by permission of Dutton Signet, a division of Penguin Books USA Inc.

Woody Guthrie. "Pastures of Plenty." Words and music by Woody Guthrie. TRO–Copyright © 1960 (renewed), 1963 (renewed) by Ludlow Music, Inc., New York, NY Used by permission.

John Steinbeck. "The Leader of the People," from *The Long Valley,* by John Steinbeck. Copyright 1938; © renewed 1966 by John Steinbeck. Used by permission of Viking Penguin, a division of Penguin Books USA, Inc.

N.P. Langford. From "The Wonders of the Yellowstone." *Scribner's Monthly,* May, 1871.

Clarence E. Dutton. From *Tertiary History of the Grand Canyon District.* Geological Survey, 1882, Government Printing Office.

John Muir. From "Explorations in the Great Tuolumne Cañon." Reprinted with permission of Sierra Club Books.

Mary Austin. From *The Land of Little Rain,* by Mary Austin. Albuquerque: University of New Mexico Press, 1974.

Edward Abbey. From *Desert Solitaire.* Reprinted by permission of Don Congdon Associates, Inc. Copyright © 1968 by Edward Abbey.

Joseph Wood Krutch. From *The Desert Year.* Reprinted with permission of The Trustees of Columbia University in the City of New York. All rights reserved.

Ann Zwinger. "Of Red-tailed Hawks and Black-tailed Gnatcatchers," from *The Mysterious Lands,* by Ann Haymond Zwinger. Copyright © 1989 by Ann Haymond Zwinger. Used by permission of Dutton Signet, a division of Penguin Books USA Inc.

From *A Sand County Almanac: And Sketches Here and There* by Aldo Leopold. Copyright 1949, 1977 by Oxford University Press, Inc. Reprinted by permission of Oxford University Press, Inc. and the Aldo Leopold Shack Foundation.

T.H. Watkins. "Little Deaths." Reprinted with permission of Sierra Club Books.

Wallace Stegner. From *The Sound of Mountain Water,* by Wallace Stegner. Copyright © 1969 by Wallace Stegner. Used by permission of Doubleday, a division of Bantam Doubleday Dell Publishing Group, Inc.

Preamble to the Wilderness Act, September 3, 1964.

Richard Shelton. From *Going Back to Bisbee,* by Richard Shelton. The University of Arizona Press. Copyright © 1992.

John Daniel. From *The Trail Home.* Copyright © 1992 by John Daniel. Reprinted by permission of Pantheon Books, a division of Random House, Inc.

Pam Houston. Reprinted from *Cowboys are My Weakness,* by Pam Houston with the permission of W.W. Norton & Company, Inc. Copyright © 1992 by Pam Houston.

Gretel Ehrlich. "Rules of the Game: Rodeo," from *The Solace of Open Spaces,* by Gretel Ehrlich. Copyright © 1985 by Gretel Ehrlich. Used by permission of Viking Penguin, a division of Penguin Books USA Inc.

Ruth Rudner. From *Greetings from Wisdom, Montana,* by Ruth Rudner. Fulcrum Publishing, Inc., 350 Indiana St., #350, Golden, CO 80401 (303) 277-1623.

Charles Bowden. From *Blue Desert,* by Charles Bowden. The University of Arizona Press. Copyright © 1986.

Gary Snyder. "Hay for the Horses," from *Riprap and Cold Mountain Poems,* by Gary Snyder. Copyright © 1965 by Gary Snyder. Reprinted by permission of North Point Press, a division of Farrar, Straus & Giroux, Inc.

William Stafford. "Witness." Reprinted by permission of the Estate of William Stafford.

Wallace Stegner. From *The American West as Living Space.* Copyright © 1987 by The University of Michigan Press.

CONTENTS

INTRODUCTION

The Native Home of Hope

This book might legitimately be called the documentary history of a region that poet Archibald MacLeish once called "a country in the mind." The items we have chosen to include, then, are designed to reveal the essence of perhaps the oldest and most enduring visionary place in our national history. This is a daunting task, and in an attempt to facilitate understanding, we have opted for simplicity as the framework on which to hang our sublimely eclectic gathering of paintings, drawings, photographs, stories, essays, memoirs, songs, and poems. The selections are organized and presented, for the most part, in a roughly chronological and thematic manner, beginning with a section devoted to the West's first residents, the Native Americans, then moving more or less predictably through the various periods of exploration, conquest, settlement, and development up to our own times. It is our hope that anyone who might be moved to sit down and go through the book from start to finish will get a pretty firm grasp of the major movements and events in the history of the West.

The simple, direct organization of the book belies the material it presents. Americans (if one includes the first Americans, and one does) have been picturing the West with words and graphic art for thousands of years—and even in the less than two hundred years of its existence as an American political entity, the West has been blessed (or cursed) by the production of more art and literature than possibly any single region of the country. From this stunning abundance, we have selected not only such "standard" items as excerpts from the work of Elizabeth B. Custer, say, or that of Andy Adams or Mary Austin, however necessary and enjoyable they are, but such diverse and lesser known writers as railroad man Harry French, memoirist Milton Shatraw, Josephine Johnson, or historian Don Russell, each of whom brings a distinctly individual and sometimes idiosyncratic flavor to the discussion. Much the same could be said for the illustrations, from the crude symbolic evocations of prehistoric times to the sophisticated and sometimes jarring power of modern American Indian paintings. The scope and calculated diversity of this documentation illustrates as nothing less varied could, I think, the extraordinary power this place has always had to move us, stir our imaginations, people our story with heroes and villains, reveal both the best and the worst that is in us as a people, and invest our future with hope.

Which is not to say that we have always—or even very frequently—understood it and what it has meant to us. Many of the selections here demonstrate this, too, for all their value as art, literature, or just good journalism. For example, Frederic Remington handsomely evoked the look and spirit of man-and-horse in motion, as well as the broad sweep of the land in which the cowhand labored, but he was not himself a cowboy and we would not look to him to discover the reality of the cowhand's life or why we should honor it; for that, the art of Will James, who spent much of his life looking at the back end of a cow, is a more reliable source.

For the most part, we Americans have not much honored the prophets of truth in the West, of which there were a few even in the age of Buffalo Bill. John Wesley Powell, for one, not only led the first exploring expedition through the Grand Canyon in 1869, thereby amplifying the nation's perception of the West as adventure; he also went on to write one of the most important documents in the history of government publications: *Report on the Lands of the Arid Region of the United States,* a scientific cautionary tale written in 1878 that warned the federal government and western settlers alike that there simply was not enough water in the Great West to nourish all the dreams of limitless settlement that it had inspired. Truth was inconvenient to the dreams of boomers, however; the government refused to listen and the settlement of the West went right along in its exploitive, helter-skelter tradition. In his own time, and in most of ours, it was not the warning that was remembered and celebrated, but the adventure of his Grand Canyon expedition.

Powell's exercise in reality may have gone all but unnoticed, but a happier fate was enjoyed by a young historian named Frederick Jackson Turner. It is symbolically convenient that in Chicago on the evening of July 17, 1893, just a few hours after the last performance of the day of "Buffalo Bill's Wild West" and "Congress of Rough Riders of the World" in the same city, Turner got up to speak before something called the World's Congress of Historians and Historical Students. "Buffalo Bill's Wild West," a huge circus-like entertainment which had been touring the nation and the world for ten years by then, represented just about every distortion and misconception of the nature of the West common to the day (or our own day, for that matter)—a lively and irresistible melange of myth, theatrics, and exaggeration, emphasizing blazing six-guns, outlaws, dashing cavalry, brave army scouts (starring, of course, the white-goateed William F. Cody—Buffalo Bill—himself), howling Indians, and horsemanship. Turner, on the other hand, gave that same West its first serious discussion as an integral part of the American story—a part, in fact, Turner said, that contributed mightily to the very nature of what it meant to be an American.

His Chicago talk that evening was called "The Significance of the Frontier in American History," and by the turn of the century a whole generation of historians had adopted his thesis. The various waves of frontier conquest and settlement by traders, farmers, and cattlemen, Turner declared, represented a kind of social evolution. "The result is," he said, "that to the frontier the American intellect owes its striking characteristics. That coarseness and strength combined with acuteness and inquisitiveness; that practical, inventive turn of mind, quick to find expedients; that masterful grasp of material things, lacking material things, lacking in the artistic but powerful to effect great ends; that restless, nervous energy." This "frontier individualism," he insisted, "from the beginning has promoted democracy."

Much of Turner's thesis did not stand the the test of time. As later historians have demonstrated, the American character was shaped a good deal less by the challenge of establishing economic and political institutions in the middle of a howling wilderness than by the intellectual and political baggage the frontiersmen and women brought with them (at least, the Anglo-Saxons among them) across the Atlantic—the inheritance of hundreds of years of European experience as already tested and refined on the earlier frontiers of New England and the mid-Atlantic colonies.

There are numerous other points at which modern historiography has successfully punctured Turner's thesis. Still, however wrong Turner may have been in many of his assumptions, his importance is nevertheless immense. When he stood up before that group of historians in Chicago in 1893, it was the first time that the frontier—for which we may conveniently read, the West—began to be taken seriously. It had acquired dignity and meaning. It was now not just the province of adventurers or a section of landscape over which one had to pass in order to get to someplace better. It was a *frontier,* a place of honor and importance, where the very character of Crevecoeur's "this new man, this American," was established. The dream of possibility continued to fire the imaginations of entire armies of western boomers, who discerned in the Great West places in which Turner's thesis of succession from primitivism to civilization might still be acted out. Indeed, the West, with all its space and richness of opportunity, they believed, was destined to be the greatest cauldron of progress and democracy in history.

Such a dream . . . a dream that was largely meaningless even as it was articulated. Both the readings and the illustrations in this book reveal that the story of the western experience was—and remains—a complex and often contradictory narrative. It is punctuated by moments of high endeavor, like the incomparable journey of Lewis and Clark, and lifelong epochs of numb endurance, like Emma Mitchell New's somber, moving account of life on the Kansas frontier. It is sullied by an ugly bigotry, as in the treatment accorded the Mexican-American peoples of the Southwest, marked by a sometimes startling tolerance, as among black and white cowhands who judged one another as much by the amount of gumption possessed by any given individual as by the color of his skin. It is measured by cooperation for the common good, as among the Mormons of Utah encountered by Richard Burton, and by the kind of rank individualism practiced by the thugs described in Larry McMurtry's *Lonesome Dove.* It is seen as possessed of a terrible rural loneliness in Willa Cather's *O Pioneers!* and of a dangerous, crowded, industrial carelessness in Frank Crampton's *Deep Enough.* It is relieved by high good humor, as in Gene Fowler's account of the mule he called the Senator, and cloaked in nearly unbearable melancholy, as in C.C. Goodwin's bleak elegy, "The Prospector." It is suffused in an adventurous glow or dimmed by misery, bubbles with stories of uncommon bravery and craven cowardice, violence and serenity, hilarity and fury, selflessness and greed. And throughout the whole wide panorama this book gives you of Indians, explorers, conquerors, mountain men, cowboys, prospectors, railroad men, settlers, outlaws, and lawmen, there is everywhere a sense of lives lived hugely, actions and individuals alike enlarged to epic proportions by the dimensions of the enormous, diverse, and beautiful landscape in which they appear.

Little wonder the story has for so long and in so many ways been the province of romance. This land of stories great and small retains its fascination for us, and this book is enriched by those stories and by the illustrations that match them. But there are other selections here, those that speak of limits and consequences and the need to respect a world not of our own making. These are included because it is important that we not misunderstand the history of this place, or let romance be its final interpretation. To do so is to deny its history, diminish its importance, and even subvert it as a legitimate place of hope.

Consider, for example, what this exercise in democracy-building meant to the Native Americans. The American West was a region already generously peopled when the first Spanish conquistadors wandered north from Mexico in the middle of the sixteenth century and the first English settlers arrived on Chesapeake Bay in the beginning years of the seventeenth century. Recent estimates put the number of Native American people in what would become the United States at anywhere from five to ten million, and fully half this number must have resided in the land that stretched west from the Mississippi River. The West, then, was not a great vacancy waiting to be filled by civilization's blessings; it was, rather, a montage made up of territorial possessions that may have lacked the formality of European institutions but were no less valid in the minds and hearts of those who held them.

These people did not know that the West was lost and in need of "discovery." Some of their ancestors had come here, after all, as long as 25,000 years ago across the Bering Land Bridge, moving south into the midcontinent of America, spreading, multiplying, splitting into language groups and extended families, bands, tribes, societies, establishing trade routes and currency exchange, complex systems of religion, government, and community, engaging in wars of expansion and trade dominance, building technologically sophisticated irrigation systems and great cities made of earth. And, through most of these long centuries, listening to what the land and its wild creatures had to tell them about the proper way of living.

That was what they might have been able to tell their conquerors, if their conquerors had stopped to listen. They did not stop, and the frequently grisly details of the bloody conflict that accompanied the march of European and later American civilization across and through the hundreds of individual Native American societies comprise one of the saddest tales in human history. The tale is sad not only because the conflict was so brutal, so one-sided (most of the time, anyway), and so utterly destructive to the resident cultures, but because it helped to define just how far we had failed the best that was in us as a civilization.

Similarly, in encouraging and promoting an economy almost entirely dependent on resource exploitation—mining, logging, grazing, and agribusiness—financed and controlled by institutions on both coasts, we were not creating a proud, self-sufficient regional civilization, but establishing an enormous colony packed by industrialized urban enclaves, whose land, economy, and society would be largely controlled by the perceived needs of people and institutions in San Francisco, Chicago, New York, and elsewhere—not excluding Edinburgh, London, and Paris.

Bernard DeVoto called the West the Plundered Province as late as the mid-1930s, and while his portrait was somewhat exaggerated for effect, it still cut close to the truth of the matter, and up to very recent times it still would resonate with a powerful measure of uncomfortable truth. But if the Turnerian dream of human civic and social progress is less than sublimely validated by the history of the West, does it mean that the West is doomed forever to be a place where such dreams go to die? I don't think so, and I don't think so because there has been a new kind of dream growing in the West over the past several years, a vision given weight and definition by the selections we have chosen for the final two sections of this book—"Scenes of Wonder and Curiosity" and "Living in the New West." The new dream has in many respects been brought to the West by a stream of in-migrants over the past several years. Many of these are generally young, well-educated, and highly skilled people who moved West during the boom years of the 1970s and early 1980s in search of jobs. Unlike most of the transients who have marked time in the West in the past, many of these new people stuck even when the jobs themselves went away or changed, stuck because they found they liked living there. Other newcomers intended to stick all along, coming in search not merely of jobs, but of a quality of life they felt was missing in the urban enclaves of the eastern and western thirds of the nation—quiet, safety, stability, friendliness, a healthy social and physical environment in which to bring up children and plan for a sustainable future. Together with the old-time stickers who also have seen in the West something more than a place to satisfy brief dreams of wealth, these new westerners are helping to change the West in ways we are only now learning how to measure.

It is people like these who have brought new life and ferment to college towns like Missoula and Bozeman, Montana; Tucson and Tempe, Arizona; Boulder, Colorado; Logan, Utah; Albuquerque, New Mexico—enriching the cultural content of the region and supporting the development of a wide variety of new, technologically sophisticated opportunities that have nothing to do with extraction and everything to do with education and communication. It is people like these who are helping to support a whole new generation of western American writers who have declared their independence from the old school. "Serious writers about the West," Wallace Stegner once wrote, "have often had to celebrate the scenery for the lack of the social complexities out of which most fiction is made. Geography, at least, is one matter in which a Westerner can excel and in which he takes pride. History is another." Modern western writers of fiction might argue that complexity is human and therefore discoverable in any community, from the hogans of a Navajo village to the boarded-up storefronts of a western mining town gone bust. And anyone familiar with novels like *The Big Rock Candy Mountain* or *Recapitulation* or any number of his short stories knows that Stegner himself had little trouble finding strands of intricacy in the western experience out of which to weave his own fiction.

Like Stegner, dozens of western writers of both fiction and nonfiction have long since abandoned the stereotypes of romance, and in the hands of an artist like Larry McMurtry, even the protocols of the old "thud-and-blunder" school of western fiction can be raised to epic dimensions that shoot-'em-up writers like Zane Grey could not have imagined. Many others, like John Daniel or Richard Shelton, are coming at the West from the inside as well as the outside now, giving us not merely a sense of what it is as a place but of what it means to them and others who have chosen to call it home.

As well, a population of new westerners are helping to guide the West into the beginnings of a period of economic transition that is as potentially revolutionary as anything it has ever known in the past—from a boom-and-bust society to one of sustainable economies.

Not a little of this transformation has been the result of a rise in environmental consciousness in the West among the same kinds of people who are helping to change so much else in the region, people working from the grassroots up to satisfy the growing hunger for a more viable future.

Do not mistake me. The old doctrines that see the land and its resources as commodities to be used, and if necessary, used up still dominate land use in the West. Nevertheless, I am persuaded that their power is waning, and if this book of art and literature does nothing more, I will be satisfied if it provides support for yet one more vision. This one holds that a new generation of stewards is coming, one which recognizes that without a healthy environment there is no healthy economy. In this new vision the old dreams will be replaced by something new, perhaps something wise, something that will vindicate the faith that the character of the land still can shape the character of those who came to take it from the wind and that the West today will remain, as Wallace Stegner has described it at its best, "the native home of hope."

—T. H. Watkins
Washington, D.C.

FIRST PEOPLES

Songs and Ritual Chants

For decades, there were so many white scholars at work among Native American peoples that the typical Navajo family was said to consist of one man, one woman, three children, and an anthropologist. The material these irritatingly ubiquitous investigators recorded included chants, songs, and myths that combined ritual with language in some of the most moving poetry and prose any culture ever produced. Here is a sampling.

"The Birth of Dawn" (Pawnee)

Earth our Mother, breathe forth life
all night sleeping
now awakening
in the east
now see the dawn

Earth our Mother, breathe and waken
leaves are stirring
all things moving
new day coming
life renewing

Eagle soaring, see the morning
see the new mysterious morning
something marvelous and sacred
though it happens every day
Dawn the child of God and Darkness

Creation Myth (Luther Standing Bear, Lakota Sioux)

Our legends tell us that it was hundreds and perhaps thousands of years ago since the first man sprang from the soil in the midst of the great plains. . . . In time the rays of the sun hardened the face of the earth and strengthened the man and he bounded and leaped about, a free and joyous creature. From this man sprang the Lakota nation. . . . We are of the soil and the soil is of us.

"Rain Song" (Sia)

White floating clouds
Clouds like the plains
Come and water the earth.
Sun, embrace the earth
That she may be fruitful.
Moon, lion of the north,
Bear of the west,
Badger of the south,
Wolf of the east,
Eagle of the heavens, shrew of the earth,
Elder war hero,
Warriors of the six mountains of the world,
Intercede with the cloud people for us,
That they may water the earth.

"A Prayer of the Night Chant" (Navajo)

House made of Dawn.
House made of evening light.
House made of the dark cloud.
House made of male rain.
House made of dark mist.
House made of female rain. . . .
May it be beautiful before me.
May it be beautiful behind me.
May it be beautiful below me.
May it be beautiful above me.
May it be beautiful all around me.

In beauty it is finished.

BARRY LOPEZ
"The Stone Horse"

Many people have seen the prehistoric and historic Indian petroglyphs (images chipped into raw rock) and pictographs (rock paintings) scattered throughout the West from the coast of Washington to the deserts of New Mexico. Fewer have seen intaglios, enormous images that evoke a special mystery. Award-winning writer Barry Lopez (Men and Wolves *and* Arctic Dreams) *discovered this one in Southern California.*

I

The deserts of southern California, the high, relatively cooler and wetter Mojave and the hotter, dryer Sonoran to the south of it, carry the signatures of many cultures. Prehistoric rock drawings in the Mojave's Coso Range, probably the greatest concentration of petroglyphs in North America, are at least 3,000 years old. Big-game-hunting cultures that flourished six or seven thousand years before that are known from broken spear tips, choppers, and burins left scattered along the shores of great Pleistocene lakes, long since evaporated. Weapons and tools discovered at China Lake may be 30,000 years old; and worked stone from a quarry in the Calico Mountains is, some argue, evidence that human beings were here more than 200,000 years ago.

Because of the long-term stability of such arid environments, much of this prehistoric stone evidence still lies exposed on the ground, accessible to anyone who passes by—the studious, the acquisitive, the indifferent, the merely curious. Archaeologists do not agree on the sequence of cultural history beyond about 12,000 years ago, but it is clear that these broken bits of chalcedony, chert, and obsidian, like the animal drawings and geometric designs etched on walls of basalt throughout the desert, anchor the earliest threads of human history, the first record of human endeavor here.

Western man did not enter the California desert until the end of the eighteenth century, 250 years after Coronado brought his soldiers into the Zuni pueblos in a bewildered search for the cities of Cibola. The earliest appraisals of the land were cursory, hurried. People traveled *through* it, en route to Santa Fe or the California coastal settlements. Only miners tarried. In 1823 what had been Spain's became Mexico's and in 1848 what had been Mexico's became America's; but the bare, jagged mountains and dry lake beds, the vast and uniform plains of creosote bush and yucca plants, remained as obscure as the northern Sudan until the end of the nineteenth century.

Before 1940 the tangible evidence of twentieth-century man's passage here consisted of very little—the hard tracery of travel corridors; the widely scattered, relatively insignificant evidence of mining operations; and the fair expanse of irrigated fields at the desert's periphery. In the space of a hundred years or so the wagon roads were paved, railroads were laid down, and canals and high-tension lines were built to bring water and electricity across the desert to Los Angeles from the Colorado River. The dark mouths of gold, talc, and tin mines yawned from the bony flanks of desert ranges. Dust-encrusted chemical plants stood at work on the lonely edges of dry lake beds. And crops of grapes, lettuce, dates, alfalfa, and cotton covered

BARRIE ROKEACH. *Early North American Indian Intaglio, Blythe, California.* Photograph. Courtesy of the artist. © Barrie Rokeach 1994.

the Coachella and Imperial valleys, north and south of the Salton Sea, and the Palo Verde Valley along the Colorado.

These developments proceeded with little or no awareness of earlier human occupations by cultures that preceded those of the historic Indians—the Mohave, the Chemehuevi, the Quechan. (Extensive irrigation began to actually change the climate of the Sonoran Desert, and human settlements, the railroads, and farming introduced many new, successful plants and animals into the region.)

During World War II, the American military moved into the desert in great force, to train troops and to test equipment. They found the clear weather conducive to year-round flying, the dry air and isolation very attractive. After the war, a complex of training grounds, storage facilities, and gunnery and test ranges was permanently settled on more than three million acres of military reservations. Few perceived the extent or significance of the destruction of aboriginal sites that took place during tank maneuvers and bombing runs or in the laying out of highways, railroads, mining districts, and irrigated fields. The few who intuited that something like an American Dordogne Valley lay exposed here were (only) amateur archaeologists; even they reasoned that the desert was too vast for any of this to matter.

After World War II, people began moving out of the crowded Los Angeles basin into homes in Lucerne, Apple, and Antelope valleys in the western Mojave. They emigrated as well to a stretch of resort land at the foot of the San Jacinto Mountains that included Palm Springs, and farther out to old railroad and military towns like Twentynine Palms and Barstow. People also began exploring the desert, at first in military-surplus jeeps and then with a variety of all-ter-

COLORPLATE I

Feather Bonnet. (Assiniboine or Gros Ventre). c. 1885. Eagle feathers, wool cloth, ermine and weasel skins.
Length: 28 in. Buffalo Bill Historical Center. Gift of Mr. and Mrs. Richard A. Pohrt.

Scout Jacket. (Sioux). Late 19th c. Buffalo skin. Courtesy of America Hurrah, New York. *The inside view of a rare jacket, made from part of an earlier ceremonial Ghost Dance jacket.*

Scout Jacket. (Sioux). Late 19th c. Buffalo skin with quill work. Courtesy of America Hurrah, New York. *This outside view of the same jacket demonstrates the exquisite decorative quill work of the Sioux.*

COLORPLATE 6

Teepee Liner. (Sioux). Late 19th/early 20th c. Painted muslin. Courtesy of America Hurrah, New York.

COLORPLATE 7 (bottom, opposite page)

Miniature Teepee. (Sioux). Late 19th c. Painted muslin. Courtesy of America Hurrah, New York. *A marvelously detailed miniature teepee probably made as a special gift for a child. The earliest Plains Indian art tended to be "picture writing," as direct and simple as the petroglyphs and pictographs still visible throughout much of the West. By the last half of the 19th century, however, exposure to such professional white artists as Karl Bodmer and George Catlin had given the Indians a better grasp of realistic portraiture. While the art on garments and teepees still told the old tribal stories of battles fought and won, famines survived and great hunts accomplished, it often did so with a more certain eye for reality.*

COLORPLATE 8

Medicine Shield. (Sioux). Date unknown. Deerskin stretched around willow hoop, brass bells, cropped feathers, painted decoration. Robert Hull Fleming Museum, University of Vermont, Burlington. Ogden B. Read Collection.

COLORPLATE 9

GEORGE CATLIN. *Prairie Meadows Burning*. 1832. Oil on canvas. 11 x 14 ¹/8 in. National Museum of American Art, Washington, D.C. *George Catlin is best known for his intimate portraits of Plains Indian life in the 1830s, but he also captured moments of spectacular action, as in this scene. Prairie fires were quite common; in fact, they were often set by the Indians themselves to encourage the thicker, healthier regrowth of native grasses—but once started, such fires, pushed along by the ever-present winds, were impossible to control.*

COLORPLATE 10

ALFRED JACOB MILLER. *The Trapper's Bride*. Mid-19th c. Oil. 25 x 30 in. Joslyn Art Museum, Omaha, Nebraska.
The fur-trading-and-trapping "mountain men," the West's first entrepreneurs, often embraced the culture and the people of the various Indian tribes with whom they dealt. After years of a wild, free life, many of them could never successfully return to the "civilized" cultures from which they had sprung.

rain and off-road vehicles that became available in the 1960s. By the mid-1970s, the number of people using such vehicles for desert recreation had increased exponentially. Most came and went in innocent curiosity; the few who didn't wreaked a havoc all out of proportion to their numbers. The disturbance of previously isolated archaeological sites increased by an order of magnitude. Many sites were vandalized before archaeologists, themselves late to the desert, had any firm grasp of the bounds of human history in the desert. It was as though in the same moment an Aztec library had been discovered intact various lacunae had begun to appear.

The vandalism was of three sorts: the general disturbance usually caused by souvenir hunters and by the curious and the oblivious; the wholesale stripping of a place by professional thieves for black-market sale and trade; and outright destruction, in which vehicles were actually used to ram and trench an area. By 1980, the Bureau of Land Management estimated that probably 35 percent of the archaeological sites in the desert had been vandalized. The destruction at some places by rifles and shotguns, or by power winches mounted on vehicles, was, if one cared for history, demoralizing to behold.

In spite of public education, land closures, and stricter law enforcement in recent years, the BLM estimates that, annually, about 1 percent of the archaeological record in the desert continues to be destroyed or stolen.

2

A BLM archaeologist told me, with understandable reluctance, where to find the intaglio. I spread my Automobile Club of Southern California map of Imperial County out on his desk, and he traced the route with a pink, felt-tip pen. The line crossed Interstate 8 and then turned west along the Mexican border.

"You can't drive any farther than about here," he said, marking a small X. "There's boulders in the wash. You walk up past them."

On a separate piece of paper he drew a route in a smaller scale that would take me up the arroyo to a certain point where I was to cross back east, to another arroyo. At its head, on higher ground just to the north, I would find the horse.

"It's tough to spot unless you know it's there. Once you pick it up . . ." He shook his head slowly, in a gesture of wonder at its existence.

I waited until I held his eye. I assured him I would not tell anyone else how to get there. He looked at me with stoical despair, like a man who had been robbed twice, whose belief in human beings was offered without conviction.

I did not go until the following day because I wanted to see it at dawn. I ate breakfast at 4 A.M. in El Centro and then drove south. The route was easy to follow, though the last section of road proved difficult, broken and drifted over with sand in some spots. I came to the barricade of boulders and parked. It was light enough by then to find my way over the ground with little trouble. The contours of the landscape were stark, without any masking vegetation. I worried only about rattlesnakes.

I traversed the stone plain as directed, but, in spite of the frankness of the land, I came on the horse unawares. In the first moment of recognition I was without feeling. I recalled later being startled, and that I held my breath. It was laid out on the ground with its head to the east, three times life size. As I took in its outline I felt a growing concentration of all my senses, as though my attentiveness to the pale rose color of the morning sky and other peripheral images had now ceased to be important. I was aware that I was straining for sound in the windless air and I felt the uneven pressure of the earth hard against my feet. The horse, outlined in a standing profile on the dark ground, was as vivid before me as a bed of tulips.

I've come upon animals suddenly before, and felt a similar tension, a precipitate heightening of the senses. And I have felt the inexplicable but sharply boosted intensity of a wild moment in the bush, where it is not until some minutes later that you discover the source of electricity—the warm remains of a grizzly bear kill, or the still moist tracks of a wolverine.

But this was slightly different. I felt I had stepped into an unoccupied corridor. I had no familiar sense of history, the temporal structure in which to think: This horse was made by Quechan people three hundred years ago. I felt instead a headlong rush of images: people hunting wild horses with spears on the Pleistocene veld of southern California; Cortés riding across the causeway into Montezuma's Tenochtitlán; a short-legged Comanche, astride his horse like some sort of ferret, slashing through cavalry lines of young men who rode like farmers. A hoof exploding past my face one morning in a corral in Wyoming. These images had the weight and silence of stone.

When I released my breath, the images softened. My initial feeling, of facing a wild animal in a remote region, was replaced with a calm sense of antiquity. It was then that I became conscious, like an ordinary tourist, of what was before me, and thought: This horse was probably laid out by Quechan people. But when, I wondered? The first horses they saw, I knew, might have been those that came north from Mexico in 1692 with Father Eusebio Kino. But Cocopa people, I recalled, also came this far north on occasion, to fight with their neighbors, the Quechan. And *they* could have seen horses with Melchior Díaz, at the mouth of the Colorado River in the fall of 1540. So, it could be four hundred years old. (No one in fact knows.)

I still had not moved. I took my eyes off the horse for a moment to look south over the desert plain into Mexico, to look east past its head at the brightening sunrise, to situate myself. Then, finally, I brought my trailing foot slowly forward and stood erect. Sunlight was running like a thin sheet of water over the stony ground and it threw the horse into relief. It looked as though no hand had ever disturbed the stones that gave it its form.

The horse had been brought to life on ground called desert pavement, a tight, flat matrix of small cobbles blasted smooth by sand-laden winds. The uniform, monochromatic blackness of the stones, a patina of iron and magnesium oxides called desert varnish, is caused by long-term exposure to the sun. To make this type of low-relief ground glyph, or intaglio, the artist either selectively turns individual stones over to their lighter side or removes areas of stone to expose the lighter soil underneath, creating a negative image. This horse, about eighteen feet from brow to rump and eight feet from withers to hoof, had been made in the latter way, and its outline was bermed at certain points with low ridges of stone a few inches high to enhance its three-dimensional qualities. (The left side of the horse was in full profile; each leg was extended at 90 degrees to the body and fully visible, as though seen in three-quarter profile.)

I was not eager to move. The moment I did I would be back in the flow of time, the horse no longer quivering in the same way before me. I did not want to feel again the sequence of quotidian events—to be drawn off into deliberation and analysis. A human being, a four-footed animal, the open land. That was all that was present—and a "thoughtless" understanding of the very old desires bearing on this particular animal: to hunt it, to render it, to fathom it, to subjugate it, to honor it, to take it as a companion.

What finally made me move was the light. The sun now filled the shallow basin of the horse's body. The weighted line of the stone berm created the illusion of a mane and the distinctive roundness of an equine belly. The change in definition impelled me. I moved to the left, circling past its rump, to see how the light might flesh the horse out from various points of view. I circled it completely before squatting on my haunches. Ten or fifteen minutes later I chose another view. The third time I moved, to a point near the rear hooves, I spotted a stone tool at my feet. I stared at it a long while, more in awe than disbelief, before reaching out to pick it up. I turned it over in my left palm and took it between my fingers to feel its cutting edge. It is always difficult, especially with something so portable, to rechannel the desire to steal.

I spent several hours with the horse. As I changed positions and as the angle of the light continued to change I noticed a number of things. The angle at which the pastern carried the hoof away from the ankle was perfect. Also, stones had been placed within the image to suggest at precisely the right spot the left shoulder above the foreleg. The line that joined thigh and hock was similarly accurate. The muzzle alone seemed distorted—but perhaps these stones had been moved by a later hand. It was an admirably accurate representation, but not what a breeder would call perfect conformation. There was the suggestion of a bowed neck and an undershot jaw, and the tail, as full as a winter coyote's, did not appear to be precisely to scale.

The more I thought about it, the more I felt I was looking at an individual horse, a unique combination of generic and specific detail. It was easy to imagine one of Kino's horses as a model, or a horse that ran off from one of Coronado's columns. What kind of horses would these have been, I wondered? In the sixteenth century the most sought-after horses in Europe were Spanish, the offspring of Arabian stock and Barbary horses that the Moors brought to

Iberia and bred to the older, eastern European strains brought in by the Romans. The model for this horse, I speculated, could easily have been a palomino, or a descendant of horses trained for lion-hunting in North Africa.

A few generations ago, cowboys, cavalry quartermasters, and draymen would have taken this horse before me under consideration and not let up their scrutiny until they had its heritage fixed to their satisfaction. Today, the distinction between draft and harness horses is arcane knowledge, and no image may come to mind for a blue roan or a claybank horse. The loss of such refinement in everyday conversation leaves me unsettled. People praise the Eskimo's ability to distinguish among forty types of snow but forget the skill of others who routinely differentiate between overo and tobiano pintos. Such distinctions are made for the same reason. You have to do it to be able to talk clearly about the world.

For parts of two years I worked as a horse wrangler and packer in Wyoming. It is dim knowledge now; I would have to think to remember if a buckskin was a kind of dun horse. And I couldn't throw a double-diamond hitch over a set of panniers—the packer's basic tie-down—without guidance. As I squatted there in the desert, however, these more personal memories seemed tenuous in comparison with the sweep of this animal in human time. My memories had no depth. I thought of the Hittite cavalry riding against the Syrians 3,500 years ago. And the first of the Chinese emperors, Ch'in Shih Huang, buried in Shensi Province in 210 B.C. with thousands of life-size horses and soldiers, a terra-cotta guardian army. What could I know of what was in the mind of whoever made this horse? Was there some racial memory of it as an animal that had once fed the artist's ancestors and then disappeared from North America? And then returned in this strange alliance with another race of men?

Certainly, whoever it was, the artist had observed the animal very closely. Certainly the animal's speed had impressed him. Among the first things the Quechan would have learned from an encounter with Kino's horses was that their own long-distance runners—men who could run down mule deer—were no match for this animal.

From where I squatted I could look far out over the Mexican plain. Juan Bautista de Anza passed this way in 1774, extending El Camino Real into Alta California from Sinaloa. He was followed by others, all of them astride the magical horse; *gente de razón*, the people of reason, coming into the country of *los primitivos*. The horse, like the stone animals of Egypt, urged these memories upon me. And as I drew them up from some forgotten corner of my mind—huge horses carved in the white chalk downs of southern England by an Iron Age people; Spanish horses rearing and wheeling in fear before alligators in Florida—the images seemed tethered before me. With this sense of proportion, a memory of my own—the morning I almost lost my face to a horse's hoof—now had somewhere to fit.

I rose up and began to walk slowly around the horse again. I had taken the first long measure of it and was looking now for a way to depart, a new angle of light, a fading of the image itself before the rising sun, that would break its hold on me. As I circled, feeling both heady and serene at the encounter, I realized again how strangely vivid it was. It had been created on a barren bajada between two arroyos, as nondescript a place as one could imagine. The only plant life here was a few wands of ocotillo cactus. The ground beneath my shoes was so hard it wouldn't take the print of a heavy animal even after a rain. The only sounds I had heard here were the voices of quail.

The archaeologist had been correct. For all its forcefulness, the horse is inconspicuous. If you don't care to see it you can walk right past it. That pleases him, I think. Unmarked on this bleak shoulder of the plain, the site signals to no one; so he wants no protective fences here, no informative plaque, to act as beacons. He would rather take a chance that no motorcyclist, no aimless wanderer with a flair for violence and a depth of ignorance, will ever find his way here.

The archaeologist had given me something before I left his office that now seemed peculiar—an aerial photograph of the horse. It is widely believed that an aerial view of an intaglio provides a fair and accurate depiction. It does not. In the photograph the horse looks somewhat crudely constructed; from the ground it appears far more deftly rendered. The photograph is of a single moment, and in that split second the horse seems vaguely impotent. I watched light pool in the intaglio at dawn; I imagine you could watch it withdraw at dusk and sense the same animation I did. In those prolonged moments its shape and so, too, its general character changed—noticeably. The living quality of the image, its immediacy to the eye, was brought out by the light-in-time, not, at least here, in the camera's frozen instant.

Intaglios, I thought, were never meant to be seen by gods in the sky above. They were meant to be seen by people on the ground, over a long period of shifting light. This could even be true of the huge figures on the Plain of Nazca in Peru, where people could walk for the length of a day beside them. It is our own impatience that leads us to think otherwise.

This process of abstraction, almost unintentional, drew me gradually away from the horse. I came to a position of attention at the edge of the sphere of its influence. With a slight bow I paid my respects to the horse, its maker, and the history of us all, and departed.

3

A short distance away I stopped the car in the middle of the road to make a few notes. I could not write down what I was thinking when I was with the horse. It would have seemed disrespectful, and it would have required another kind of attention. So now I patiently drained my memory of the details it had fastened itself upon. The road I'd stopped on was adjacent to the All American Canal, the major source of water for the Imperial and Coachella valleys. The water flowed west placidly. A disjointed flock of coots, small, dark birds with white bills, was paddling against the current, foraging in the rushes.

I was peripherally aware of the birds as I wrote, the only movement in the desert; and of a series of sounds from a village a half-mile away. The first sounds from this collection of ramshackle houses in a grove of cottonwoods were the distracted dawn voices of dogs. I heard them intermingled with the cries of a rooster. Later, the high-pitched voices of children calling out to each other came disembodied through the dry desert air. Now, a little after seven, I could hear someone practicing on the trumpet, the same rough phrases played over and over. I suddenly remembered how as children we had tried to get the rhythm of a galloping horse with hands against our thighs, or by fluttering our tongues against the roofs of our mouths.

After the trumpet, the impatient calls of adults, summoning children. Sunday morning. Wood smoke hung like a lens in the trees. The first car starts—a cold eight-cylinder engine, of Chrysler extraction perhaps, goosed to life, then throttled back to murmur through dual mufflers, the obbligato music of a shade-tree mechanic. The rote bark of mongrel dogs at dawn, the jagged outcries of men and women, an engine coming to life. Like a thousand villages from West Virginia to Guadalajara.

I finished my notes—where was I going to find a description of the horses that came north with the conquistadors? Did their manes come forward prominently over the brow, like this one's, like the forelocks of Blackfeet and Assiniboine men in nineteenth-century paintings? I set the notes on the seat beside me.

The road followed the canal for a while and then arced north, toward Interstate 8. It was slow driving and I fell to thinking how the desert had changed since Anza had come through. New plants and animals—the MacDougall cottonwood, the English house sparrow, the chukar from India—have about them now the air of the native-born. Of the native species, some—no one knows how many—are extinct. The populations of many others, especially the animals, have been sharply reduced. The idea of a desert impoverished by agricultural poisons and varmint hunters, by off-road vehicles and military operations, did not seem as disturbing to me, however, as this other horror, now that I had been those hours with the horse. The vandals, the few who crowbar rock art off the desert's walls, who dig up graves, who punish the ground that holds intaglios, are people who devour history. Their self-centered scorn, their disrespect for ideas and images beyond their ken, create the awful atmosphere of loose ends in which totalitarianism thrives, in which the past is merely curious or wrong.

I thought about the horse sitting out there on the unprotected plain. I enumerated its qualities in my mind until a sense of its vulnerability receded and it became an anchor for something else. I remembered that history, a history like this one, which ran deeper than Mexico, deeper than the Spanish, was a kind of medicine. It permitted the great breadth of human expression to reverberate, and it did not urge you to locate its apotheosis in the present.

Each of us, individuals and civilizations, had been held upside down like Achilles in the

DIANE COOK.
*Petroglyphs, Horseshoe
Canyon, Canyonland
National Park, Utah.*
Photograph. ©1988
Diane Cook.

River Styx. The artist mixing his colors in the dim light of Altamira; an Egyptian ruler lying still now, wrapped in his byssus, stored against time in a pyramid; the faded Dorset culture of the Arctic; the Hmong and Samburu and Walbiri of historic time; the modern nations. This great, imperfect stretch of human expression is the clarification and encouragement, the urging and the reminder, we call history. And it is inscribed everywhere in the face of the land, from the mountain passes of the Himalayas to a nameless bajada in the California desert.

Small birds rose up in the road ahead, startled, and flew off. I prayed no infidel would ever find that horse.

GEORGE CATLIN

From *Letters and Notes on the Manners, Customs, and Condition of the North American Indians*

Long Hair

George Catlin, the Pennsylvania-born artist who spent much of the 1830s among the Pawnee and Comanche tribes, is well known for his luminous paintings of Native Americans, several of which appear in this book. His writings are less familiar, but his Letters and Notes on the Manners, Customs, and Condition of the North American Indians, *first published in 1841, shows him to have been a precise and sympathetic reporter. Here, he describes an attribute of the Crow that he found particularly fascinating.*

Since my last Letter, nothing of great moment has transpired at this place; but I have been continually employed in painting my portraits and making notes on the character and customs of the wild folks who are about me. I have just been painting a number of the Crows, fine looking

and noble gentlemen. They are really a handsome and well-formed set of men as can be seen in any part of the world. There is a sort of ease and grace added to their dignity of manners, which gives them the air of gentlemen at once. I observed the other day, that most of them were over six feet high, and very many of these have cultivated their natural hair to such an almost incredible length, that it sweeps the ground as they walk; there are frequent instances of this kind amongst them, and in some cases, a foot or more of it will drag on the grass as they walk, giving exceeding grace and beauty to their movements. They usually oil their hair with a profusion of bear's grease every morning, which is no doubt one cause of the unusual length to which their hair extends; though it cannot be the sole cause of it, for the other tribes throughout this country use the bear's grease in equal profusion without producing the same results. The Mandans, however, and the Sioux, of whom I shall speak in future epistles, have cultivated a very great growth of the hair, as many of them are seen whose hair reaches near to the ground.

This extraordinary length of hair amongst the Crows is confined to the men alone; for the women, though all of them with glossy and beautiful hair, and a great profusion of it, are unable to cultivate it to so great a length; or else they are not allowed to compete with their lords in a fashion so ornamental (and on which the men so highly pride themselves), and are obliged in many cases to cut it short off.

The fashion of long hair amongst the men, prevails throughout all the Western and North Western tribes, after passing the Sacs and Foxes; and the Pawnees of the Platte, who, with two or three other tribes only, are in the habit of shaving nearly the whole head.

The present chief of the Crows, who is called "Long-hair," and has received his name as well as his office from the circumstance of having the longest hair of any man in the nation, I have not yet seen: but I hope I yet may ere I leave this part of the country. This extraordinary man is known to several gentlemen with whom I am acquainted, and particularly to Messrs. Sublette and Campbell, of whom I have before spoken, who told me they had lived in his hospitable lodge for months together; and assured me that they had measured his hair by a correct means, and found it to be ten feet and seven inches in length; closely inspecting every part of it at the same time, and satisfying themselves that it was the natural growth.

On ordinary occasions it is wound with a broad leather strap, from his head to its extreme end, and then folded up into a budget or block, of some ten or twelve inches in length, and of some pounds weight; which when he walks is carried under his arm, or placed in his bosom, within the folds of his robe; but on any great parade or similar occasion, his pride is to unfold it, oil it with bear's grease and let it drag behind him, some three or four feet of it spread out upon the grass, and black and shining like a raven's wing.

It is a common custom amongst most of these upper tribes, to splice or add on several lengths of hair, by fastening them with glue; probably for the purpose of imitating the Crows, upon whom alone Nature has bestowed this conspicuous and signal ornament.

FRANCIS LA FLESCHE
"The Omaha Buffalo Medicine Men"

Francis La Flesche, an Omaha Indian trained as an interpreter of Plains Indian language and customs in the 1880s by the famous white anthropologist, Alice Fletcher, went on to take a law degree and join the Bureau of American Ethnography. He also was a frequent contributor to the prestigious Journal of American Folklore, *where this memoir appeared in 1890.*

Among the bluffs of the Missouri River Valley, there stood an Indian village, the inhabitants of which were known as the Omahas. Although missionaries had been among these Indians, many were yet in their savage state. The traders, who were present long before the advent of the missionaries, taught the people nothing that would elevate them above their superstitions and strange beliefs; and the echoes of the Indians' religious and war songs still resounded through the hills, and in their ignorance they were happy.

In this village many of the days of my childhood were spent. By the lodge fire I have often sat, with other little boys, listening to the stories handed down by my forefathers, of their battles with the Sioux, the Cheyennes, and the Pawnees; to the strange tales told of the great "medicinemen," who were able to transform themselves into wild animals or birds, while attacking or fleeing from their enemies; of their power to take the lives of their foes by supernatural means; and of their ability to command even the thunder and lightning, and to bring down the rain from the sky. Like all other little savages of my age, I, too, loved to dream of the days when I should become a warrior, and be able to put to shame and to scalp the enemies of my people. But my story is to be about the buffalo medicinemen.

It was on a hot summer day that a group of boys were playing by the brook which ran by this Omaha village, a game for which I cannot find an English name. I was invited to join them; so I took part in the gambling for feathers, necklaces of elk-teeth, beads, and other valueless articles, which were the treasures of the Indian boy. In the village, preparations were going on for the annual summer hunt, and all the people were astir in various occupations. Here and there sat women in the shade of their tents or sod houses, chatting over their work. Warriors were busy making bows and arrows, shaping the arrowshafts and gluing the feathers to them; while in the open spaces or streets a number of young men were at play gambling as we were, but using a different game. Now and then a noisy dispute arose over the game of the young men, but by the interference of the older men peace would be restored.

Towards the afternoon our game grew to be quite interesting, there being but one more stake to win, and the fight over it became exciting, when suddenly we were startled by the loud report of a pistol. We dropped our sticks, scrambled up the bank of the brook, and in an instant were on the ridge, looking in the direction of the sound to see what it meant. It was only a few young men firing with a pistol at a mark on a tree and some noisy little boys watching them. One of our party suggested going up there to see the shooting, but he was cried down, as he was on the losing side of our game and accused of trying to find some excuse to break up the sport. We were soon busy again with our gambling, and points were made and won back again, when we heard three shots in succession; we were a little uneasy, although the shouts and laugh of the men as they joked quieted us, so that we went on with the game. Then came another single loud report, a piercing scream, and an awful cry of a man: "Hay-ee!" followed by the words, *"Ka-gae ha, wanunka ahthae ha!* (O friends! I have committed murder!)" We dropped our sticks and stared at one another. A cold chill went through me, and I shivered with fright. Before I could recover myself, men and women were running about with wild shouts, and the whole village seemed to be rushing to the spot, while above all the noise could be heard the heartrending wail of the man who had accidentally shot a boy through the head. The excitement was intense. The relatives of the wounded boy were preparing to avenge his death, while those of the unfortunate man who had made the fatal shot stood ready to defend him. I made my way through the crowd to see who it was that was killed. Peering over the shoulders of another boy, I saw on the ground a dirty-looking little form and recognized it as one of my playmates. Blood was oozing from a wound in the back of his head and from one just under the right eye, near the nose. The sight of blood sickened me, as it did the other boys, and I stepped back as quickly as I could.

A man just then ordered the women to stop wailing and the people to stand back. Soon there was an opening in the crowd, and I saw a tall man come up the hill, wrapped in a buffalo robe, and pass through the opening to where the boy lay; he stooped over the child, felt of his wrists, then of his breast. "He is alive," the man said; "set up a tent, and take him in there." The little body was lifted in a robe and carried by two men into a large tent which was hastily erected. A young man was sent in haste to call the buffalo medicine men of another village (the Omahas lived in three villages, a few miles apart). It was not long before the medicine men came galloping over the hills on their horses, one or two at a time, their long hair streaming over their naked backs. They dismounted before the tent and went in one by one, where they joined the buffalo doctors of our village, who had already been called. A short consultation was held, and soon the sides of the tent were thrown open to let in the fresh air, and also that the people might witness the operation. Then began a scene rarely if ever witnessed by a white man.

All the medicine men sat around the boy, their eyes gleaming out of their wrinkled faces. The man who was first to try his charms and medicines on the patient began by telling in a loud voice how he became possessed of them; how in a vision he had seen the buffalo which had revealed to him the mysterious secrets of the medicine and of the charm song he was taught to sing when using the medicine. At the end of every sentence of this narrative the boy's father thanked the doctor in terms of relationship. When he had recited his story from beginning to end and had compounded the roots he had taken from his skin pouch, he started his song at the top of his voice, which the other doctors, twenty or thirty in number, picked up and sang in unison, with such volume that one would imagine it could have been heard many miles. In the midst of the chorus of voices rose the shrill sound of the bone whistle accompaniment, imitating the call of an eagle. After the doctor had started the song, he put the bits of root into his mouth, grinding them with his teeth, and, taking a mouthful of water, he slowly approached the boy, bellowing and pawing the earth, after the manner of an angry buffalo at bay. All eyes were upon him with an admiring gaze. When within a few feet of the boy's head, he paused for a moment, drew a long breath, and with a whizzing noise forced the water from his mouth into the wound. The boy spread out his hands and winced as though he was again hit by a ball. The man uttered a series of short exclamations, "He! he! he!" to give an additional charm to the medicine. It was a successful operation, and the father and the man who had wounded the boy lifted their spread hands towards the doctor to signify their thanks. During this performance all of the medicine men sang with energy the song which had been started by the operator. There were two women who sang, as they belonged to the corps of doctors.

The next morning the United States Indian agent came into the village, driving a handsome

horse and riding in his shining buggy. He first went to the chief and demanded that the wounded boy be turned over to him. He was told that none but the parents of the child could be consulted in the matter; and if he wanted the boy, he had better see the father. The agent was said to be a good man, and before he offered his services to the government as Indian agent he had studied medicine, so that he could be physician to the Indians as well as their agent. I had attended the mission school for a while and learned to speak a little of the white man's language; and as the government interpreter was not within reach, the agent took me to the parents of the boy, who were by the bedside of their sick one. On our way to the place we heard the singing and the noises of the medicine men, and the agent shook his head, sighed, and made some queer little noises with his tongue, which I thought to be expressive of his feelings. When our approach was noticed, everyone became silent; not a word was uttered as we entered the tent, where room had already been made for us to sit, and we were silently motioned to the place. We sat down on the ground by the side of the patient, and the agent began to feel of the pulse of the boy. The head medicine man, who sat folded up in his robe, scowled and said to me, "Tell him not to touch the boy." The agent respected the request and said that unless the boy was turned over to him and was properly treated, death was certain. He urged that a sick person must be kept very quiet and free from any kind of excitement, for that would weaken him and lessen the chances of recovery. All this I interpreted in my best Omaha, and the men listened with respectful silence. When I had finished, the leader said, "Tell him that he may ask the father of the boy if he would give up the youth to be cared for by the white medicine man." The question was asked, and a deliberate "No" was the answer. Then the medicine man said, "He may ask the boy if he would prefer to be doctored by the white man." While I was translating this to the agent, the boy's father whispered in his child's ear. I then interpreted the agent's question to the boy. He held out his hand to me, and said with an effort, "Who is this?" He was told that it was "Sassoo," one of his friends. I held his hand and repeated the question to him, and he said, "My friend, I do not wish to be doctored by the white man." The agent rose, got into his buggy, and drove off, declaring that the boy's death was certain, and indeed it seemed so. The boy's head was swollen to nearly twice its natural size, and looked like a great blue ball; the hollows of his eyes were covered up, so that he could not see, and it made me shudder to look at him.

Four days the boy was treated in this strange manner. On the evening of the third day the doctors said that he was out of danger and that in the morning he would be made to rise to meet the rising sun and to greet the return of life.

I went to bed early, so that I could be up in time to see the great ceremony. In the morning I was awakened by the singing and approached the tent, where already a great crowd had assembled, for the people had come from the other villages to witness the scene of recovery. There was a mist in the air, as the medicine men had foretold there would be; but as the dawn grew brighter and brighter, the fog slowly disappeared, as if to unveil the great red sun that was just visible over the horizon. Slowly it grew larger and larger, while the boy was gently lifted by two strong men, and when up on his feet, he was told to take four steps toward the east. The medicine men sang with a goodwill the mystery song appropriate to the occasion, as the boy attempted this feeble walk. The two men by his side began to count, as the lad moved eastward, "*Win* (one), *numba* (two), *thab'thin* (three)"; slower grew the steps; it did not seem as if he would be able to take the fourth; slowly the boy dragged his foot and made the last step; as he set his foot down, the men cried, "*duba* (four)," and it was done. Then was sung the song of triumph, and thus ended the first medicine incantation I witnessed among the Omahas.

Before the buffalo medicine men disbanded, they entered a sweat lodge and took a bath, after which the fees were distributed. These consisted of horses, robes, blankets, bears'-claw necklaces, eagle feathers, beaded leggings, and many other articles much valued by Indians. The friends of the unfortunate man who shot the boy had given nearly half of what they possessed, and the great medicine men went away rejoicing. One or two, however, remained for a time with the boy, and in about thirty days he was up again, shooting sticks, and ready to go and witness another pistol practice.

FREDERIC REMINGTON

From "A Sergeant of the Orphan Troop"
Ahead of the Skirmish Line

After the Civil War ended in 1865, the American military turned its efforts toward the removal and control of the Indians who inconvenienced white settlement in the land that lay west of the Mississippi. Among the chroniclers of the subsequent thirty-year conflict was artist Frederic Remington, who, like George Catlin, was better known for his art than for his writings. But he was a pretty fair storyteller, too, as can be seen in this sample from Harper's New Monthly Magazine *of 1897.*

─────────────

"We have been fighting the Indians all day here," said the officer, putting down his glass and turning to the two "non-coms." "The command has gone around the bluffs. I have just seen Indians up there on the rim-rocks. I have sent for troops, in the hope that we might get up there. Sergeant, deploy as skirmishers, and we will try."

At a gallop the men fanned out, then forward at a sharp trot across the flats, over the little hills, and into the scrub pine. The valley gradually narrowed until it forced the skirmishers into a solid body, when the lieutenant took the lead, with the command tailing out in single file. The signs of the Indians grew thicker and thicker—a skirmisher's nest here behind a scrub-pine bush, and there by the side of a rock. Kettles and robes lay about in the snow, with three "bucks" and some women and children sprawling about, frozen as they had died; but all was silent except the crunch of the snow and the low whispers of the men as they pointed to the telltales of the morning's battle.

As the column approached the precipitous rim-rock the officer halted, had the horses assembled in a side cañon, putting Corporal Thornton in charge. He ordered Sergeant Johnson to again advance his skirmish-line, in which formation the men moved forward, taking cover behind the pine scrub and rocks, until they came to an open space of about sixty paces, while above it towered the cliff for twenty feet in the sheer. There the Indians had been last seen. The

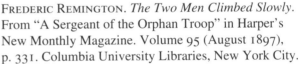

FREDERIC REMINGTON. *The Two Men Climbed Slowly.* From "A Sergeant of the Orphan Troop" in Harper's New Monthly Magazine. Volume 95 (August 1897), p. 331. Columbia University Libraries, New York City.

soldiers lay tight in the snow, and no man's valor impelled him on. To the casual glance the rim-rock was impassable. The men were discouraged and the officer nonplussed. A hundred rifles might be covering the rock fort for all they knew. On closer examination a cutting was found in the face of the rock which was a rude attempt at steps, doubtless made long ago by the Indians. Caught on a bush above, hanging down the steps was a lariat, which, at the bottom, was twisted around the shoulders of a dead warrior. They had evidently tried to take him up while wounded, but he had died and had been abandoned.

After cogitating, the officer concluded not to order his men forward, but he himself stepped boldly out into the open and climbed up. Sergeant Johnson immediately followed, while an old Swedish soldier by the name of Otto Bordeson fell in behind them. They walked briskly up the hill, and placing their backs against the wall of rock, stood gazing at the Indian.

With a grin the officer directed the men to advance. The sergeant, seeing that he realized their serious predicament, said,

"I think, lieutenant, you had better leave them where they are; we are holding this rock up pretty hard."

They stood there and looked at each other. "We's in a fix," said Otto.

"I want volunteers to climb this rock," finally demanded the officer.

The sergeant looked up the steps, pulled at the lariat, and commented: "Only one man can go at a time; if there are Indians up there, an old squaw can kill this command with a hatchet; and if there are no Indians, we can all go up."

The impatient officer started up, but the sergeant grabbed him by the belt. He turned, saying, "If I haven't got men to go, I will climb myself."

"Stop, lieutenant. It wouldn't look right for the officer to go. I have noticed a pine-tree the branches of which spread over the top of the rock," and the sergeant pointed to it. "If you will make the men cover the top of the rim-rock with their rifles, Bordeson and I will go up;" and turning to the Swede, "Will you go, Otto?"

"I will go anywhere the sergeant does," came his gallant reply.

"Take your choice, then, of the steps or the pine-tree," continued the Virginian; and after a rather short but sharp calculation the Swede declared for the tree, although both were death if the Indians were on the rim-rock. He immediately began sidling along the rock to the tree, and slowly commenced the ascent. The Sergeant took a few steps up the cutting, holding on by the rope. The officer stood out and smiled quizzically. Jeers came from behind the soldiers' bushes—"Go it, Otto! Go it, Johnson! Your feet are loaded! If a snow-bird flies, you will drop dead! Do you need any help? You'd make a hell of a sailor!" and other gibes.

The gray clouds stretched away monotonously over the waste of snow, and it was cold. The two men climbed slowly, anon stopping to look at each other and smile. They were monkeying with death.

At last the sergeant drew himself up, slowly raised his head, and saw snow and broken rock. Otto lifted himself likewise, and he too saw nothing. Rifle-shots came clearly to their ears from far in front—many at one time, and scattering at others. Now the soldiers came briskly forward, dragging up the cliff in single file. The dull noises of the fight came through the wilderness. The skirmish-line drew quickly forward and passed into the pine woods, but the Indian trails scattered. Dividing into sets of four, they followed on the tracks of small parties, wandering on until night threatened. At length the main trail of the fugitive band ran across their front, bringing the command together. It was too late for the officer to get his horses before dark, nor could he follow with his exhausted men, so he turned to the sergeant and asked him to pick some men and follow on the trail. The sergeant picked Otto Bordeson, who still affirmed that he would go anywhere that Johnson went, and they started. They were old hunting companions, having confidence in each other's sense and shooting. They ploughed through the snow, deeper and deeper into the pines, then on down a cañon where the light was failing. The sergeant was sweating freely; he raised his hand to press his fur cap backward from his forehead. He drew it quickly away; he stopped and started, caught Otto by the sleeve, and drew a long breath. Still holding his companion. he put his glove again to his nose, sniffed at it again, and with a mighty tug brought the startled Swede to his knees, whispering, "I smell Indians; I can sure smell 'em, Otto—can you?"

Otto sniffed, and whispered back, "Yes, plain!"

"We are ambushed! Drop!" and the two soldiers sunk in the snow. A few feet in front of them lay a dark thing; crawling to it, they found a large calico rag, covered with blood.

"Let's do something, Carter; we's in a fix."

"If we go down, Otto, we are gone; if we go back, we are gone; let's go forward," hissed the sergeant.

Slowly they crawled from tree to tree.

"Don't you see the Injuns?" said the Swede, as he pointed to the rocks in front, where lay their dark forms. The still air gave no sound. The cathedral of nature, with its dark pine trunks starting from gray snow to support gray sky, was dead. Only human hearts raged, for the forms which held them lay like black bowlders.

"Egah—lelah washatah," yelled the sergeant.

Two rifle-shots rang and reverberated down the cañon; two more replied instantly from the soldiers. One Indian sunk, and his carbine went clanging down the rocks, burying itself in the snow. Another warrior rose slightly, took aim, but Johnson's six-shooter cracked again, and the Indian settled slowly down without firing. A squaw moved slowly in the half-light to where the buck lay. Bordeson drew a bead with his carbine.

"Don't shoot the woman, Otto. Keep that hole covered; the place is alive with Indians;" and both lay still.

A buck rose quickly, looked at the sergeant, and dropped back. The latter could see that he had him located, for he slowly poked his rifle up without showing his head. Johnson rolled swiftly to one side, aiming with his deadly revolver. Up popped the Indian's head, crack went the six-shooter; the head turned slowly, leaving the top exposed. Crack again went the alert gun of the soldier, the ball striking the head just below the scalp-lock and instantly jerking the body into a kneeling position.

Then all was quiet in the gloomy woods.

Elizabeth B. Custer

From *Following the Guidon*

"Corral of the Captives"

On November 17, 1868, General George Armstrong Custer's Indian-fighting Seventh Cavalry captured an entire Cheyenne village in a brutal surprise attack on the banks of the Washita River in western Kansas. The aftermath of the raid was recounted by his talented wife Elizabeth in Following the Guidon, *published in 1890. Her matter-of-fact presentation of the Indian captives as interesting, although clearly inferior, beings was typical of the era.*

The squaws had some small sense of humor. When, on one of our visits, an officer whom they knew well took his wife in to see the prisoners, one of them asked by a sign if that was his wife. He, being full of fun, shook his head, and placing two fingers in his mouth, made the Indian sign for "sister." The squaw carefully scrutinized the wife's face, she trying not to flinch while the brown fingers passed over the skin; when the examination was finished, the squaw made a sign that she knew the statement was not true, and, as she shook her head decisively, a gleam came into her eyes as if of triumph in her keenness of perception.

The buttons of the lady's habit, her whip, with a dog's head on the handle (at sight of which the squaw bow-wowed), and finally the visitor's curls were closely examined, and great curiosity and surprise were evinced when the hair was pulled straight and the curl resumed its form on being released.

After many visits to the corral, which really added greatly to the interest of our life, we came to feel at home with these dusky strangers; and even the woman who at first would only stand by the sentinel and look down, because, as she said, she chose to die some other death than that by disembowelling, summoned courage to enter the tents and look at the ever-interesting, ever-new object to a woman, the pappoose. I at last forgot the knife that at first, in my excited state, I had almost seen gleaming in the folds of the blanket, and we even stood quietly while the bent and odious old squaws crooned and smoothed our faces. The uniform kindness with which these prisoners had been treated had convinced them that the white man meant to keep his word. In the councils that were constantly held, General Custer gave them the news of the negotiations that were going on regarding the delivering up of white captives to our people, and they knew that each event of that kind hastened their release.

One day an orderly from the post rode hurriedly up to our tent in camp, and dismounting, gave the compliments of the commanding officer of the garrison, and asked that General Custer should come to the post at once, as the Indian prisoners had made trouble, and no one could understand their desires further than that they kept calling for "Ouchess," meaning "Creeping Panther," a name they had given General Custer some time before. The two miles were soon accomplished, and General Custer found a sorry state of affairs and intense excitement prevailing. The officers in charge explained that as constant rumors were circulated of parties of hostile Indians hovering around the post and the corral, with the intention of rescuing the captives, and as it was feared that the three chiefs were preparing to attempt an escape, it had been thought best to remove the latter from their tent to the guard-house adjoining. The sergeant and guard had gone to them, but being unable to make any signs that the Indians could understand, they had attempted to force them to go into the prison. With the suspiciousness natural to the race, the braves had resisted with all their strength. All the women and children, witnessing the encounter, surrounded the officer, who had joined the soldiers as soon as trouble seemed imminent, and while he and the sergeant and men were trying to make their exit with the three chiefs, a general fight had taken place. The chiefs quickly drew from the folds of their

Captured Indian Chiefs: Fat Bear, Dull Knife, Big Head—in Travelling Costume. From *Following the Guidon* by Elizabeth B. Custer. New York, Harper & Brothers, 1890. General Research Division, New York Public Library, Astor, Lenox and Tilden Foundations.

blankets the knives they had been allowed to eat with. These had been surreptitiously sharpened and polished, and they flashed right and left as the braves plunged to and fro in their struggles. The squaws, similarly armed, threw themselves with wild fury upon the guard. An old squaw singled out the officer in charge, sprang upon him, and plunged her knife down the back of his neck with unerring aim. One of the chiefs leaped upon the sergeant and stabbed and gashed him in so horrible a manner that his life was despaired of. The remainder of the guard came to the rescue, but not before one chief, Big Head, had fallen dead, and another, Dull Knife, was mortally wounded by a bayonet thrust through the body. The third, Fat Bear, was felled by the butt of a musket, but was uninjured. The outside guard, by firing in, had quelled the mutiny among the women. When General Custer reached the corral the excitement was still intense, but he insisted upon entering the stockade alone, and talking with the prisoners. The women were running about, making frantic gestures, angrily and revengefully menacing the guard and the sentinel on his beat. As soon as General Custer appeared they closed around him, asking vehemently if they were all to be shot. He quieted them by his decision of manner, and his assurances that they were now safe, and asked what was the meaning of their violent conduct. They told him that they had asked again and again to have him as interpreter, for when the soldiers had come in to take the chiefs, they could neither understand nor be understood. They had supposed that the braves were being forced out to be hanged, and the special dread of an Indian is to die such a death. General Custer had learned to treat the Indians with the patience that children require, and he told them, in endeavoring to conciliate and quiet the still agitated women, what the real intention of the guard was, how friendly the men had constantly been up to that time, and that their brusque conduct when resisted was not to be marvelled at, for that soldiers were drilled to quick, peremptory ways. The men had no intention, he assured them, of injuring any one; they only wanted to remove the three chiefs to the inside of the guard-house, and they could not talk with them, not having been out on the campaign the winter before.

This talk had at once a perceptible effect. Some of the older women crouched down to croon and moan over the dead, as is their custom; others walked about wailing and gesticulating in the expressive manner of the Indian. Many of them had gashed their legs horribly, in commemoration of the dead, and their leggings constantly irritated the wounds. One old squaw had been shot in the leg in the *mêlée*, and another exhibited her blanket with bullet-holes in it; but there was not much pity felt among the soldiers, whose lives had been imperilled, for these old viragos, who had fought so furiously.

General Custer went into the cell where the dying chief lay, and explained in the same manner the cause of the misunderstanding and disaster. The old warrior told the general how much they had wished, through all the imprisonment, that they had been confined within the limits of the cavalry camp, among the soldiers who had captured them, and who, during the past winter, had learned to talk with them by signs; he complained that the "Walk-a-heaps," as they called the infantry, who now had them in keeping, did not understand them at all.

After this unfortunate affair there was no more visiting the stockade on the part of the women. The very hands that had smoothed our faces and stroked our hair had too skilfully wielded the knives that we had all the time suspected them of carrying under their garments. They were now more dissatisfied, suspicious, and restless than ever, and when at last the news came that the white captives were released, and that they, in turn, would be sent back to their tribe, there was general rejoicing.

WOODEN LEG

"Young Men, Go Out and Fight Them"

General Custer's Indian-fighting days came to an end on June 24, 1876, when the entire Seventh Cavalry was obliterated by an army of Plains Indians under the command of Sitting Bull. Among the Indian fighters was an eighteen-year-old Northern Cheyenne named Wooden Leg. His oral account of the battle captures the terrible violence and surreal confusion that characterized the fighting for warrior and soldier alike.

In my sleep I dreamed that a great crowd of people were making lots of noise. Something in the noise startled me. I found myself wide awake, sitting up and listening. My brother too awakened, and we both jumped to our feet. A great commotion was going on among the camps. We heard shooting. We hurried out from the trees so we might see as well as hear.

The shooting was somewhere at the upper part of the camp circles. It looked as if all of the Indians there were running away toward the hills to the westward or down toward the village. Women were screaming and men were letting out war cries. Through it all we could hear old men calling: "Soldiers are here! Young men, go out and fight them."

We ran to our camp and to our home lodge. Everybody there was excited. Women were hurriedly making up little packs for flight. Some were going off northward or across the river without any packs. Children were hunting for their mothers. Mothers were anxiously trying to find their children. I got my lariat and my six-shooter. I hastened on down toward where had been our horse herd. . . .

My father had caught my favorite horse from the herd brought in by the boys and Bald Eagle. I quickly emptied out my war bag and set myself at getting ready to go into battle. I jerked off my ordinary clothing. I jerked on a pair of new breeches that had been given to me by an Uncpapa Sioux. I had a good cloth shirt, and I put it on. My old moccasins were kicked off and a pair of beaded moccasins substituted for them.

My father strapped a blanket upon my horse and arranged the rawhide lariat into a bridle. He stood holding my mount. "Hurry," he urged me.

The air was so full of dust I could not see where to go. But it was not needful that I see that far. I kept my horse headed in the direction of movement by the crowd of Indians on horseback. I was led out around and far beyond the Uncpapa camp circle. Many hundreds of Indians on horseback were dashing to and fro in front of a body of soldiers. The soldiers were on the level valley ground and were shooting with rifles. Not many bullets were being sent back at them, but thousands of arrows were falling among them. I went on with a throng of Sioux until we got beyond and behind the white men. By this time, though, they had mounted their horses and were hiding themselves in the timber. . . .

Suddenly the hidden soldiers came tearing out on horseback, from the woods. I was around on that side where they came out. I whirled my horse and lashed it into a dash to escape from them. All others of my companions did the same. But soon we discovered they were not following us. They were running away from us. They were going as fast as their tired horses could carry them across an open valley space and toward the river. We stopped, looked a moment, and then we whipped our ponies into swift pursuit. A great throng of Sioux also were coming after them. A distant position put them among the leaders in the chase. The soldier horses moved slowly, as if they were very tired. Ours were lively. We gained rapidly on them.

I fired four shots with my six-shooter. I do not know whether or not any of my bullets did harm. I saw a Sioux put an arrow into the back of a soldier's head. Another arrow went into his shoulder. He tumbled from his horse to the ground. Others fell dead either from arrows or from stabbings or jabbings or from blows by the stone war clubs of the Sioux. Horses limped or staggered or sprawled out dead or dying.

Our war cries and war songs were mingled with many jeering calls, such as: "You are only boys. You ought not to be fighting. We whipped you on the Rosebud. You should have brought more Crows or Shoshones with you to do your fighting."

Little Bird and I were after one certain soldier. Little Bird was wearing a trailing warbonnet. He was at the right and I was at the left of the fleeing man. We were lashing him and his horse with our pony whips. It seemed not brave to shoot him. Besides, I did not want to waste my bullets. He pointed back his revolver, though, and sent a bullet into Little Bird's thigh. Immediately I whacked the white man fighter on his head with the heavy elk-horn handle of my pony whip. The blow dazed him. I seized the rifle strapped on his back. I wrenched it and dragged the looping strap over his head. As I was getting possession of this weapon, he fell to the ground. I did not harm him further. I do not know what became of him. The jam of oncoming Indians swept me on. . . .

I returned to the west side of the river. Lots of Indians were hunting around there for dead soldiers or for wounded ones to kill. I joined in this search. I got some tobacco from the pockets of one dead man. I got also a belt having in it a few cartridges. All of the weapons and clothing and all other possessions were being taken from the bodies. The warriors were doing this. No old people nor women were there. They all had run away to the hill benches to the westward.

I went to a dead horse, to see what might be found there. Leather bags were on them, behind the saddles. I rummaged into one of these bags. I found there two pasteboard boxes. I broke open one of them. "Oh, cartridges!"

There were twenty of them in each box, forty in all. Thirty of them were used to fill up the vacant places in my belt. The remaining ten I wrapped into a piece of cloth and dropped them down into my own little kit bag. Now I need not be so careful in expending ammunition. Now I felt very brave. . . .

The shots quit coming from the soldiers. Warriors who had crept close to them began to call out that all of the white men were dead. All of the Indians then jumped up and rushed forward. All of the boys and old men on their horses came tearing into the crowd. The air was full of dust and smoke. Everybody was greatly excited. It looked like thousands of dogs might look if all of them were mixed together in a fight. All of the Indians were saying these soldiers also went crazy and killed themselves. I do not know. I could not see them. But I believe they did so. . . .

I took one scalp. As I went walking and leading my horse among the dead, I observed one face that interested me. The dead man had a long beard growing from both sides of his face and extending several inches below the chin. He had also a full mustache. All of the beard hair was of a light yellow color, as I now recall it. Most of the soldiers had beards growing, in different lengths, but this was the longest one I saw among them. I think the dead man may have been thirty or more years old. "Here is a new kind of scalp," I said to a companion. I skinned

COLORPLATE 11

THOMAS MORAN. *Mist in Kanab Canyon, Utah.* 1892. Oil on canvas. 44 3/8 x 38 3/8 in.
National Museum of American Art, Washington, D.C.

COLORPLATE 12

ALBERT BIERSTADT. *A Storm in the Rocky Mountains—Mt. Rosalie*. 1866. Oil on canvas. 83 x 142 ¹/₄ in. The Brooklyn Museum.

COLORPLATE 13 (top, opposite page)

THOMAS MORAN. *The Grand Canyon of the Yellowstone*. 1893–1901. Oil on canvas. 96 ¹/₂ x 168 ³/₈ in. National Museum of American Art, Washington, D.C. Gift of George D. Pratt. *Thomas Moran's sweeping renditions of various scenes on the upper reaches of the Yellowstone River—which he visited in 1871 as a member of the exploring expedition of Ferdinand V. Hayden—helped persuade Congress to establish Yellowstone National Park, the country's first, in 1872. Three years later, Moran ventured into the canyon country of the Southwest as an artist for John Wesley Powell's ongoing exploration of the Colorado River Plateau. From this experience he produced many huge canvases of the Grand Canyon, then went on to depict many other grand landscapes in other parts of the West.*

COLORPLATE 14 (bottom, opposite page)

THOMAS MORAN. *Chasm of the Colorado*. 1873–1874. Oil on canvas. 84 ³/₈ x 144 ³/₄ in. U.S. Department of the Interior, Office of the Secretary. On loan to the National Museum of American Art, Washington, D.C.

COLORPLATE 15 (following spread)

THOMAS MORAN. *Badlands of Dakota*. 1901. Oil on canvas. 20 x 30 in. Private collection. Courtesy of Spanierman Gallery, New York City.

COLORPLATE 16

GEORGE CATLIN. *Buffalo Chase, Bull Protecting Cow and Calf.* 1832–1833. Oil on canvas. 24 x 29 in. National Museum of American Art, Washington, D.C. Gift of Mrs. Joseph Harrison, Jr. *The buffalo was the essential beast of the Plains Indian culture—a kind of supermarket on hooves whose meat, innards, sinew, hide, and bones all went to satisfy the protocols of survival. And buffalo-hunting scenes like this became the staple of any artist worthy of the name.*

COLORPLATE 17

ARTIST UNKNOWN. *Buffalo Hunt*. c. 1880. Oil. 23 x 32 in. Courtesy of America Hurrah, New York.

COLORPLATE 18

GEORGE CATLIN. *Portraits of Grizzly Bear and Mouse, Life Size.* 1846–1848. Oil on canvas. 26 ¹/₂ x 32 ¹/₂ in.. National Museum of American Art, Washington, D.C. *The other great beast of the West was its largest and—next to humans— its most efficient predator, the Grizzly. In this marvelous bit of whimsy, George Catlin proved himself not without humor.*

KICKING BEAR. *Battle of Little Big Horn.* 1898. Courtesy of The Southwest Museum, Los Angeles. Photo #N30454.

one side of the face and half of the chin, so as to keep the long beard yet on the part removed. I got an arrow shaft and tied the strange scalp to the end of it. . . .

I waved my scalp as I rode among our people. The first person I met who took special interest in me was my mother's mother. She was living in a little willow dome lodge of her own. "What is that?" she asked me when I flourished the scalp stick toward her. I told her. "I give it to you," I said, and I held it out to her. She screamed and shrank away. "Take it," I urged. "It will be good medicine for you." Then I went on to tell her about my having killed the Crow or Shoshone at the first fight up the river, about my getting the two guns, about my knocking in the head two soldiers in the river, about what I had done in the next fight on the hill where all of the soldiers had been killed. We talked about my soldier clothing. She said I looked good dressed that way. I had thought so too, but neither the coat nor the breeches fit me well. The arms and legs were too short for me. Finally she decided she would take the scalp. She went then into her own little lodge. . . .

There was no dancing nor celebrating of any kind in any of the camps that night. Too many people were in mourning, among all of the Sioux as well as among the Cheyennes. Too many Cheyenne and Sioux women had gashed their arms and legs, in token of their grief. The people generally were praying, not cheering. There was much noise and confusion, but this was from other causes. Young men were going out to fight the first soldiers now hiding themselves on the hill across the river from where had been the first fighting during the morning. . . .

I did not go back that afternoon nor that night to help in fighting the first soldiers. Late in the night, though, I went as a scout. Five young men of the Cheyennes were appointed to guard our camp while other people slept. These were Big Nose, Yellow Horse, Little Shield, Horse Road and Wooden Leg. One or other of us was out somewhere looking over the country all the time. Two of us went once over to the place where the soldiers were hidden. We got upon hill points higher than they were. We could look down among them. We could have shot among them, but we did not do this. We just saw that they yet were there.

Five other young men took our duties in the last part of the night. I was glad to be relieved. I did not go to my family group for rest. I let loose my horse and dropped myself down upon a thick pad of grassy sod.

JOHN G. NEIHARDT

From *A Cycle of the West*
"High Noon on the Little Horn"

Nebraska poet John G. Neihardt—who also transcribed and edited the autobiography of a Holy Man of the Oglala Sioux, Black Elk Speaks *(1930)—began writing a cycle of "songs" about the western experience in 1912. In 1949, the five songs were published in* A Cycle of the West. *In this excerpt from "Song of the Indian Wars," Neihardt finds epic poetry as the Battle of the Little Bighorn commences.*

                    Now it came to pass,
That late June morning on the Greasy Grass,
Two men went fishing, warriors of the Sioux;
And, lonesome in the silence of the two,
A youngster pictured battles on the sand.
Once more beneath the valor of his hand
The execrated troopers, blotted out,
Became a dust. Then, troubled with a doubt,
He ventured: "Uncle, will they find us here—
The soldiers?" 'Twas a buzzing in the ear
Of Red Hawk where he brooded on his cast.
"The wind is coming up," he said at last;
"The sky grows dusty." "Then the fish won't bite,"
Said Running Wolf. "There may be rain tonight,"
Said Red Hawk, falling silent. Bravely then
The youngster wrought himself a world of men
Where nothing waited on a wind of whim,
But everything, obedient to him,
Fell justly. All the white men in the world
Were huddled there, and round about them swirled
More warriors than a grownup might surmise.
The pony-thunder and the battle-cries,
The whine of arrows eager for their marks
Drowned out the music of the meadowlarks,
The rising gale that teased the cottonwoods
To set them grumbling in their whitened hoods,
The chatter of a little waterfall.
These pebbles—see!—were Crazy Horse and Gall;
Here Crow King raged, and Black Moon battled there!
This yellow pebble—look!—was Yellow Hair;
This drab one with a little splotch of red,
The Gray Fox, Crook! Ho ho! And both were dead;
And white men fell about them every place—
The leafage of the autumn of a race—
Till all were down. And when their doom was sealed,
The little victor danced across the field
Amid the soundless singing of a throng.
The brief joy died, for there was something wrong

Black Elk. Photograph. South Dakota State Historical Society, Pierre.

About this battle. Mournfully came back
That other picture of a dawn attack—
The giant horses rearing in the fogs
Of their own breath; the yelping of the dogs;
The screaming rabble swarming up the rise;
The tangled terror in his mother's eyes;
The flaming lodges and the bloody snow.
Provokingly oblivious of woe,
The two still eyed the waters and were dumb.

"But will they find us, Uncle? Will they come?"

Now Red Hawk grunted, heaving at his line,
And, wrought of flying spray and morning-shine,
A spiral rainbow flashed along the brook.
"Hey hey!" said Red Hawk, staring at his hook,
"He got my bait! Run yonder to the bluff
And catch some hoppers, Hohay. Get enough
And you shall see how fish are caught today!"

Half-heartedly the youngster stole away
Across a brawling riffle, climbed the steep
And gazed across the panoramic sweep
Of rolling prairie, tawny in the drouth,
To where the Big Horns loomed along the south,
No more than ghosts of mountains in the dust.
Up here the hot wind, booming gust on gust,

Made any nook a pleasant place to dream.
You could not see the fishers by the stream;
And you were grown so tall that, looking down
Across the trees, you saw most all the town
Strung far along the valley. First you saw
The Cheyennes yonder opposite the draw
That yawned upon the ford—a goodly sight!
So many and so mighty in a fight
And always faithful brothers to the Sioux!
Trees hid the Brulé village, but you knew
'Twas half a bow-shot long from end to end.
Then Ogalalas filled a river bend,
And next the Minneconjoux did the same.
A little farther south the Sans Arc came,
And they were neighbors to the Hunkpapas.—
The blackened smoke-vents, flapping in the flaws,
Were like a startled crow flock taking wing.—
Some Ogalalas played at toss-the-ring
And many idlers crowded round to see.—
The grazing ponies wandered lazily
Along the flat and up the rolling west.

Now, guiltily remembering his quest,
He trotted farther up the naked hill,
Dropped down a gully where the wind was still—
And came upon a hopping army there!
They swarmed, they raged—but Hohay didn't care;
For suddenly it seemed the recent climb
Had been a scramble up the height of time
And Hohay's name was terror in the ears
Of evil peoples. Seizing weeds for spears,
He charged the soldiers with a dreadful shout.
The snapping of their rifles all about
Might daunt a lesser hero. Never mind;
His medicine made all their bullets blind,
And 'twas a merry slaughter. Then at last
The shining glory of the vision passed,
And hoppers were but hoppers as before,
And he, a very little boy once more,
Stood dwarfed and lonely on a windy rise.
The sun was nearly up the dusty skies.
'Twas white with heat and had a funny stare—
All face! The wind had blown away its hair.
It looked afraid; as though the sun should fear!

Now, squinting downward through the flying blear,
He scanned the town. And suddenly the old
Remembered dawn of terror struck him cold.
Like startled ants that leave a stricken mound
In silence that is felt as panic sound
By one who sees, the squaws and children poured
Along the valley northward past the ford;
And men were chasing ponies every place,
While many others ran, as in a race,
To southward.

Hohay, taking to his heels,
Made homeward like a cottontail that feels
A kiote pant and whimper at his tail.
He reached the bluff rim, scrambled to the vale
And crossed the stream. The fishermen were gone.
A hubbub in the village led him on
Pell-mell among the snatching underwood,
Till, checked as by a wall of sound, he stood
Apant and dripping in the howling town.

A bent old man there hobbled up and down
Upon a staff and sang a cackling song
Of how his heart was young again and strong;
But no one heeded. Women ran with guns
And bows and war clubs, screaming for their sons
And husbands. Men were mounting in a whirl
Of manes and tails to vanish in a swirl
Of scattered sand; and ever louder blew
The singing wind of warriors riding through
To battle. Hohay watched them, mouth agape,
Until he felt a hand upon his nape
That shoved him north, and someone shouted *"Run!"*
He scampered.

ERSKINE WOOD

"An Officer's Son With Chief Joseph"

In 1877, after leading his pursuers across much of Montana, Chief Joseph of the Nez Perce surrendered the desperate remnants of his band to General Nelson A. Miles. One of Miles's officers was Charles Erskine Scott Wood, who sympathized deeply with the Indians. In the 1890s, he sent his teenaged son Erskine to spend two autumns with Joseph and his people on the Colville Reservation in Idaho. Erskine recalled the experience in 1976.

When you ask me to describe the family life of Joseph and his culture, please remember that I was only a boy thirteen and fourteen years old when I spent the nine months with him, on two separate visits in 1892 and 1893. In this way I participated in the two fall deer hunts of those years when we laid in our supply of venison and smoked it on racks over the tepee fires. Those hunts occurred in November in the mountains whither we moved from the pleasant little Nespelem Valley, where was our main camp. The band would split up into groups of four or five families, hunting in different parts of the mountains, and I, of course, always was with Joseph's group, where I participated in the arduous work of the hunt along with the men.

We used to get up long before daylight each morning and take a sweat bath to get the human scent off our bodies so the game we were hunting could not smell us. Joseph always took part in these along with the rest of us. I only mention this to show that Joseph mingled freely in all that his men did. Soon after daylight we would be off hunting.

Of course, all the menial housework was left to the squaws. Joseph's life was occupied in handling any of his band's affairs with the agency, such as issuing rations, clothing, etc., or any

EDWARD S. CURTIS. *Hinmaton-Yalaktit ("Chief Joseph")*. 1980 from 1903 negative. Orotone. 23 x 19 in. National Portrait Gallery, Smithsonian Institution, Gift of Jean-Antony du Lac.

special matters. As I remember it, he had a little grain patch and threshed the grain by spreading it out and walking the horses round and round through it to thresh it out onto the canvas spread beneath their hooves. But there wasn't too much of that. Of course, he would moderate and settle any possible disputes, of which there were very few.

He kept a calendar. It was a bunch of ten or twelve little white, smooth sticks, each the size of a pencil, and on each stick, for whatever current month or year it was, he would file a little mark for that day, and on Sundays he would bore a little hole and color it with red. This calendar, since each stick was four-sided and eight or ten inches long, must have carried perhaps two or three years.

I have not mentioned Joseph's family. He had two wives. The elder was Wawin-Tip-Yay-La-Tal-E-Cotsot, and the younger was Iyat-Too-We-A-Net-En-My. They slept together with Joseph and lived in perfect harmony, the two women doing all the household work like cooking, mending clothing, making moccasins, taking down and putting up the tepees when on the move, and all such necessary chores. There also lived in our tepee a boy about a year older than I named Cool-Cool-Smool-Smool. He and I together had the job of looking after Chief Joseph's pony herd of perhaps fifty horses, driving them to water hemmed in by a pool in the Nespelem River and there catching fresh horses for the next day's use and turning the others back into the herd. And, of course, we and the other boys played games together, but we never had much to do with the girls that I saw—maybe I was too young. I should add in describing tepee life that Joseph shared his tepee with another family.

You ask me to speak of Joseph's culture. Of course, you cannot expect a boy of fourteen to penetrate an Indian's inner beliefs and feelings, but this much I can say well and truthfully: Joseph, when I knew him, was about fifty years old and was a very handsome man with noble features, a beautiful forelock rising from his forehead and then falling a little off to his left side, fine eyes, and a pleasant voice; and as even I could tell from the minimum knowledge of his language that I picked up, he was an eloquent man with an eloquent voice. Two heavy braids of black hair hung down his shoulders, one in front of each. In speech he was moderate but clear and unmistakable, and whatever he said was respected and listened to. He disliked obscenity and on one occasion reproved it. He was unquestionably looked up to by his people as their chief.

By the way, they never called him Joseph; they always referred to him as Hin-Mah-Too-Yah-Lat-Kekht, meaning Thunder Rolling in the Mountains. His advice, his decisions had always proved right. His advice in 1877 had been not to go to war with the whites, for he knew their might and that they were too strong; and yet when this advice was ignored, he made the important decision of his life: to remain with his people and lead them, not desert them in their extremity; and all through the bitter following years he continued their chief because there was no one like him, and they knew it. And so on, back to their old place in the north. They looked to him and trusted him as their chief. Why? Because of the integrity of his character.

My parting with Joseph was sad. It was sad anyway, but the memory of it is sadder because of two mistakes I made, and one in particular has haunted me. We were on the banks of the Columbia River waiting for me to cross in a dugout canoe to the other side, to the conveyance that was to take me back to civilization. I had with me some fishberries, a poisonous berry which when boiled in water produced a brown liquid that would kill lice. My father had given them to me in case I needed them (which I did). Joseph asked me to leave those berries with him, but I declined, fearing to leave an unknown poison in his unaccustomed hands. He said no more. I think I made a mistake.

The other was this: my father had written me to say to Joseph that if there was anything that he could do for him to let him know and my father would try to do it. I related this to Joseph, and I expected him to ask my father to prevail on the government to give back to Joseph part of his own original land or something of that sort. But instead, all Joseph asked for was a good stallion to improve the breed of his pony herd. I looked upon Joseph as such a great chief that I thought such a request was petty and that he ought to ask for a piece of the Wallowa Valley or something grand, so I simply said to Joseph, "No, that's not what my father meant." Joseph said no more, and I have reproached myself to this day that I was such a fool. A fine stallion would have been a magnificent gift to Joseph and would really have improved his breed of horses.

Here I will end. He took me—the son of his former soldier-enemy—and treated me as a son. What more can I say?

JOHN (FIRE) LAME DEER

From *Lame Deer: Seeker of Visions*

"The Green Frog Skin"

In spite of sometimes violent attempts at suppression, replacement, or dilution, much of the cultural identity of Native American people has persisted through decades of poverty and abuse. This endurance may be a testament to the healing strength of pride and anger; both certainly can be discerned in the provocative commentary of Lame Deer, a twentieth-century Sioux Holy Man whose words were transcribed by Richard Erdoes in 1972.

The green frog skin—that's what I call a dollar bill. In our attitude toward it lies the biggest difference between Indians and whites. My grandparents grew up in an Indian world without money. Just before the Custer battle the white soldiers had received their pay. Their pockets were full of green paper and they had no place to spend it. What were their last thoughts as an

Beatien Yazz. *Bird and Bear*. Courtesy School of American Research, Santa Fe, New Mexico.

Indian bullet or arrow hit them? I guess they were thinking of all that money going to waste, of not having had a chance to enjoy it, of a bunch of dumb savages getting their paws on that hard-earned pay. That must have hurt them more than the arrow between their ribs.

The close hand-to-hand fighting, with a thousand horses gally-hooting all over the place, had covered the battlefield with an enormous cloud of dust, and in it the green frog skins of the soldiers were whirling around like snowflakes in a blizzard. Now, what did the Indians do with all that money? They gave it to their children to play with, to fold those strange bits of colored paper into all kinds of shapes, making them into toy buffalo and horses. Somebody was enjoying that money after all. The books tell of one soldier who survived. He got away, but he went crazy and some women watched him from a distance as he killed himself. The writers always say he must have been afraid of being captured and tortured, but that's all wrong.

Can't you see it? There he is, bellied down in a gully, watching what is going on. He sees the kids playing with the money, tearing it up, the women using it to fire up some dried buffalo chips to cook on, the men lighting their pipes with green frog skins, but mostly all those beautiful dollar bills floating away with the dust and the wind. It's this sight that drove that poor soldier crazy. He's clutching his head, hollering, "Goddam, Jesus Christ Almighty, look at them dumb, stupid, red sons of bitches wasting all that dough!" He watches till he can't stand it any longer, and then he blows his brains out with a six-shooter. It would make a great scene in a movie, but it would take an Indian mind to get the point.

The green frog skin—that was what the fight was all about. The gold of the Black Hills, the gold in every clump of grass. Each day you can see ranch hands riding over this land. They have a bagful of grain hanging from their saddle horns, and whenever they see a prairie-dog hole they toss a handful of oats in it, like a kind little old lady feeding the pigeons in one of your city parks. Only the oats for the prairie dogs are poisoned with strychnine. What happens to the prairie dog after he has eaten this grain is not a pleasant thing to watch. The prairie dogs are poisoned, because they eat grass. A thousand of them eat up as much grass in a year as a cow. So if the rancher can kill that many prairie dogs he can run one more head of cattle, make a little more money. When he looks at a prairie dog he sees only a green frog skin getting away from him.

For the white man each blade of grass or spring of water has a price tag on it. And that is the trouble, because look at what happens. The bobcats and coyotes which used to feed on prairie dogs now have to go after a stray lamb or a crippled calf. The rancher calls the pest-control officer to kill these animals. This man shoots some rabbits and puts them out as bait with a piece of wood stuck in them. That stick has an explosive charge which shoots some cyanide into the mouth of the coyote who tugs at it. The officer has been trained to be careful. He puts a printed warning on each stick reading, "Danger, Explosive, Poison!" The trouble is that our dogs can't read, and some of our children can't either.

And the prairie becomes a thing without life—no more prairie dogs, no more badgers, foxes, coyotes. The big birds of prey used to feed on prairie dogs, too. So you hardly see an eagle these days. The bald eagle is your symbol. You see him on your money, but your money is killing him. When a people start killing off their own symbols they are in a bad way.

*　　*　　*

I made up a new proverb: "Indians chase the vision, white men chase the dollar." We are lousy raw material from which to form a capitalist. We could do it easily, but then we would stop being Indians. We would just be ordinary citizens with a slightly darker skin. That's a high price to pay, my friend, too high. We make lousy farmers, too, because deep down within us lingers a feeling that land, water, air, the earth and what lies beneath its surface cannot be owned as someone's private property. That belongs to everybody, and if man wants to survive, he had better come around to this Indian point of view, the sooner the better, because there isn't much time left to think it over.

N. Scott Momaday

From "An American Land Ethic"

In a numinous essay on the power of the Native American sense of interdependence with the land and its creatures, Pulitzer Prize–winning novelist N. Scott Momaday (House Made of Dawn, *awarded 1969*) *finds a mystic connection to his own Kiowa ancestors.*

One night a strange thing happened. I had written the greater part of *The Way To Rainy Mountain*—all of it, in fact, except the epilogue. I had set down the last of the old Kiowa tales, and I had composed both the historical and the autobiographical commentaries for it. I had the sense of being out of breath, of having said what it was in me to say on that subject. The manuscript lay before me in the bright light, small, to be sure, but complete; or nearly so. I had written the second of the two poems in which that book is framed. I had uttered the last word, as it were. And yet a whole, penultimate piece was missing. I began once again to write.

During the first hours after midnight on the morning of November 13, 1833, it seemed that the world was coming to an end. Suddenly the stillness of the night was broken; there were brilliant flashes of light in the sky, light of such intensity that people were awakened by it. With the speed and density of a driving rain, stars were falling in the universe. Some were brighter than Venus; one was said to be as large as the moon.

I went on to say that that event, the falling of the stars on North America, that explosion of

Leonid meteors which occurred 137 years ago, is among the earliest entries in the Kiowa calendars. So deeply impressed upon the imagination of the Kiowas is that old phenomenon that it is remembered still; it has become a part of the racial memory.

"The living memory," I wrote, "and the verbal tradition which transcends it, were brought together for me once and for all in the person of Ko-sahn." It seemed eminently right for me to deal, after all, with that old woman. Ko-sahn is among the most venerable people I have ever known. She spoke and sang to me one summer afternoon in Oklahoma. It was like a dream. When I was born she was already old; she was a grown woman when my grandparents came into the world. She sat perfectly still, folded over on herself. It did not seem possible that so many years—a century of years—could be so compacted and distilled. Her voice shuddered, but it did not fail. Her songs were sad. An old whimsy, a delight in language and in remembrance, shone in her one good eye. She conjured up the past, imagining perfectly the long continuity of her being. She imagined the lovely young girl, wild and vital, she had been. She imagined the Sun Dance:

There was an old, old woman. She had something on her back. The boys went out to see. The old woman had a bag full of earth on her back. It was a certain kind of sandy earth. That is what they must have in the lodge. The dancers must dance upon the sandy earth. The old woman held a digging tool in her hand. She turned towards the south and pointed with her lips. It was like a kiss, and she began to sing:

> *We have brought the earth,*
> *Now it is time to play;*
> *As old as I am, I still have the feeling of play.*

That was the beginning of the Sun Dance.

By this time I was back into the book, caught up completely in the act of writing. I had projected myself—imagined myself—out of the room and out of time. I was there with Ko-sahn in the Oklahoma July. We laughed easily together; I felt that I had known her all of my life—all of hers. I did not want to let her go. But I had come to the end. I set down, almost grudgingly, the last sentences:

It was—all of this and more—a quest, a going forth upon the way to Rainy Mountain. Probably Ko-sahn too is dead now. At times, in the quiet of evening, I think she must have wondered, dreaming, who she was. Was she become in her sleep that old purveyor of the sacred earth, perhaps, that ancient one who, old as she was, still had the feeling of play? And in her mind, at times, did she see the falling stars?

For some time I sat looking down at these words on the page, trying to deal with the emptiness that had come about inside of me. The words did not seem real. The longer I looked at them, the more unfamiliar they became. At last I could scarcely believe that they made sense, that they had anything whatsoever to do with meaning. In desperation almost, I went back over the final paragraphs, backwards and forwards, hurriedly. My eyes fell upon the name Ko-sahn. And all at once everything seemed suddenly to refer to that name. The name seemed to humanize the whole complexity of language. All at once, absolutely, I had the sense of the magic of words and of names. Ko-sahn, I said. And I said again KO-SAHN.

Then it was that that ancient, one-eyed woman Ko-sahn stepped out of the language and stood before me on the page. I was amazed, of course, and yet it seemed to me entirely appropriate that this should happen.

"Yes, grandson," she said. "What is it? What do you want?"

"I was just now writing about you," I replied, stammering. "I thought—forgive me—I thought that perhaps you were . . . that you had. . . ."

"No," she said. And she cackled, I thought. And she went on. "You have imagined me well, and so I am. You have imagined that I dream, and so I do. I have seen the falling stars."

"But all of this, this *imagining*," I protested, "this has taken place—is taking place in my

DIANE COOK. *Spider Rock, Canyon de Chelly*. Photograph. © 1987 Diane Cook.

mind. You are not actually here, not here in this room." It occurred to me that I was being extremely rude, but I could not help myself. She seemed to understand.

"Be careful of your pronouncements, grandson," she answered. "You imagine that I am here in this room, do you not? That is worth something. You see, I have existence, whole being, in your imagination. It is but one kind of being, to be sure, but it is perhaps the best of all kinds. If I am not here in this room, grandson, then surely neither are you."

"I think I see what you mean," I said meekly. I felt justly rebuked. "Tell me, grandmother, how old are you?"

"I do not know," she replied. "There are times when I think that I am the oldest woman on earth. You know, the Kiowas came into the world through a hollow log. In my mind's eye I have seen them emerge, one by one, from the mouth of the log. I have seen them so clearly, how they were dressed, how delighted they were to see the world around them. I *must* have been there. And I must have taken part in that old migration of the Kiowas from the Yellowstone to the Southern Plains, for I have seen antelope bounding in the tall grass near the Big Horn River, and I have seen the ghost forests in the Black Hills. Once I saw the red cliffs of Palo Duro Canyon. I was with those who were camped in the Wichita Mountains when the stars fell."

"You are indeed very old," I said, "and you have seen many things."

"Yes, I imagine that I have," she replied. Then she turned slowly around, nodding once, and receded into the language I had made. And then I imagined I was alone in the room.

*　*　*

Ko-sahn could remember where my grandmother was born. "It was just there," she said, pointing to a tree, and the tree was like a hundred others that grew up in the broad depression of the Washita River. I could see nothing to indicate that anyone had ever been there, spoken so much as a word, or touched the tips of his fingers to the tree. But in her memory Ko-sahn could see the child. I think she must have remembered my grandmother's voice, for she seemed for a long moment to listen and to hear. There was a still, heavy heat upon that place; I had the sense that ghosts were gathering there.

And in the racial memory, Ko-sahn had seen the falling stars. For her there was no distinction between the individual and the racial experience, even as there was none between the mythical and the historical. Both were realized for her in the one memory, and that was of the land. This landscape, in which she had lived for a hundred years, was the common denominator of everything that she knew and would ever know—and her knowledge was profound. Her roots ran deep into the earth, and from those depths she drew strength enough to hold still against all the forces of chance and disorder. And she drew therefrom the sustenance of meaning and of mystery as well. The falling stars were not for Ko-sahn an isolated or accidental phenomenon. She had a great personal investment in that awful commotion of light in the night sky. For it remained to be imagined. She must at last deal with it in words; she must appropriate it to her understanding of the whole universe. And, again, when she spoke of the Sun Dance, it was an essential expression of her relationship to the life of the earth and to the sun and moon.

In Ko-sahn and in her people we have always had the example of a deep, ethical regard for the land. We had better learn from it. Surely that ethic is merely latent in ourselves. It must now be activated, I believe. We Americans must come again to a moral comprehension of the earth and air. We must live according to the principle of a land ethic. The alternative is that we shall not live at all.

JAMES WELCH

"Thanksgiving at Snake Butte"

James Welch, a Blackfeet/Gros Ventre Indian of Montana, has written several highly acclaimed novels, including Fools Crow, *the depiction of the Blackfeet Indian experience in the last third of the nineteenth century, and* The Indian Lawyer, *a novel of modern Indian life. Here, he lets poetry evoke the sadness of a vanished way of life.*

In time we rode that trail
up the butte as far as time
would let us. The answer to our time
lay hidden in the long grasses
on the top. Antelope scattered

through the rocks before us, clattered
unseen down the easy slope to the west.
Our horses balked, stiff-legged,
their nostrils flared at something unseen
gliding smoothly through brush away.

On top, our horses broke, loped through
a small stand of stunted pine, then jolted
to a nervous walk. Before us lay
the smooth stones of our ancestors, the fish,
the lizard, snake and bent-kneed

bowman—etched by something crude,
by a wandering race, driven by their names
for time: its winds, its rain, its snow
and the cold moon tugging at the crude figures
in this, the season of their loss.

William Clift. *Factory Butte, Utah.* 1975. Photograph. Courtesy William Clift. © William Clift.

Leslie Marmon Silko

From *Almanac of the Dead*

The Return of the Giant Snake

In the books Storyteller, Ceremony, *and* Almanac of the Dead, *Leslie Marmon Silko, of Pueblo Indian ancestry, has established herself as one of the most important Native American writers at work today. In this excerpt from her epic novel that follows the Native American experience from prehistoric times to the present, one of her central characters expresses the perennial yearning of his people for redemption from the terrible weight of history.*

Sterling hiked over the little sand hills across the little valley to the sandstone cliffs where the family sheep camp was. The windmill was pumping lazily in the afternoon breeze, and Sterling washed his face and hands and drank. The taste of the water told him he was home. "Home." Even thinking the word made his eyes fill with tears. What was "home"? The little stone shack seemed to be deserted although Sterling had found an empty Vienna sausage can on the little wood-burning stove. On the shelf there were two coffee cans; inside he had found dry pinto beans and some sugar.

Sterling didn't think what he was experiencing was depression; it felt more like shock. For three days Sterling lay stunned; he could barely swallow water. On the fourth day Sterling awoke and no longer felt exhausted, but he had felt different. He didn't have the heart to look at his magazines anymore. He didn't even glance in the direction of his shopping bags. The magazines referred to a world Sterling had left forever, a world that was gone, that safe old world that had never really existed except on the pages of *Reader's Digest* in articles on reducing blood cholesterol, corny jokes, and patriotic anecdotes.

Sterling cooked beans in the tin coffeepot and went for a walk in the field of sunflowers below the windmill. He had never spent so much time before alone with the earth; he sat below the red sandstone cliffs and watched the high, thin clouds. Far in the distance, he could hear jet airplanes, Interstate 40, and the trains. But Sterling found it was easy to forget that world in the distance; that world no longer was true. He purposely kept his mind focused on the things he could see or touch; he avoided thinking about the day before or even the hour before, and he did not think about tomorrow. He watched the tiny black ants busily gather food for the ant pile. Aunt Marie and the old people had believed the ants were messengers to the spirits, the way snakes were. The old people used to give the ants food and pollen and tiny beads as gifts. That way the ants carried human prayers directly underground. Sterling had spooned out a few cooked beans on the ant hill, but he couldn't think of a prayer to say, or even a message to send to the spirits of the earth. But the ants didn't worry about prayers or messages; they swarmed excitedly over the beans. Sterling watched them work for a long time; sometimes the ant workers had almost been crushed under beans they were carrying. The ants worked steadily, and by sundown they had taken all the beans underground. Sterling did not understand why, but the success of the ants had lifted his spirits. He wished he had listened more closely to Aunt Marie and her sisters, for he might have understood better the connection between human beings and ants.

The next day Sterling got up before dawn and took a bath in the shallow creek Laguna people call "the river." Sterling gasped as the cold river clay squeezed between his toes and the cold water reached his ankles. He washed his hair with soapweed root left behind by some sheepherder too poor or too stingy to buy real shampoo. The day after that, Sterling had walked for two or three hours along the river enjoying the smell of the willows. When he stopped to rest, he realized he had walked north almost as far as the mine road. The open-pit uranium mine had been closed for years. Sterling walked away from the shoulder of the road in the weeds although there were no signs of any traffic, or other human beings for miles.

Sterling knew what was at the mine, but he wasn't afraid. Without realizing what he was doing, Sterling had been walking in the exact direction of the mine road where the shrine of the giant snake was. Sterling knew the visit to the giant snake was what he must do, before anything else, even before he went to buy food.

Sterling felt stronger as he walked along. The wild purple asters were blooming, and Sterling could smell Indian tea and bee flowers; in the distance, he heard the field larks call. As long as Sterling did not face the mine, he could look out across the grassy valley at the sandstone mesas and imagine the land a thousand years ago, when the rain clouds had been plentiful and the grass and wildflowers had been belly high on the buffalo that had occasionally wandered off the South Plains. Lecha had talked about the Lakota prophecy while they were driving from Tucson. Lecha said that as a matter of fact, the buffalo were returning to the Great Plains, just as the Lakota and other Plains medicine people had prophesied. The buffalo herds had gradually outgrown and shifted their range from national parks and wildlife preserves. Little by little the buffalo had begun to roam farther as the economic decline of the Great Plains had devastated farmers and ranchers and the small towns that had once served them. Sterling had to smile when he thought of herds of buffalo grazing among the wild asters and fields of sunflowers below the mesas. He did not care if he did not live to see the buffalo return; probably the herds would need another five hundred years to complete their comeback. What mattered was that after all the groundwater had been sucked out of the Ogalala Aquifer, then the white people and their cities of Tulsa, Denver, Wichita, and Des Moines would gradually disappear and the Great Plains would again host great herds of buffalo and those human beings who knew how to survive on the annual rainfall.

Sterling still had two miles to walk, but already the mountains of grayish-white tailings loomed ahead. He had not understood before why the old people had cried when the U.S. government had opened the mine. Sterling was reminded of the stub left after amputation when he looked at the shattered, scarred sandstone that remained; the mine had devoured entire mesas. "Leave our Mother Earth alone," the old folks had tried to warn, "otherwise terrible things will happen to us all." Before the end of the war, the old folks had seen the first atomic explosion— the flash brighter than any sun—followed weeks later by the bombs that had burned up a half a million Japanese. "What goes around, comes around." Now he was approaching the shrine of the giant snake.

Ceramic Plate from San Ildefonso showing Plumed Serpent with lightning arrow tongue. Signed Tony and Juanita. c. 1900. Courtesy School of American Research, Santa Fe, New Mexico.

Sterling tried to remember more of the stories the old people used to tell; he wished he had listened more closely because he vaguely recalled a connection the giant snake had with Mexico. Tucson was too close to Mexico. Tucson was Mexico, only no one in the United States had realized it yet. Ferro had called the exploding car bomb outside Tucson police head-quarters his "announcement" that Tucson wasn't United States territory anymore. Sterling had been terrified of Ferro from the start because Aunt Marie and the old people used to talk about how fierce the Mexican tribes were—how quickly and casually they had killed.

Long time ago, long before the Europeans, the ancestors had lived far to the south in a land of more rain, where crops grew easily. But then something terrible had happened, and the peo-ple had to leave the abundance and flee far to the north, to harsh desert land. Hundreds of years before the Europeans had appeared, sorcerers called Gunadeeyahs or Destroyers had taken over in the South. The people who refused to join the Gunadeeyahs had fled; the issue had been the sorcerers' appetite for blood, and their sexual arousal from killing. Aunt Marie and the oth-ers had been reluctant to talk about sorcery in the presence of young children, and Sterling had not paid much attention to what his playmates had told him about the Gunadeeyahs. Still Sterling knew the Destroyers robbed graves for human flesh and bones to make their fatal "powders." Aunt Marie had cautioned Sterling and the other children always to be careful around Mexicans and Mexican Indians because when the first Europeans had reached Mexico City they had found the sorcerers in power. Montezuma had been the biggest sorcerer of all. Each of Montezuma's advisors had been sorcerers too, descendants of the very sorcerers who had caused the old-time people to flee to Pueblo country in Arizona and New Mexico, thou-sands of years before. Somehow the offerings and food for the spirits had become too bloody, and yet many people had wanted to continue the sacrifices. They had been excited by the sacrifice victim's feeble struggle; they had lapped up the first rich spurts of hot blood. The Gunadeeyah clan had been born.

Sterling wished for a drink of water. No wonder the blood sacrifices and the blood-spilling had stopped when the people reached this high desert plateau; every drop of moisture, every drop of blood, each tear, had been made precious by this arid land. The people who had fled north to escape the bloodshed made rules once they were settled. On the rare occasions when the sacred messengers had to be dispatched to the spirit world, the eagles and macaws had been gently suffocated by the priests; not one drop of blood had been spilled. Permission had to be asked and prayers had to be made to the game animals before the hunters brought them home.

The people were cautioned about disturbing the bodies of the dead. Those who touched the dead were easily seduced by the Gunadeeyahs, who craved more death and more dead bodies to open and consume.

Now the old story came back to Sterling as he walked along. The appearance of Europeans had been no accident; the Gunadeeyahs had called for their white brethren to join them. Sure enough the Spaniards had arrived in Mexico fresh from the Church Inquisition with appetites whetted for disembowelment and blood. No wonder Cortés and Montezuma had hit it off together when they met; both had been members of the same secret clan.

Sterling made his way up a sandy hill and then slid down the crumbling clay bank of a small arroyo. He tore a cuff on his pants crawling through the barbed-wire fence that marked the mine boundaries. Ahead all he could see were mounds of tailings thirty feet high, uranium waste blowing in the breeze, carried by the rain to springs and rivers. Here was the new work of the Destroyers; here was destruction and poison. Here was where life ended. What had been so remarkable about the return of the giant snake had been how close the giant snake was to the mountains of tailings. Two mine employees from Laguna had discovered the giant stone snake on a routine check for erosion of the tailings. Sterling had heard Aunt Marie and the others talking excitedly about a giant stone snake. At first Sterling had thought a fossil snake had been found, but then he had realized the stone snake was only an odd outcropping of sandstone. Sterling remembered his skepticism about the giant snake. He had not believed the mine employees who swore there had never been anything at the foot of the tailings before—nothing but sand and a few weeds. Sterling had thought that probably the strange sandstone formation had been lying there for hundreds of years and no one had noticed it; or if they had, the people had lost track of the rock formation after the mining began. But Aunt Marie and the others had pointed out the sheep camps nearby and the road that passed within a hundred yards of the giant stone snake. Rabbit hunters familiar with the area had come to agree with the miners, sheepherders, and the others. No way had they overlooked a sandstone snake thirty feet long! Overnight, the giant stone snake had appeared there. The old folks said Maahastryu had returned. Sterling had forgotten all about the stone snake after that. He had heard Aunt Marie talk about the stone snake from time to time with her nieces; but back then, talk about religion or spirits had meant nothing to Sterling, drinking beer with his section-gang buddies. Back then Sterling used to say he only believed in beer and big women bouncing in water beds. For Sterling, the stone snake had been a sort of joke, and he had forgot all about the snake until the Hollywood film crew had tried to film it and all hell had broken loose.

Sterling was not sure how much farther he had to walk; he had been to the snake shrine only a few times, and the last time, Sterling had been in the backseat of a tribal police car as they had raced to stop the movie people from filming the stone snake. Suddenly there it was. The stone snake's head was raised dramatically and its jaws were open wide. Sterling felt his heart pound and the palms of his hands sweat. The ground near the snake's head was littered with bits of turquoise, coral, and mother-of-pearl; there were streaks of cornmeal and pollen on the snake's forehead and nose where those who came to pray had fed the spirit being.

Sterling had no idea what to do; he had no idea why he had walked all that distance to the stone snake. He sat down near the snake to rest. He had to think. What had happened to him? What had happened to his life? Education, English, a job on the railroad, then a pension; Sterling had always worked hard on self-improvement. He had never paid much attention to the old-time ways because he had always thought the old beliefs were dying out. But Tucson had changed Sterling. In Africa the giant snakes talked to the people again, and the buffalo ran free again on the Great Plains. Sterling felt haunted—he would never forget the child Seese had lost. Marching through his brain day and night were Lecha's "armies" of Lakotas and Mohawks; Sterling saw them over and over in dreams; ghost armies of Lakota warriors, ghost armies of the Americas leading armies of living warriors, armies of indigenous people to retake the land. Sterling tried to forget the blood and the gunshots. He tried to forget everything Lecha had told him because she and the others at the meeting in Tucson were crazy. "Rambo of the Homeless," "Poor People's Army," the Barefoot Hopi and Wilson Weasel Tail—the world was not like that. Tucson had only been a bad dream.

When the giant stone snake had first reappeared, Aunt Marie and the old folks had argued

COLORPLATE 19

JAMES WALKER. *The Vaquero.* c. 1877. Oil on canvas. Bancroft Library, University of California, Berkeley. *Of those who supplanted the Native American cultures, the Spanish-Mexican occupants of the Southwest and California came closest to replicating the Indians' symbiotic relationship to the land. No matter; like the nomadic existence of the Indians, the insular pastoral society of the Hispanic people did not long survive the arrival of the American Anglos.*

COLORPLATE 20

KARL BODMER. *Landscape with Herd of Buffalo on the Upper Missouri.* 1833. Watercolor on paper. 9 5/8 x 12 3/8 in.
Joslyn Art Museum, Omaha, Nebraska. Gift of the Enron Art Foundation.

COLORPLATE 21

ALFRED JACOB MILLER. *The Lost "Green-Horn."* 1837. Watercolor. 9 7/16 x 12 5/16 in. Walters Art Gallery, Baltimore, Maryland. *Alfred Jacob Miller painted the life of the fur trapper with fidelity and almost impressionistic grace—and sometimes subtle impact. As the relentlessly empty horizon of this painting suggests, getting lost on the featureless High Plains was no small matter.*

COLORPLATE 22

EMANUEL GOTTLIEB LEUTZE. *Westward the Course of Empire Takes Its Way*. (Mural study, U.S. Capitol). 1861. Oil on canvas. 33 1/4 x 43 3/8 in. National Museum of American Art, Washington, D.C. Bequest of Sara Carr Upton. *The continental impulse that drove people west was called, among other things, "Manifest Destiny"—the proposition that fate had somehow willed it that North America be conquered and occupied by the people of the United States from sea to shining sea. In spite of (or perhaps because of) its too often cruel consequences—both to the Native Americans whose cultures were overrun and to the pioneers themselves, who suffered terrible ordeals along the way—the impulse was given an almost religious character in paintings and lithographs, as it was in songs, stories, and jingoistic histories.*

COLORPLATE 23

ALBERT BIERSTADT. *The Oregon Trail.* 1869. Oil on canvas. 31 x 49 in. Butler Institute of American Art, Youngstown, Ohio.

COLORPLATE 24

ALFRED JACOB MILLER. *Green River Rendezvous.* 1837. Oil on canvas. 26 x 37 in. American Heritage Center, University of Wyoming, Laramie. Copyright restricted. *During the height of the fur-trapping industry (and it was an industry, after all) in the 1830s and early 1840s, trappers and Indians alike would "rendezvous" at various locations every spring to trade goods and stories, drink, carouse, and engage in other therapeutic behavior not unlike that of Las Vegas conventioneers today. One of the most popular spots for such meetings was a beautiful "hole," or valley, along the Green River in Wyoming.*

COLORPLATE 25

JOHN MIX STANLEY. *Oregon City on the Willamette River.* c. 1850–1852. Oil on canvas. 26 ¹/₂ x 40 in.
Amon Carter Museum, Fort Worth, Texas.

COLORPLATE 26

ALFRED JACOB MILLER. *Fort Laramie.* 1851. Oil on canvas. 18 x 27 in. From the Collection of Gilcrease Museum, Tulsa, Oklahoma.

over the significance of the return of the snake. Religious people from all the pueblos and even the distant tribes had come to see the giant stone snake. The snake was so near the tailings it appeared as if it might be fleeing the mountains of wastes. This had led to rumors that the snake's message said the mine and all those who had made the mine had won. Rumors claimed the snake's head pointed to the next mesa the mine would devour, and Sterling had believed the mine had won. But the following year uranium prices had plunged, and the mine had closed before it could devour the basalt mesa the stone snake had pointed at.

Sterling sat for a long time near the stone snake. The breeze off the junipers cooled his face and neck. He closed his eyes. The snake didn't care if people were believers or not; the work of the spirits and prophecies went on regardless. Spirit beings might appear anywhere, even near open-pit mines. The snake didn't care about the uranium tailings; humans had desecrated only themselves with the mine, not the earth. Burned and radioactive, with all humans dead, the earth would still be sacred. Man was too insignificant to desecrate her.

Sterling didn't show himself in Laguna for a long time, and then only to buy food. He had held his breath, but the Tribal Council had ignored him. His grandnephews and grandnieces let him stay at the sheep camp, but they didn't trust him with sheep right away. There was gossip and speculation about what had happened to Sterling in Tucson. Sterling didn't look like his old self anymore. He had lost weight and quit drinking beer. The postmaster reported Sterling had let go all his magazine subscriptions. Sterling didn't care about the rumors and gossip because Sterling knew why the giant snake had returned now; he knew what the snake's message was to the people. The snake was looking south, in the direction from which the twin brothers and the people would come.

RIM OF CHRISTENDOM

Frederick Jackson Turner

From "The Significance of the Frontier in American History"

Studious and somewhat unprepossessing, historian Frederick Jackson Turner nevertheless was an ambitious young man, and when he stood up before the annual meeting of the American Historical Association in Chicago in 1893 he fully intended to startle his audience with an essay that treated the frontier as an integral and formative part of the American story. Even he was astonished, however, at the eagerness with which his thesis was accepted by most of his fellow historians for the next two generations.

In a recent bulletin of the Superintendent of the Census for 1890 appear these significant words: "Up to and including 1880 the country had a frontier of settlement, but at present the unsettled area has been so broken into by isolated bodies of settlement that there can hardly be said to be a frontier line. In the discussion of its extent, its westward movement, etc., it can not therefore, any longer have a place in the census reports." This brief official statement marks the closing of a great historic movement. Up to our own day American history has been in a large degree the history of the colonization of the Great West. The existence of an area of free land, its continuous recession, and the advance of American settlement westward, explain American development.

Behind institutions, behind constitutional forms and modifications, lie the vital forces that call these organs into life and shape them to meet changing conditions. The peculiarity of Amercian institutions is, the fact that they have been compelled to adapt themselves to the changes of an expanding people—to the changes involved in crossing a continent, in winning a wilderness, and in developing at each area of this progress out of the primitive economic and political conditions of the frontier into the complexity of city life. . . .

American social development has been continually beginning over again on the frontier. This perennial rebirth, this fluidity of American life, this expansion westward with its new opportunities, its continuous touch with the simplicity of primitive society, furnish the forces dominating American character. The true point of view in the history of this nation is not the Atlantic coast, it is the great West. . . .

Moving westward, the frontier became more and more American. As successive terminal moraines result from successive glaciations, so each frontier leaves its traces behind it, and when it becomes a settled area the region still partakes of the frontier characteristics. Thus the advance of the frontier has meant a steady movement away from the influence of Europe, a steady growth of independence on American lines. And to study this advance, the men who grew up under these conditions, and the political, economic, and social results of it, is to study the really American part of our history.

PAUL HORGAN

From *Great River*

"The River of Palms"

By the time Americans ventured across the Mississippi River in the beginning of the nineteenth century, the Spanish had already "conquered" the American West. Some of the first moments of the Spanish conquest, which began even before English settlers arrived in the New World, are brought to life in Paul Horgan's magnificent history, Great River: The Rio Grande in North American History *(1954).*

As it came to the sea at the Gulf of Mexico the river turned from side to side in looping bends and dragging effort like a great ancient dying snake. The land was white with sea shells and crusty with salty sand. On the low dunes hard tall ranks of grass stood up in thin blades that cut if touched. The sky was low, even in sunlight. Air over the sea thickened and thinned as wind and moisture played. Someone watching the sea where the river flowed its brown water into salty gray waves that broke shoreward forever, someone looking and idly turning his head, saw the low lines of the whole world—pale horizon, vapory sky, wide-shadowed green sea, the mist-white shore with its reed huts scattered close to the river, and the drying nets, and the powdery browns of the people moving at what they did. Warm in the fall, the days expected nothing new. The search for clams, crabs, oysters went on, and the dwellers watched for signs that the edible root of the sand dunes was coming into season. Now and then a memory of outrage by other people inland, or from up and down the coast, returned and brought caution. Enemies always came on foot. Sometimes all their dogs and children and women came too, and waited in the land haze for the outcome of battle. On some days the distance was blue with

misty heat and the aisles of palm trees along the river could be taken for smoke far away.

Looking to the land for food and protection, and to the sky for weathers that told the immediate future, the beach people kept no guard seaward, where the water birds dived with sounds
like splintering rock, and the clouds now met and hung over everything and again separated
and travelled like misty pearls and trailed shadows like mother of pearl over the waters that
were never still, and yet always the same, forever long as anyone remembered, forever and forever.

Yet the sea, the light, the clouds, had the power of making image and marvel out of nothing,
phantoms to loom and fade. Perhaps it was so with the vision of change that became visible on
the sea one day.

One, then another, and another, and another, sharp cloud came clear of the horizon. They
moved close on the surface of the water. They rested on dark bulks. They came toward shore,
all four of them. They were not clouds, then, but houses on the water, with trees standing out of
them holding up great mats in the air. All four moving slowly could turn in accord like birds.
Each time they turned they crossed a line nearer to the beach. Before long they were moving in
the water that was made brown by the run of the river into the sea. The mats were shaken and
changed, the bulks drifted, and all four came into the arms of the river, and in the moving houses were men amazingly decorated. Voices stranger than any before echoed across the water.

Twenty-seven years after Columbus's first discoveries, it was a day in the autumn of 1519
Anno Domini when four ships of Jamaica stood in through the veils of sea air to the mouth of
the Rio Grande, and the point of view was about to be changed for the next three hundred years
from that of the river Indian to that of the European soldiers, sailors, civil servants and friars—
for surely chaplains came too—on board the little fleet.

With their coming, the golden haze of the Indian story along the river began to lift. Hitherto,
the river people had been without individuality. Time was unrecorded and experience was halted within each generation. There was no way of setting down the past and of letting it recede.
The ancient people were trapped in an eternity of the present tense.

Now against the moving backdrop of the civilized world, the little fleet dropped anchor in
the brown river water, and someone on board recorded the act. Leo X was Pope, the earthly
source of all legitimate authority. The Emperor Charles V, King of Spain, was planning to go to
Germany to preside at hearings of Martin Luther. In England Henry VIII was King, and the
righteous author of an essay condemning Luther for defection from the Faith. In France, as
guest and employee of Francis I, Leonardo da Vinci died. Ferdinand Magellan was nearing

Tierra del Fuego in his first voyage around the globe. There were no European colonies anywhere in North America. Deep in Mexico, to the south, the passion to conquer smoldered like hidden coals under the courtesy with which the Captain-General Hernando Cortés approached the Emperor Montezuma high in his capital.

The four ships of the little fleet were under the command of Captain Alonso Alvarez de Pineda. With him were two hundred and seventy Spanish men-at-arms. They had been afloat since the previous spring. Their orders, issued by Francisco Garay, governor of Jamaica, directed them to coast along the shores of Florida as far as they might in order to find a water passage to the Orient. For a while the term Florida signified the whole immense crescent of the Gulf of Mexico. Pineda logged rivers and bays, but he had not found the strait for Cathay when in August he came upon other Spaniards already ashorte at Veracruz.

There was an incident at Veracruz. Pineda anchored his fleet in the harbor. The ships were reported to the Spanish commander ashore—Cortés, who at once went with fifty soldiers to investigate. No newcomers were welcome on that shore. Cortés had already sunk his own ships. His men were ready with his own spirit to take Mexico, for by now they had seen with him the gifts brought with soft messages by ambassadors from Montezuma; and they lusted for such a country. The feathered ambassadors had laid before Cortés an image of the sun, beautifully chased, of pure gold, the size of a carriage wheel, alone worth more than twenty thousand crowns; a larger disc, of silver, which was the moon; a helmet full of raw gold to the value of three thousand crowns; thirty excellently modelled gold figures of ducks, dogs, lions, deer, monkeys and tigers; ornaments—rods, collars, plumes of feathers, fans, all done in gold or silver; headdresses of precious green parrot feathers. The Emperor's messages in presenting the gifts said that he would not welcome the Spaniards in his capital. In return, Cortés gave the ambassadors three shirts of Holland cloth and a Venetian glass cup to take to their lord, with the answer that having come so far, he could not fail his own monarch the Emperor Charles V by not pressing forward to visit the ruler of Mexico in his palace. Mexico was rich. The soldiers knew it now for a fact in their own terms. Was every unknown land in the new world a treasure house? An ancient theme sounded again fatefully. Cortés wanted none to help, and none to share, in the ravishment of Mexico. Coming to the Veracruz beach with his soldiers to see who anchored offshore and what was wanted, he did not see Pineda, but met a notary and two soldiers from the anchored fleet, who in ceremony took possession of these lands for Governor Garay of Jamaica.

Cortés at once had them arrested and denuded. Putting three of his own men in the clothes of the captives, he sent them in the landing party's own boat to hail the ships to send ashore. A small boat with twelve men in it put in to the beach, and four came from it through the surf carrying crossbows and guns. Cortés's men sprang out of hiding and surrounded them. The small boat pushed off in alarm, and as it reached the nearest anchored ship, the fleet was already making sail. It departed.

So Cortés knew from his captives that the coasting expedition was also charged with laying claim to lands; and Pineda knew that a ruthless and powerful campaign was afoot in Mexico. Plunging heavily northward, the four ships travelled along the barren coast which at that season was also mild. There were no signs of other Spaniards, there were nothing but naked brown staring creatures as Pineda brought the squadron to the mouth of the river that reached inland and showed its course by its aisle of palm trees. The tallest masts of the vessels reached as high as the highest palms. At rest, the ships looked heavy and swollen, with their high bows and bulging sides and tall, suddenly narrowed housing at the stern where rows of windows framed in gilt carving flashed slowly when the hulls veered. Either under sail, or with sail furled as now, the ships looked to be nodding forward, across their own bowsprits.

Seen close to, their mystery vanished. Their clinker-built planking was crusted with barnacles. When an unloading port in the side was opened, and men leaned out gazing, a wave of foul air was let go. What looked like a cloud on the horizon was dirty coarse sailcloth with faded heraldic painting on it. The hulls were perhaps a third as long as the masts were high. A small boat was launched over the side to bring Pineda ashore. It was then proper style to step into the surf when the boat grounded and, drawing a sword, slash the blade into the waves, stating at the same time that these waters, and this land, and all in their provinces, now came under the possession of His Most Catholic Majesty.

Company from the ships followed the captain ashore. They were in general slender and muscular people, not very tall, but finely proportioned. Their heads were narrow, their faces oval, their hands and fingers long, their shoulders sloping. Moving with grace, and a certain suggestion of repose, they yet could in an instant flare into violence, sparring with blade or pike swift and deadly. Their skin was tough and swarthy, taking the light with a faint tarnish of gold, and turning in shadow with warm darks that suggested embers buried but alive and ardent. They kept their dark hair cropped like caps hugging their tall skulls. Many of them, even youths, wore mustaches that curved out about the mouth to meet sharply pointed beards under the lower lip. The lips were exposed, ruddy and sharply scrolled. These swarthy faces flashed alive with startling whites—the whites of eyes set off by the piercing black of their pupils, and the whites of teeth showing through lips parted for the breath of interest. Their eyes were set deep and often showed black shadows under the carved shell of their brows. In the faces of old men, the eyes were like black gems that reflected suffering, resignation and irony from the world all about them. The eyelids roofed over from a little curved fold deep in the socket. In the faces of young men, the eyes, suggesting a taste for life to be both given and taken, shone with calm animal charm. Above metal gorget or velvet collar a white ruffle of starched linen, sometimes edged with lace, gleamed along the dark jaws, bony or bearded, of those lean, perfervid faces.

Those men were not all dressed alike. Some—the leaders, the elders—wore shining pieces of armor at the neck, the breast, the arms, the thighs. Others wore chain-mail shirts, hauberks, under their ordinary shirts of Holland linen. Some had jackets of many layers of quilted cotton, that could turn or break the blow of an arrow. Some wore metal helmets shaped like deep slices of melon, that were morions, and others had hats of leather and felt shaped like little round boxes with tufted brims and jeweled brooches and expensive feathers from eastern Africa. There were suits of brocade or velvet, stained and worn from travel, padded and puffed at the shoulders and elbows. The hips and loins were covered with trunks made of leather or heavy cloth, slashed and puffed to show other stuff and color beneath. Their legs looked long and slender and ceremonial, encased in tight thick hose that reached to the groin. Soft leather boots were worn either rippled up tight on the thighs or loosely pulled down about the calves in many folds. Shoes were flat-soled-and-heeled, and had puffed and slashed toes revealing contrasting color. Everyone had cloaks, some with embroidery of gold and silver bullion, some plain, but all voluminous and expressive in gesture, whether thrown about the face for warmth or secrecy, or lifted by a sword at the rear like the rooster's tail, and all hanging as richly from the shoulders of a hungry private soldier as from those of a hereditary gentleman.

At the waist, aslant the codpiece, nestled the dagger with hilt turned to receive the left hand instantly. At the left side, from a baldric of leather studded variously with precious stones, or gold, silver or brass rivets, hung the sword with basket guard, silver wire-wrapped hilt, and a cross guard below the grip that signified when necessary the crucifix. The private soldiers carried a variety of tall weapons—pikes, halberds, spears, lances—and some had maces, including the morning star from Germany with its long-spiked ball dangling from a length of chain. A platoon handled the heavy crossbows that with their carved and colored ornaments, graceful curved bows and stout thongs at a glance suggested some sort of plectral instrument for music. A few elite soldiers handled the heavily chased flintlock muskets bound to walnut or blackthorn stocks with thick bands of copper, brass and silver. A hardly bearded youngster in white hose and quilted body mail, with indifference masking pride, might carry the royal standard on a tall pole tipped with silk streamers and a sharp iron point.

They gave in the light every color as they came out of the foul ships and crossed to the shore. They found the Indians friendly in their leathery nakedness. A sizable squatters' town reached along the river at the mouth. Supplies must be at hand. The beach was wide and sloped gently, so gently that the tidal marks of certain seasons showed far back in the sharp-grassed marshes. The air was balmy. As far inland as could be seen the ground was flat and easy to explore. Pineda's ships were ready for overhaul. Here he ordered them careened.

The Spanish company spent forty days about the mouth of the Rio Grande, which they called the Rio de las Palmas. While some of the men worked on the ships—scraping barnacles, recaulking, repairing—others went into the country. They traded with the Indians, though for what and with what nobody said. Travelling eighteen miles upriver from the mouth, they found forty Indian towns—wattled reed and mud houses to come to for sea food seasons, and to leave when the roots and berries inland were ready to be eaten. There was no report of seeds planted and crops raised for food. Pineda told in sweeping general terms of the whole land he had seen, from Florida to Veracruz, and found it good, at peace, productive, healthful. He saw Indians with gold ornaments but did not say where. But of all the places he had seen he chose the River of Palms to recommend for colonization when at the end of forty days, the ships were floated, and the expeditioners embarked for their return to Jamaica, four and a third centuries ago, laden with the most desirable cargo of their time—knowledge of new lands.

WILLA CATHER

From *Death Comes for the Archbishop*

"The Lady"

From the beginning of Spanish settlement until the American conquest of 1846–1848, priests, soldiers, and rancheros *made up the ruling class of the American Southwest. In this excerpt from* Death Comes for the Archbishop *(1927), a romantic fictional biography of Bishop Jean Baptist Lamy of Santa Fé, novelist Willa Cather gives us a glimpse into the complex culture that prevailed in the pre-American years.*

Antonio Olivares's funeral was the most solemn and magnificent ever seen in Santa Fé, but Father Vaillant was not there. He was off on a long missionary journey to the south, and did not

STUART DAVIS. *New Mexico Gate.* 1923. Oil on linen. Roswell Museum and Art Center, Roswell, New Mexico. Gift of Mr. and Mrs. Donald Winston and Mr. and Mrs. Samuel H. Marshall. © Estate of Stuart Davis/VAGA, New York 1994.

reach home until Madame Olivares had been a widow for some weeks. He had scarcely got off his riding-boots when he was called into Father Latour's study to see her lawyer.

Olivares had entrusted the management of his affairs to a young Irish Catholic, Boyd O'Reilly, who had come out from Boston to practise law in the new Territory. There were no steel safes in Santa Fé at that time, but O'Reilly had kept Olivares's will in his strong-box. The document was brief and clear: Antonio's estate amounted to about two hundred thousand dol= lars in American money (a considerable fortune in those days). The income therefrom was to be enjoyed by "my wife, Isabella Olivares, and her daughter, Inez Olivares," during their lives, and after their decease his property was to go to the Church, to the Society for the Propagation of the Faith. The codicil, in favour of the Cathedral fund, had, unfortunately, never been added to the will.

The young lawyer explained to Father Vaillant that the Olivares brothers had retained the leading legal firm of Albuquerque and were contesting the will. Their point of attack was that Señora Inez was too old to be the daughter of the Señora Olivares. Don Antonio had been a promiscuous lover in his young days, and his brothers held that Inez was the offspring of some temporary attachment, and had been adopted by Doña Isabella. O'Reilly had sent to New Orleans for an attested copy of the marriage record of the Olivares couple, and the birth certificate of Señorita Inez. But in Kentucky, where the Señora was born, no birth records were kept; there was no document to prove the age of Isabella Olivares, and she could not be per- suaded to admit her true age. It was generally believed in Santa Fé that she was still in her early forties, in which case she would not have been more than six or eight years old at the date when Inez was born. In reality the lady was past fifty, but when O'Reilly had tried to persuade her to admit this in court, she simply refused to listen to him. He begged the Bishop and the Vicar to use their influence with her to this end.

Father Latour shrank from interfering in so delicate a matter, but Father Vaillant saw at once that it was their plain duty to protect the two women and, at the same time, secure the rights of the Propaganda. Without more ado he threw on his old cloak over his cassock, and the three men set off through the red mud to the Olivares' hacienda in the hills east of the town.

Father Joseph had not been to the Olivares' house since the night of the New Year's party, and he sighed as he approached the place, already transformed by neglect. The big gate was propped open by a pole because the iron hook was gone, the court-yard was littered with rags and meat bones which the dogs had carried there and no one had taken away. The big parrot cage, hanging in the *portale*, was filthy, and the birds were squalling. When O'Reilly rang the bell at the outer gate, Pablo, the banjo player, came running out with tousled hair and a dirty shirt to admit the visitors. He took them into the long living-room, which was empty and cold, the fire-place dark, the hearth unswept. Chairs and window-sills were deep in red dust, the glass panes dirty, and streaked as if by tear-drops. On the writing-table were empty bottles and sticky glasses and cigar ends. In one corner stood the harp in its green cover.

Pablo asked the Fathers to be seated. His mistress was staying in bed, he said, and the cook had burnt her hand, and the other maids were lazy. He brought wood and laid a fire.

After some time, Doña Isabella entered, dressed in heavy mourning, her face very white against the black, and her eyes red. The curls about her neck and ears were pale, too—quite ashen.

After Father Vaillant had greeted her and spoken consoling words, the young lawyer began once more gently to explain to her the difficulties that confronted them, and what they must do to defeat the action of the Olivares family. She sat submissively, touching her eyes and nose with her little lace handkerchief, and clearly not even trying to understand a word of what he said to her.

Father Joseph soon lost patience and himself approached the widow. "You understand, my child," he began briskly, "that your husband's brothers are determined to disregard his wishes, to defraud you and your daughter, and, eventually, the Church. This is no time for childish vanity. To prevent this outrage to your husband's memory, you must satisfy the court that you are old enough to be the mother of Mademoiselle Inez. You must resolutely declare your true age; fifty-three, is it not?"

Doña Isabella became pallid with fright. She shrank into one end of the deep sofa, but her blue eyes focused and gathered light, as she became intensely, rigidly animated in her corner,—her back against the wall, as it were.

"Fifty-three!" she cried in a voice of horrified amazement. "Why, I never heard of anything so outrageous! I was forty-two my last birthday. It was in December, the fourth of December. If Antonio were here, he would tell you! And he wouldn't let you scold me and talk about business to me, either, Father Joseph. He never let anybody talk about business to me!" She hid her face in her little handkerchief and began to cry.

Father Latour checked his impetuous Vicar, and sat down on the sofa beside Madame Olivares, feeling very sorry for her and speaking very gently. "Forty-two to your friends, dear Madame Olivares, and to the world. In heart and face you are younger than that. But to the Law and the Church there must be a literal reckoning. A formal statement in court will not make you any older to your friends; it will not add one line to your face. A woman, you know, is as old as she looks."

"That's very sweet of you to say, Bishop Latour," the lady quavered, looking up at him with tear-bright eyes. "But I never could hold up my head again. Let the Olivares have that old money. I don't want it."

Father Vaillant sprang up and glared down at her as if he could put common sense into her drooping head by the mere intensity of his gaze. "Four hundred thousand pesos, Señora Isabella!" he cried. "Ease and comfort for you and your daughter all the rest of your lives. Would you make your daughter a beggar? The Olivares will take everything."

"I can't help it about Inez," she pleaded. "Inez means to go into the convent anyway. And I don't care about the money. *Ah, mon père, je voudrais mieux être jeune et mendiante, que n'être que vieille et riche, cerres, oui!*"

Father Joseph caught her icy cold hand. "And have you a right to defraud the Church of what is left to it in your trust? Have you thought of the consequences to yourself of such a betrayal?"

Father Latour glanced sternly at his Vicar. *"Assez,"* he said quietly. He took the little hand Father Joseph had released and bent over it, kissing it respectfully. "We must not press this any further. We must leave this to Madame Olivares and her own conscience. I believe, my daughter, you will come to realize that this sacrifice of your vanity would be for your soul's peace. Looking merely at the temporal aspect of the case, you would find poverty hard to bear. You would have to live upon the Olivares's charity, would you not? I do not wish to see this come about. I have a selfish interest; I wish you to be always your charming self and to make a little *poésie* in life for us here. We have not much of that."

Madame Olivares stopped crying. She raised her head and sat drying her eyes. Suddenly she took hold of one of the buttons on the Bishop's cassock and began twisting it with nervous fingers.

"Father," she said timidly, "what is the youngest I could possibly be, to be Inez's mother?"

The Bishop could not pronounce the verdict; he hesitated, flushed, then passed it on to O'Reilly with an open gesture of his fine white hand.

"Fifty-two, Señora Olivares," said the young man respectfully. If I can get you to admit that, and stick to it, I feel sure we will win our case."

"Very well, Mr. O'Reilly." She bowed her head. As her visitors rose, she sat looking down at the dust-covered rugs. "Before everybody!" she murmured, as if to herself.

When they were tramping home, Father Joseph said that, as for him, he would rather combat the superstitions of a whole Indian pueblo than the vanity of one white woman.

"And I would rather do almost anything than go through such a scene again," said the Bishop with a frown. "I don't think I ever assisted at anything so cruel."

Boyd O'Reilly defeated the Olivares brothers and won his case. The Bishop would not go to the court hearing, but Father Vaillant was there, standing in the malodorous crowd (there were no chairs in the court room), and his knees shook under him when the young lawyer, with the fierceness born of fright, poked his finger at his client and said:

"Señora Olivares, you are fifty-two years of age, are you not?"

Madame Olivares was swathed in mourning, her face a streak of shadowed white between folds of black veil.

"Yes, sir." The crape barely let it through.

The night after the verdict was pronounced, Manuel Chavez, with several of Antonio's old friends, called upon the widow to congratulate her. Word of their intention had gone about the town and put others in the mood to call at a house that had been closed to visitors for so long. A considerable company gathered there that evening, including some of the military people, and several hereditary enemies of the Olivares brothers.

The cook, stimulated by the sight of the long *sala* full of people once more, hastily improvised a supper. Pablo put on a white shirt and a velvet jacket, and began to carry up from the cellar his late master's best whisky and sherry, and quarts of champagne. (The Mexicans are very fond of sparkling wines. Only a few years before this, an American trader who had got into serious political trouble with the Mexican military authorities in Santa Fé, regained their confidence and friendship by presenting them with a large wagon shipment of champagne— three thousand, three hundred and ninety-two bottles, indeed!)

This hospitable mood came upon the house suddenly, nothing had been prepared beforehand. The wine glasses were full of dust, but Pablo wiped them out with the shirt he had just taken off, and without instructions from anyone he began gliding about with a tray full of glasses, which he afterward refilled many times, taking his station at the sideboard. Even Doña Isabella drank a little champagne; when she had sipped one glass with the young Georgia captain, she could not refuse to take another with their nearest neighbour, Ferdinand Sanchez, always a true friend to her husband. Everyone was gay, the servants and the guests, everything sparkled like a garden after a shower.

Father Latour and Father Vaillant, having heard nothing of this spontaneous gathering of friends, set off at eight o'clock to make a call upon the brave widow. When they entered the court-yard, they were astonished to hear music within, and to see light streaming from the long row of windows behind the *portale*. Without stopping to knock, they opened the door into the *sala*. Many candles were burning. Señors were standing about in long frock-coats buttoned over full figures. O'Reilly and a group of officers from the Fort surrounded the sideboard, where Pablo, with a white napkin wrapped showily about his wrist, was pouring champagne. From the other end of the room sounded the high tinkle of the harp, and Doña Isabella's voice:

> *"Listen to the mocking-bird,*
> *Listen to the mocking-bird!"*

The priests waited in the doorway until the song was finished, then went forward to pay their respects to the hostess. She was wearing the unrelieved white that grief permitted, and the yellow curls were bobbing as of old—three behind her right ear, one over either temple, and a little row across the back of her neck. As she saw the two black figures approaching, she dropped her arms from the harp, took her satin toe from the pedal, and rose, holding out a hand to each. Her eyes were bright, and her face beamed with affection for her spiritual fathers. But her greeting was a playful reproach, uttered loud enough to be heard above the murmur of conversing groups:

"I never shall forgive you, Father Joseph, nor you either, Bishop Latour, for that awful lie you made me tell in court about my age!"

The two churchmen bowed amid laughter and applause.

HARVEY FERGUSSON

From *Followers of the Sun*

A View from Inside the Old Order

The society of the rancheros, *in which cattle fiefdoms the size of small European countries were owned by men with virtually absolute power over the peons and* vaqueros *who did the work, was an extraordinarily rigid, insular, and self-involved culture. In a moment from* Wolf Song *(1921), the first in his epic triology of novels about the Southwest,* Followers of the Sun *(1949), Harvey Fergusson suggests the insecurity that lay beneath all the bluster and arrogance.*

When Don Solomon Salazar came in they all stopped talking and smoking. They waited his pleasure. In this house he the father was God. He had the majesty of a God, tall, erect and dignified with the human mystery of his mouth hidden behind fierce white mustachios. His nose commanded and his eyes defied. His belly bulged with many years of good living. He was dressed in leather but his wealth supported his dignity with a blue serape worth two hundred dollars and a towering black and silver sombrero. A long white scar crossed his cheek from ear to nose.

It was one of many scars that were livid on the pale polished leather of his aging skin and bloody still in his aging memory. He was a walking record of Indian battles—whooping, yelling battles of terrific dust and noise, of soul-satisfying excitement—battles fought with arrows, lances, muskets, knives and swords, battles of great glory and little blood. He fought them over endlessly in words while his household listened in drowsy respectful obedience as they listened to the priest chanting Latin. He liked to begin more than half a century before when the Comanches wiped out the first settlement of Taos and galloped away to the mountains with screaming Spanish women in their arms and Spanish scalps at their belts. A few survivors got to Mexico City and these returned and built the walled town. When the Comanches came again they were ready for them. Don Solomon's father was among those who built the town so the Don knew all about that mighty battle. The Comanches were beaten—they were all but annihilated. How many were killed? God knows, but the slaughter was awful. Dead Comanches littered the valley and blood ran ankle deep in the roads and they came back to the town with cartloads of scalps and plunder. . . .

Never after that had wild Indians attacked the town but all through the youth of Don Solomon life had been a long series of skirmishes with Indians who came to raid the herds. Don Solomon had killed Comanches, Apaches and Navajos. He had been shot with arrows in fourteen places, carried a bullet in his left leg and had three knife scars, including one on the back of his neck made by an Apache who tried to scalp him while he lay stunned. The prick of the knife brought him to. He strangled the Apache and scalped him with his own knife. It was his favorite story. His great yellow hands worked when he told it. He could still crumple a silver plate between them.

Well, all that was a long time ago. The Indians were still bad, to be sure, but they seldom raided the principal settlements of New Mexico. Along the Rio Grande from Taos to El Paso the Mexican power sat firm, crops were growing, sheep herds were multiplying into tens of thousands, young men were getting fat and lazy with nothing to fight, devoting their time to cock-pits, monte and the girls. Don Solomon was disgusted with the younger generation. The girls were as bad as the boys. The way they flirted with the gringos! It was revolting. And the gringos were coming more every year with their wagonloads of cheap goods from St. Louis, taking all the money out of the country. They trapped beaver in all the Mexican streams against the Mexican law, bribed the *alcalde* right here in Taos and sold their stolen peltries for Mexican dollars! Then they gave *bailes*, got drunk and made free with the women. . . . Let some gringo lay a finger on his wife or daughter! . . . But the terrible part of it was the women seemed to like them.

And the government? There wasn't any government! Ever since the revolution Mexico City had been a puddle of corruption and in Santa Fe the upstart Armijo, who began life stealing sheep, sat in the governor's palace, looted the treasury to buy Indian girls and sold guns to the Apaches.

For his services against the Indians the government had granted Don Solomon a great tract of land across the mountains. He was to establish there a colony as a bulwark against the gringos and the wild Indians of the prairies. . . . He might as well have tried to colonize the moon. Nobody wanted to go. He was too old himself and young men had no courage any more. . . . What could a man do? Don Solomon rode his acres, drank his wine, cursed man and trusted God.

Now he sat serenely chatting among his family and friends. He told his wife the lambing was good this year and that his herders had killed a wolf and the chile crop was an inch above

CHARLES C. NAHL.
Vaqueros Roping a Steer.
Oil on canvas. 42 x 51 in.
Courtesy of The
Anschutz Collection,
Denver, Colorado.

the ground. He clapped his hands and two Indian girls brought silver pitchers of thick chocolate, silver cups and plates heaped with hot sweet cakes. They all ate, dipping their cakes into thick brown dripping chocolate, munching and talking. Warmed and comforted he stretched his legs, rolled a cigarette and called for a light, graciously bade Ambrosio to smoke—which the younger would never have done without permission. . . . It was an evil and a changing world but here in his thick-walled house were peace and order he had created.

Suddenly they all stopped eating and listened. From the plaza came faintly to their ears a growing rumpus. Dogs barked, a man shouted. Then an Indian chant—a chant not of peaceful pueblos but of wild Indians, riding. "Hai, hai, hai! Haiyai, haiyai, haiyai!"

"Bang!" went a gun. A man shouted.

"Eeowgh! yough!" It was the shrill yell of Apaches!

Don Solomon got to his feet with an agility that he thought he had lost forever. He hurried out and across the *placita*, followed by all the others. The old *portero*, Juan Garcia, who had been with the family twenty years, had opened the double doors a crack and was looking out. He turned to meet them.

"*Indios?*" Don Solomon demanded, incredulous but eager.

Juan spread his hands and wrinkled his nose.

"Gringos!" he snorted in disgust. "*Indios blancos!*"

The Don looked out and saw a band of trappers riding into the plaza with a great dust and thunder of hooves, yelling like Indians as they always did when drunk. One of them had shot his pistol into the air.

Don Solomon, disgusted, turned away. He did not want to see gringos. They had no place in the completed pattern of his life. He snorted and went back to his chocolate and his cigarette.... A gringo was something he could neither fight nor love.

Peering through the door opened a crack, with her *reboso* drawn up to hide all but her eyes, Lola watched mountain men ride by. Childlike she sorted them and picked one—a tall lean young man with sunbleached hair blowing wild from under his hat, bleached eyebrows showing like scars against the deep red of his face, eyes bright blue, alert and roaming—she sorted them and picked that one for hers. . . .

He was a strange man from far away, a brave man who went up and down the earth alone with a gun in his hands and fought for his life. He was a wild man, hard to catch and hard to hold, a man uncomforted who slept alone on the hard ground—a man aching with need of all a woman had to give.

He was dirty, to be sure, but he could be washed and his skin would be so white and his hair so golden.

She would have liked to run out and bid them all come in and give them chocolate and cake. *Pobercitos!* They never had chocolate and cake. . . .

O sweetness she would like to give where sweetness so was needed!

William Brandon

"Bernalillo County"

Since the conquest of 1846, the relationship between Anglos and Mexican-Americans in the Southwest has remained both troubled and complex. But, as historian William Brandon suggests in this personal memoir, for some, at least, the quiet democracy of childhood could transcend prejudice.

W. R. Leigh. *Greased Lightning*. Oil. 28 x 22 in. The Harmsen Collection.

When I was seven years old we went to live on a little ranch in Bernalillo County, New Mexico. Nothing could have made me happier since at the time I had an ambition to be a cowboy. I haven't entirely gotten over the ambition yet.

In Bernalillo County I got to be a cowboy. I had a horse named Buddy, and there was a cow, and sometimes a calf, and a four-acre field for me to round it, or them, up in. I often spent all day riding herd on the cow while she grazed. She was a well-herded cow, but it spoiled her. She would try to come along with Buddy and my brother Cal and me when we went to school. When we came back in the evening she would be bitter and spiteful and get bloated on purpose, and Cal and I would have to run her up and down until long after dark to unbloat her.

I also had a pair of beat-up chaps and what was supposed to be a cowboy hat. In style, the hat was more William S. Hart than Tom Mix. It looked as if it had been handed down to me after William S. Hart had used it for sacking up potatoes. But I thought it was pretty fine, although I got bow-ears from it. I was gratified to get bow-legged, and I am still bow-legged today and secretly proud of it. I'm still bow-eared too, but you have to take one thing with another.

The world is big and someplace in it there may be better country for growing up in, but surely none a kid could like better for growing up in if he happened to have an ambition to be a cowboy. Nowadays malevolent psychologists tell us that childhood is not a happy time at all but only looks that way from a distance. Clearly they were never cowboys in New Mexico at the age of nine or ten. Great and terrible events were abroad in the land in those years: the Teapot Dome loomed over New Mexico; the Bursum Bill lurked and menaced; the McNary-Haugen Bill was defeated; the Santa Fe yards in Albuquerque caught fire. But I lived in bliss in spite of everything. The only genuine unhappiness I have ever been able to remember from that life was when we moved away. Then I had to let Buddy be sold. I can't think of it yet without a lump in my throat. I was eleven then and a good deal too big to cry, and naturally cowboys didn't anyway; but I went out behind the adobe feed shed and wept as I never had before and hope I never do again. But the pain of an ending can't outweigh the previous joys of being. Otherwise we'd all sensibly strangle ourselves in our infancy.

It happened, more or less by accident, that Buddy was not only a real cow horse but also a professional cutting horse. Sometimes in the spring and fall I reluctantly permitted him to be rented out for that purpose to legitimate cowboys, who always praised him highly. Once, a polo player from the cavalry team down at Fort Bliss, at El Paso, came up to see him and wanted to buy him.

With all these accomplishments Buddy had considerable contempt for me and frequently put me in my place, which was head over heels in the ditch. That horse must have thrown me nine thousand times by the most conservative estimate. He wouldn't carry double, so whenever we wanted a little rodeo my brother Cal and I had only to hop on him both at once and he would pitch in great shape.

There was a boy named Jesús Gonzalez who had a long-legged white mare, very fast, and she could outrun Buddy with a leg to spare once she got started, but when we had races we raced to a mark and back again, and Buddy would sometimes win because of the turn. He was as handy as a pocket in a shirt. But he was too handy for me. When he would skid behind and peel himself around in one of those remarkable quick turns and take out again with a bound, he would often as not leave me going straight ahead. So he was disqualified for a lot of races he won, merely because I didn't come back to the starting line with him. I think he thought it was unfair and that he was overhandicapped to begin with, but he kept trying, and now and then he would win with me still on him, technically.

Like any intelligent horse, Buddy didn't like to leave home. A mystic spot about a hundred yards down the road from our gate represented the outermost limits of home to him, and here he would want to turn back. I would haul him around with both hands and start him out again. Then he would turn around again. Then I would break a stick off a cottonwood limb and whack him. Then he would back down in the ditch and flatten his ears. Then I would kick him and whack him and he wouldn't move, and at this point Cal would always appear, to jeer at my humiliation. Thinking about it, I can't understand why I loved that damned horse. But I did. I still do.

Whenever Buddy was left out to pasture for a few days without being used, he forgot that he was supposed to be broke and gentle. He wouldn't let himself be caught up, and when he *was* caught up he wouldn't let himself be saddled. All of this was a battle, and he would rear back and plunge and kick sideways at you when you tried to tighten up the cinch, and for the first little bit after you got on him he would dance and kick up and try to get his head down so he could buck and throw you off. If he got his head down he always unloaded me, because when he really wanted to cut loose he could buck quite handsomely, at least so it seemed to me. It seemed to me he went eleven feet in the air every jump, and stayed up there sunfishing for five minutes at a time. Now I could never ride worth a plugged nickel, which should be evident, since most of the time I should have spent learning was instead spent bouncing on the ground, and it may be that to someone else Buddy would only have seemed a mite skittish. I never saw the great bucking horse Midnight, but I saw Five Minutes to Midnight once at Madison Square Garden, and all I know is that his bucking form sure looked familiar. My private opinion is that he was one of Buddy's students.

The way I caught Buddy up when he didn't want to be caught was to go down the road to a neighbor named Jeff, who was a real cowboy, and ask him to do it. Jeff would bring his rope, back Buddy into a fence corner, and spin out a loop and rope him, as easy as shutting a door. It was always a scene of great drama and excitement, because the loop would sing in the air, and Buddy would whirl gigantically this way and that, wanting to dodge it. Jeff wore cowboy boots and had a steeldust horse, and although he was a grown man, he was simple and kindly and put on no airs and treated Cal and me as equals. When he got time off he liked to ride up on the mesa, and sometimes he let me go along with him.

Our place was across the Rio Grande from Albuquerque, and behind us was the mesa, and beyond that three extinct volcanoes, all in a row. We never rode toward the river and Albuquerque, but always toward the mesa. Along the irrigation ditches there were trees, and there were square adobe houses garlanded with red peppers, and sand and chaparral. Sometimes the horses would walk or trot and sometimes Jeff would say, "Let's go!" and we would lope, and if a car went by in sight on the road Jeff would wave and we would let the horses run to show off.

Up on the mesa there were seas of rippled sand and islands of half-buried cactus. Jeff would always ride to the rim of the mesa and dismount and squat on his toes and look out over the river. Away across the river there were the Sandia Mountains—the Watermelons—veiled with magic colors that dissolved as the sun sank low, and the river was stippled with green along its edges and split into numerous winding ribbons, and the sky was streaked with rust. When the sun was setting the three volcanoes burned as if they were on fire. Then the afterglow leached through the air, the clearest light in the world, as delicate as a distant echo, and Jeff would get up and swing on his steeldust horse again and we would ride home. I stayed in the saddle on Buddy, because I wasn't too sure I'd be able to get back aboard him again without a lot of trouble that would be embarrassing.

Jeff seldom said anything. Once he told me his steeldust horse wouldn't let anyone else ride him. I suppose now that he was warning me in case I had any ideas about stealing a ride on him. At the time I thought he was only stating an objective fact, and I always treated the steeldust horse with great respect. Aside from that, and "Let's go!" and an occasional "Sure" in answer to some question, I can't remember Jeff saying anything, except very rarely. One of the last times we rode up on the mesa he made a remark voluntarily. I thought I was big enough then to dismount, too; so I did, and sat down on the warm sand and looked at the valley. Jeff, after a while, celebrated the occasion by making an observation about the view we had gone up there so often to see. He said, "Sure is quiet."

Jeff's father lived with him. He was a stumpy old man, bald-headed, and he always wore a flat-crowned hat. He called it a Texas hat. I know that he felt undressed without his hat, because one time when he had come down to our place to help out in some crisis, and my mother asked him to come in for a cup of coffee, he said he couldn't because he had come in such a hurry he hadn't brought his hat.

Cal and I went to a one-room school a mile or so away, although while we were there another room was added on. There were comparatively few Anglos among the pupils, and in the lower grades lessons were taught in both English and Spanish. At recess and at noon hour the bigger kids who had ridden horses to school rigged up makeshift bucking straps with burrs and ropes and had rodeos. I didn't like to participate because I didn't like to stick Buddy in the flanks with burrs and because I'd just as soon he kept it confidential that I was the sorriest rider in the school's history. It was ignominious to prove it in front of the girls. Another occupation at recess was hunting horned toads. They would weep tears of blood, and since we all believed in *brujas*, or witches, those miraculous tears were awesome and moving and gave rise to metaphysical discussions.

We learned to swim in an *acequia madre*, a mother irrigation ditch. Hollywood can have its blue-tiled, kidney-shaped pools, clear and sparkling, and the Cote d'Azur can have its sapphire Mediterranean, and you can even have your shade-dappled old swimming hole down the creek, but give me my muddy *acequia* on a desert-hot day, with José and Jesús and Maria and Cal, and our big old dog Turk chasing a water snake, and a watermelon waiting in the cool under the bank to be busted when we got out.

Old Turk was killed by a rattlesnake one August day when we were exploring along the bed of the Rio Grande. We were there because we'd been told to keep away, with fearsome stories of quicksand, and Turk got killed, and it was a lesson to us. Rattlesnakes were said to be blind during dog days, when they were shedding their skins, and at that time they would strike without warning.

I think people in a big empty country get a special kind of affection for it. I think most of the people there, grown-ups as well as the kids, even those who didn't particularly want to be cowboys, felt more than an ordinary tenderness for the sunburnt land and the blazing sky around them. They didn't rhapsodize about it and you wouldn't expect them to, any more than you'd expect the Queen of England to walk along striking matches on her thumbnail. But sometimes something was said.

One graduation day at school, or rather evening, when parents came and various unlucky pupils had pieces to speak, José, dressed up in his narrowest overall pants and a black sateen shirt, was waiting for his turn to recite. While he was waiting he was looking out the window at nighthawks sailing against the last ivory color of the afterglow. The teacher called on him and he didn't hear her, so she snapped him to. Then more kindly, since parents were present, she asked him what he had been dreaming about. José said with a flashing smile, "I was watching a bird fly." He explained it seriously, and as if he expected everyone to understand, and everyone seemed to understand.

Nighthawks always make me think of New Mexico.

RITA MAGDALENO

"Hermanita"

Today's generation of Mexican-American writers is especially aware of the inequality between the Chicano and Anglo societies, and much of their writing reverberates with a very modern— and largely justified—anger. Still, the best of these writers reach into the wellsprings of tradition to create a literature. Among these is Rita Magdaleno, whose wrenching "Hermanita" carries the power of some ancient story written out of the earth itself.

We were old enough. Sí, old enough to go con mi Papá. That night, the moon was coming up like a mistake, like an eye punched out, swollen like a calabacita, so soft and puffy. It was the bluish color of a little plum squeezed too hard. Sí, the moon was a mistake coming up that night in Grover Canyon over the tailings of Inspiration Mine and all the stripped hills; over gray horses in the next canyon and the sad little songs that José strummed on his guitar; over the jojoba and the Alamo trees; over the two Holly Berry and our small back porch. It was winter, November, our back yard ice cold. And you, hermanita, went to sleep forever. Señor, why did you take her? I got down on my knees and prayed, "Oh, sweet Jesus, you are so kind. Por favor, Dios, give us your blessings and deliver us from evil." But my Mama still opened her legs and let the little death slide again. You, coming wet and red into the house, into the big brown hands de la Señora Flores. Pobrecita, mi hermanita. I prayed and prayed for you.

That night, after everyone fell asleep, Papá came. "Come on, wake up . . . Shhh. Carmen y Chayo, levántense. Get up." And we put on our shoes, wrapped white blankets around our shoulders como Indias, like little ghosts con ponchos. It was like a holy ceremony and we were putting on white vestments. We were following our Papá out to the back yard in Grover Canyon. Hush! Callado . . . calladito, quiet. Shhh! And I saw the pale bruised moon. She hung above us as we made our little procession into the night, la Noche Triste.

Hermanita, you never got a name. That night, we wrapped you in a little silk scarf, slipped you back into the earth, into Grover Canyon, into Nuestra Madre. Our Mother—la Mujer Buena. Buena, Good Mother. Sí, we slipped you into la tierra bendita because there was no money to bury you, pobrecita. It nearly broke my father's heart, his big corazón. He was a

COLORPLATE 27

CHARLES M. RUSSELL. *Cowboy Camp During the Roundup (Utica Picture)*. c. 1885–1887. Oil on canvas.
23 1/2 x 47 1/4 in. Amon Carter Museum, Fort Worth, Texas. *Like the annual rendezvous of the mountain men, the spring roundups of the cattle industry—though usually a little more sedate and businesslike—were occasions for letting loose with a little rambunctious behavior. As cowboy artist Charles M. Russell illustrated in one of his most purely documentary paintings, however, among the very real chores was roping and breaking in horses that had gone a little wild over the winter, a practice that led to the development of the rodeo as a sporting event.*

COLORPLATE 28

ARTIST UNKNOWN. *Pikes Peak or Bust.* 1870. Oil on canvas. 18 x 24 in. Courtesy Colorado Historical Society, Denver. *The "Pikes Peak" on the wagon cover in this anonymous rendition was in Colorado—eastern Kansas at the time—and the occasion that spurred travel to that country was the discovery of gold in 1858. The result was the biggest gold rush since that to California in 1849. Many people succumbed along the way—though very few from the kinds of attacks depicted here. It was nearly a thousand miles from the Mississippi and Missouri river towns to the Colorado gold fields, and most people who died did so because they drowned while fording streams, drank bad water, or simply got lost, wandering away from water sources and grass for their animals.*

COLORPLATE 29

WILLIAM DE LA MONTAGNE CARY. *The Upper Missouri*. 1875. Oil on canvas. 14 5/8 x 27 3/8 in. The Rockwell Museum, Corning, New York. *Of the five greatest rivers of the West—the Colorado, the Rio Grande, the Yellowstone, the Columbia, and the Missouri—none was more romantically compelling than the Missouri, not least because, unlike the others, it was navigable along most of its length. No one captured its particular beauty better than William Cary, a peripatetic artist who wandered through much of the West in the 1860s and 1870s.*

COLORPLATE 30 (following spread)

THOMAS MORAN. *Cliffs of the Upper Colorado River, Wyoming Territory*. 1882. Oil on canvas. 16 x 24 in. National Museum of American Art, Washington, D.C. Ranger Fund.

COLORPLATE 31 (top)

ALBERT BIERSTADT. *Surveyor's Wagon in the Rockies.* 1830–1902. Oil on paper on canvas. 7 3/4 x 12 7/8 in. St. Louis Art Museum. Gift of Lionberger Davis.

COLORPLATE 32 (bottom)

THOMAS P. OTTER. *On the Road.* 1860. Oil on canvas. 22 x 45 3/8 in. The Nelson-Atkins Museum of Art, Kansas City, Missouri. Purchase: Nelson Trust.

COLORPLATE 33

SETH EASTMAN. *Ballplay of the Sioux on the St. Peters River in Winter.* 1848. Oil on canvas. 25 3/4 x 35 1/4 in.
Amon Carter Museum, Fort Worth, Texas.

COLORPLATE 34

WALTER UFER. *Where the Desert Meets The Mountain*. 1920. Oil on canvas. 36 x 40 in. Courtesy of The Anschutz Collection, Denver, Colorado.

B. J. O. NORDFELDT.
Still Life with Santo. Oil
on canvas. 40 x 28 in.
Courtesty of The
Anschutz Collection,
Denver, Colorado.

good father, hermanita. He took his shovel and cut the ground open, made a little hole in the earth for you. The land in our back yard was so hard, muy duro. Clank, clank . . . cold shovel in my ear.

That winter, I was almost thirteen and my eyes were as black as ripe olives. Hermanita, I wonder what color your eyes would have been. Sí, almost thirteen; almost a woman—I was old enough. Es la verdad. Como mi Papá me dijo a mí y a Carmen, "Don't go to sleep tonight. We're going to bury your little sister. You are old enough to help me." And I was proud pa' ayudar a mi Papá, proud to help him. Sí, I was old enough. That' what he told me. And it's the truth . . . es la verdad.

TOWARD THE BIG SKY

Meriwether Lewis and William Clark

From *The Journals of Lewis and Clark*

Crossing the Continental Divide

From a purely American perspective, the history of the West began in 1803 when Meriwether Lewis and William Clark set out to discover a practicable route to the Pacific Ocean across the newly purchased Louisiana Territory. The following excerpt from their journals recounts their triumphant crossing of the Continental Divide in the fall of 1805—the first time white men had ever traversed this monumental ridge.

———————

[Lewis]

Monday August 26th. 1805. we proceeded to a fine spring on the side of the mountain where I had lain the evening before I first arrived at the Shoshone Camp. here I halted to dine and graize our horses. there being fine green grass on that part of the hillside which was moistened by the water of the spring while the grass on the other parts was perfectly dry and parched with the sun.

I directed a pint of corn to be given each Indian who was engaged in transporting our baggage and about the same quantity to each of the men which they parched pounded and made into supe. one of the women who had been assisting in the transportation of the baggage halted at a little run about a mile behind us, and sent on the two pack horses which she had been conducting by one of her female friends. I enquired of Cameahwait the cause of her detention, and was informed by him in an unconcerned manner that she had halted to bring fourth a child and would soon overtake us; in about an hour the woman arrived with her newborn babe and passed us on her way to the camp apparently as well as she ever was.

It appears to me that the facility and ease with which the women of the aborigines of North America bring fourth their children is reather a gift of nature than depending as some have supposed on the habitude of carrying heavy burthens on their backs while in the state of pregnacy. if a pure and dry air, an elivated and cold country is unfavourable to childbirth, we might expect every difficult incident to that operation of nature in this part of the continent; again as the snake Indians possess an abundance of horses, their women are seldom compelled like those in other parts of the continent to carry burthens on their backs, yet they have their children with equal convenience, and it is a rare occurrence for any of them to experience difficulty in childbirth. I have been several times informed by those who were conversant with the fact, that the indian women who are pregnant by whitemen experience more difficulty in childbirth than when pregnant by an Indian. if this be true it would go far in suport of the opinion I have advanced.

on our near approach we were met by a number of young men on horseback. Cameahwait requested that we would discharge our guns when we arrived in sight of the Village, accordingly when I arrived on an eminence above the village in the plain I drew up the party at open order in a single rank and gave them a runing fire discharging two rounds. they appeared much gratified with this exhibition. we then proceeded to the village or encampment of brush lodges 32 in number. we were conducted to a large lodge which had been prepared for me in the cen-

White Salmon Trout. From *William Clark Journal*, March 16, 1806. (Voorhis #2). Missouri Historical Society, St. Louis.

ter of their encampment which was situated in a beautifull level smooth and extensive bottom near the river about 3 miles above the place I had first found them encamped. here we arrived at 6 in the evening arranged our baggage near my tent and placed those of the men on either side of the baggage facing outwards. I found Colter here who had just arrived with a letter from Capt. Clark in which Capt. C. had given me an account of his perigrination and the description of the river and country

from this view of the subject I found it a folly to think of attemp[t]ing to decend this river in canoes and therefore determined to commence the purchase of horses in the morning from the indians in order to carry into execution the design we had formed of passing the rocky Mountains. I now informed Cameahwait of my intended expedition overland to the great river which lay in the plains beyond the mountains and told him that I wished to purchase 20 horses of himself and his people to convey our baggage. he observed that the Minnetares had stolen a great number of their horses this spring but hoped his people would spear me the number I wished. I also asked a guide, he observed that he had no doubt but the old man who was with Capt. C. would accompany us if we wished him and that he was better informed of the country than any of them. matters being thus far arranged I directed the fiddle to be played and the party danced very merily much to the amusement and gratification of the natives, though I must confess that the state of my own mind at this moment did not well accord with the prevailing mirth as I somewhat feared that the caprice of the indians might suddenly induce them to withhold their horses from us without which my hopes of prosicuting my voyage to advantage was lost; however I determined to keep the indians in a good humour if possible, and to loose no time in obtaining the necessary number of horses. I directed the hunters to turn out early in the morning and indeavor to obtain some meat. I had nothing but a little parched corn to eat this evening.

*   *   *

[Clark]

September 2nd. Monday 1805. proceded up on the Creek, proceded on thro' thickets in which we were obliged to Cut a road, over rockey hill Sides where our horses were in [per]peteal danger of Slipping to their certain distruction & up & Down Steep hills, where Several horses fell, Some turned over, and others Sliped down Steep hill Sides, one horse Crippeled & 2 gave out.

September 3rd. Tuesday 1805. hills high & rockey on each Side, in the after part of the day the high mountains closed the Creek on each Side and obliged us to take on the Steep Sides of those Mountains, So Steep that the horses Could Scur[ce]ly keep from Slipping down, Several sliped & Injured themselves verry much, with great dificuelty we made [blank space in MS.] miles & Encamped on a branch of the Creek we assended after crossing Several Steep points & one mountain, but little to eate

The mouintains to the East Covered with Snow. we met with a great misfortune, in haveing our last Th[er]mometer broken, by accident This day we passed over emence hils and Some of the worst roads that ever horses passed, our horses frequently fell Snow about 2 inches deep when it began to rain which termonated in a Sleet [storm]

* * *

September 4th. Wednesday 1805. a verry cold morning every thing wet and frosed, Groun[d] covered with Snow, we assended a mountain & took a Divideing ridge which we kept for Several Miles & fell on the head of a Creek which appeared to run the Course we wished to go

prosued our Course down the Creek to the forks about 5 miles where we met a part[y] of the Tushepau nation, of 33 Lodges about 80 men 400 Total and at least 500 horses, those people rec[e]ved us friendly, threw white robes over our Sholders & Smoked in the pipes of peace, we Encamped with them & found them friendly but nothing but berries to eate a part of which they gave us, those Indians are well dressed with Skin shirts & robes, they [are] Stout & light complected more So than Common for Indians, The Chief harangued untill late at night, Smoked in our pipe and appeared Satisfied. I was the first white man who ever wer on the waters of this river.

September 5th. Thursday. 1805. we assembled the Chiefs & warriers and Spoke to them (with much dificuel[t]y as what we Said had to pass through Several languages before it got into theirs, which is a gugling kind of language Spoken much thro the throught [throat]) we informed them who we were, where we came from, where bound and for what purpose &c. &c. and requested to purchase & exchange a fiew horses with them, in the Course of the day I purchased 11 horses & exchanged 7 for which we gave a fiew articles of merchendize, those people possess ellegant horses.

September 6th. Friday 1805. took a Vocabelary of the language litened our loads & packed up, rained contd. untill 12 oClock

all our horses purchased of the flat heads *(oote-lash-shutes)* we Secured well for fear of their leaveing of us, and Watched them all night for fear of their leaving us or the Indians prosuing & Steeling them.

[Lewis]

Monday September 9th. 1805. two of our hunters have arrived, one of them brought with him a redheaded woodpecker of the large kind common to the U States. this is the first of the kind I have seen since I left the Illinois. just as we were seting out Drewyer arrived with two deer. we continued our rout down the valley about 4 miles and crossed the river; it is hear a handsome stream about 100 yards wide and affords a considerable quantity of very clear water, the banks are low and it's bed entirely gravel. the stream appears navigable, but from the circumstance of their being no sammon in it I believe that there must be a considerable fall in it below. our guide could not inform us where this river discharged itself into the columbia river, he informed us that it continues it's course along the mountains to the N. as far as he knew it and that not very distant from where we then were it formed a junction with a stream nearly as large as itself which took it's rise in the mountains near the Missouri to the East of us and passed through an extensive valley generally open prarie which forms an excellent pass to the

Missouri. the point of the Missouri where this Indian pass intersects it, is about 30 miles above the *gates of the rocky Mountain*, or the place where the valley of the Missouri first widens into an extensive plain after entering the rockey Mountains. the guide informed us that a man might pass to the missouri from hence by that rout in four days.

we continued our rout down the W. side of the river about 5 miles further and encamped on a large creek which falls in on the West. as our guide inform[ed] me that we should leave the river at this place and the weather appearing settled and fair I determined to halt the next day rest our horses and take some scelestial Observations. we called this Creek *Travellers rest*.

JOHN WESLEY POWELL

From *Exploration of the Colorado River of the West*

Among his many accomplishments, scientist John Wesley Powell founded both the Bureau of American Ethnography and the U.S. Geological Survey in 1879. But he is best remembered for leading an expedition down the Colorado River through the Grand Canyon in 1869. His account of this harrowing journey, Exploration of the Colorado River of the West *(1875), was a best-seller. Its concluding pages demonstrate why.*

August 13.—We are three quarters of a mile in the depths of the earth, and the great river shrinks into insignificance, as it dashes its angry waves against the walls and cliffs, that rise to the world above; they are but puny ripples, and we but pigmies, running up and down the sands, or lost among the boulders.

We have an unknown distance yet to run; an unknown river yet to explore. What falls there are, we know not; What rocks beset the channel, we know not; what walls rise over the river, we know not. Ah, well! we may conjecture many things. The men talk as cheerfully as ever; jests are bandied about freely this morning; but to me the cheer is somber and the jests are ghastly.

With some eagerness, and some anxiety, and some misgiving, we enter the cañon below, and are carried along by the swift water through walls which rise from its very edge. They have the same structure as we noticed yesterday—tiers of irregular shelves below, and, above these, steep slopes to the foot of marble cliffs. We run six miles in a little more than half an hour, and emerge into a more open portion of the cañon, where high hills and ledges of rock intervene between the river and the distant walls. Just at the head of this open place the river runs across a dike; that is, a fissure in the rocks, open to depths below, has been filled with eruptive matter, and this, on cooling, was harder than the rocks through which the crevice was made, and, when these were washed away, the harder volcanic matter remained as a wall, and the river has cut a gate-way through it several hundred feet high, and as many wide. As it crosses the wall, there is a fall below, and a bad rapid, filled with boulders of trap; so we stop to make a portage. Then on we go, gliding by hills and ledges, with distant walls in view; sweeping past sharp angles of rock; stopping at a few points to examine rapids, which we find can be run, until we have made another five miles, when we land for dinner. . . .

August 14.—At daybreak we walk down the bank of the river, on a little sandy beach, to take a view of a new feature in the cañon. Heretofore, hard rocks have given us bad river; soft rocks, smooth water; and a series of rocks harder than any we have experienced sets in. The river enters the granite!

We can see but a little way into the granite gorge, but it looks threatening.

After breakfast we enter on the waves. At the very introduction, it inspires awe. The cañon is narrower than we have ever before seen it; the water is swifter; there are but few broken rocks in the channel; but the walls are set, on either side, with pinnacles and crags; and sharp, angular buttresses, bristling with wind and wave polished spires, extend far out into the river.

Ledges of rocks jut into the stream, their tops sometimes just below the surface, sometimes rising few or many feet above; and island ledges, and island pinnacles, and island towers break the swift course of the stream into chutes, and eddies, and whirlpools. We soon reach a place where a creek comes in from the left, and just below, the channel is choked with boulders, which have washed down this lateral cañon and formed a dam, over which there is a fall of thirty or forty feet; but on the boulders we can get foothold, and we make a portage. . . .

About eleven o'clock we hear a great roar ahead, and approach it very cautiously. The sound grows louder and louder as we run, and at last we find ourselves above a long, broken fall, with ledges and pinnacles of rock obstructing the river. There is a descent of, perhaps, seventy five or eighty feet in a third of a mile, and the rushing waters break into great waves on the rocks, and lash themselves into a mad, white foam. We can land just above, but there is no foot-hold on either side by which we can make a portage. It is nearly a thousand feet to the top of the granite, so it will be impossible to carry our boats around, though we can climb to the summit up a side gulch, and, passing along a mile or two, can descend to the river. This we find on examination; but such a portage would be impracticable for us, and we must run the rapid, or abandon the river. There is no hesitation. We step into our boats, push off and away we go, first on smooth but swift water, then we strike a glassy wave, and ride to its top, down again into the trough, up again on a higher wave, and down and up on waves higher and still higher, until we strike one just as it curls back, and a breaker rolls over our little boat. Still, on we speed, shooting past projecting rocks, till the little boat is caught in a whirlpool, and spun around several times. At last we pull out again into the stream, and now the other boats have passed us. The open compartment of the "Emma Dean" is filled with water, and every breaker rolls over us. Hurled back from a rock, now on this side, now on that, we are carried into an eddy, in which we struggle for a few minutes, and are then out again, the breakers still rolling over us. Our boat is unmanageable, but she cannot sink, and we drift down another hundred yards, through breakers; how, we scarcely know. We find the other boats have turned into an eddy at the foot of the fall, and are waiting to catch us as we come, for the men have seen that our boat is swamped. They push out as we come near, and pull us in against the wall. We bail our boat, and on we go again.

The walls, now, are more than a mile in height—a vertical distance difficult to appreciate. Stand on the south steps of the Treasury building, in Washington, and look down Pennsylvania Avenue to the Capitol Park, and measure this distance overhead, and imagine cliffs to extend to that altitude, and you will understand what I mean; or, stand at Canal street, in New York, and look up Broadway to Grace Church, and you have about the distance; or, stand at Lake street bridge, in Chicago, and look down to the Central Depot, and you have it again.

A thousand feet of this is up through granite crags, then steep slopes and perpendicular cliffs rise, one above another, to the summit. The gorge is black and narrow below, red and gray and flaring above, with crags and angular projections on the walls, which, cut in many places by side cañons, seem to be a vast wilderness of rocks. Down in these grand, gloomy depths we glide, ever listening, for the mad waters keep up their roar; ever watching, ever peering ahead, for the narrow cañon is winding, and the river is closed in so that we can see but a few hundred yards, and what there may be below we know not; but we listen for falls, and watch for rocks, or stop now and then, in the bay of a recess, to admire the gigantic scenery. And ever, as we go, there is some new pinnacle or tower, some crag or peak, some distant view of the upper plateau, some strange shaped rock, or some deep, narrow side cañon. Then we come to another broken fall, which appears more difficult than the one we ran this morning.

A small creek comes in on the right, and the first fall of the water is over boulders, which have been carried down by this lateral stream. We land at its mouth, and stop for an hour or two to examine the fall. It seems possible to let down with lines, at least a part of the way, from point to point, along the right hand wall. So we make a portage over the first rocks, and find footing on some boulders below. Then we let down one of the boats to the end of her line,

John Wesley Powell. Photograph. U. S. Geological Survey.

when she reaches a corner of the projecting rock, to which one of the men clings, and steadies her, while I examine an eddy below. I think we can pass the other boats down by us, and catch them in the eddy. This is soon done and the men in the boats in the eddy pull us to their side. On the shore of this little eddy there is about two feet of gravel beach above the water. Standing on this beach, some of the men take the line of the little boat and let it drift down against another projecting angle. Here is a little shelf, on which a man from my boat climbs, and a shorter line is passed to him, and he fastens the boat to the side of the cliff. Then the second one is let down, bringing the line of the third. When the second boat is tied up, the two men standing on the beach above spring into the last boat, which is pulled up alongside of ours. Then we let down the boats, for twenty five or thirty yards, by walking along the shelf, landing them again in the mouth of a side cañon. Just below this there is another pile of boulders, over which we make another portage. From the foot of these rocks we can climb to another shelf, forty or fifty feet above the water.

On this bench we camp for the night. We find a few sticks, which have lodged in the rocks. It is raining hard, and we have no shelter, but kindle a fire and have our supper. We sit on the rocks all night, wrapped in our ponchos, getting what sleep we can.

*   *   *

August 29. We start very early this morning. The river still continues swift, but we have no serious difficulty, and at twelve o'clock emerge from the Grand Cañon of the Colorado.

We are in a valley now, and low mountains are seen in the distance, coming to the river below. We recognize this as the Grand Wash.

A few years ago, a party of Mormons set out from St. George, Utah, taking with them a boat, and came down to the mouth of the Grand Wash, where they divided, a portion of the party crossing the river to explore the San Francisco Mountains. Three men—Hamblin, Miller, and Crosby—taking the boat, went on down the river to Callville, landing a few miles below the mouth of the Rio Virgen. We have their manuscript journal with us, and so the stream is comparatively well known.

To night we camp on the left bank, in a *mesquite* thicket.

The relief from danger, and the joy of success, are great. When he who has been chained by wounds to a hospital cot, until his canvas tent seems like a dungeon cell, until the groans of those who lie about, tortured with probe and knife, are piled up, a weight of horror on his ears that he cannot throw off, cannot forget, and until the stench of festering wounds and anesthetic drugs has filled the air with its loathsome burthen, at last goes out into the open field, what a world he sees! How beautiful the sky; how bright the sunshine; what "floods of delirious music" pour from the throats of birds; how sweet the fragrance of earth, and tree, and blossom! The first hour of convalescent freedom seems rich recompense for all—pain, gloom, terror.

Something like this are the feelings we experience to night. Ever before us has been an unknown danger, heavier than immediate peril. Every waking hour passed in the Grand Cañon has been one of toil. We have watched with deep solicitude the steady disappearance of our scant supply of rations, and from time to time have seen the river snatch a portion of the little left, while we were ahungered. And danger and toil were endured in those gloomy depths, where ofttimes the clouds hid the sky by day, and but a narrow zone of stars could be seen at night. Only during the few hours of deep sleep, consequent on hard labor, has the roar of the waters been hushed. Now the danger is over; now the toil has ceased; now the gloom has disappeared; now the firmament is bounded only by the horizon; and what a vast expanse of constellations can be seen!

FRANCIS PARKMAN

From *The Oregon Trail*

"The Buffalo Camp"

In 1846, Boston historian Francis Parkman took a trip West to have a look at the burgeoning westward movement. What he found was a landscape so unfamiliar to his experience as to be disgusting. In spite of his sour outlook, in The Oregon Trail *(1849) his descriptive talents give us an enduring view of what it must have been like to encounter such abundance of space and life for the first time.*

On the second day of our stay at this place, Henry went out for an afternoon hunt. Shaw and I remained in camp, until, observing some bulls approaching the water upon the other side of the river, we crossed over to attack them. They were so near, however, that before we could get under cover of the bank our appearance as we walked over the sands alarmed them. Turning round before coming within gunshot, they began to move off to the right in a direction parallel to the river. I climbed up the bank and ran after them. They were walking swiftly, and before I could come within gunshot distance they slowly wheeled about and faced me. Before they had turned far enough to see me I had fallen flat on my face. For a moment they stood and stared at the strange object upon the grass; then turning away, again they walked on as before; and I, rising immediately, ran once more in pursuit. Again they wheeled about, and again I fell prostrate. Repeating this three or four times, I came at length within a hundred yards of the fugitives, and as I saw them turning again, I sat down and leveled my rifle. The one in the center was the largest I had ever seen. I shot him behind the shoulder. His two companions ran off. He attempted to follow, but soon came to a stand, and at length lay down as quietly as an ox chewing the cud. Cautiously approaching him, I saw by his dull and jelly-like eye that he was dead.

When I began the chase, the prairie was almost tenantless; but a great multitude of buffalo

GEORGE CATLIN. *Catlin and his Indian Guide Approaching Buffalo under White Wolf Skins*. 1846–48. Oil on canvas. 20 x 27 ¹/₈ in. National Museum of American Art, Washington, D.C. Gift of Mrs. Joseph Harmsen, Jr.

had suddenly thronged upon it, and looking up I saw within fifty rods a heavy, dark column stretching to the right and left as far as I could see. I walked towards them. My approach did not alarm them in the least. The column itself consisted almost entirely of cows and calves, but a great many old bulls were ranging about the prairie on its flank, and as I drew near they faced towards me with such a grim and ferocious look that I thought it best to proceed no farther. Indeed, I was already within close rifle shot of the column, and I sat down on the ground to watch their movements. Sometimes the whole would stand still, their heads all one way; then they would trot forward, as if by a common impulse, their hoofs and horns clattering together as they moved. I soon began to hear at a distance on the left the sharp reports of a rifle, again and again repeated; and not long after, dull and heavy sounds succeeded, which I recognized as the familiar voice of Shaw's double-barreled gun. When Henry's rifle was at work there was always meat to be brought in. I went back across the river for a horse, and, returning, reached the spot where the hunters were standing. The buffalo were visible on the distant prairie. The living had retreated from the ground, but ten or twelve carcasses were scattered in various directions. Henry, knife in hand, was stooping over a dead cow, cutting away the best and fattest of the meat.

When Shaw left me he had walked down for some distance under the river bank to find another bull. At length he saw the plains covered with the host of buffalo, and soon after heard the crack of Henry's rifle. Ascending the bank, he crawled through the grass, which for a rod or two from the river was very high and rank. He had not crawled far before to his astonishment he saw Henry standing erect upon the prairie, almost surrounded by the buffalo. Henry was in his element. Quite unconscious that anyone was looking at him, he stood at the full height of his tall figure, one hand resting upon his side, and the other arm leaning carelessly on the muzzle of his rifle. His eye was ranging over the singular assemblage around him. Now and then he would select such a cow as suited him, level his rifle, and shoot her dead; then quietly reloading, he would resume his former position. The buffalo seemed no more to regard his presence than if he were one of themselves; the bulls were bellowing and butting at each other, or rolling about in the dust. A group of buffalo would gather about the carcass of a dead cow, snuffing at her wounds; and sometimes they would come behind those that had not yet fallen, and endeavor to push them from the spot. Now and then some old bull would face towards Henry with an air of stupid amazement, but none seemed inclined to attack or fly from him. For some time Shaw lay among the grass, looking in surprise at this extraordinary sight; at length he crawled cautiously forward, and spoke in a low voice to Henry, who told him to rise and come on. Still the buffalo showed no sign of fear; they remained gathered about their dead companions. Henry had already killed as many cows as we wanted for use, and Shaw, kneeling behind one of the carcasses, shot five bulls before the rest thought it necessary to disperse.

The frequent stupidity and infatuation of the buffalo seems the more remarkable from the contrast it offers to their wildness and wariness at other times. Henry knew all their peculiarities; he had studied them as a scholar studies his books, and derived quite as much pleasure from the occupation. The buffalo were a kind of companion to him, and, as he said, he never felt alone when they were about him. He took great pride in his skill in hunting. He was one of the most modest of men; yet in the simplicity and frankness of his character, it was clear that he looked upon his preëminence in this respect as a thing too palpable and well established to be disputed. But whatever may have been his estimate of his own skill, it was rather below than above that which others placed upon it. The only time that I ever saw a shade of scorn darken his face was when two volunteer soldiers, who had just killed a buffalo for the first time, undertook to instruct him as to the best method of "approaching." Henry always seemed to think that he had a sort of prescriptive right to the buffalo, and to look upon them as something belonging to himself. Nothing excited his indignation so much as any wanton destruction committed among the cows, and in his view shooting a calf was a cardinal sin.

Bernard DeVoto

From *Across the Wide Missouri*

Those Grizzly Mountain Men

Few American historians have been able to match the narrative and descriptive powers of Bernard DeVoto. In the following excerpt from Across the Wide Missouri, *his 1947 history of the fur trade and the trappers who came to know every nook and cranny of the West during the 1830s and 1840s, he provides an evocative portrait of what life was once like for a handful of free souls in an unutterably beautiful country.*

This, then, is the mountain epicure's moment of climax. Hump and boss boil in a kettle, cracked marrow bones sizzle by the fire, there are as many ribs to roast as a man may want. Crosslegged on the ground, using only their Green River knives, the trappers eat their way through six or ten pounds of fat cow. Wellbeing overspreads them; fat cow is an intoxicant only less persuasive than the alcohol which they will not taste again till the next rendezvous—unless the partisan has brought a couple of curved tin kegs for Indian customers and on some noteworthy occasion can be induced to broach one. Camp is pitched near some watercourse, a small creek or a rushing mountain river, with firewood and grass at hand. If there has been no Indian sign and if there is no reason to apprehend Indians, the fire will be built up when the meal is over. Here is the winesap air of the high places, the clear green sky of evening fading to a dark that brings the stars within arm's length, the cottonwoods along the creek rustling in the wind. The smell of meat has brought the wolves and coyotes almost to the circle of firelight. They skulk just beyond it; sometimes a spurt of flame will turn their eyes to gold; they howl and attack one another, and farther out in the dark the howls of their relatives diminish over the plains. In running season there will be the bellowing of the bulls. Horses and mules crop the bunch grass at the end of their lariats or browse on leaves along the creek. The firelight flares and fades in the wind's rhythm on the faces of men in whose minds are the vistas and the annals of the entire West.

It is the time of fulfillment, the fullness of time, the moment lived for itself alone. The mountain men were a tough race, as many selective breeds of Americans have had to be; their courage, skill, and mastery of the conditions of their chosen life were absolute or they would not have been here. Nor would they have been here if they had not responded to the loveliness of the country and found in their way of life something precious beyond safety, gain, comfort, and family life. Besides the specific attributes of that way of life and its country, it is fair to point out an extremity, perhaps the maximum, of American individualism and gusto. Moreover, solitude had given them a surpassing gift of friendship and simple survival proved the sharpness of their wits. There were few books and few trappers were given to reading what there were: talk was everything. In this hour of function there was the talk of friends and equals. . . .

The Americans, and especially the Americans who live in the open, have always been story-tellers—one need recall only the rivermen, the lumberjacks, the cowmen, or in fact the loafers round any stove at a rural crossroads—but there have been no stories beyond those told by the map-minded breakers of trails, hunters of beaver, and exterminators of Indians. . . . Most of their yarning has been lost to history, but it was a chronicle of every watercourse, peak, park, and gulch in a million square miles, a chronicle of chance happening suddenly and expectation reversed, of violent action, violent danger, violent mirth, of Indians whose thought was not commensurate with white thinking and therefore inexhaustibly fascinating, a fantasy of mytho-logical beavers or grizzlies, of Welsh Indians or Munchies or the Fair God, of supernatural beings and spectral visitants and startling medicine and heroes who were cousin to Paul Bunyan. It was a shop talk, trapping, hunting, trailing, fighting Indians, escaping from Indians, the lore of animals and plants, and always the lay of the land and old fields revisited and new fields to be found, water and starvation and trickery and feasts. How Long Hatcher had lifted those Apache scalps. How one who was with us last year was eviscerated by a grizzly or gut-shot by a Blackfoot. How Old Gabe outsmarted a Blackfoot war party, or Tom Fitzpatrick lay in his crevice while the Gros Ventres looked for him, or a Delaware, one of the Ishmaels of the West, had taunted the Arikaras who were killing him piecemeal. How one's partner had wan-dered into a canyon quite unknown even to these masters of geography, how another had stolen the daughter of a Sioux medicine man or a Taos rancher, how a third had forted up behind his slaughtered horse and held off fifty Comanches. How we came into Taos or the Pueblo of Los

S. E. HOLLISTER. *The Great American Hunter and Trapper, in an encounter with a She-bear protecting her cubs in the Sierra Nevada Mountains, California.* 1863. Hand-colored litho-graph. 13 1/8 x 15 5/16 in. Bancroft Library, University of California, Berkeley.

Angeles and the willing women there and the brandy we drank and the horses we stole.

Till at last the fire sank. The mountain man rolled up in his robe or blanket on his apishemore, loaded rifle beside him, and knife and pistols within reach, and might lie awhile listening to the wind and water and the coyotes. He might wake a few hours later, kick fuel on the embers, and roast another half-dozen ribs, eating alone while his companions slept and the horses pawed at the end of their pickets. Then sleep again till a grayness ran with the wind across the sky, in the shuddering cold of a mountain dawn someone was shouting 'Leve! Leve!' and it was time for breakfast on buffalo meat and the day's hazard of hunt or trail. . . . It was a good life.

A.B. GUTHRIE, JR.

From *The Way West*

A Difficult Crossing

After the fur trappers—the "mountain men"—came the wagon trains carrying settlers. Most of them were bound for Oregon or California along trails that soon became as familiar as modern highways. But they were not without peril, as this moment from A. B. Guthrie's novel, The Way West *(1949), attests. It is the middle volume in a trilogy that began with the fur trade in* The Big Sky *(1947) and concluded with the cattle kingdom in* These Thousand Hills *(1956).*

Evans rode to the head of the line. "Good for another trip?" he joked at Hig, who sat like a bent stick on his horse. A knobby skeleton of a man, Hig was, with a face like an old white potato, but he could ride a horse or swim a stream or mend a rifle, and, what was more, he had a thinkpiece behind that withered skin.

"Good as gravy," Hig answered.

"Lead away, Dick."

They had hitched six yokes to Byrd's wagon, for it was medium heavy and the oxen either partly spent or smallish for so hard a chore.

They took the first stretch fine, barely swimming here and there, for, after all the trips across, the best course had been learnt. Glancing back as the leaders pulled up the bank of the first island, Evans thought Byrd looked like a churchman facing sin, a proper banker-churchman for the first time meeting evil in the flesh.

The next stretch went fine, too, the critters slanting up the stream and bending left and coming out like other teams before them.

While the oxen caught their wind, Evans made his horse step back. "Just one more hitch," he said to Byrd.

"I honestly believe it looks worse than it is."

"It ain't so bad. Scare you, Mrs. Byrd?"

She said it didn't.

"Just hang on."

Evans walked his horse back and nodded at Dick, and Dick led off again.

It happened suddenly, close to shore. It happened all at once, without warning or good reason, like something bursting into an easy dream. The team was going all right, the wagon rolling safe above the muscled ripple, and then a leader slipped and thrashed for footing, and the hungry current took it and wrenched its mate along.

They descended on Evans, their legs scrambling the water into spray, the weight of them dragging the second yoke out of line. "Gee!" he hollered out of habit and poked with his stick and beyond the tangle of them saw Hig and the hold-rope taut and Hig's horse floundering with the pull on it. "Gee."

Nellie wouldn't hold. She broke before the thrashing push of them, frightened now and unsteady in the tear of water. The line clear back to the wheel yoke skewed to the pull, slanting the wagon below the come-out trail, slanting toward the ripple, slanting off to wicked depths.

The wagon began to skid, half sailing, half grinding over gravel. It was swinging like the tail of crack-the-whip, dragging the wheelers with it, bending the yokes into an arc that it yanked to a straight line, angled up into the tide. The swing squeezed Nellie toward the lower shore, into swimming water she couldn't swim against.

Too late the leaders found their feet. Every yoke was off the course, some trying to swim, some trying to set themselves, and all of them wild and all being beaten back. The landing place was drawing off.

Evans heard Hig shouting and Byrd crying out, in words that lost shape in the rush of water. His eye glimpsed people on the shore and Dick moving with his horse. And then the swinging wagon caught on an unseen boulder and the current tore at it and the upstream wheels lifted. Wrenched between the rock and wash, the wagon flopped over on its side.

For a flash, it seemed to Evans, things happened slow and sharp to see—Byrd grabbing for his woman and missing and she pitching out and he climbing like a squirrel up the side and she floating feathery as a hen tossed into a pond.

It wasn't a pond, this water. It was power and muscle to shame the power and muscle of a man. It was fury. It was the cold fury of the offended land. It rushed at arms and legs and tried to wrench the body over—and ahead of him was just the opened mouth of Mrs. Byrd, the hen's beak opened for a final squawk above the dragging feathers.

The beak went down, but underneath his hand, underneath the rippled water, he saw the blinking blue of cloth. He struck for it and caught a hold and squared around and tried for shore. It wasn't far away. It was a hop, skip and jump without an anvil in one hand. It was the stroke of an oar on peaceful water. It was here. It was streaming here, almost where he could reach it, and he never could. He hadn't strength enough, or wind. He hadn't legs and arms enough to take him over. Beyond, above the waves that lapped his face, he saw the people huddled, watching, and the wagon washed close to the bank and the oxen struggling and one yoke safe on land and Nellie standing near.

He lost them as a wave washed up. There was the water around him and the near-far shore and the sunshine dazzling to wet eyes and heaviness in arms and legs and strangles in the throat. There was the water and the power of water and the voice of it and over it another voice, over it, "Lije! Lije!"

The voice of Summers and the person of him, busy with his horse, and his arm swinging and a rope looping out, and his own arm catching for it and missing and catching it lower down.

Summers pulled him in, easy so as not to break his holds, and slid from his horse and drew Mrs. Byrd farther up the bank. The folks came running, Byrd in the lead, crying, "Ruth! Ruth!"

"She can't be dead," Evans panted at him. "Ain't had long enough to drown."

"Ruth!"

Dick said, "Easy," and turned Mrs. Byrd over on her stomach and lifted her at the middle to get the water out.

"You all right, Lije?" It was Becky, scolding him with her eyes for he didn't know what.

"Winded, is all."

They stood by, mostly quiet, while Summers worked on Mrs. Byrd. "She's comin' round," he said. "I kin feel the life in her."

He turned her over, and she opened her eyes, and Byrd leaned down and pulled her dress so it wouldn't show her leg. "Are you all right, Ruth?"

She didn't answer right away. Her eyes looked big and washed-out, and they traveled from face to face as if to ask what she was doing on the ground with people looking down on her. Of a sudden her eyes filled and her face twisted, and Evans switched his gaze.

She was all right, though, except for the crying. Directly she got up, helped by Byrd and

Emigrant Train Crossing the River. Photograph. Nebraska State Historical Society.

Weatherby, and let them lead her toward the wagons.

"She'd best lay down awhile," Becky said, and followed them to spread a blanket. The women trailed off with her.

"Poor way you picked to git to Oregon," Summers said to Evans then. His smile said something different.

"What's the loss?"

"Ain't had time to count."

Hig shook his head, as if still unbelieving. "I don't think there's a thing except a cracked tongue and some plunder wet."

"Not a critter?"

"Don't seem reasonable, but that wagon kind of coasted into shore. I hung to the rope and the team done the best it could, and she kind of coasted."

"What did Byrd do?"

"Just rode 'er out."

"I swear! What's holdin' the wagon now?"

"Team's still hitched."

Byrd was coming back from the wagons.

"Anything wrong?" Evans asked as he came into hearing.

"No. I think she's all right. I forgot to thank you. I just came to thank you."

"Fergit it! Just happens I can swim."

"I can't forget it, ever. I want you to know that." When Evans couldn't think of more to say, Byrd faced around and walked away.

"Funny nigger," Summers said, watching him. "But still I reckon you got thanks comin', Lije."

"Owe some myself." He turned away from the faces fastened on him. Across the river the other wagons waited. "We'll camp here. There's more outfits to bring across and Byrd's wagon to haul out and fix, and the wood we put in the boxes'll give us fires. You all think that's best?"

Their heads said they did.

"And it'll give the stock another fill of grass," Summers added. "There's more hard goin' ahead."

Horace Greeley

From *An Overland Journey*

"The Home of the Buffalo"

In 1859, newspaper publisher Horace Greeley ("Go West, young man, go West") decided to go west himself. His An Overland Journey from New York to San Francisco in the Summer of 1859 *(1860) is still the best account we have of transcontinental stagecoach travel. Here, among other things, Greeley talks about the millions of buffalo. In less than thirty years, almost all of them would be gone, annihilated by commercial hide hunters and the human occupation of wild habitat.*

May 29, 1859.

We are near the heart of the buffalo region. The stages from the west that met us here this evening report the sight of millions within the last two days. Their trails checker the prairie in every direction. A company of Pike's Peakers killed thirteen near this point a few days since. Eight were killed yesterday at the next station west of this by simply stampeding a herd and driving them over a high creek bank, where so many broke their necks. Buffalo meat is hanging or lying all around us, and a calf two or three months old is tied to a stake just beside our wagons. He was taken by rushing a herd up a steep creek bank, which so many could not possibly climb at once; this one was picked out in the melee as most worth having, and taken with a rope. Though fast-tied and with but a short tether, he is true game, and makes at whoever goes near him with desperate intent to butt the intruder over. We met or passed today two parties of Pike's Peakers who had respectively lost three oxen or steers, stampeded last night by herds of buffalo. The mules at the express stations have to be carefully watched to preserve them from a similar catastrophe—to their owners.

I do not like the flesh of this wild ox. It is tough and not juicy. I do not forget that our cookery is of the most unsophisticated pattern—carrying us back to the age of the building of the Pyramids, at least—but I would much rather see an immense herd of buffalo on the prairie than eat the best of them.

The herbage hereabout is nearly all the short, strong grass known as the buffalo grass, and is closely fed down; we are far beyond the stakes of the land surveyor—beyond the usual haunts of white men. The Santa Fé trail is far south of us; the California is considerably north. Very probably, the buffalo on Solomon's Fork were never hunted by white men till this spring. Should one of these countless herds take a fancy for a manhunt, our riflemen would find even the express wagons no protection.

Though our road is hardly two months old, yet we passed two graves on it today. One is that of an infant, born in a tent of the wife of one of the stationmasters on her way to his post, and which lived but a day; the other that of a Missourian on his way to Pike's Peak, who was accidentally shot in taking a rifle from his wagon. His party seems to have been singularly unfortunate. A camp or two further on, a hurricane overtook them and tore their six wagons into oven wood; they were able to make but three passable wagons out of the remains. Their loss in other property was serious, and they sustained much bodily harm. One more of them was buried a camp or two further on.

Those whom we meet here coming down confirm the worst news we have had from the Peak. There is scarcely any gold there; those who dig cannot average two shillings per day; all who can get away are leaving; Denver and Auraria are nearly deserted; terrible sufferings have been endured on the Plains, and more must yet be encountered; hundreds would gladly work for their board, but cannot find employment—in short, Pike's Peak is an exploded bubble,

which thousands must bitterly rue to the end of their days. Such is the tenor of our latest advices. I have received none this side of Leavenworth that contradict them. My informant says all are getting away who can, and that we shall find the region nearly deserted. That is likely, but we shall see.

A young clerk with whom I conversed at supper gave me a little less discouraging account; but even he, having frozen his feet on the winter journey out, had had enough of gold-hunting, and was going home to his parents in Indiana, to stick to school for a few years. I commended that as a wise resolution. Next morning, after we had started on our opposite ways, I was apprised by our conductor that said clerk was a woman! I had not dreamed of such a thing; but his more practical or more suspicious eyes had seen through her disguise at once. We heard more of her at Denver—quite enough more—but this may as well be left untold.

Mrs. Frank Leslie

"Thirty-three Hundred Miles in a Pullman Hotel Car"

In 1862, with the aid of federal land grants and low-interest loans, the Union Pacific Railroad began building from the east, the Central Pacific Railroad from the west; seven years later, their lines were joined to form the transcontinental railroad. In 1877, Mrs. Frank Leslie, publisher and editor of Frank Leslie's Illustrated Newspaper, *provided a glowing account of what westward travel was like in a Pullman "hotel car"—at least for those who could pay the fare.*

It sounds appalling. Still more appalling were the accounts of friends who had gone before us, following the setting sun at twenty miles an hour.

COLORPLATE 40

C. C. A. CHRISTENSEN. *The Handcart Company.* 1900. Oil on canvas. 25 3/8 x 38 5/16 in. Courtesy Museum of Church History and Art, Salt Lake City. *After Brigham Young led the first contingent of Mormons across the plains and established the state of Deseret in the valley of the Great Salt Lake in 1847, thousands of the "Saints" would flee the fleshpots of gentile civilization to join their brothers and sisters in Utah. Among them were about three thousand impoverished pilgrims—most of them British and Scandinavian immigrants—who joined "handcart companies" and hauled their few worldly goods across the plains and mountains with the power of their own muscles.*

COLORPLATE 41

JOSEPH BECKER. *Snow Sheds on the Central Pacific Railroad in the Sierra Nevada Mountains*. Oil on canvas. 19 x 26 in. From the Collection of Gilcrease Museum, Tulsa, Oklahoma. *Perhaps the harshest of the many harsh realities of building the Central Pacific Railroad across the Sierra Nevada in the 1860s were the winter snows that could and often did obliterate the tracks—often by avalanches. The solution was the snowshed, scores of which were constructed along the twisting route across the mountains. The Chinese in the foreground are not some strange anomaly; it was these immigrants who had built both the railroad and the sheds.*

COLORPLATE 42

Sallie Cover. *Homestead of Ellsworth L. Ball*. c. 1880–1890. Oil on canvas. 19 ¹/₂ x 23 in.
Nebraska State Historical Society, Lincoln.

"You will be worn out with fatigue. You will be cramped and stiff with the confinement. You will turn blacker than the Ethiop with tan and cinders and be rasped like a nutmeg grater with alkali dust. You can never sleep a wink for the jarring and noise of the train, and never will be able to dress and undress and bathe yourselves like Christians. Above all, your nearest and dearest, under the influence of the fatigue and the monotony and the discomfort, will be ready to turn and rend you before you get down into the Sacramento Valley—and *you* will desire nothing better than to make a burnt offering of them and everyone else insane enough to shut himself up seven days and nights in a railway car!"

"Scenery?" I venture to suggest.

"Oh, the scenery is grand at the end of the route—Echo and Weber Canyons, of course, and the Wasatches. But the plains! So dry and brown and monotonous—you'll hate the sight of them before you're twelve hours out from Omaha!"

This was the sketch held up to us. What is the reality? Look through *my* glasses—not *coleur de rose*, I assure you—and take twenty-four hours on the Pullman hotel car as a fair sample of the rest.

Peep in at us by lamplight, when Howells is majestically working his way between the berths, making them up in strict rotation, regardless of the prayers of sleepy wretches whose numbers come last on his list.

Howells is a severe autocrat who patronizes the women and condescends to be playful with the men. His daily life is passed in struggles to suppress our light baggage and keep track of lost penknives, sketchbooks, gloves, and purses. Berth after berth is spread with fresh, clean sheets and heavy rugs, piled with little square pillows, and duly shut in with voluminous curtains; while under each are stowed the occupant's belongings—the satchel, the half-cut magazine that is never read, the portfolio and sketchbooks, a pair of slippers, or a whiskbroom.

We are divided by a curtain across the aisle: four women, each rejoicing in "a whole section all to herself," at one end; and at the other, the turbulent masculine element, "doubled up," so to speak, in upper and lower berths and making night gleeful in their own peculiar fashion.

And do you sleep? The springy roll of the cars, the slight monotonous rocking of your easy, roomy bed, and the steady roar and rattle of the train lull you into dreamland as a child is rocked by his nurse's lullaby. There is a little struggle with sleep at first, for the mysterious moonlit country is so full of fascination. A dark shape slides swift and shadowy across the picture, vanishing with great flying leaps. It may be a prairie wolf, a coyote, or a mountain lion. Another faintly outlined shadow points a motionless cone up to the stars. It is a Shoshone tepee, the moonlight falling on its smoke-stained, ragged skins and the ashes of its smoldering fire. Your eyes shut lazily and forget to open again. But they shut in a picture of those melancholy, awful wastes that will be a part of you henceforward.

Then the waking—perhaps with a flash of new-risen sunshine across your pillows, or only the first scarlet streak of dawn above the tawny divides. You draw the blankets and rugs closer round your shoulders, for it is chilly, and, pushing the pillows higher, you lie staring out for the next hour or two upon the shifting wonder of the Great Plains. There is no sign of life among the other sleepers; nothing stirring but Howells, who will presently pull open the curtains of the berth with a bland, "Wake up—open your eyes, lady!"

And then the womanly soul gives itself up to one great problem—how to dive into the washroom with the greatest expedition, eluding other candidates and locking them out in triumph.

If you step out on the back platform, you can investigate the process of breakfast and have a chat with the cook. Our car is the last of the train, and its tiny kitchen opens on the platform, the steps of which are guarded by strong iron gates. In the tiny cupboard adjoining, where the caterer reigns supreme, is an incredible store of potted meats and vegetables, preserves and fruit, and close-packed dainties of all sorts. The portly chef almost fills up his small quarters and risks knocking down an army of saucepans at every turn of his elbow; but he moves deftly and beams upon us over his little stove while he turns the beefsteaks and stirs the mushroom sauce.

At nine o'clock Howells fastens the little tables in place, lays the white cloths and napkins, and we slip into our places. Breakfast comes by dainty courses: fish, fresh-caught at the last station on our way; beefsteak and *champignons*; hot rolls and cornbread; broiled chicken on

Pullman Car Interior. Engraving. From *Leslie's Illustrated Weekly.* 1876. General Research Division. New York Public Library, Astor, Lenox and Tilden Foundations.

toast; and potatoes stewed in cream or fried Saratoga fashion, with the best of coffee and tea, or a glass of milk, half cream. You eat with an appetite unknown east of Missouri, and meanwhile your eyes are drinking in their fill of the great, solid sea of the plains, new-bathed in morning sunshine.

Breakfast is scarcely over before you rush to the platform to see some wonderful line of buttes, or look for antelopes, or watch a slow emigrant train winding past; or else, in a fit of sudden industry, you spread your little table with sketchbook and pencils and work out, as much as the almost imperceptible jar of the car will let you, the last group of Indians sketched at Elko or Evanston.

The party scatters into groups, twos and threes, as parties inevitably will. Somebody scribbles notes in a tiny book; another hurries off a file of postal cards to drop at the next station. Lady Bountiful opens her workbox to darn a rent in a flounce or a coat sleeve; and Madame brings out her French *brochure* to read, when anyone will let her.

At the further end of the car, in the gentlemen's quarters, the tiny smoking room has always a tenant or two; and so we drift our several ways and dream or work away the miles until the sun is high overhead and Howells announces luncheon.

Our little table is set this time with sandwiches and a salad, or some biscuits and a dish of fruit, never very long ignored, though everyone declares that he is "not the least bit hungry." An hour afterward, perhaps, the train stops for dinner and twenty minutes at the wayside station; we rush for our hats and the blessed opportunity of a "constitutional" on the platform while the rest of the hungry passengers besiege the dining room.

The afternoon is never a minute too long. If it should be, there is the couch in the middle section, with its bright rugs and fresh pillows. We see freaks of architecture among the ochery-red buttes; we slide through miles of prairie dog villages, alive with frisky little tenants; we throw silver "bits" and handfuls of crackers and cakes to painted squaws, reaching up greedy hands at every station; we whistle herds of cattle off the track, and the sportsmen impotently pop their pistols at fleet-limbed antelopes skimming by like shadows; and never for one second do we grow tired of it all.

Now the afternoon light is getting low, and Howells and the little tables come on the scene again. We sip our oyster soup, discuss turkey and antelope steaks and quail, and trifle with ice cream and *café noir*. When the wild cloudy masses in the west are flushed and hot with the sunset's last fires, we take our places on the platform again and keep them until the stars are out and the moon is high above the snow peaks of the Rockies.

Inside, the lamps are lit and swinging overhead. Between the windows, the looking glasses are slid up on their panels, and a candle behind each burns in a bright reflector. You will join the group at cards yonder, and I shall order a table laid for me at the farthest end, away from the clatter and laughter and fun, and shall scribble a half-dozen letters to tell the friends at home how I have gained five pounds already, how I am burnt brown as an Indian by the western sun and wind, and how the rarest and richest of all my journeyings is this three thousand miles by rail.

ROBERT LOUIS STEVENSON

From *Across the Plains*

"Fellow-Passengers"

Not everyone could afford a Pullman hotel car for transcontinental railroad travel. In fact, most could not—including British novelist Robert Louis Stevenson, who joined the cars traveling west to San Francisco in 1879 and limned a colorful, though not entirely gentle, portrait of his fellow-passengers in this selection from Across the Plains *(1911).*

———————————

At Ogden we changed cars from the Union Pacific to the Central Pacific line of railroad. The change was doubly welcome; for, first, we had better cars on the new line; and, second, those in which we had been cooped for more than ninety hours had begun to stink abominably. Several yards away, as we returned, let us say from dinner, our nostrils were assailed by rancid air. I have stood on a platform while the whole train was shunting; and as the dwelling-cars drew near, there would come a whiff of pure menagerie, only a little sourer, as from men instead of monkeys. I think we are human only in virtue of open windows. Without fresh air, you only require a bad heart, and a remarkable command of the Queen's English, to become such another as Dean Swift; a kind of leering, human goat, leaping and wagging your scut on mountains of offence. I do my best to keep my head the other way, and look for the human rather than the bestial in this Yahoo-like business of the emigrant train. But one thing I must say, the car of the Chinese was notably the least offensive.

The cars on the Central Pacific were nearly twice as high, and so proportionally airier; they were freshly varnished, which gave us all a sense of cleanliness as though we had bathed; the seats drew out and joined in the centre, so that there was no more need for bed boards; and there was an upper tier of berths which could be closed by day and opened at night.

I had by this time some opportunity of seeing the people whom I was among. They were in rather marked contrast to the emigrants I had met on board ship while crossing the Atlantic. They were mostly lumpish fellows, silent and noisy, a common combination; somewhat sad, I should say, with an extraordinary poor taste in humour, and little interest in their fellow-creatures beyond that of a cheap and merely external curiosity. If they heard a man's name and business, they seemed to think they had the heart of that mystery; but they were as eager to know that much as they were indifferent to the rest. Some of them were on nettles till they learned your name was Dickson and you a journeyman baker; but beyond that, whether you were Catholic or Mormon, dull or clever, fierce or friendly, was all one to them. Others who were not so stupid, gossiped a little, and, I am bound to say, unkindly. A favourite witticism was for some lout to raise the alarm of 'All aboard!' while the rest of us were dining, thus contributing his mite to the general discomfort. Such a one was always much applauded for his high spirits. When I was ill coming through Wyoming, I was astonished—fresh from the eager humanity on board ship—to meet with little but laughter. One of the young men even amused himself by incommoding me, as was then very easy; and that not from ill-nature, but mere clodlike incapacity to think, for he expected me to join the laugh. I did so, but it was phantom merriment. Later on, a man from Kansas had three violent epileptic fits, and though, of course, there were not wanting some to help him, it was rather superstitious terror than sympathy that his case evoked among his fellow-passengers. 'Oh, I hope he's not going to die!' cried a woman; 'it would be terrible to have a dead body!' And there was a very general movement to leave the man behind at the next station. This, by good fortune, the conductor negatived.

There was a good deal of story-telling in some quarters; in others, little but silence. In this society, more than any other that ever I was in, it was the narrator alone who seemed to enjoy the narrative. It was rarely that any one listened for the listening. If he lent an ear to another man's story, it was because he was in immediate want of a hearer for one of his own. Food and the progress of the train were the subjects most generally treated; many joined to discuss these who otherwise would hold their tongues. One small knot had no better occupation than to worm out of me my name; and the more they tried, the more obstinately fixed I grew to baffle them. They assailed me with artful questions and insidious offers of correspondence in the future; but I was perpetually on my guard, and parried their assaults with inward laughter. I am sure Dubuque would have given me ten dollars for the secret. He owed me far more, had he understood life, for thus preserving him a lively interest throughout the journey. I met one of my fellow-passengers months after, driving a street tramway car in San Francisco; and, as the joke was now out of season, told him my name without subterfuge. You never saw a man more chapfallen. But had my name been Demogorgon, after so prolonged a mystery he had still been disappointed.

There were no emigrants direct from Europe—save one German family and a knot of Cornish miners who kept grimly by themselves, one reading the New Testament all day long through steel spectacles, the rest discussing privately the secrets of their old-world, mysterious race. Lady Hester Stanhope believed she could make something great of the Cornish; for my part, I can make nothing of them at all. A division of races, older and more original than that of Babel, keeps this close, esoteric family apart from neighbouring Englishmen. Not even a Red Indian seems more foreign in my eyes. This is one of the lessons of travel—that some of the strangest races dwell next door to you at home.

The rest were all American born, but they came from almost every quarter of that Continent. All the States of the North had sent out a fugitive to cross the plains with me. From Virginia, from Pennsylvania, from New York, from far western Iowa and Kansas, from Maine that borders on the Canadas, and from the Canadas themselves—some one or two were fleeing in quest of a better land and better wages. The talk in the train, like the talk I heard on the steamer, ran upon hard times, short commons, and hope that moves ever westward. I thought of my shipful from Great Britain with a feeling of despair. They had come 3000 miles, and yet not far enough. Hard times bowed them out of the Clyde, and stood to welcome them at Sandy Hook. Where were they to go? Pennsylvania, Maine, Iowa, Kansas? These were not places for immigration, but for emigration, it appeared; not one of them, but I knew a man who had lifted up his heel and left it for an ungrateful country. And it was still westward that they ran. Hunger, you would have thought, came out of the east like the sun, and the evening was made of edible gold. And, meantime, in the car in front of me, were there not half a hundred emigrants from the opposite quarter? Hungry Europe and hungry China, each pouring from their gates in search of provender, had here come face to face. The two waves had met; east and west had alike failed; the whole round world had been prospected and condemned; there was no El Dorado anywhere; and till one could emigrate to the moon, it seemed as well to stay patiently at home. Nor was there wanting another sign, at once more picturesque and more disheartening; for, as we continued to steam westward toward the land of gold, we were continually passing other emigrant trains upon the journey east; and these were as crowded as our own. Had all

Railroad passengers.
Denver Public Library.
Western History
Department.

these return voyagers made a fortune in the mines? Were they all bound for Paris, and to be in Rome by Easter? It would seem not, for, whenever we met them, the passengers ran on the platform and cried to us through the windows, in a kind of wailing chorus, to 'Come back.' On the plains of Nebraska, in the mountains of Wyoming, it was still the same cry, and dismal to my heart, 'Come back!' That was what we heard by the way 'about the good country we were going to'. And at that very hour the Sand-lot of San Francisco was crowded with the unemployed, and the echo from the other side of Market Street was repeating the rant of demagogues.

If, in truth, it were only for the sake of wages that men emigrate, how many thousands would regret the bargain! But wages, indeed, are only one consideration out of many; for we are a race of gipsies, and love change and travel for themselves.

HARRY FRENCH

From "The Rowdy Brakeman"

For decades, the steam locomotive was the great machine of its age, and in the West, as elsewhere, those who worked on the railroad acquired a certain air of distinction and romance. Being a "railroad man" was, in fact, not without its colorful adventures, as Harry French's memoir, dictated in the 1930s, illustrates vividly.

Hunnewell was the shipping point for all the LL&G cattle trade. The location of this cow town gave it many advantages for cattlemen shipping directly to the stockyards in Kansas City. The saving in time (as compared to Dodge City) became an important factor, and Hunnewell flourished.

The downtown section, as I remember it, had one hotel, two stores, one barber shop, a couple of dance halls, and eight or nine saloons. The town was Dodge City on a smaller scale. There was no Bat Masterson to control the casual use of firearms, so there was more shooting than I ever saw in Dodge City. Because of the nearby Indian reservation, where they could not be pursued by the local law enforcement authorities, the cowboys took more liberties than they would have elsewhere. The men of Hunnewell more than lived up to their reputation as hell-raisers.

We railroadmen had the usual trouble keeping lights lit at night when cowboys were on a rampage. We would often get messages from the agent at Hunnewell, advising us to show no lights entering town. These were not idle warnings. A bevy of saloons faced the railroad tracks, and a light on our train—headlight, hand lantern, or caboose marker—was almost certain to draw a few practice shots.

While running into Hunnewell, I recommended the hiring of my elder brother as a brakeman. He was detailed to my crew, and in about three months I succeeded in making a passably good brakeman out of him. He had been warned about showing a light in Hunnewell; but one night when we entered the town, he forgot to put out his hand lantern. As he started to climb down off a box car, a pistol roared. The shooter must have been a couple of blocks away. Brother's light went out. He always claimed that the bullet had to pass between his legs in order to hit his lantern, but this point is debatable.

Brother threw the switch, and after our train was sidetracked, he reset it for the main line. We put our engine away in total darkness and then cleaned up ready for supper, but my brother did not show up. The other brakeman, a former cowboy, after a tour of all the saloons, notified me that he could not find him. An intensive search of the town failed to locate him. Daylight the next morning brought him walking into town carrying his bedroll. He had passed the night in a culvert a couple of miles from that "shootin'est" town.

And it *was* a shooting town. It was not uncommon for a group of whiskey-mad cowboys to take a violent dislike to some particular saloon or store. They would mount their ponies, shoot up the town, and ride their horses full tilt into the offending saloon or place of business. Bartenders and clerks made themselves scarce. One spree lasted for three days and nights. It was more than a riot—the cowboys owned the town. They knocked the heads off sugar barrels so that the ponies might eat their fill. Guns blazed day and night.

Finally, the agent sent a wire to Wellington advising the sheriff of conditions. The sheriff assembled a few militia and a number of deputies, and headed for Hunnewell. I was the conductor of the special train. On arrival the sheriff lined up the militia and deputies, and ordered the cowboys to disperse. He and his "tin soldiers and toy men" were roundly jeered. Some fool fired a gun and a real fight started. The militia's first volley killed several cowboys and took much of the fight out of the others. By sundown the fight was over, and most of the cowboys were in Indian Territory.

My return trip to Wellington was to be as a fast stock train. (Fast was about thirty miles an hour.) Leaving town, I climbed into the cupola, where I could have the train under observation. On top of the caboose there was a stranger. I climbed out and asked him where he was going.

"As far as your damn train goes," was the surly reply.

I told him what the fare would be. Passengers on freight trains were not uncommon, and riding was permitted. But this stranger's hand slid down to his hip to produce the longest, ugliest six-shooter I have ever seen.

"This is my fare, runt," he growled.

While I did not like the reference to my size (about five foot six), that gun and his disposition convinced me they were all the fare he needed.

My rear brakeman, who had been building a fire in the caboose stove, missed me. Thinking something might be wrong with the train, he climbed the ladder on the front end of the caboose. This put him behind the gunman. When the brakeman's head cleared the top of the caboose, he saw the man toying with his huge shooting iron.

My brakeman took no chances. Softly, he continued climbing. A short brake club dangled at his wrist. The roar of the train silenced his two swift steps, and he swung his club in a short arc, ending on the gunman's derby hat. Mr. Gunman went down. His weapon dropped to the roof of

Charles Russell. *In Without Knocking*. 1909. Oil on canvas. 20 1/8 x 29 7/8 in. Amon Carter Museum, Fort Worth, Texas.

the caboose and fired as it hit. The bullet made a hole in the cupola but did no other damage. I grabbed the gunman to keep him from rolling off the speeding train, and we tied him, unconscious, to the running board on top of the caboose, where he rode until we arrived at Wellington.

The sheriff came down at our invitation and looked over the prisoner.

"Which one of you took him?" he asked.

I motioned to the brakeman. "He was the artist with the brake club," I said. "All I did was look at the gun."

"You'll get a big share of the reward," the sheriff told the brakeman. "There's about two thousand dollars on his head."

The brakeman had been very unconcerned about his prisoner until he found out that he had captured a genuine bad man, one that was wanted in several localities for murder. Only then was he afraid. The day that the reward was divided marked the end of my brakeman's railroading. He took his share (about fifteen hundred dollars) and purchased a whole farm outfit—teams, wagons, horses, plows. The last I heard, he was located on a homestead at Burden, Kansas.

I kept the gun as a souvenir. At least I kept it until luck ran against me in a poker game. Easy come—easy go.

DIPS, SPURS, AND ANGLES

Vicente Pérez Rosales

From *We Were 49ers!*

The Mexican War of 1846–1848 cost 11,000 American lives, but when huge deposits of gold were discovered in the newly acquired possession of California early in 1848, it was considered a bargain. Some 80,000 goldseekers rushed to California in 1849 in one of the largest mass migrations in human history. Among them were about 7,000 Chileans, including Vicente Pérez Rosales, who provided a lively picture of the early excitement in his diary.

———————

At the crack of dawn we were up, getting the horses ready, and rolling up the bedding. Then with good heart and satisfaction we left the river in the same order as we had used the day before. The freshness of the morning, the beautiful appearance of the country through which we were passing, totally uncultivated and without a suggestion of a human habitation anywhere; the flowers, the birds, the trees, all new to us; all of this made us willing to overlook the difficulties we began to encounter toward noontime. It was hot, and the mud forced us to push the carts by hand at almost every step of the way.

The appearance of the country had changed completely. The soil was no longer covered with grass. Here and there were outcroppings of granite, and the farther one went the more rugged it became. We were soon climbing and descending slopes that we would have consigned to Barabbas if they had not been covered with the most spectacular flowers. Actually it seemed as though we were travelling through a garden richly cultivated, with as many wild flowers as there are cultivated ones in Chile. At the end of a march of about five leagues we ran into an arroyo or small creek. It had so little water, and that was so dispersed in a swamp, that it was possible to do but little toward satisfying our thirst.

We took a short rest there, and when we were ready to start again so as to catch up with the carts, which had gone on ahead a long way with the rest of our party, we noticed with dismay that our little dray horse was bleeding at his shoulder joint. It was due to the harness, which had certainly not been made by skilled London leather workers. It was plain we would not have a horse at all if we went on this way. The problem deserved some thought. The carts were too far ahead for us to reach them and get back again; and even if we had reached them they could not have stopped without adding a heavy expense for us. We could not stay where we were because we had no food and did not know the country. The sensible thing seemed to be to abandon the big van, but in that case we would lose our bedding and our most essential tools. We had to decide at once, so we made up our minds to pull the cart ourselves and give the horse a chance to recuperate. We tied ropes to the front and rear hooks, and César, Federico, Jorge, and I took hold of them. We sent Cipriano on ahead, and began a long climb that would not end until we reached a spot two leagues from Sutter's mill, where we were due to arrive the following day.

The road became steeper and more tortuous every moment, and we were very much afraid a wheel might break. Although the axle was iron, as were also the wheel rims, the iron was so

California Gold Diggers: Mining Operations on the Western Shore of the Sacramento River. c. 1850. Hand-colored lithograph. 8 3/8 x 12 1/8 in. Bancroft Library, University of California, Berkeley.

worn it could give way any minute. The hills with their ups-and-downs followed one another endlessly and the bogs between them made the job even harder.

Our courage would have been shot all to hell by the heat, mud, and exhaustion if it had not been that we knew how we looked. Imagining how our friends in Santiago would laugh if they could see us slaving away like this kept us laughing like lunatics. So we kept on, boasting to one another of our strength and skill, and inventing reasons to explain away any missteps we made.

We soon realized that not knowing the road would have been no handicap to us. There was a trail of bottles strewn along the whole way. If you want to locate a Yankee, all you need do is follow the empty cognac bottles and you are sure to find him.

After about four hours of this we caught sight of our carts parked on a high plateau that was covered with grass. The view revived our spirits—but that did not last long, for a short distance farther on we found a swamp blocking our way. In it a troop of Yankees were swearing like frogs around a cart that had broken down, and another that was sunk deep in the mud.

Our recourse at this juncture was to take a brief rest, and then, recommending ourselves with all our hearts to our absent Dulcineas, we charged into the nasty barrier and, fighting tooth and nail, triumphantly pulled our contraption through to the other side of the muck, arriving more proud of ourselves than if we had won a battle.

There never was for anyone in this world a more laborious task than we had in covering the few hundred yards we had to cross to reach the carts. But this day was full of anticlimaxes. The carts had only stopped briefly to rest the animals, and then had gone on their insolent way, leaving us with no choice but to let them go and fall to the ground on our backs, panting like worn-out oxen.

Fifteen minutes later we were on the go again and, after two hours of travel, we came upon the carts. They were at the bottom of a valley formed by the hill we had just passed and another hill that lay ahead. They were set up for the night, and a fire was going. The place seemed to be a rendezvous for travellers because the trail forked there. The trail on the right went off toward a mining area called Dry Diggings, and the trail to the left went to Sutter's mill. Many people, some on foot, some on horseback, and some with carts, already occupied the better part of the area.

What a friar's night of self-mortification we spent there, after filling ourselves with biscuit and rice!

Of course if we had not had in view the great difficulties we still had to overcome before reaching our third camping spot, we would have followed our course more happily.

Although the trail was awful, the hill we were climbing was very nice. The flowers and trees, changing at every step and becoming more abundant, would have made the journey enchanting for those who can travel like lords. I grew tired counting the varieties of oaks and pines—and they grow in size as you get into the Sierra. The many creeks, each with fine water, made it possible for us to enjoy frequent and plentiful flour-soup *culpeus*. Inasmuch as the carts could not make so good a showing as they had the day before because the trail was so difficult, our Yankee drivers were glad to make a short day of it; and we camped in midafternoon with our disintegrating cart on the bank of the nearest fork of a stream called Weber Creek.

This Weber was one of the numberless adventurers who had reached this creek in the early days as he looked for gold; and, finding it had no name, he gave it his own.

We were just as tired as we had been the day before, but we felt happier because we had overcome the first difficulties of the trip. We spread out our ragged bedding, left Garcés to cook some rice for us, and then the rest of us seized shovels, pans, and *poruñas* and began to pan the sands of the creek with much talking and enthusiasm. We immediately struck gold! Cipriano and Urbina said they would not need any more in Chile than they found. At the cry of "gold," the cooking was deserted and everyone, fully dressed and with shoes on, dashed into the water. In a moment we were all busy trying, as best we could, to learn how to operate the heavy yet delicate Chilean gold pan. All were happy to see one or two glints of accidentally trapped gold. Urbina, though, found the equivalent of a gold escudo.

In spite of our pleasure in the light work and our general high spirits, we decided the prudent thing to do was to take to our beds. It made no sense to get so wet for so little, after such a hard day. So we went back to our oak tree and our rice, triumphantly carrying the first gold the California placers had yielded to us.

WILLIAM SWAIN

On Mining at the South Fork of Feather River

For all the frenzy of the Gold Rush, after the first few months of 1848 there simply was not enough gold in California to support the glorious dreams of the tens of thousands of prospectors who scuttled over the Sierra Nevada. Most could expect modest results at best after months of numbing, exhausting work. This is the eloquent lesson in William Swain's letter home to his brother.

January 6, 1850
You may have some curiosity to know something about our location and dwelling. Our house is a log cabin, sixteen by twenty feet. It is covered with boughs of cedar and is made of nut pine logs from one to two feet in diameter, so that it is quite a blockhouse. It has a good door made of cedar boards hewn out of cedar logs, but no window. It faces the south and is on the north side of the river. In the east end is a family fireplace, in which large backlogs are burning night and day. At the west end is a bedstead framed into the logs of the cabin and running from side to side. The cords of the bedstead are strips of rawhide, crossing at every three inches, thus forming a bottom tight enough to hold large armfuls of dry breaks gathered from the sides of the mountains, which make a substitute for feather beds. On these are our blankets and buffalo skins. Altogether it makes a comfortable bed. Moore has a bunk in one of the other corners. Over the fireplace are our rifles, which are ever ready, cocked and primed, and frequently yield us good venison. In the other corner may be seen our cupboard with its contents, which consist

Head of Auburn Ravine.
Daguerreotype. California State
Library, Sacramento. California
Section.

of a few wooden and tin dishes, bottles, knives and forks and spoons, tin frying pan, boiler, and coffee pot.

Around the sides of the cabin at various points are the few articles of clothing belonging to the different members of the company. Under the bed are five cakes of tallow, under the bunk are three or four large bags of flour. Along the point of the roof is a line of dried beef and sixty or seventy pounds of suet. And out at the corner of the house in a large trough made of pine may be found salt beef in the pickle, in abundance.

At ten in the evening you might see in this cabin, while everything is still, a fire blazing up from the mass of fuel in the large fireplace, myself and Hutchinson on one end of the bedstead, Lt. Cannon on the other, Mr. Bailey stretched before the fire in his blankets on the ground floor, and Moore in his bunk. On the roof the incessant rain keeps up its perpetual patter, while the foaming stream howls out a requiem of the rushing torrent as it dashes on its way to the valley. And here, wakeful and listless, are the members of other circles too. But often the mind is far away, filled with other scenes, far distant homes, and relatives.

In front of our cabin a mountain rises from the edge of the river two thousand feet and hides the sun till ten o'clock in the day. Its top is often covered with snow. The live oak and numerous other mountain evergreens, besides the pine and cedar, green as spring, are loaded with snow near the mountain top and dripping with rain on its side and base. And this is only a specimen of the hills and scenery on all sides of us.

The following is a list of prices current per pound when we arrived at Long's Bar: pork, $1.25; beans from 75 cents to $1; sugar, 75 cents; coffee, 50 cents; tea, $2.50; saleratus, $6; vinegar, $5; pickaxes and tin pans, $8 apiece; coffee pots, $6 to $8; frying pans $6.

These prices were caused by the rains which commenced six weeks earlier this year than last and consequently found the merchants in the mines without having laid in their winter's stock.

*   *   *

There was some talk between us of your coming to this country. For God's sake think not of it. Stay at home. Tell all whom you know that are thinking of coming that they have to sacrifice everything and face danger in all its forms, for George, thousands have laid and will lay their bones along the routes to and in this country. Tell all that "death is in the pot" if they attempt to cross the plains and hellish mountains. Say to Playter [a Youngstown resident] never to think of the journey; and as for you, *stay at home*, for if my health is spared, I can get enough for both of us.

My health has been extremely good since I arrived here. I am fifteen pounds heavier than when I left home and measured six feet last evening. A slight attack of rheumatism in the left hip has given me some trouble for a few days.

You may think from the tenor of this letter that I am sick of my job, but not so. I have not seen the hour yet when I regretted starting for California, nor have any one of our little party ever regretted that we undertook the enterprise. I have seen hard times, faced the dangers of disease and exposure and perils of all kinds, but I count them nothing if they enable me to place myself and family in comfortable circumstances.

Now you will think that there is a contradiction in the advice that I gave you and others about coming to California and the declaration of my own satisfaction that I have performed the journey. The fact is that gold is plenty here and the accounts received before I left home did not exaggerate the reality. Therefore I am glad that I am here. But the time is past—if it ever existed—when fortunes could be obtained for picking them up. Gold is found in the most rocky and rough places, and the streams and bars that are rich are formed of huge rocks and stones. In such places, you will see, it requires robust labor and hard tugging and lifting to separate the gold from the rock. But this is nothing to the risk of life run in traveling to this country. Therefore, if I was at home and knew all the circumstances, I think I should stay at home; but having passed those dangers in safety, I thank God that I am here in so favorable circumstances. . . .

I hope soon to send for my letters, and God grant that they may bring no sad intelligence from home, for I almost dread to hear from that happy home, fearing that our neighborhood may have been the theater of cholera.

You are better acquainted with the state of things around San Francisco Bay than I am, and therefore I say nothing about them.

I have felt great anxiety about my wife and child, as I left them no means to live upon for so long a time, expecting to send home means before this; and also, their necessities might embarrass you. I hope that you will see that they are provided for, and if I can remunerate you for any trouble you may have, I shall feel willing to do so and ever feel grateful for your kindness. Give my love to Mother, if she is yet living, and say to her that I often, very often, think of her. Tell Sabrina *not* to be overanxious about me, for I shall be careful of my health, and as soon as I can get the rocks in my pocket I shall hasten home as fast as steam can carry me.

Write often, for I may sometime or another get your letters.

Mark Twain

From *Roughing It*

"All that Glitters . . ."

Like his most renowned fictional character, Huckleberry Finn, Samuel Clemens, who used the pen name Mark Twain, "lit out for the territories" in 1862. His destination was the western part of Utah Territory—present-day Nevada—where prospectors from California had spilled over the mountains and discovered large deposits of silver. In Roughing It, *published ten years later, Twain exposed his own splendidly mindless infatuation with prospecting.*

After leaving the Sink, we traveled along the Humboldt river a little way. People accustomed to the monster mile-wide Mississippi, grow accustomed to associating the term "river" with a high degree of watery grandeur. Consequently, such people feel rather disappointed when they stand on the shores of the Humboldt or the Carson and find that a "river" in Nevada is a sickly rivulet which is just the counterpart of the Erie canal in all respects save that the canal is twice as long and four times as deep. One of the pleasantest and most invigorating exercises one can contrive is to run and jump across the Humboldt river till he is overheated, and then drink it dry.

On the fifteenth day we completed our march of two hundred miles and entered Unionville, Humboldt county, in the midst of a driving snow-storm. Unionville consisted of eleven cabins and a liberty-pole. Six of the cabins were strung along one side of a deep canyon, and the other five faced them. The rest of the landscape was made up of bleak mountain walls that rose so high into the sky from both sides of the canyon that the village was left, as it were, far down in the bottom of a crevice. It was always daylight on the mountain tops a long time before the darkness lifted and revealed Unionville.

We built a small, rude cabin in the side of the crevice and roofed it with canvas, leaving a corner open to serve as a chimney, through which the cattle used to tumble occasionally, at night, and mash our furniture and interrupt our sleep. It was very cold weather and fuel was scarce. Indians brought brush and bushes several miles on their backs; and when we could catch a laden Indian it was well—and when we could not (which was the rule, not the exception), we shivered and bore it.

I confess, without shame, that I expected to find masses of silver lying all about the ground. I expected to see it glittering in the sun on the mountain summits. I said nothing about this, for some instinct told me that I might possibly have an exaggerated idea about it, and so if I betrayed my thought I might bring derision upon myself. Yet I was as perfectly satisfied in my own mind as I could be of anything, that I was going to gather up, in a day or two, or at furthest a week or two, silver enough to make me satisfactorily wealthy—and so my fancy was already busy with plans for spending this money. The first opportunity that offered, I sauntered carelessly away from the cabin, keeping an eye on the other boys, and stopping and contemplating the sky when they seemed to be observing me; but as soon as the coast was manifestly clear, I fled away as guiltily as a thief might have done and never halted till I was far beyond sight and call. Then I began my search with a feverish excitement that was brimful of expectation— almost of certainty. I crawled about the ground, seizing and examining bits of stone, blowing

Colorado miners, Ocean Grove. Photograph. Denver Public Library. Western History Department.

the dust from them or rubbing them on my clothes, and then peering at them with anxious hope. Presently I found a bright fragment and my heart bounded! I hid behind a boulder and polished it and scrutinized it with a nervous eagerness and a delight that was more pronounced than absolute certainty itself could have afforded. The more I examined the fragment the more I was convinced that I had found the door to fortune. I marked the spot and carried away my specimen. Up and down the rugged mountain side I searched, with always increasing interest and always augmenting gratitude that I had come to Humboldt and come in time. Of all the experiences of my life, this secret search among the hidden treasures of silver-land was the nearest to unmarred ecstasy. It was a delirious revel. By and by, in the bed of a shallow rivulet, I found a deposit of shining yellow scales, and my breath almost forsook me! A gold mine, and in my simplicity I had been content with vulgar silver! I was so excited that I half believed my overwrought imagination was deceiving me. Then a fear came upon me that people might be observing me and would guess my secret. Moved by this thought, I made a circuit of the place, and ascended a knoll to reconnoiter. Solitude. No creature was near. Then I returned to my mine, fortifying myself against possible disappointment, but my fears were groundless—the shining scales were still there. I set about scooping them out, and for an hour I toiled down the windings of the stream and robbed its bed. But at last the descending sun warned me to give up the quest, and I turned homeward laden with wealth. As I walked along I could not help smiling at the thought of my being so excited over my fragment of silver when a nobler metal was almost under my nose. In this little time the former had so fallen in my estimation that once or twice I was on the point of throwing it away.

The boys were as hungry as usual, but I could eat nothing. Neither could I talk. I was full of dreams and far away. Their conversation interrupted the flow of my fancy somewhat, and annoyed me a little, too. I despised the sordid and commonplace things they talked about. But as they proceeded, it began to amuse me. It grew to be rare fun to hear them planning their poor little economies and sighing over possible privations and distresses when a gold mine, all our own, lay within sight of the cabin and I could point it out at any moment. Smothered hilarity began to oppress me, presently. It was hard to resist the impulse to burst out with exultation and reveal everything; but I did resist. I said within myself that I would filter the great news through my lips calmly and be serene as a summer morning while I watched its effect in their faces. I said:

"Where have you all been?"

"Prospecting."

"What did you find?"

"Nothing."

"Nothing? What do you think of the country?"

"Can't tell, yet," said Mr. Ballou, who was an old gold miner, and had likewise had considerable experience among the silver mines.

"Well, haven't you formed any sort of opinion?"

"Yes, a sort of a one. It's fair enough here, may be, but overrated. Seven thousand dollar ledges are scarce, though. That Sheba may be rich enough, but we don't own it; and besides, the rock is so full of base metals that all the science in the world can't work it. We'll not starve, here, but we'll not get rich, I'm afraid."

"So you think the prospect is pretty poor?"

"No name for it!"

"Well, we'd better go back, hadn't we?"

"Oh, not yet—of course not. We'll try it a riffle, first."

"Suppose, now—this is merely a supposition, you know—suppose you could find a ledge that would yield, say, a hundred and fifty dollars a ton—would that satisfy you?"

"Try us once!" from the whole party.

"Or suppose—merely a supposition, of course—suppose you were to find a ledge that would yield two thousand dollars a ton—would *that* satisfy you?"

"Here—what do you mean? What are you coming at? Is there some mystery behind all this?"

"Never mind. I am not saying anything. You know perfectly well there are no rich mines here—of course you do. Because you have been around and examined for yourselves. Anybody would know that, that had been around. But just for the sake of argument, suppose— in a kind of general way—suppose some person were to tell you that two-thousand-dollar ledges were simply contemptible—contemptible, understand—and that right yonder in sight of this very cabin there were piles of pure gold and pure silver— oceans of it—enough to make you all rich in twenty-four hours! Come!"

"I should say he was as crazy as a loon!" said old Ballou, but wild with excitement, nevertheless.

"Gentlemen," said I, "I don't say anything—*I* haven't been around, you know, and of course don't know anything—but all I ask of you is to cast your eye on *that*, for instance, and tell me what you think of it!" and I tossed my treasure before them.

There was an eager scramble for it, and a closing of heads together over it under the candlelight. Then old Ballou said:

"Think of it? I think it is nothing but a lot of granite rubbish and nasty glittering mica that isn't worth ten cents an acre!"

So vanished my dream. So melted my wealth away. So toppled my airy castle to the earth and left me stricken and forlorn.

Moralizing, I observed, then, that "all that glitters is not gold."

Mr. Ballou said I could go further than that, and lay it up among my treasures of knowledge, that *nothing* that glitters is gold. So I learned then, once for all, that gold in its native state is but dull, unornamental stuff, and that only lowborn metals excite the admiration of the ignorant with an ostentatious glitter. However, like the rest of the world, I still go on underrating men of gold and glorifying men of mica. Commonplace human nature cannot rise above that.

ANONYMOUS

"Culture on Bitter Creek"

There was almost nothing the average western working man would rather do than puncture someone's pretentiousness, and all "tenderfeet" were fair game for this intellectual exercise. The cautionary tale this unfortunate and anonymous young man relates appeared in the Lake City *(Colorado)* Mining Register *for October 8, 1880.*

———————

Perhaps every person who is somewhat advanced in life can remember some incident of his early years which he would really like to forget, something that resulted from the freshness and vast inexperience of youth. I remember one which I have spent a good deal of time trying to forget. Just before the Union Pacific railroad reached the Bitter Creek country, I made my first overland trip to the Pacific coast. I staged it from the then terminus of the Union Pacific to the Central Pacific, which was pushing east. The stage broke down on Bitter creek, and the passengers had to walk to the next station. I grew tired of walking before I reached the station, and coming late in the afternoon, to where some teamsters were camped, I concluded to stop with them for the night. On asking their permission to do so, they assented so heartily that I felt at home at once. Life in the west was something new to me. I was young and buoyant, and just out of college. I was fond of talking. I thought it would be novel and delightful to sleep out with these half-savage ox-drivers, with no shelter but the vaulted, star-gemmed heavens. There were four teamsters, and as many wagons, while thirty-two oxen grazed around in the vicinity. Of the teamsters, one was a giant in stature, and wore a bushy black beard; another was shorter, but powerfully built, and one-eyed; the third was tall, lank and hame-jawed; while the fourth was a wiry, red-headed man. In my thoughts I pitied them, on account of the hard life they led, and spoke to them in a kind tone, and endeavored to make my conversation constructive. I plucked a flower, and, pulling it to pieces mentioned the name of the parts—pistils, stamen, calyx, and so on—and remarked that it must be indigenous to the locality, and spoke of the plant being ondogenous, in contradiction exogenous, and they could see that it was not cryptogamous. In looking at some fragments of rock my thoughts wandered off into geology, and among other things I spoke of the tertiary and carboniferous periods, and of the pterodactyl, icthyosaurus and dinothorium. The teamsters looked at me, and then at each other, but made no response. We squatted down around the frying-pan to take supper, as the big fellow, with his right hand slapped or sort of larruped, a long piece of fried bacon over a piece of bread in his left hand, sending a drop of hot grease into my left eye, he said to the one-eyed man:

"Bill, is my copy of Shakespere in yo' wagon? I missed it to-day."

"No. My Tennerson and volum' of the Italian poets is in thar—no Shakespere."

The lank-looking teamster, biting off a piece of bread about the size of a saucer, in a voice which came huskily through the bread:

"Jake, did yer ever read that volum' of po'ms that I writ?"

"No, but hev often hearn tell on 'em."

"Yer mean 'Musin's of an Idle Man?'" spoke up the red-headed man, addressing the poet.
"Yes."

"Hev read every line in it a dozen times," said the teamster with the red hair, and as he sopped a four-inch swath, with a piece of bread, across a frying-pan, he repeated some lines.

"Them's they," nodded the poet. "The Emp'ror of Austry writ me a letter highly complimentin' them po'ms."

"They're very tochin'," added the wiry man.

I took no part in these remarks. Somehow I did not feel like joining in.

The wiry man having somewhat satisfied himself rolled up a piece of bacon rind into a sort of single-barreled opera glass, and began to squint through it towards the southern horizon.

"What yer doin', Dave?" asked the stout man.

"Takin' observations on the North star. Want to make some astronomical calkilations when I git later to Sackrymenter."

"Well, yer needn't ter made that tel'scope. I could er tuk yo' observations for yer, bein' as I have but one eye."

"Git that yer durned old carboniferous pterdacky," yelled the hame-jawed driver to an ox that was licking a piece of lariat.

"I give a good deal of my time to 'stronomy when I was in Yoorup," remarked the tall man.

"Over thar long?" asked one.

"Good while. War Minister to Roosky. Then I spent some time down ter Rome."

"Rome!" exclaimed the tall individual. "Was born thr. My father was a sculptor."

"Good sculptor?"

"Yes."

"Well, one wouldn't er thought it, ter look at yer."

"I never was in Yoorup," remarked the one-eyed man. "When I ocypied the cheer of ancient languages in Harvard College my health failed, and the fellers what hired me wanted me ter go ter Yoorup for an out, but I concluded ter come west ter look—hold upthar, yer infernal old flea-bitten ichthyosaurus," he bawled to an ox that was chewing a wagon cover.

I felt hot and feverish, and a long way from home.

"I got ready once ter go ter Rome—wanted ter complete my studies thar—but give it up," said the one called Dave.

"What fer?".

"They wanted me ter run fur guv'ner in Virginny."

"Yer beat 'em?"

"Thunder, yes."

"Why didn't yer stay thar?"

COLORPLATE 47

FREDERIC REMINGTON. *The Coming and Going of the Pony Express.* 1900. Oil on canvas. 27 x 40 in.
From the Collection of Gilcrease Museum, Tulsa, Oklahoma.

COLORPLATE 48 (top)

CHARLES M. RUSSELL. *Bruin not Bunny Turned the Leaders.* 1924. Oil. 24 x 36 in. From the Collection of Gilcrease Museum, Tulsa, Oklahoma. *Charles M. Russell may have lacked in professional training when compared to artists such as Remington, but if there was a more prolific and agile interpreter of the western scene, his name is lost to history. Russell painted in both oils and watercolors, sketched in pencil, pen and ink, charcoal, and even crayon, and every now and then he whipped up something in clay. None of his work is more treasured by those who own it than his illustrated letters, insouciant explosions of vernacular prose and swiftly-drawn vignettes sent to friends, relatives, and sometimes total strangers on the occasion of holidays, birthdays, anniversaries, or no occasion at all.*

COLORPLATE 49 (right)

CHARLES M. RUSSELL. *A Game Country.* Illustrated letter, March 4, 1917. Watercolor and ink on paper. 11 x 8 ½ in. The Rockwell Museum, Corning, New York.

COLORPLATE 50

CHARLES M. RUSSELL. *A Mix Up*. 1910. Oil on canvas. 30 x 48 in. The Rockwell Museum, Corning, New York.

"Well, when my job as guv'ner give out they 'lected me 'Piscopal bishop an' I hurt my lungs preachin'. Come west for my lungs."

"Found 'em?"

"Well, I'm improvin'."

I did not rest well that night. As day came on, and the men began to turn over in their blankets and yawn, the tall one said:

"Hello, Bill. How yer makin' it?"

"O, I'm indigenous."

"An' Dave?"

"I'm endogenous."

"An' you, Lanky, yer son of a sculptor?"

"Exogenous."

"How do you feel, Jake?" inquired one of the three who had responded.

"Cryptogamous, sir, cryptogamous."

I walked out a few steps to a little stream, to get a drink. I felt thirsty, and I ached. Then I heard a voice from the blankets.

"Wonder if them durned ole dinother'ums of ourn are done grazin'?"

Then a reply.

"I guess they've got to the tertiary period."

I walked a little piece on the road, to breathe the morning air.

I kept on.

Grub Time at a Wyoming Roundup. 1898. Photograph. Wyoming State Museum, Cheyenne. Stimson Collection.

GENE FOWLER

From *Timber Line*

"The Amorous Senator"

The burro was the independent miner's best friend, and some of the descendants of those crit-ters who carried the prospector's grub and tools during the glory days of mining can still be seen now and then, peeking shyly over desert hilltops. Denver-born newspaperman Gene Fowler immortalized his own beast in Timberline: A Story of Bonfils and Tammen *(1933).*

───────────

The Senator was the finest animal I ever owned. He was sturdy of back and strong of will. Occasionally he seemed sullen with captivity—I think an enforced celibacy weighed on his mind—but withal, the Senator was an effervescent fellow, unbroken in spirit and possessed of a flair for life.

The Senator was a mouse-colored burro, with one lop-ear which lent his port side a docile quality, entirely misleading, if not actually libelous. The other great ear stood like a member of the Coldstream Guards, forever hearkening to some oracular summons inaudible to humans. I am sure he was clairvoyant, for he could foretell a rattlesnake half a mile away. No doubt he had stemmed from Balaam's beast.

At sunrise, the Senator was as loquacious as any chanticleer, and he sang the dawn in terms of the soul undaunted. Most critics eschew the brayings of a burro, holding that the bestial *bel canto* is unmusical, quite, as the cascading hee-haws roll through glens where the quivering aspens dance in a west wind. But when the Senator cut loose with stentorian treble, I swear there was launched a commanding voice that would have won him top billing at the Metropolitan—at La Scala of Milan, even—had he deigned to become civilized, to bow, to scrape, to barter the brave pleasures of the wilderness for the perfumed ateliers of Park Avenue, his high mountain trail for a pent-house and a salon of dyspeptic fawners. He per-formed vocally in the Chinese scale of quarter notes, this Bing Crosby of the crags.

Somehow, it seemed the Senator was re-born each morning. By noon he had attained a sort of middle-age, and forthwith began to act rather foolishly and sophomoric. It was hard to curb him from a beckoning mesa, where trollop-eyed Jennies were waiting like spiders for just such a blade as the Senator.

Then, at nightfall—his one upright ear giving him a unicorn profile against the moon—the Senator seemed to be smelling Death. But he did not cringe. He stood statuesquely and would have presented a kingly mien, were it not for the pendulous ear. This blemish robbed him of majesty, and perhaps imbued a twilight tinge of inferiority. Artists unwittingly have revealed this quality in crippled rulers by their very effort to gloss over deformity, emphasizing, rather than concealing in stone or canvas, the regal funks.

Thus, the boomerangs of flattery so frequently have resulted in non-payment of royal bills, imprisonment in dungeons, market-place flagellations, disgrace and banishment. All of which does not prove that monarchs are stupidly ungrateful; rather, it defines the artist as a traitor to his craft whenever he counterfeits a rose where the wart or wen has priority.

I, too, endeavored to correct a noble infirmity, the Senator's auricular lassitude, by applica-tion of birch-splints. He roundly booted me into a cold and shallow creek for my pains. The Senator wanted no pity, and of pity he gave none. A gentleman, and my first tutor.

He stood still enough—outwardly—as the night stars came, but his hackamore was askew with straining, his tether-rope taut with yearning.

The Senator had legs of the Queen Anne period of furniture, and his feet were as dainty as Cinderella's—albeit more lethal. He had porphyry eyes that looked wistfully toward the far mesa, where the wild burros herded. When distant throatings of the wanton Jennies rode the wind with nymph-like invitations, the Senator would mumble love ditties. His body was Prometheus; his soul, Orpheus.

I did not quite understand him . . . then.

I was nine years old when I assumed ownership of the Senator. I believe he was six or upwards; but no one knew for certain—nor cared, either, since the day the Senator almost amputated the exploring hand of Tom Aldrich, who had said such matters could be determined beyond dispute by an examination of equine teeth.

Aside from a dose of the Senator's heels the time I played plastic surgeon on his flaccid ear, he and I got along together. The Senator had served in Axel Carr's small pack-train, carrying crates of dynamite from Empire, thirty miles away, to Red Mountain. He was named in honor of Senator ("Silver Dollar") Tabor, who had grubstaked Carr, as well as my grandpa and a hundred other prospectors in Leadville days. During a laborious era of powder-toting, the Senator had *two* upright ears, and had sampled the joys of fatherhood.

One autumn evening Carr's cabin went to Heaven with a grand roar, and Carr with it. Fragments of Carr were found every few minutes after the mysterious detonation—a leg, as I recall it, being the largest recoverable part of the confetti-like decedent. It was hanging, in a weird yuletide fashion, from the top branch of a Douglas fir tree.

The Senator had escaped whole—but his left ear had been slapped down by the blast—and I took him over in fee simple.

How glad the days! How sweet the smell of the pines, and how caressing the wind against the smooth cheeks of nine! We would ride along the old Mormon Road, where Brigham Young, Joseph Smith and other whiskered saints had trod during the long-ago pilgrimage to their Utah Canaan. I would sit astride the Senator—well back on his maltese rump—a Sir Launcelot, listening to the Merlin-tones of the great winds. There were voices, prophecies, soothsayings that only a child might understand—men have forfeited the right to dwell in enchanted places.

And often I looked at timber line, some three thousand feet above our remote valley. Timber line, above which no trees grow. From a distance, timber line is a strangely level hedge. The peaks rise baldly, a congregation of tonsured monks. Red Mountain was a fat, jovial fellow with a pink sandstone pate—a Franz Hals' portrait, a Falstaff of the range. To the east of Red Mountain lay the mesa, where the bawdy Jennies kicked up their heels at convention and domesticity.

At timber line, once you are there, a measureless rug of white sheep's wool quite frequently is spread beneath your feet. There you will find your hedge greatly changed. The trees are gnarled, stunted, rheumatic. There the whirlwinds have their home. And you come to feel that timber line is symbolic of something, a barrier perhaps—you never quite know what it means, but you sense that timber line is a frontier, where the work of man leaves off and that of God begins.

Seldom is there foliage on the storm-facing bosoms of the strained, tenacious old trees that have breasted a century or more of prevailing winds. The mountaintops have a climate entirely their own, seasons exclusively their own, and weather as fickle as the vows of diplomats. If you scale a peak crowned by an acre or so of tableland, you will encounter amazing paradoxes. You have climbed through a violence of upthrusting winds—mostly from the east—which have endeavored to hurl you from crag to ravine; then suddenly you win the flat summit and stand in an area so calm as to be uncanny. The nearby gale, mounting a corkscrew to heaven, rockets past your peak to wrestle with the stars. And it is a vastly impressive experience to stand in the calm zone, hearing the unruly cry of the great wind, and with never a whisper of it straying through your young hair. At timber line you become Olympian.

There are times, too, above timber line, when an electric storm actually touches you, and it is not at all dangerous—I have no scientific basis for saying so—even though your young hair stands on end, and sparks pop from your finger-tips when you flex your knuckles. You are shaking hands with Jove himself, and a very merry fellow he is up there.

And again, to be above timber line, when tarnished clouds are spilling snow on cabins thousands of feet below—but above and about you there is no snow! Only the sunlight, and here and there a peak, rising island-like, from the cloud-sea. All these are wonderful things. But they belong to a past, to a boyhood, and I believe I was talking about the Senator.

Where are his grandly lecherous bones today?

The Senator waited one noon for Grandma to hang out the sugar-sack dishcloths; and he promptly ate them, gobbling every one of them with gargantuan optimism. This gluttony was an overt act. It was my first intimation that Fate does not travel a direct and simple route, but moves along oblique lines. An assassin kills a prince in a provincial town, and a world war is born. A burro eats Grandma's dish-clouts, and . . . well, the old lady was a person of dominance and occasional choler.

"The burro must go," she said; "he's destructive."

The fabric-sated Senator now was braying in delirious crescendo, his great trowel of an ear cocked toward the mesas.

"I never liked him anyway," Grandma said; "he's shameless."

Grandpa had had another futile day of blasting the granite hill for gold. (He had had twelve years of futile days—but was there not always a Tomorrow?)

Grandpa was busy, putting half a dozen yellow sticks of dynamite into the oven, to dry the powder for next day's salvos. "You might of known better'n hang anything near that jackass," Grandpa said. "How was he to know?"

"*Must* you put that dynamite in the oven?" Grandma asked. "It drives me crazy."

"Keep your shirt on," Grandpa said. "I know my business."

These good folk were a bit critical of each other. It seems that General Lew Wallace, when Governor of New Mexico, had consulted Grandma in a literary way. He had given her a warmly-autographed copy of *Ben Hur*. Since that time, Grandma and Grandpa had been a bit critical of each other. Heigho!

Grandpa was handling the sticks like a farmer placing eggs in an incubator. "There's not the slightest danger. We die when our time comes."

"That's what Axel Carr thought," Grandma said. "It's tempting Providence. Anyway, get rid of that burro. What good is he?"

I lay in my bunk, listening. I heard the Senator braying right lustily. I heard Grandma pronounce his doom. I heard Grandpa grunt and go out to drive the Senator away, like a grim father giving the gate to an erring son. I did not cry when he turned the Senator loose upon a wide world. But I did hope the log cabin would blow up, like Carr's, myself with it. I planned to slip from my bunk and set off the powder in the oven. I waited a while for it to go off of its own accord. Then it was too late, for Grandpa returned, grumbling, took the powder from the oven and laid it aside for the next of his countless Tomorrows.

"Women are a problem," he was saying to himself.

For a week thereafter I wandered the Mormon Road afoot. It was small fun. I fashioned spears from lodge-pole pine. I roamed the groves, hurling javelins at chipmunks, pretending they were Saracens. But the joys of crusading were ephemeral. I kept asking Grandpa if he had run across the Senator, during the trips up and down the trail.

One evening in late spring, Grandpa said: "I seen the Senator today. He was on the mesa with the other Jacks and Jennies."

"How did he look? Homesick?"

Grandpa stuck a stout hand into his beard. An hour-glass stream of ore dust spilled from his pancake hat. "Depends on what you call homesick. I dunno. Come with me tomorrow. I think I'm nearing a lode."

I went to bed, but couldn't sleep. Just to see the Senator would be something. Maybe . . . but it's hard to dream when an argument is in progress near one's bed. Near one's soul. Grandma and Grandpa were having a few words in regard to a pan of Grandpa's personal sour-dough, from which he made his own biscuits. Somebody had thrown it away. It was a breed of pastry second to none, in the opinion of this gritty old citizen of the hills. I fell asleep during these log-cabin recriminations. I remember vaguely having heard a reference to General Wallace's amateur standing as a biscuit connoisseur.

"Just leave his name out of it," Grandma was saying. "The General had background."

Next morning we went toward the claim. "I'm likely to get into the vein today," Grandpa said. "We'll be richer'n all hell, and you can have a pony. A dozen ponies."

We finally reached the mesa. In the distance were about forty burros of various conformations. Some were grazing, others immobile, their ears vaned toward us querulously. Standing guard, a Lucifer of pride and apparently monarch of the whole herd, was the Senator. Beside him was the most dissipated, flea-bitten Jenny I ever had seen, frisking and cavorting like any old scut.

I ran with all speed, stumbling over boulders, but never slackening. Grandpa was howling: "You got no rope! You got to have a rope."

The Senator appraised me rather coldly, in the manner of a friend to whom you have lent money. "Senator!" I called. "Senator!"

I don't think titles meant much to him. He turned philosophically; then, with a most obscene gesture, lifted his heels, snorted and galloped swiftly off, the herd following him like sycophants. I felt whittled-down. I could sense, even at nine, that the Senator's affections were not for me, but with that unwholesome Jenny—that Moll Flanders of the mesa—whose sly countenance haunts me even to my forty-third year. God, what a strumpet!

I limped back to Grandpa. "Won't he ever come home?"

The old man lifted his pack. "I guess not, son. And I guess you're too young to take telling. But when you grow up, remember what I say: don't ever expect anything that's in love to listen to reason." . . .

I've often wondered if Love killed the Senator, or if the Senator killed Love.

Gold Seekers, Goldfield, Nevada. 1905. Photograph. Wyoming State Museum, Cheyenne. Stimson Collection.

JOHN TAYLOR WALDORF

From *A Kid on the Comstock*

"Taking a Chance"

Virginia City, Nevada, like most western mining towns, went from boom to bust in a mere hand-ful of years. Founded with the discovery of the great Comstock Lode in 1859, it was only a cut or two above ghost town status by the turn of the century. Reporter John Taylor Waldorf remembers in A Kid on the Comstock: Reminiscences of a Virginia City Childhood *(1968).*

In my day on the Comstock almost everybody took an active interest in some kind of specula-tion. The babies were barred, of course, but I've seen infants making a faro chip do duty as a teething ring. We small boys went further and played cards for matches. Sometimes we got blooded and bet such treasures as tops and marbles. One budding plunger wagered his hat and went home bareheaded, but I shall not mention his name because his father robbed him of fame by retrieving the hat and incidentally bringing about the "lammin'" of the winner for gambling.

Our dads wanted to do all the gambling themselves. The stronger the game, the better they liked it, and they all seemed to be inspired by the prehistoric gambler who said, "Money won't grow in your hand." Still, this was to be expected. They risked their lives every time they went to work, and when a man gambles with what God gave him, he isn't apt to hesitate over stak-ing what he has picked up for himself.

The favorite game with our fathers was stocks. We little fellows didn't understand it, but we thought it would be made plain when we grew up. Since then we've come to the conclusion we never will be old enough to master it. I got my wisdom free of cost, but some of my friends

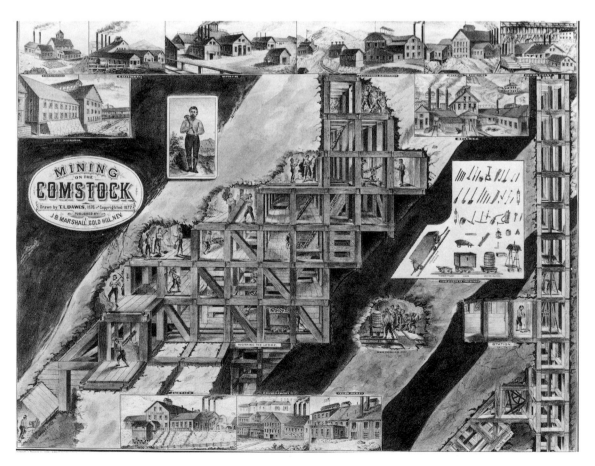

T. L. DAWES. *Mining on the Comstock.* 1876–77. Hand-colored lithograph. 20 1/2 x 27 1/8 in. Bancroft Library, University of California, Berkeley.

paid dearly for theirs. It is still as much of a mystery to me as it was in the days when the sight of a crowd around a stock board filled us with contempt. I remember the first crowd of that kind that I ever ran into. One of the neighbor's boys was with me. He burrowed his way through a jam of excited men, but soon came back to me snorting with disgust. "Aw," he said, "I thought it was a fight!"

How anybody could become interested in a game where you couldn't watch the dealer was beyond our powers of comprehension, but Virginia City was like every other place. The grown-up folks didn't believe that wisdom could come from the mouths of babes. Women as well as men put their all in stocks. When the newspaper came flying over the fence or banged against the front door, they seized it and turned hastily to the market page. Though the front page told of the death of the nation's greatest statesman or the blowing up of a czar, it made no difference. They paid no attention to the news until they had looked over the stock quotations.

If their eyes were weak, they would get the children to read to them. One kind-hearted lady used to call to me almost every day, "Johnny, come over like a good boy and tell me what's in the paper." I knew what that meant. She wanted to know about stocks. Many a day on her account I missed precious opportunities to have fun, but I'm entitled to no credit for that. It was her pies and cakes that lured me.

I would sit in her kitchen half an hour at a time reading such jargon as "Andes, 25 cents bid, 27 cents asked"; or "Bullion, opened 42, closed 41 3/4"; going through the long list, following it up with the sales, and closing the recital with mining news about dips, spurs, angles, winzes, up-raises, cross-cuts, inclines, and what not. The dear lady understood it all, but my expert knowledge was confined to pie and cake. Her stock of these commodities was always of superior quality, but the demand always exceeded the visible supply. If I had posted a board, it would often have read: "Cake opened strong, and all offerings found ready takers. Pie, one piece bid: two pieces asked. Extension work at the mouth of the shaft may become necessary in the near future."

I didn't need to go to the neighbors to hear stock talk. Dad got the fever soon after he struck the camp. Mother used to say to me, "Some day we're going back East," but for years none of the stocks in which Dad invested showed any disposition to furnish us with the price of transportation. All the while I was throwing out my little chest and informing every small boy I met that "we" were going back East.

Finally, "our" Ophir took a boom. Dad's holdings rose in value to $10,000 and mother began to talk of buying a farm. I was a real king, as far as feelings went. The stock kept going upward. Dad was worth $15,000 for at least a minute. He wanted $20,000, the clock ticked a few times; the bottom fell out of Ophir, and Mother's dream farm fell with it, for Dad was broke. The next day a kid across the street yelled to me, "You ain't so stuck up now. Goin' back East! Maybe you're goin' to Gold Hill." That was kind! From where we lived, it was almost a mile to Gold Hill.

Everybody had a hard luck story. Some had their goods packed when the crash came. I knew little fellows who got no Christmas presents because their dad had to pay an assessment on Confidence or Justice or some other mine with a sarcastic name. My dad never let the fever get that kind of a hold on him. He would sooner lose part of his stock than ignore Christmas. At least once a year he made me so happy that I forgot all about back East and the terrible day when Ophir wrecked our hopes.

Speaking of Ophir, "Old Doc," a neighborhood celebrity, used to say: "She reminds me of an old woman I knew in Missouri. This woman used to sit suckin' a gin bottle. When she started in, all she owned was a little patch of ground with a cabin on it, but with every drink she kept growin' richer and richer, and about the time she had the bottle straight up in the air she owned the whole state of Missouri. Then without any warnin' she'd slide unter the table, and that ended the performance. You don't catch me buyin' any Ophir!"

Some people had better luck than we. A few made their pile and went away. This helped the game, for those who stayed behind took hope and decided not to break themselves of the habit of carrying a few gold pieces to the broker's office every payday. Many a man delved in the depths year after year, earning his bread in more sweat than the prophets ever dreamed of, and got nothing out of his wage save board and lodgings. Some of these unfortunates economized to buy a few more shares of stock or to pay assessments on what they had.

What a nightmare those assessments were! The young felt them as well as the old, even though small boys were barred from the game. A father might be fond of his offspring, but the constant levying of assessments on his stock didn't improve his patience with a child who got noisy while he was studying the quotations in the paper. No doubt many a "lammin'" that was administered down in our neighborhood had its inception in a meeting of mining magnates. I remember at least one youngster who was wise in his generation. I saw him come dashing out the front door of his home with the toe of his dad's boot pursuing him closely. When he reached me he took a long breath and said: "Gee, I wish Kentuck would declare a dividend."

ISABELLA L. BIRD

From *A Lady's Life in the Rocky Mountains*
"The Blight of Mining"

For all the excitement that the mining industry in the West engendered, it was first and fore-most an industry—and left no prettier stamp upon the land than most industry. Isabella L. Bird, who traveled the Rocky Mountain mining region with her engineer husband in the 1880s, found a good deal of ugliness to report in her letters home, as in this November 1886 sample.

Boulder

The answer regarding a horse (at the end of my former letter) was given to the landlord outside the hotel, and presently he came in and asked my name and if I were the lady who had crossed from Link's to South Park by Tarryall Creek; so news travels fast. In five minutes the horse was at the door, with a clumsy two-horned side-saddle, and I started at once for the upper regions. It was an exciting ride, much spiced with apprehension. The evening shadows had darkened over Georgetown, and I had 2,000 feet to climb, or give up Green Lake. I shall forget many things, but never the awfulness and hugeness of the scenery. I went up a steep track by Clear Creek, then a succession of frozen waterfalls in a widened and then narrowed valley, whose frozen sides looked 5,000 feet high. That is the region of enormous mineral wealth in silver. There are the "Terrible" and other mines whose shares you can see quoted daily in the share lists in the *Times*, sometimes at cent per cent premium, and then down to 25 discount.

These mines, with their prolonged subterranean workings, their stamping and crushing mills, and the smelting works which have been established near them, fill the district with noise, hubbub, and smoke by night and day; but I had turned altogether aside from them into a still region, where each miner in solitude was grubbing for himself, and confiding to none his finds or disappointments. Agriculture restores and beautifies, mining destroys and devastates, turning the earth inside out, making it hideous, and blighting every green thing, as it usually blights man's heart and soul. There was mining everywhere along that grand road, with all its destruction and devastation, its digging, burrowing, gulching, and sluicing; and up all along the seemingly inaccessible heights were holes with their roofs log supported, in which solitary and patient men were selling their lives for treasure. Down by the stream, all among the icicles, men were sluicing and washing, and everywhere along the heights were the scars of hardly-passable trails, too steep even for pack-jacks, leading to the holes, and down which the miner packs the ore on his back. Many a heart has been broken for the few finds which have been

Mining town, Creede, Colorado. c.1890. Photograph. Henry Ford Museum and Greenfield Village.

made along those hill sides. All the ledges are covered with charred stumps, a picture of desolation, where nature had made everything grand and fair. But even from all this I turned. The last miner I saw gave me explicit directions, and I left the track and struck upwards into the icy solitudes—sheets of ice at first, then snow, over a foot deep, pure and powdery, then a very difficult ascent through a pine forest, where it was nearly dark, the horse tumbling about in deep snowdrifts. But the goal was reached, and none too soon.

At a height of nearly 12,000 feet I halted on a steep declivity, and below me, completely girdled by dense forests of pines, with mountains red and glorified in the sunset rising above them, was Green Lake, looking like water, but in reality a sheet of ice two feet thick. From the gloom and chill below I had come up into the pure air and sunset light, and the glory of the unprofaned works of God. It brought to my mind the verse, "The darkness is past, and the true light now shineth"; and, as if in commentary upon it, were the hundreds and thousands of men delving in dark holes in the gloom of the twilight below.

> *O earth, so full of dreary noises!*
> *O men, with wailing in your voices,*
> *O delved gold, the wailer's heap,*
> *God strikes a silence through you all,*
> *He giveth His beloved sleep.*

It was something to reach that height and see the far-off glory of the sunset, and by it to be reminded that neither God nor His sun had yet deserted the world. But the sun was fast going down, and even as I gazed upon the wonderful vision the glory vanished, and the peaks became sad and gray. It was strange to be the only human being at that glacial altitude, and to descend again through a foot of untrodden snow and over sloping sheets of ice into the darkness, and to see the hill sides like a firmament of stars, each showing the place where a solitary man in his hole was delving for silver.

Frank A. Crampton

From *Deep Enough*

Cave-in

If western mining was an ugly business on the surface, it was often lethal underground. Safety standards were lax, to say the least; maiming and death from explosions, cave-ins, and poisoned air were common. Nothing, however, could match the horror of being trapped underground, as demonstrated by this powerful story from Frank Crampton's classic memoir, Deep Enough: A Working Stiff in the Western Mine Camps *(1956).*

———————————

As we were going down the drift, we heard yells coming from the tunnel and saw men running toward the mouth. In a few seconds there came the sounds of breaking timbers, then a grinding rumble, followed by a depressing silence and a violent rush of air as if a big blast had gone, or an over-pressured air line had broken. Our carbide lamps went out but we did not need light to know that the tunnel had caved.

Our carbide lamps lighted again, we looked at each other and, without a word, headed back to where we had left the bohunks. By the time we got to the cross-cuts the bohunks had their candles going again and I could size them up. Fear was written on every face, as I know it must have been on mine, but there was no sign of panic. All of us knew we were in for trouble, and there was not one who wasn't scared stiff. We were caught behind a tunnel full of rock that would take a lot of days to muck out and timber. A caved-in adit, with no other exit from the workings, was bad—rotten surveying and management had taken care of that.

There was almost nothing we could do to help. The little that we might do would waste our strength, and we were going to need all we had. Relays of hard-rock stiffs outside, working in twenty-minute shifts, would break through, sooner or later, and it was up to us to last it out if we could; our chances were much better if we did nothing.

There was no immediate danger where we were. We could hear the ground working and still coming down into the tunnel. Caving had stopped at the drift end where we were; a few feet more might sluff, but even if that happened, only a few tons would come, and it would not block the tunnel any more than it already was. The workings had a lot of bad ground but none between the four hundred and the fifteen hundred foot stations; we would keep away from the bad ground deeper into the mine unless we were driven back by water.

The workings were heavy with dead powder smoke and the smell of water-soaked timber. With thousands of feet of drifts and cross-cuts in the workings, it might be some time before the danger from mine gasses would become serious. Water dripping from the roof and coming out of the walls would furnish us more than we needed to drink. Although the water was a blessing in one way, its constant dripping from above would keep our clothing soaked. It would give us a lot of trouble, moreover, if it did not drain through the caved ground and backed up into the workings. This danger was somewhat offset by the grade of the drift, which was steep (about four inches each hundred feet toward the mouth of the tunnel).

Food was our greatest problem. When we took inventory of the graveyard lunches, which had not been eaten, we found that the lunch buckets contained less than we had expected. But we knew that with water men could last much longer than with food and no water.

Candles and snuffs were collected and put in an empty powder case. Knives, candle holders, and miscellaneous junk were deposited in the owners' lunch buckets, to be claimed later. We all kept our watches, money, plug tobacco, snoose, and matches. When the inventory and collection were over, the lunch buckets and candles were cached down the drift where they would not be a temptation and could be guarded against raids.

We were going to be in darkness long before the stiffs working in the tunnel could reach us. By burning one candle at a time there would be enough to give light less than four days. The carbide lamps that Steve, Bob, and I carried could be kept lighted a few hours with the unburned carbide in them and with the reserve we carried with us in tins. We hoped to get everything prepared for the wait ahead before resorting to candles.

Our first consideration was to make our waiting place as comfortable as we could while we were fresh. The intersection of cross-cuts and the drift at the twelve-hundred station was selected as the safest place. The ground was good and there was no danger from sluffs or caves. Moreover, the level of the drift floor here was over three feet higher than at the closed end of the caved-in tunnel. There were more than three miles of workings below the twelve-hundred station, and they would hold a hell of a lot of water. It would take a long time before it reached us or became deep enough to drive us back to the far end of the workings where the ground was loose and dangerous.

The bohunks were divided into three groups, one of five and two of six. Lots were drawn to determine who would occupy each of the three locations. The five group drew the drift, and the six groups drew the cross-cuts. Steve, Bob, and I had already selected the drift below the intersection.

When we realized what we were up against, we had wasted no time worrying and had gotten down to cases in a hurry. Everything was under control, the food and light situations were taken care of, the location of our new homes decided, and there was nothing left but to start building. While Steve and Bob were getting the home work under way, I went down the drift to size things up and to take a good look at the cave-in.

When I reached the five-hundred station, I paced the distance to the caved ground. It was eighty feet. Four hundred twenty feet of a caved-in tunnel lay between us and daylight. If all of the tunnel had caved, it would take no less than three weeks before the stiffs on the relays of rescue workers could break through. It would be longer if mucking was difficult. It would also depend on whether a lot of spilling had to be done, and how much work it would take to get sets in to hold the ground. The stiffs would not do a fancy job, a hole to get through would be enough, but they would make sure that the hole would not close behind them. It could be more than three weeks—a lot longer than I cared to think about. It might be less if some of the timber put in during the past few days had held. The thought was encouraging, but I didn't dare let that hope take over.

Faint sounds came through the caved ground, or the rock walls. I didn't know which, and it didn't matter. The sounds told me that the stiffs were on their way. I would have known it anyway, even had I heard no sounds. They were giving it everything they had. The sounds were a reminder that we had sent no signals, and it suddenly dawned on me that a message must be gotten to the stiffs outside to let them know that we were alive.

As I knelt to send a message on the compressed-air line, I realized that there was no pond of water under me; water coming down the drift was flowing through openings in the caved ground. It was a welcome discovery. Then I signalled—tap-tap, a pause, tap-tap-tap—and hoped the compressed-air line was not so badly broken that a message would not go through. Then I waited. There was an answer—tap-tap, a pause, tap-tap—faintly. From the sound I knew the line had been badly bashed and damaged but messages would go through. Then, to let the stiffs know we were all alive I signalled "twenty," and when the reply came I got up and went back to where the bohunks were working.

Work on our new homes went fast. Lagging and timber from the cross-cuts was used without cutting, and a couple of ore cars made it easy to get it to the job without manhandling. Our homes were to be platforms, one in each cross-cut and two in the drift, one above and one below the intersection. Barriers erected at the end of each platform made a hollow square of the intersection and we hoped it would discourage the bohunks from wandering around and visiting. The location of our platform on the lower side of the hollow square at the intersection, with the barriers between us and the bohunks, gave control of almost any situation—panic, demoralization, or a rush for food. We did not misjudge the bohunks, we did not expect trouble, and there was never any sign of it, but anything could have happened under the increasing tensions of passing hours and days.

Toilets were built in a corner at the end of each platform and against its barrier, with empty powder cases used as thunder-mugs. Burned carbide from a pile in the cross-cut near the lockers was used as a deodorant. The bohunks got fresh drinking water by dipping it from the trench along the tracks, before the water went under the platforms. Our water was taken from the eleven-hundred station cross-cut, much below our platform and away from anything that might flow down the drift. From the survey station in the roof of the intersection we fastened wire and hung an empty cap-box to the lower end. A lighted candle in the cap-box threw light into the drift and the cross-cuts.

It was six hours from the time of the cave-in before everything was completed, and then there was nothing more to do but wait. Before sending the bohunks to their platform homes, we all had a piece of sandwich meat and some bread. Somehow, while the work of home-building had been going on, three of the bohunks had fashioned crude musical instruments. Two were made from powder cases to which necks had been attached, and each had four strings made from tightly drawn rawhide shoe laces, taken from the bohunk's high work boots. The third was a flute, fashioned from a piece of pipe with a four inch long crack. One end was plugged and the other had a very creditable mouthpiece.

The bohunks began making a holiday of the situation. The groups would take turns chanting to the deep bass notes of the powder-case instruments, or to the high-pitched flute. When a chant ended, peals of laughter would follow, punctuated by comments passed between one group and another. We couldn't understand much, but what we did was enough to leave no questions that it was profane and ribald.

Steve, Bob, and I joined the festivities as best we could. Sometimes the chants went on for a long time. Then there would be quiet until some of the bohunks became restless or could not sleep, and started it all over again. It was good that the bohunks had found something to do, and their antics broke the monotony, for them as well as for us. It was not easy to wait and do nothing.

Dragging hours were not made shorter by the routine of giving signals on the compressed-air line. Each succeeding hour interval passed slower than the preceding one. Watching the candle to see that it burned to its bottom, and no more, then waiting for the split-second to put in a new one, lighted quickly as the burning candle flickered out, was a strained diversion. It made us more aware of time than did the signalling. When half of the candles had been burned, we knew that darkness would come sooner than we had expected. The candles were cheap and of an inferior grade and burned rapidly. Oncoming darkness was nothing to look forward to.

At first we doled out food in small portions, but the allowances were increased when we found that the meat and bread were beginning to go bad. The muggy-warm dampness and the gasses from the dead powder smoke were no doubt responsible; both had already begun to affect us also. On the second day, what was left of the food was divided and eaten. The food did more harm than good: it was in worse condition than we had suspected, although there was no odor of spoilage. After it was down a short time, all of us began to retch, and we lost it all. The retching continued for hours. It would have been better had we thrown it away; strength was lost to each of us for having eaten it.

Every hour Steve, Bob, and I took alternate turns going down the drift to signal and to listen for the sounds of work that seemed to be getting closer. At first there had been no blasting, and the sounds seemed to be coming rapidly closer. On the second day there were sounds of machine drilling, then, after a short silence, a few shots. As time passed, the machines drilled longer as the sounds came closer, and the shots were heavier. The longer drilling and heavier shooting were discouraging. It was not difficult to guess what was happening. The stiffs working to get to us, had passed the loose broken ground near the tunnel mouth, and were hitting large blocks of caved rock as they came closer. The blocks must be huge, or the blasting would not have been so heavy; unless there was a damned good reason, the blasting would be held to light-loaded holes. Our guess of three weeks to break through was raised. Only by a miracle, we thought, could the stiffs get to us in time.

The third day was less than half over when an extra heavy shot sent a concussion through the workings that put out our lighted candle. Before that no one had given a thought to matches, no one smoked in the mine at any time; we chewed plug or used snoose. The only time

matches were used was to light lamps or candles and that had not been necessary except imme-diately after the cave-in. Every stiff carried a few in a pocket or in some battered-up metal case. All were useless. The water in our water-soaked clothing had ruined the loose ones, and dampness had gotten into the metal containers where others were kept. There was no way to get a candle going again, or a snuff, and two shifts of light remained in them if they could be burned.

Waiting with light was bad enough. Without it, everything was changed. There was less con-versation, and the music and chants from the bohunk's quarters were heard less frequently, then not at all. The darkness made us realize our trouble acutely. When we had light, what we were up against seemed as if it were an unreal dream; without light, it was a nightmare and far from unreal.

During the time we had had light our ears had become accustomed to sounds of the stiffs working to get to us through the caved tunnel, of men turning and groaning, and of heavy breathing and snoring, all expected and therefore unnoticed. In the darkness a new sound was heard. Whether any of us had noticed the ticking of watches, all twenty of them, I don't know, probably as unnoticed as other sounds we had become accustomed to. But with darkness, sounds from our watches, irregular and at random, were as loud as a boiler factory in which a drum corps was practicing.

Not many hours of darkness passed before I had stood the new noise as long as I could. I crawled over the barricade and told the bohunks to hand over their watches. Not one of them hesitated. No doubt the noise had been as unbearable to them as it had been to me.

When I crawled back to our platform, with the boiler factory going full blast in my pockets, Steve and Bob handed me their timepieces without a word. Then I crawled down the drift to the eleven-hundred cross-cuts, felt the floor for a hole deep enough with water to cover the watches and drown the noise, found one, and dumped the mess into it. I made my way back to our platform and dozed off, in the silence of usual and noticed sounds. The boiler-factory

Fifth Vein of Argentiferous Galena, 500-foot level, Tombstone Consolidated Mines Company. c. 1904. Photograph. Arizona Historical Society, Tucson.

drum-corps situation was solved.

Our clothing, clear to the skin, was waterlogged. The continual dripping of water from the roof could not be stopped, and there was nothing in the workings with which to make a shelter to turn it away from us. When we lay in some position for a while, the part of our bodies not facing the mine roof would warm up, and the water-soaked clothing also. When we turned again, which was often, the dripping water from the roof would chill us again in a matter of moments. It was as if we were being boiled in cold water.

Water-soaked clothing was softening otherwise hard flesh all over my body, and the flesh became so loosened that it would slip and crawl over the meat underneath whenever I moved. In addition, my injured legs were swelling and becoming increasingly painful. It was not my legs, though, that gave the most trouble: it was the flesh loosened from the meat and muscle underneath. Changing from one position to another became impossible, as impossible as it was to remain in one position longer than a few minutes at a time.

My teeth were chattering almost constantly, as if I had malaria, a result of the wet, cold, water-logged clothing. My jaws were so tired and sore that I tied a bandanna around my head and chin to keep them from moving, and to stop the agony. It didn't stop the jaws in their effort to chatter; the bandanna loosened and had to be retied time after time, until finally, from sheer and hopeless weariness, I gave up trying and let them chatter as they would.

Occasionally the movement of my jaws would stop. Whenever it did, I could hear the chattering of the teeth of the stiffs around me. They were having the same trouble as I was, both from their cold-boiled flesh and chattering teeth. I was sorry for them, but I was glad to know that I was not the only one who was having the same kind of troubles.

Weakness and exhaustion were overtaking us long before it should. Water-logged clothing and bad air that was getting worse were bad enough, much too bad, but the spoiled food was getting in its best work. We had plenty of water, but only a few had held it down since the food was eaten. It took several days before all of us were over that jolt. By the time we were all again able to hold the water we drank, our weakness was so great that nerves, already strung to high pitch, had all but reached the breaking point.

*   *   *

I was in a dazed and nightmarish doze when the break-through was made. A sudden rush of ice-cold air brought me out of it, momentarily, and I could hear voices down the drift, but they did not seem to get nearer, and I went off into unconsciousness again. The next I knew was when I heard the voice of John T, shouting over and over, "Cover up your eyes, here we come with lights."

There was no chance of my putting anything over my eyes. I was so weak I couldn't move. I do not think any of the other stiffs could either. Then, as the stiffs who had worked to get to us came closer, we knew it was not a dream. And then I heard sobs, deep-breathing sobs, trying to be held back, but breaking out nonetheless, for the strength to hold them back was gone. Then I was sobbing, too, and tears running down and smarting my tender-skinned face.

C. C. GOODWIN

"The Prospector"

The life of the mining frontier—like that of the average miner—was short, and not always sweet. It lasted, roughly, from 1848 to 1905, when the last major discovery of gold took place in Goldfield, Nevada. This lugubrious poem by C.C. Goodwin, first published in 1872, may have lacked in art, but it remained true to the melancholy that colored the memories of many who had lived through those times.

W. R. FREEMAN. *The Prospector*. 1882. Oil. 36 x 29 in. Arizona
Historical Society Museum, Tucson, Arizona. Southern
Arizona Division.

How strangely tonight our memory flings
From the face of the past the shadowy wings,
And we see far back through the mist and tears,
Which make the record of twenty years;
From the beautiful days in the Golden State,
When life seemed taking a lease of Fate;
From the wondrous visions of "long ago"
To the naked shade that we call "now."
Those halcyon days; there were four of us then—
Ernest and Ned, wild Tom and Ben.
Now all are gone; Tom was first to die;
We held his hands, closed his glazed eyes,
And many a tear o'er his grave we shed,
As we tenderly pillowed his curly head,
In the shadows deep of the pines that stand
Forever solemn, forever fanned
By the winds that steal through the Golden Gate
And spread their balm o'er the Golden State.
And the others, too, they all are dead!
By the turbid Gila perished Ned;
Brave, noble Ernest, he was lost
Amid Montana's ice and frost:
And Bennie's life went out in gloom
Deep in the Comstock's vaults of doom,
And we are left, the last of all,
And as tonight the cold snows fall,
And barbarous winds around us roar,
We think the long past o'er and o'er:
What we have hoped and suffered, all,
From the twenty years roll back the pall,
From the dusty, thorny, weary track,
As the torturous path we follow back.
In our childhood's home they think us, there,

A failure, or lost, till our name in the prayer
At eve is forgot. Well, they cannot know
That our toil through heat, through tempest and snow,
While it seemed for naught but a portion of pelf,
Was more for them, far more, than ourself.
Well, well, as our hair turns slowly to snow,
The places of childhood more distantly grow.
And our dreams are changing; 'tis home no more.
But shadowy hands from the other shore
Stretch nightly down, and it seems as when
We lived with Tom, Ned, Ernest, and Ben.
And the mountains of earth seem dwindling down
And the hills of Eden, with golden crown,
Rise up, and we think, in the last great day
Will our claims above bear a fine assay?
From the slag of earth and the baser stains
Will Death's crucible show of precious grains
Enough to give us a standing above
In the mansions of Peace, in the cradle of Love?
And thus do we dream while the tempests beat
While fall on our casement the ice and sleet,
And the fierce winds moan as they sweep the nights
Of these desolate hills, through these desolate nights;
So changed is life since the bright days when
We lived with Tom, Ned, Ernest, and Ben.

THE HIRED MAN
ON HORSEBACK

ANDY ADAMS

From *The Log of a Cowboy*

"Dodge"

The cattle industry, as old as America itself, did not enter the realm of romance until the post–Civil War era, when Texas cowboys began driving herds north to railheads at Abilene, Dodge City, and other Central Plains towns. One of the cowboys was Andy Adams, who went on to fictionalize his experience in a series of stories and novels, the best of which was The Log of a Cowboy *(1903), the story of a single cattle drive. Here, the boys pause for a little fun.*

———————

"I've been in Dodge every summer since '77," said the old cowman, "and I can give you boys some points. Dodge is one town where the average bad man of the West not only finds his

COLORPLATE 51

FRANK TENNEY JOHNSON. *The Deputy Sheriff*. 1929. Oil on canvas. Private collection.

COLORPLATE 53

Frank Tenney Johnson. *The Morning Shower.* 1927. Oil on canvas. 36 x 28 in. The Rockwell Museum, Corning, NY.

COLORPLATE 52 (opposite page)

N. C. Wyeth. *The Lee of the Grub-Wagon.* 1904. Oil on canvas. 38 x 26 in. Buffalo Bill Historical Center,
Cody, Wyoming. Gift of John M. Schiff.

COLORPLATE 54

FRANK TENNEY JOHNSON. *Riders of the Dawn*. 1935 . Oil on canvas. 48 x 60 in.
Courtesy of The Anschutz Collection, Denver, Colorado.

COLORPLATE 55

CHARLES M. RUSSELL. *Free Trappers.* 1911. Oil on canvas. 33 x 24 in. Courtesy of Montana Historical Society, Helena. Mackay Collection.

COLORPLATE 56 (top)

HENRY FARNEY. *The Sorceror*. 1903. Oil on canvas. 22 x 40 in. From the Collection of Gilcrease Museum,
Tulsa, Oklahoma.

COLORPLATE 57 (bottom)

CHARLES SCHREYVOGEL. *The Last Drop*. 1900. Oil on canvas. 16 x 20 in. Private collection.
Photograph courtesy of the Gerald Peters Gallery, Santa Fe, New Mexico.

COLORPLATE 58

W. H. D. KOERNER. *Hard Winter*. 1932. Oil on canvas. 29 x 41 ¹/8 in. Buffalo Bill Historical Center, Cody, Wyoming.
For all his relative obscurity, it is entirely possible that W. H. D. Koerner, one of The Saturday Evening Post*'s illustrators
in the 1920s and 1930s, reached many more millions than Remington, Russell, or any other painter of things western.
The* Post *had a weekly circulation of 3 million copies and an assumed readership of at least 10 million, and over fifteen
years Koerner produced more than five hundred illustrations of western scenes. Along the way, his biographer,
W. H. Hutchinson has written, Koerner gave us much of what we think we remember about the actual West: "Given a
willing audience of millions exposed many, many times each year for many years to the work of a single artist in a
particular field, it is reasonable to expect that artist to have had a significant effect in creating the popular conceptions
of the period and the subjects he portrayed—on that assumption the case for Koerner as a leading image-maker of the
Western mythos rests."*

Dude and a waitress taking the prize for dancing "Bull Calves" Medley on the Grand Piano. Harper's Magazine. Engraving.

equal, but finds himself badly handicapped. The buffalo hunters and range men have protested against the iron rule of Dodge's peace officers, and nearly every protest has cost human life. Don't ever get the impression that you can ride your horses into a saloon, or shoot out the lights in Dodge; it may go somewhere else, but it don't go there. So I want to warn you to behave yourselves. You can wear your six-shooters into town, but you'd better leave them at the first place you stop, hotel, livery, or business house. And when you leave town, call for your pistols, but don't ride out shooting; omit that. Most cowboys think it's an infringement on their rights to give up shooting in town, and if it is, it stands, for your six-shooters are no match for Winchesters and buckshot; and Dodge's officers are as game a set of men as ever faced danger."

*   *   *

We were enjoying ourselves immensely over at the Lone Star dance hall, when an incident occurred in which we entirely neglected the good advice of McNulta, and had the sensation of hearing lead whistle and cry around our ears before we got away from town.

Quince Forrest was spending his winnings as well as drinking freely, and at the end of a quadrille gave vent to his hilarity in an old-fashioned Comanche yell. The bouncer of the dance hall of course had his eye on our crowd, and at the end of a change, took Quince to task. He was a surly brute, and instead of couching his request in appropriate language, threatened to throw him out of the house. Forrest stood like one absent-minded and took the abuse, for physically he was no match for the bouncer, who was armed, moreover, and wore an officer's star. I was dancing in the same set with a red-headed, freckled-faced girl, who clutched my arm and wished to know if my friend was armed. I assured her that he was not, or we would have had notice of it before the bouncer's invective was ended. At the conclusion of the dance, Quince and The Rebel passed out, giving the rest of us the word to remain as though nothing was wrong. In the course of half an hour, Priest returned and asked us to take our leave one at a time without attracting any attention, and meet at the stable. I remained until the last, and noticed The Rebel and the bouncer taking a drink together at the bar,—the former apparently in a most amiable mood. We passed out together shortly afterward, and found the other boys mounted and awaiting our return, it being now about midnight. It took but a moment to secure our guns, and once in the saddle, we rode through the town in the direction of the herd. On the outskirts of the town, we halted. "I'm going back to that dance hall," said Forrest, "and have one round at least with that whore-herder. No man who walks this old earth can insult me, as he did, not if he has a hundred stars on him. If any of you don't want to go along, ride right on to camp, but I'd like to have you all go. And when I take his measure, it will be the signal to the rest of you to put out the lights. All that's going, come on."

There were no dissenters to the programme. I saw at a glance that my bunkie was heart and soul in the play, and took my cue and kept my mouth shut. We circled round the town to a vacant lot within a block of the rear of the dance hall. Honeyman was left to hold the horses; then, taking off our belts and hanging them on the pommels of our saddles, we secreted our six-shooters inside the waistbands of our trousers. The hall was still crowded with the revelers when we entered, a few at a time, Forrest and Priest being the last to arrive. Forrest had changed hats with The Rebel, who always wore a black one, and as the bouncer circulated around, Quince stepped squarely in front of him. There was no waste of words, but a gun-barrel flashed in the lamplight, and the bouncer, struck with the six-shooter, fell like a beef. Before the bewildered spectators could raise a hand, five six-shooters were turned into the ceiling. The lights went out at the first fire, and amidst the rush of men and the screaming of women, we reached the outside, and within a minute were in our saddles. All would have gone well had we returned by the same route and avoided the town; but after crossing the railroad track, anger and pride having not been properly satisfied, we must ride through the town.

On entering the main street, leading north and opposite the bridge on the river, somebody of our party in the rear turned his gun loose into the air. The Rebel and I were riding in the lead, and at the clattering of hoofs and shooting behind us, our horses started on the run, the shooting by this time having become general. At the second street crossing, I noticed a rope of fire belching from a Winchester in the doorway of a store building. There was no doubt in my mind but we were the object of the manipulator of that carbine, and as we reached the next cross street, a man kneeling in the shadow of a building opened fire on us with a six-shooter. Priest reined in his horse, and not having wasted cartridges in the open-air shooting, returned the compliment until he emptied his gun. By this time every officer in the town was throwing lead after us, some of which cried a little too close for comfort. When there was no longer any shooting on our flanks, we turned into a cross street and soon left the lead behind us. At the outskirts of the town we slowed up our horses and took it leisurely for a mile or so, when Quince Forrest halted us and said, "I'm going to drop out here and see if any one follows us. I want to be alone, so that if any officers try to follow us up, I can have it out with them."

As there was no time to lose in parleying, and as he had a good horse, we rode away and left him. On reaching camp, we secured a few hours' sleep, but the next morning, to our surprise, Forrest failed to appear. We explained the situation to Flood, who said if he did not show up by noon, he would go back and look for him. We all felt positive that he would not dare to go back to town; and if he was lost, as soon as the sun arose he would be able to get his bearings. While we were nooning about seven miles north of the Saw Log, some one noticed a buggy coming up the trail. As it came nearer we saw that there were two other occupants of the rig besides the driver. When it drew up old Quince, still wearing The Rebel's hat, stepped out of the rig, dragged out his saddle from under the seat, and invited his companions to dinner. They both declined, when Forrest, taking out his purse, handed a twenty-dollar gold piece to the driver with an oath. He then asked the other man what he owed him, but the latter very haughtily declined any recompense, and the conveyance drove away.

"I suppose you fellows don't know what all this means," said Quince, as he filled a plate and sat down in the shade of the wagon. "Well, that horse of mine got a bullet plugged into him last night as we were leaving town, and before I could get him to Duck Creek, he died on me. I carried my saddle and blankets until daylight, when I hid in a draw and waited for something to turn up. I thought some of you would come back and look for me sometime, for I knew you would n't understand it, when all of a sudden here comes this livery rig along with that drummer—going out to Jetmore, I believe he said. I explained what I wanted, but he decided that his business was more important than mine, and refused me. I referred the matter to Judge Colt, and the judge decided that it was more important that I overtake this herd. I'd have made him take pay, too, only he acted so mean about it."

After dinner, fearing arrest, Forrest took a horse and rode on ahead to the Solomon River. We were a glum outfit that afternoon, but after a good night's rest were again as fresh as daisies. When McCann started to get breakfast, he hung his coat on the end of the wagon rod, while he went for a bucket of water. During his absence, John Officer was noticed slipping something into Barney's coat pocket, and after breakfast when our cook went to his coat for his tobacco, he unearthed a lady's cambric handkerchief, nicely embroidered, and a silver mounted garter. He looked at the articles a moment, and, grasping the situation at a glance, ran his eye over the outfit for the culprit. But there was not a word or a smile. He walked over and threw the articles into the fire, remarking, "Good whiskey and bad women will be the ruin of you varmints yet."

WILL JAMES

From *Lone Cowboy: My Life Story*

Sleepering

Like Andy Adams, Will James (born Ernest Dufault in Quebec) spent some time in the saddle, then made his living for the rest of his life from that experience—both as an artist and as a writer. His illustrated children's book, Smoky, *is still widely read. Much of the rest of his work was fiction as well—including most of his "autobiography,"* Lone Cowboy *(1930). It still made for good storytelling, as this excerpt demonstrates.*

I don't know what Bopy would of thought if he'd knowed of me hiring out as a "long rope" artist. Maybe he'd felt the same way I did at the time, because then in that country it seemed like the only big wrong in appropriating cattle was getting caught doing it. It was still less wrong to steal cattle from a sheep outfit. Anyway, that's how I was made to feel, and it wasn't long when I was as much against the sheepman as any cowman could of been.

What turned the cowman against the sheepman from the first is that the sheepman came in the country after the cowman had found it, claimed his part and made the range safe against the Indian. The cowman had fought for it for all he was worth and soon as he had the Indian tamed down and raids was getting far apart, why here comes the sheepman to tramp down the grass the cowman had fought for. The blatting woollies and the herders had no respect for the cowman's territory and not only tramped down his grass, but brought in a lot of loco and other poison weeds.

There's many a part of the range country right to-day where the cowman still mixes it with the sheepman, and that'll always be, I guess, as long as there's open country and cattle and sheep.

The old cowman I was riding for was pretty sore at all sheepmen and he kept a stirring me up about 'em till I got to thinking it was sure fine to sort of get even with 'em for him. It was a lot of fun getting by with it too, and being I liked the old cowman so much made me try to please him all the more. While pleasing him I was getting in good with that brown-headed niece of his too. Far as she knowed, I wasn't doing anything out of the way, but just the usual riding for her uncle, and what her uncle had to say that was good about me sure smoothed things.

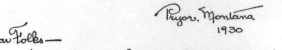

Pryor, Montana
1930

Dear Folks—

Here's a long story for you with no names in it to speak of ~ So, you won't be bothered by the names of the creeks and cow camps you might never heard of ~ And of riders you wouldn't know ~ But if you have been in the cow country and are acquainted with the lay of it you'll have a lot of fun recognizing the spots where I drifted thru ~ If you don't know the cow country I think you'll like to come out and get lost in it for a spell ~ You'll know it by the time you ride with me thru these pages ~ The whole West ~ from the Far North to the South —

There's more than plain riding and covering territory in this story ~ There's the sunshine, rains, blizzards and crosses of life on the range, ~ from the times I first remember ~ my raising amongst cowboys and trappers ~ my teachings from them, the open country and animals ~ More teachings after I'd growed up while always sitting on a horse ~ Sowing my wild oats ~ reaping 'em ~ cutting my wisdom teeth on sharp edges of experience, and then finally lining out to ride for High Points ——

Here's a gentle horse for you Climb on and follow me.

— WILL JAMES

WILL JAMES. *Illustrated letter.* 1930. From *Lone Cowboy: My Life Story* by Will James. New York, Charles Scribner's Sons.

All around, I got to thinking I was pretty smart. The old man would ride with me once in a while and sort of coach me as to the tricks of the rustling game. He knowed many tricks and I don't think I could ever got a better teacher in that line. His work wasn't coarse in nothing he done, wether it was picking out the cattle or making over an iron. In picking out cattle, he warned me never to take a "marker" (an animal that could easy be recognized by odd markings). When he changed a brand he didn't use no knife, no hot iron, nor wet blanket. He had a little bottle of some acid, which parts he'd get at different stores and mix. By dipping a twig in that acid he could work over the old brand and spread out with the new one. In a few hours the new brand would show up in a scaly ridge and look as old as the first one it blended with. There'd even be gray hairs showing and that brand would stand inspection from the outside of the hide as well as from the inside, in case trouble come and the animal would have to be killed and skinned to show evidence. It takes a burned brand a few months before it shows a ridge inside a hide.

But the old man didn't do much brand altering. He would had to have too many registered brands and that would throw suspicion, with as little a herd as he had. He done most of his work on young stock, "sleepering."

"Sleepering" is taking an unbranded calf and earmarking him with the same earmark the mother has and turning him loose *unbranded*. The earmark is that of the outfit he belongs to and draws no attention, and if a rider is not on the watch he'll take it for granted, on account of the earmark, that the calf *is* branded. If that goes over well and it's not noticed that the calf is unbranded, the rustler will then get the calf when he's about six months and wean it away from its mammy and slap on his iron. The earmark can be changed then to go with his own cattle.

Sleepering is where I came in at. I was of an age that nobody suspicioned much and, being a stranger, none of the closest outfits ever got to know that I was any more than just a rider drifting thru, and they didn't connect me with the old man. Even my string of horses was strange to that country. I was very careful to dodge meeting riders, and when I took my rope down to catch a calf to earmark, it was always well out on a big flat. The earmarking was done mighty quick and the calf was soon let go to his mother again.

I got a big thrill out of doing that, something like what, I guess, most kids would get when stealing watermelons when there's danger of getting a shot of coarse salt while making a getaway. My work was more dangerous than that because there'd be something a heap more penetrating than coarse salt coming my way if I was caught with my rope on somebody else's animal. It'd been bullets.

Realizing that, only seemed to make me work all the more interesting and, besides, I got to thinking I wasn't really doing any wrong. I wasn't stealing, I was just making it easy for the other feller to do that. Another thing was that some of them sleeper calves would be noticed and branded in time by the right owner while the other feller was waiting for 'em to grow to maverick size so he could get away with 'em.

Everything was coming along fine. Besides my wages, I was getting extra money for every fresh piece of right ear I brought in. I was riding good fast horses and the few scares I'd had from riders bumping onto me didn't amount to much, not excepting once, and that time sure made up for the others. I was just bending over a calf and earmarking late one evening, when my horse turns and looks up. I looked up too and, not over twenty feet from me, was a rider.

At the sight I fell flat behind the tied calf. It was too late for me to try to get away, so, seeing it was too dark for the rider to see what I looked like, I was going to run a bluff. I shot, not with intentions to hit but close enough by him so he'd know I wasn't shooting blank cartridges. That shot seemed to work well and in the next minute the rider had turned his horse and disappeared. . . . That rider had been mighty foolish coming up on a feller like he had me. He'd showed lack of experience with rustlers.

But, with that rider coming up on me and turning tail, it seemed like it wasn't many days later when that country got full of riders. I'd see one or two at a distance pretty near every day and I got to thinking that that one I scared sure must of spread the news of what he'd seen. Another thing was that the far scattered cattle, which I worked the most on, was brought closer and where the riders could keep a better eye on 'em.

"That's sure tough on us," says the old man. "Watching the cattle the way they are now, we better lay off a spell on account they'll notice the fresh earmarks if we keep on, and get onto the fact that somebody's sleepering. As it is now, I figger they just think you was fixing to work over a brand when that rider spotted you."

Anyway, as the old man said, our play was over for a while. There was nothing to do now but wait and hope that all the sleepers wasn't found out so there'd be a few to run out when they was big enough. In the meantime, with a little acid, we would work on the few grown stuff that was missed, or the furthest ones out, and change brands to suit so there'd also be cows to tally up some when the sleepers had growed to mavericks and the appropriating brand was put on 'em. . . . Too many big calves and not enough cows to go with 'em brings suspicion to any outfit.

But I didn't stay to help the old man do any brand changing. I'd been with him quite a while now and I'd got a hankering to see new country again. I told the old man I might be back again later and help him brand the big calves, but I never did get to come back.

Cowboy Ballads

There probably has been more balladry attached to the trade of the cowhand than to any other in our history, much of it grotesquely romanticized. The selections here, however, carry as much truth as poetry—even Curley Fletcher's wildly boastful "The High Lopin' Cowboy" (1930) or Henry Knibbs's outlandish "Boomer Johnson" (1930) emerged from real experience. (The authors and dates of both "The Wrangler Kid" and "Git Along Little Dogies" are not known.)

"The High Lopin' Cowboy"

I been ridin' fer cattle the most of my life.
I ain't got no family, I ain't got no wife,
I ain't got no kith, I ain't got no kin,
I allus will finish what ere I begin.
I rode down in Texas where the cowboys are tall,
The State's pretty big but the hosses er small.
Fer singin' to cattle, I'm hard to outdo;
I'm a high-lopin' cowboy, an' a wild buckeroo.

I rode in Montana an' in Idaho;
I rode for Terasus in old Mexico.
I rope mountain lion an' grizzly bear,
I use cholla cactus fer combin' my hair.
I cross the dry desert, no water between,
I rode through Death Valley without no canteen.
At ridin' dry deserts I'm hard to outdo;
I'm a high-lopin' cowboy an' a wild buckeroo.

Why, I kin talk Spanish and Injun to boot,
I pack me a knife and a pistol to shoot.
I got no Señorita, an' I got no squaw.
I got no sweetheart, ner mother-in-law.
I never been tied to no apron strings,
I ain't no devil, but I got no wings.
At uh dodgin' the ladies, I'm hard to outdo;
I'm a high-lopin' cowboy, an' a wild buckeroo.

I drink red whiskey, an' I don't like beer,
I don't like mutton, but I do like steer.
I will let you alone if you leave me be,
But don't you get tough an' crawl on me.
I'll fight you now at the drop of a hat,
You'll think you're sacked up with a scratchin' wild cat.
At rough ready mixin' I'm hard to outdo;
I'm a high-lopin' cowboy, an' a wild buckeroo.

"Boomer Johnson"

Now Mr. Boomer Johnson was a gettin' old in spots,
But you don't expect a bad-man to go wrestlin' pans and pots;
But he'd done his share of killin' and his draw was gettin' slow,
So he quits a-punchin' cattle and he takes to punchin' dough.

Our foreman up and hires him, figurin' age had rode him tame,
But a snake don't get no sweeter just by changin' of its name.
Well, Old Boomer knowed his business—he could cook to make you smile,
But say, he wrangled fodder in a most peculiar style.

THOMAS EAKINS. *Home Ranch*. 1888. Oil on canvas.
24 x 20 in. Philadelphia Museum of Art. Given by Mrs.
Thomas Eakins and Miss Mary Adeline Williams.

He never used no matches—left 'em layin' on the shelf;
Just some kerosene and cussin' and the kindlin' lit itself.
And, pardner, I'm allowin' it would give a man a jolt.
To see him stir *frijoles* with the barrel of his Colt.

Now killin' folks and cookin' ain't so awful far apart;
That must 'a' been why Boomer kept a-practicin' his art;
With the front sight of his pistol he would cut a pie-lid slick,
And he'd crimp her with the muzzle for to make the edges stick.

He built his doughnuts solid, and it sure would curl your hair,
To see him plug a doughnut as he tossed it in the air.
He bored the holes plumb center every time his pistol spoke,
Till the can was full of doughnuts and the shack was full of smoke.

We-all was gettin' jumpy—but he couldn't understand
Why his shootin' made us nervous when his cookin' was so grand.
He kept right on performin', and it weren't no big surprise,
When he took to markin' tombstones on the covers of his pies.

They didn't taste no better and they didn't taste no worse,
But a-settin' at that table was like ridin' in a hearse:
You didn't do no talkin' and you took just what you got,
So we et till we was foundered just to keep from gettin' shot.

Us at breakfast one bright mornin', I was feelin' kind of low,
When Old Boomer passed the doughnuts and I tells him plenty, "No!
All I takes this trip is coffee, for my stomach is a wreck,"
I could see the itch for killin' swell the wattles on his neck.

Scorn his grub? He strings some doughnuts on the muzzle of his gun,
And he shoves her in my gizzard and he says, "You're takin' one!"
He was set to start a graveyard, but for once he was mistook:
Me not wantin' any doughnuts, I just up and salts the cook.

Did they fire him? Listen, pardner, there was nothin' left to fire,
Just a row of smilin' faces and another cook to hire.
If he joined some other outfit and is cookin'—what I mean,
It's where they ain't no matches and they don't need kerosene.

"The Wrangler Kid"

The grass fire swooped like a red wolf pack,
   On the wings of a west wind dry.
It's red race left the scorched plains black
   'Neath a sullen, smoky sky.

And the wagon boss of the Bar-Y-Cross
   He rallied his roisterous crew.
"Boys, shoot some steers, and hang the loss,
   An' split them smack in two!"

They split six steers, with the blood side down,
   They'd ragged them to and fro.
But the grass fire laughed like a demon clown
   At a devil's three-ringed show.

The flame draft drove like a wind from hell,
   Across the drags they drew.
"It's no use boys!" came the foreman's yell.
   "She's roarin' right on through."

They scattered, then, from the headfires path,
   To close in from the sides.
And some stayed on to fight its wrath,
   Some fled to save their hides.

Now one who stayed was the Wrangler Kid,
   His whisker fuzz scorched black,
And he battled hard, as the others did,
   But the fire still pushed them back.

It pushed them back as the wind veered round
   Till trapped, they faced its sweep,
At the edge of a gully that split the ground,
   Too wide for a horse to leap.

'Twas down from the saddle dropped boss and men,
   And into the gulley they fled.
Safe now the men, but their horses then
   Were left to the grass fire's hell.

What! lives there a man who loves life less
   Than the dumb-brute horse he rides?
The Wrangler Kid stayed shelterless
   On the bank at the horses' side.

And he cut them free from the drags they drew,
　　Through the flames he spurred alone.
To-day the Kid bears scars, 'tis true,
　　Brands of the Red God's own.

"Git Along Little Dogies"

As I was a-walkin', one mornin' for pleasure,
　　I spied a young cowboy a-lopin' along:
His hat was throw'd back, and his spurs was a -jingle,
　　And as he rid by he was singin' this song.

　　Tip-pee ti-yi-yo, git along little dogies;
　　It's your misfortune and none o' my own,
　　Yip-pee ti-yi-yo, git along little dogies,
　　The plains o' Wyoming will be your new home.

First thing in the spring we round-up all the dogies;
　　We ear-mark, and brand 'em, and bob off their tails;
Then wrangle our hosses, load up the chuck wagon,
　　And throw the wild snuffy bunch on the North trail.

Some boys ride the long North trail just for the pleasure,
　　But soon find they figgered most terrible wrong;
Them dogies are kinky, and try for to scatter
　　All over the plains, as we roll 'em along.

BILL ANTON. *No Mulies.*
1990. Pencil on paper.
18 x 29 in. Courtesy of
the artist.

It's whoo-pee, and yip-pee, whilest drivin' the dogies;
    Oh how I wish that they'd ramble alone.
It's punchin', and yippin', "Git on little dogies,"
    For you know Wyoming will soon be your home.

Your maws was all raised-up away down in Texas,
    Whar sandburrs, and cacti, and jimpson-weed grow.
We'll fill you on prick'y-pear, catclaw, and cholla,
    Then roll you along the trail for Idaho.

Oh, you'll soon be soup for ol' Uncle Sam's Injuns,
    It's "Beef, heap good beef," I hear 'em all cry.
So git along, ramble on, roll little dogies,
    You'll all be beef-stew in the sweet by and by.

J. Frank Dobie

From *Coronado's Children*

Post Hole Banks

Not all the folklore of the cattle trade was confined to cowhands and their antics. In the following selection from Coronado's Children: Tales of Lost Mines and Buried Treasures of the Southwest *(1930), the renowned Texas folklorist J. Frank Dobie tells of an odd financial device resorted to by many a Texas ranch owner, this time with mixed results.*

I used to hear the early settlers tell how a cow and calf was legal tender for ten dollars. Even if a man paid in gold—say forty dollars for a horse—he might say he gave "four cows and calves" for it. So the banks were logically just cowpens.—Brushy Joe's Reminiscences.

"The methods of business were in keeping with the primitive conditions of society," says a chronicler of the open range of southern Texas. "There were no banks in the country. Consequently every ranch home was the depository of more or less money. The coin, if of considerable amount, was put in saddle bags, morrals, etc., and secreted in remote corners of the house or up under the roof or it was buried; it could be brought forth from its hiding place as occasion demanded. . . . In buying stock the ranchmen brought the money in gold and silver to where the animals were to be received and there paid it out dollar by dollar. They generally carried the gold in leather belts buckled around their waists, but the silver, being more bulky, was carried in ducking sacks on a pack horse or mule. . . . It was a matter of current knowledge that one thousand dollars in silver weighed sixty-two and one-half pounds. . . .

"One time a rancher near the line between Karnes and Goliad counties decided to bury a considerable amount of money that he had on hand. Choosing an especially dark night, he went down to the cowpen and, after removing one of the fence posts, dropped his bag of gold in the post hole. He then replaced the post and went to bed satisfied that he had put his treasure where moth and rust could not corrupt nor thieves break through and steal. After a year or two had gone by, he needed the money and went to get it. He had failed to mark the particular post under which it was buried and time had obliterated all trace of his work. There was but one thing for him to do and he did it.

HOWARD POST. *Holding Pen.* 1987. Oil on canvas. 66 x 62 in. Courtesy Suzanne Brown Gallery, Scottsdale, Arizona.

He dug up post after post until he came to the right one, and by that time half his pen was torn down."

I don't know whether old Tolbert forgot his post hole or not. He ranched on the Frio, and, as the saying goes, was "stingy enough to skin a flea for its hide and taller." He would never kill a maverick no matter how hungry he was for meat, but would always brand it. He never bought sugar or molasses; "sow bosom," even of the saltiest variety, was a rare luxury; he and his men made out on "poor doe"—often jerked—javelina meat, and frijoles. When he "worked" and had an outfit to feed, he always instructed the *cocinero* to cook the bread early so that it would be cold and hard, and thus go further by the time the hands got to it. He distrusted banks, and during a good part of his life there were no banks to trust. The practice of keeping money on the premises suited him finely.

When he died, none of his money could be found. So, even till this day, people dig for it around the old ranch house. One evening about twenty years ago a man who was working on the place saw two strangers in a wagon go down a ravine that runs near the ranch. He thought they were deer hunters; but when they passed him on their way out next morning, he noted that one of them had a shotgun across his knees and that they avoided conversation. While riding down the ravine a few days later, the ranch hand found that the wagon tracks led from a fresh hole under a live oak tree and that near the hole were pieces of rusted steel hinges with marks of a cold chisel on them. However, not many people believe that the two strangers got Tolbert's money.

Berry got that—and he never hunted for it either. Years ago Berry bought the Tolbert ranch and went to live on it. One day when he had nothing else for his Mexican, Pedro, to do, he told him to put some new posts in the old corral fence. Pedro worked along digging holes and putting in new posts until near ten o'clock. Then at the third post to the east from the south gate he struck something so hard that it turned the edge of his spade. He was used to digging post holes in rocky soil with a crowbar to loosen it and a tin can to dip it out, and so he went to a mesquite tree where the tools were kept and got the crowbar.

But the crowbar would no more dig into the hard substance than the spade would. The sun was mighty hot anyhow; so the Mexican went up to the house where *el señor* Berry was whittling sticks on the gallery and told him that he couldn't dig any more. "Why, *señor*," he said, "in that third hole from the south gate the devil has humped himself into a rock that nothing can get through."

Berry snorted around considerably at first, but directly he seemed to think of something and told his man, very well, not to dig any more but to saddle up and go out and bring in the main remuda. Now, only the day before they had had the main remuda in the pen and had caught out fresh mounts to keep in the little horse pasture. By this time the released horses would be scattered clear away on the back side of the pasture. The Mexican wondered why his *amo* wanted the remuda again. But it was none of his business. Well, the ride would take him all the rest of the day, and at least he would not have to dig any more post holes before *mañana*.

After Pedro had saddled his horse and drunk a *cafecita* for lunch and fooled away half an hour putting in new stirrup-leather strings and finally had got out of sight, Berry slouched down to the pens. He came back to his shade on the gallery and whittled for an hour or so longer until everything around the *jacal*, even the road-runners and Pedro's wife, was taking a siesta. Then he pulled off his spurs, which always dragged with a big clink when he walked, and went down to the pen again. The spade and the crowbar were where the Mexican had let them fall. Berry punched the crowbar down into the half-made hole. It almost bounced out of his hand, and he heard a kind of metallic thud. No, it was not flint-rock that had stopped the digging.

Berry went around back of the water trough to the huisache where his horse was tied and led him into the pen. Then he started to work. He began digging two or three feet out to one side of the hole. The dry ground was packed from the tramp of thousands of cattle and horses. He had to use the crowbar to loosen the soil. But it was no great task to remove a patch of earth two or three feet square and eighteen or twenty inches deep. Berry knew what he was about, and as he scraped the loosened earth out with his spade he could feel a flat metal surface that seemed to have rivets in it.

It was the lid of a chest. When he had uncovered it, Berry placed one of the new posts so that he could use it as a fulcrum for the crowbar. With that he levered up the end of the chest. As he suspected, it was too heavy and too tightly wedged in the soil for him to lift. He worked a chunk under the raised end of the chest and then looped a stout rope over it. Next, he mounted his horse and dallied the free end of the rope around the horn of his saddle. He had dragged cows out of the bog on that horse, and he knew that the chest was not so heavy as a cow. He had but fifty yards to drag it before he was in the brush, where undetected he could pry the lid off.

When the Mexican got back that night his *mujer* told him that Señor Berry had gone to San Antonio in the buckboard and that he had left word for the remuda to be turned back into the big pasture and for the repair of the corrals to be continued.

"They say" that the deposit Berry made at the Frost National Bank was a clean $17,000, nearly all in silver.

ROBERT M. UTLEY

From *Billy the Kid: A Short and Violent Life*
"The Execution"

Much of the story of William H. Bonney, "Billy the Kid," was false. (He did not, for example, kill twenty-one men by his twenty-first birthday.) Even so, there was enough raw truth in his murderous life to qualify him as the definitive western bad man. In his equally definitive biography, Billy the Kid: A Short and Violent Life *(1989), historian Robert M. Utley tells of the Kid's sudden end at the hands of Sheriff Pat Garrett.*

In midafternoon Poe mounted and rode up the Pecos seven miles to Sunnyside. Presenting Garrett's letter of introduction, he received a friendly welcome from Milnor Rudulph. After supper Poe broached the subject of Billy the Kid. Instantly Rudulph turned nervous and evasive. He had heard that Billy was in the area, he said, but he did not believe it. Further questioning produced only more agitated equivocation. At dusk, to his host's evident relief, Poe saddled up and rode down the river to rendezvous with his comrades.

In the darkness the three pondered their next move. The reaction of the villagers to Poe's visit, the behavior of Rudulph, and the tips from Brazil and from Poe's informant all pointed to Billy's presence somewhere around Fort Sumner. Yet the foolhardiness of such a course left all three with doubts too. At length they decided to slip into Sumner under cover of darkness, keep watch for a time on a dwelling that Garrett knew housed one of Billy's paramours, and then hunt up Pete Maxwell and talk with him. He might reveal something.

On the north edge of Sumner, the lawmen chanced across the camp of a traveler. Coincidentally, he turned out to be an old friend of Poe's, from Texas. Unsaddling here, the trio fortified themselves with coffee and then proceeded on foot. At about 9:00 P.M. they quietly took a station among the trees of a peach orchard on the northern fringe of the community. A bright moon illumined the scene. On the east side of the old parade ground were buildings that had once served as barracks for soldiers. On the west stood a line of dwellings that had housed officers. One had been fixed up as a residence for the Maxwells. Across the parade ground from the orchard, fronting the south side, the old quartermaster storehouse had been divided into rooms. At one end, hidden by officers' row, was Beaver Smith's saloon. Billy's friend Bob Campbell lived at the other end, and next door to him lived Sabal and Celsa Gutierrez.

As the lawmen crept closer to the buildings, they suddenly heard muffled voices talking in Spanish. Crouching motionless behind trees, they listened. The people were in the orchard too, not far distant, but their words could not be understood. "Soon a man arose from the ground," said Garrett, "in full view, but too far away to recognize. He wore a broad-brimmed hat, a dark vest and pants, and was in his shirt sleeves." He said something, jumped the fence, and walked into the compound.

Garrett did not recognize the figure, and learned only afterward that he was Billy the Kid. Whom he had been with and where he went after entering the old fort depends on which account one wants to accept. He may have ended up with Bob Campbell, or Celsa Gutierrez, or Deluvina Maxwell, or Jesús Silva and Francisco Lobato, among others. He is not likely to have gone to Paulita's, since she lived with her family in the big house on officers' row and since his companion seems to have been someone in one of the rooms of the old quartermaster building.

Here, after shucking his hat, vest, and boots, Billy decided that he wanted something to eat. A freshly butchered yearling hung from a rafter on Maxwell's north porch. With a butcher knife in his left hand and his Colt "self-cocker" in his right, he shuffled out in his stockinged feet to cut a slab of meat.

By now, nearly midnight, Garrett and his companions had backed out of the orchard, circled behind the officers' line on the west, and reached the Maxwell house. It was a long adobe, shadowed by porches on three sides. A picket fence with a gate separated the east face from the old parade ground. As Garrett knew, Maxwell slept in the southeast corner room. In the July heat, the door and windows stood open. Leaving Poe and McKinney outside, Garrett entered the door, walked across the room, and sat on the edge of Maxwell's bed, next to the pillow.

Outside, the two deputies waited. McKinney squatted on the ground outside the fence. Poe sat on the edge of the porch, dangling his feet in the open gateway.

Within seconds of Garrett's disappearance into Maxwell's bedroom, Poe glanced to his right and saw a figure approaching along the inside of the fence. In the moonlight, Poe recalled, "I observed that he was only partially dressed and was both bareheaded and barefooted, or rather, had only socks on his feet, and it seemed to me that he was fastening his trousers as he came toward me at a very brisk walk." Poe thought this might be Maxwell himself or one of his guests.

The man came almost face-to-face with Poe before spotting him. Startled, he recoiled, covered Poe with his pistol, and sprang to the porch, hissing "Quien es?" As he backed away, toward the door to Maxwell's bedroom, he repeated "Quien es? Quien es?"

Billie the Kid, a copy from a very old tin-type.

Billy the Kid. c. 1881. Photographic copy from an old tin-type.

Poe climbed to his feet and took several steps toward the man, telling him not to be alarmed, that they would not hurt him.

"Quien es?" the man asked again as he backed into the doorway and vanished inside.

In the minute or so since waking Maxwell, Garrett had asked whether Billy the Kid was at Fort Sumner. Agitated, Maxwell had replied that he was not at the fort but was nearby. At that moment, they heard voices outside and saw the man back around the doorframe.

Approaching the bed, the man asked, "Who are those fellows outside, Pete?"

Bolting up in his bed, Maxwell spat out, "That's him."

Suddenly aware of the dark shape next to Maxwell, the man sprang back, pointed his pistol, and again demanded, "Quien es? Quien es?"

Garrett was as startled as the intruder. He had not even thought to ready his pistol. Quickly he shifted his holster and at the same instant identified the other man. "He must have then recognized me," Garrett later conjectured, "for he went backward with a cat-like movement, and I jerked my gun and fired." The flash of exploding powder blinded Garrett, and he snapped off a second round in the direction of his target. On the verge of pulling the trigger a third time, he heard a groan and knew he had hit his mark.

Pete Maxwell sprang from his bed and hit the floor in a tangle of bedclothes, then raced for the door. Garrett had already reached the porch when Maxwell tumbled out. A startled Poe and McKinney greeted them with pistols drawn. Poe almost shot Maxwell, who shouted "Don't shoot, don't shoot" just as Garrett knocked down Poe's gun hand. "Don't shoot Maxwell," he said.

Hugging the wall outside the door, Garrett gasped, "That was the Kid that came in there onto me, and I think I have got him."

"Pat," replied Poe, "the Kid would not come to this place; you have shot the wrong man."

Garrett paused in doubt, then said, "I am sure that was him, for I know his voice too well to be mistaken."

An understandable caution restrained all the men from entering the darkened room to find out who had been shot and whether he was dead. As the Maxwell family and a scattering of townspeople began to gather, Maxwell walked down the porch to his mother's room and returned with a lighted candle. Placing it on the windowsill, he stepped aside and the lawmen peered in. "We saw a man lying stretched upon his back dead, in the middle of the room," said Poe, "with a six-shooter lying at his right hand and a butcher-knife at his left."

Venturing inside, Garrett and his deputies examined the body that now was unmistakably revealed to be Billy the Kid. Billy bore one bullet wound, in the left breast just above the heart. Garrett's bullet had killed him almost instantly.

Maxwell was certain that Billy had fired once at Garrett, and Poe and McKinney insisted that they had heard three shots. A thorough search of the room turned up only one stray bullet, in the headboard of Maxwell's bed. Examining Billy's pistol, Garrett counted five loaded cartridges; the hammer rested on the empty sixth. The empty shell did not seem to have been fired recently, and since men usually kept an empty shell under the hammer as a safety precaution, it probably had not. The report thought to have been a third shot had been Garrett's bullet ricocheting from the wall and slamming into Maxwell's headboard, the lawmen concluded. Billy's fatal second of hesitation had left the initiative to his opponent.

By now an excited crowd thronged the porch and the old parade ground beyond the fence. As word spread that the Kid had been killed, many vented their grief and anger. A sobbing Celsa Gutierrez cursed Garrett and pounded his chest. Nasaria Yerby, Abrana Garcia, Paulita Maxwell, and the Navajo woman Deluvina Maxwell wept, talked softly, and consoled one another. Armed young men shook their fists and shouted threats at Garrett and his deputies. "We spent the remainder of the night on the Maxwell premises," said Poe, "keeping constantly on our guard, as we were expecting to be attacked by the friends of the dead man."

The next morning, at Sunnyside, Milnor Rudulph and his son Charles heard the news and rode down to Fort Sumner. They found the community buzzing with confusion, anger, and controversy. Some wanted to lynch Garrett and his deputies, barricaded in a room of the Maxwell house with their guns ready for a defense. Others argued that Billy's death relieved the townspeople of a great strain and that the lawmen deserved their gratitude.

Rudulph was a sensible, widely respected, and, of particular importance at the moment, literate man. Justice of the Peace Alejandro Segura asked him to organize a coroner's jury and preside as foreman. Rudulph assented, assembled five citizens, and convened the proceedings in Pete Maxwell's bedroom, where the body still lay on the floor. Maxwell and Garrett told their stories. Rudulph then wrote out the report, and the jurors affixed their signatures or made their marks. They duly concluded that William Bonney had met death from a bullet wound in the region of the heart, inflicted by a gun in the hand of Pat F. Garrett. "And our dictum is," wrote Rudulph in Spanish, "that the act of said Garrett was justifiable homicide and we are of the opinion that the gratitude of the whole community is owed to said Garrett for his deed, and that he deserves to be rewarded."

Although many residents would have vigorously dissented had they known of Rudulph's accolade, one of the jurors who laboriously scratched an X next to his name surely agreed. He was Sabal Gutierrez, husband of Celsa Gutierrez.

The women had asked for the corpse, and after the jury completed its task they had the body carried across the parade ground to the carpenter shop. There, Poe recounted, it "was laid out on a workbench, the women placing lighted candles around it according to their ideas of properly conducting a 'wake' for the dead."

"Neatly and properly dressed," according to Garrett, the remains were placed in a coffin, which was borne to the old military cemetery that now served the community. There, on the afternoon of July 15, 1881, Fort Sumner paid final respects to Billy the Kid. Fittingly, he rested next to his old compadres of the Lincoln County War, Tom O'Folliard and Charley Bowdre.

Pat Garrett. c. 1880. Photograph.

For the two decades remaining to him, Pat Garrett basked in public acclaim as the officer who killed Billy the Kid. The deed took on an almost superhuman glow as the Kid's reputation blossomed into legend and as he came to be remembered as the frontier's most exalted outlaw.

Yet, able lawman that he was, Pat Garrett had got his man almost entirely by accident. He and his deputies thought that the fugitive was somewhere in the vicinity, but in trying to find him they encountered nothing but frustration. If the Kid had not blundered into the darkened bedroom at exactly the right moment, Pete Maxwell would have been one more frustration—like Rudulph, nervous but uninformative. Maxwell was their last hope; the next day, they doubtless would have saddled up and ridden back to Roswell.

By the most improbable coincidence of timing, therefore, Billy fell almost literally into Garrett's lap. To be sure, the sheriff kept his head, reacted with split-second decision, and shot accurately, although in the darkness he ran a great risk of shooting the wrong man. Even so, he triumphed less because of what he did than because of what his opponent failed to do. Billy had the same instant the lawman did in which to recognize his enemy and fire at him. He had his gun in hand, while Garrett's rested in his holster.

Why did he fail to pull the trigger? Fear of hitting Maxwell? Fear of hitting some unrecognized friend? Garrett himself provided as good an explanation as any: "I think he was surprised and thrown off his guard. Almost any man would have been. Kid was as cool under trying circumstances as any man I ever saw. But he was so surprised and startled, that for a second he could not collect himself. Some men cannot recover their faculties for some time after such a shock. I think Kid would have done so in a second more, if he had had the time."

COLORPLATE 59

OLAF C. SELTZER. *The Faro Layout in the Mint Saloon.* 1934. Oil on board. 4 $^1/_4$ x 6 $^1/_4$ in.
From the Collection of Gilcrease Museum, Tulsa, Oklahoma.

COLORPLATE 60 (top, left)

OLAF C. SELTZER. *Sheriff*. Watercolor on paper. 18 1/2 x 11 1/2 in. From the Collection of Gilcrease Museum, Tulsa, Oklahoma.

COLORPLATE 61 (top, right)

OLAF C. SELTZER. *Placer Miner*. Watercolor on paper. 12 x 7 in. From the Collection of Gilcrease Museum, Tulsa, Oklahoma.

COLORPLATE 62 (left)

OLAF C. SELTZER. *Sluicer*. Watercolor on paper. 12 x 7 in. From the Collection of Gilcrease Museum, Tulsa, Oklahoma.

COLORPLATE 63

E. F. WARD. *Enter the Law*. c. 1924. Oil on canvas. 21 x 28 in. From the Collection of Gilcrease Museum, Tulsa, Oklahoma.

COLORPLATE 64 (following spread)

N. C. WYETH. *The James Brothers in Missouri*. No date. Oil on canvas. 25 x 40 in.
From the Collection of Gilcrease Museum, Tulsa, Oklahoma.

COLORPLATE 65

WILLIAM DE LA MONTAGNE CARY. *Buffalo Bill on Charley*. 1881. Oil on canvas. 52 x 40 ¹/₄ in. From the Collection of Gilcrease Museum, Tulsa, Oklahoma. *The western career of William F. ("Buffalo Bill") Cody was real enough. He had been a Pony Express rider, he* did *shoot thousands of buffalo to feed the builders of the Union Pacific Railroad, he had served as an army scout during the Indian wars, and he* did *kill Cheyenne warrior chief Yellow Hair in hand-to-hand combat in the summer of 1876, five years before the portrait above was painted. But his greatest fame came with the enormous fabrication called "Buffalo Bill's Wild West."*

COLORPLATE 66

FRANK C. MCCARTHY. *Leading the Charge*. 1982. Oil. 24 x 46 in. ©1984, The Greenwich Workshop, Inc. Reproduced with the permission of The Greenwich Workshop, Inc.

COLORPLATE 67 (following page)

ARTIST UNKNOWN. *Annie Oakley: The Peerless Wing and Rifle Shot*. Poster. 1898. Lithograph on paper. 30 x 40 in. Circus World Museum, Baraboo, Wisconsin.

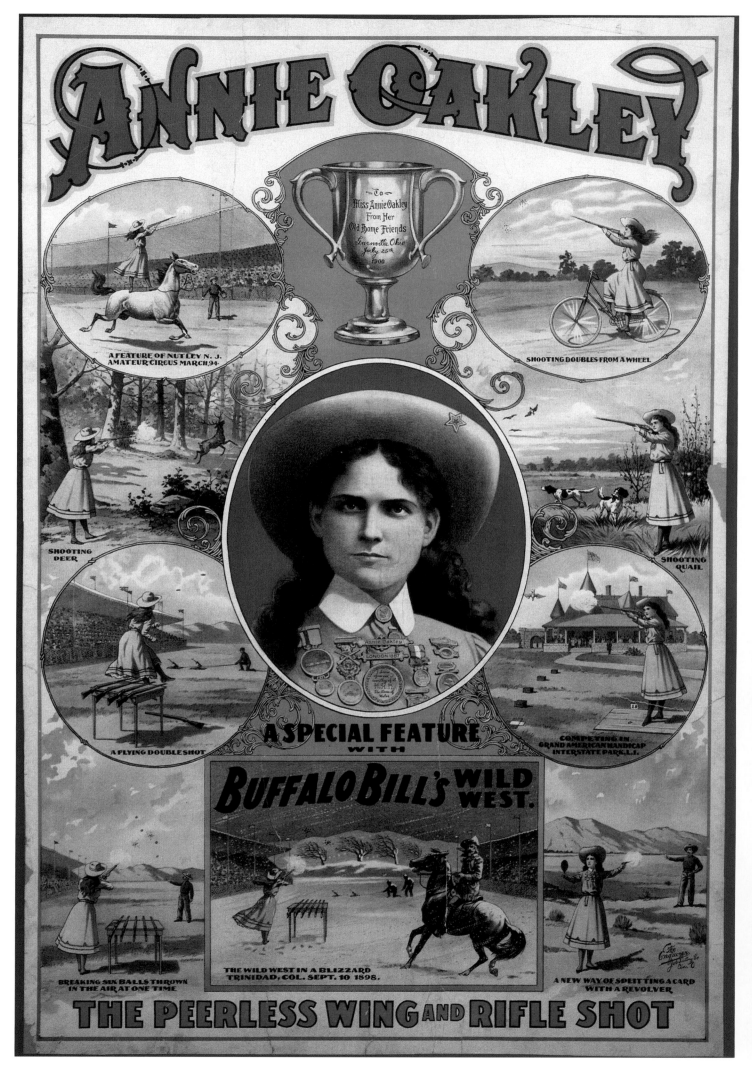

OWEN WISTER

From *The Virginian*

Pennsylvania-born and Harvard-educated, Owen Wister gained his knowledge of the cowboy's West during summer visits to a ranch in Wyoming—yet he still managed to produce what is considered the Great Ancestor of the modern cowboy novel, The Virginian *(1902). There is, however, relatively little fast-paced action or violence in Wister's novel; much of it possesses an arch humor, like this brief tale of what happens when the Virginian takes on religion.*

Our missionary did not choose Miss Wood's text. He made his selection from another of the Psalms, and when it came, I did not dare to look at anybody; I was much nearer unseemly conduct than the cow-boys. Dr. MacBride gave us his text sonorously, "'They are altogether become filthy; There is none of them that doeth good, no, not one.'" His eye showed us plainly that present company was not excepted from this. He repeated the text once more, then, launching upon his discourse, gave none of us a ray of hope.

I had heard it all often before; but preached to cow-boys it took on a new glare of untimeliness, of grotesque obsoleteness—as if some one should say, "Let me persuade you to admire woman," and forthwith hold out her bleached bones to you. The cow-boys were told that not only they could do no good, but that if they did contrive to, it would not help them. Nay, more, not only honest deeds availed them nothing, but even if they accepted this especial creed which was being explained to them as necessary for salvation, still it might not save them. Their sin was indeed the cause of their damnation, yet, keeping from sin, they might nevertheless be lost. It had all been settled for them not only before they were born, but before Adam was shaped. Having told them this, he invited them to glorify the Creator of the scheme. Even if damned, they must praise the person who had made them expressly for damnation. That is what I heard him prove by logic to these cow-boys. Stone upon stone he built the black cellar of his theology, leaving out its beautiful park and the sunshine of its garden. He did not tell them the splendor of its past, the noble fortress for good that it had been, how its tonic had strengthened generations of their fathers. No; wrath he spoke of, and never once of love. It was the bishop's way, I knew well, to hold cow-boys by homely talk of their special hardships and temptations. And when they fell he spoke to them of forgiveness and brought them encouragement. But Dr. MacBride never thought once of the lives of these waifs. Like himself, like all mankind, they were invisible dots in creation; like him, they were to feel as nothing, to be swept up in the potent heat of his faith. So he thrust out to them none of the sweet but all the bitter of his creed, naked and stern as iron. Dogma was his all in all, and poor humanity was nothing but flesh for its canons.

Thus to kill what chance he had for being of use seemed to me more deplorable than it did evidently to them. Their attention merely wandered. Three hundred years ago they would have been frightened; but not in this electric day. I saw Scipio stifling a smile when it came to the doctrine of original sin. "We know of its truth," said Dr. MacBride, "from the severe troubles and distresses to which infants are liable, and from death passing upon them before they are capable of sinning." Yet I knew he was a good man, and I also knew that if a missionary is to be tactless, he might almost as well be bad.

I said their attention wandered, but I forgot the Virginian. At first his attitude might have been mere propriety. One can look respectfully at a preacher and be internally breaking all the commandments. But even with the text I saw real attention light in the Virginian's eye. And keeping track of the concentration that grew on him with each minute made the sermon short for me. He missed nothing. Before the end his gaze at the preacher had become swerveless.

Was he convert or critic? Convert was incredible. Thus was an hour passed before I had thought of time.

When it was over we took it variously. The preacher was genial and spoke of having now broken ground for the lessons that he hoped to instil. He discoursed for a while about trout-fishing and about the rumored uneasiness of the Indians northward where he was going. It was plain that his personal safety never gave him a thought. He soon bade us good night. The Ogdens shrugged their shoulders and were amused. That was their way of taking it. Dr. MacBride sat too heavily on the Judge's shoulders for him to shrug them. As a leading citizen in the Territory he kept open house for all comers. Policy and good nature made him bid welcome a wide variety of travellers. The cow-boy out of employment found bed and a meal for himself and his horse, and missionaries had before now been well received at Sunk Creek Ranch.

"I suppose I'll have to take him fishing," said the Judge, ruefully.

"Yes, my dear," said his wife, "you will. And I shall have to make his tea for six days."

"Otherwise," Ogden suggested, "it might be reported that you were enemies of religion."

"That's about it," said the Judge. "I can get on with most people. But elephants depress me."

So we named the Doctor "Jumbo," and I departed to my quarters.

At the bunk house, the comments were similar but more highly salted. The men were going to bed. In spite of their outward decorum at the service, they had not liked to be told that they were "altogether become filthy." It was easy to call names; they could do that themselves. And they appealed to me, several speaking at once, like a concerted piece at the opera: "Say, do you believe babies go to hell?"—"Ah, of course he don't."—"There ain't no hereafter, anyway."—"Ain't there?"—"Who told yu'?"—"Same man as told the preacher we were all a sifted set of sons-of-guns."—"Well, I'm going to stay a Mormon."—"Well, I'm going to quit fleeing from temptation."—"That's so! Better get it in the neck after a good time than a poor one." And so forth. Their wit was not extreme, yet I should like Dr. MacBride to have heard it. One fellow put his natural soul pretty well into words, "If I happened to learn what they had predestinated me to do, I'd do the other thing, just to show 'em!"

And Trampas? And the Virginian? They were out of it. The Virginian had gone straight to his new abode. Trampas lay in his bed, not asleep, and sullen as ever.

"He ain't got religion this trip," said Scipio to me.

"Did his new foreman get it?" I asked.

"Huh! It would spoil him. You keep around, that's all. Keep around."

Scipio was not to be probed; and I went, still baffled, to my repose.

No light burned in the cabin as I approached its door.

The Virginian's room was quiet and dark; and that Dr. MacBride slumbered was plainly audible to me, even before I entered. Go fishing with him! I thought, as I undressed. And I selfishly decided that the Judge might have this privilege entirely to himself. Sleep came to me fairly soon, in spite of the Doctor. I was wakened from it by my bed's being jolted—not a pleasant thing that night. I must have started. And it was the quiet voice of the Virginian that told me he was sorry to have accidentally disturbed me. This disturbed me a good deal more. But his steps did not go to the bunk house, as my sensational mind had suggested. He was not wearing much, and in the dimness he seemed taller than common. I next made out that he was bending over Dr. MacBride. The divine at last sprang upright.

"I am armed," he said. "Take care. Who are you?"

"You can lay down your gun, seh. I feel like my spirit was going to bear witness. I feel like I might get an enlightening."

He was using some of the missionary's own language. The baffling I had been treated to by Scipio melted to nothing in this. Did living men petrify, I should have changed to mineral between the sheets. The Doctor got out of bed, lighted his lamp, and found a book; and the two retired into the Virginian's room, where I could hear the exhortations as I lay amazed. In time the Doctor returned, blew out his lamp, and settled himself. I had been very awake, but was nearly gone to sleep again, when the door creaked and the Virginian stood by the Doctor's side.

"Are you awake, seh?"

"What? What's that? What is it?"

"Excuse me, seh. The enemy is winning on me. I'm feeling less inward opposition to sin."

The lamp was lighted, and I listened to some further exhortations. They must have taken half an hour. When the Doctor was in bed again, I thought that I heard him sigh. This upset my composure in the dark, but I lay face downward in the pillow, and the Doctor was soon again snoring. I envied him for a while his faculty of easy sleep. But I must have dropped off myself; for it was the lamp in my eyes that now waked me as he came back for the third time from the Virginian's room. Before blowing the light out he looked at his watch, and thereupon I inquired the hour of him.

"Three," he said.

I could not sleep any more now, and I lay watching the darkness.

"I'm afeared to be alone!" said the Virginian's voice presently in the next room. "I'm afeared." There was a short pause, and then he shouted very loud, "I'm losin' my desire afteh the sincere milk of the Word!"

"What? What's that? What?" The Doctor's cot gave a great crack as he started up listening, and I put my face deep in the pillow.

"I'm afeared! I'm afeared! Sin has quit being bitter in my belly."

"Courage, my good man." The Doctor was out of bed with his lamp again, and the door shut behind him. Between them they made it long this time. I saw the window become gray; then the corners of the furniture grow visible; and outside, the dry chorus of the blackbirds began to fill the dawn. To these the sounds of chickens and impatient hoofs in the stable were added, and some cow wandered by loudly calling for her calf. Next, some one whistling passed near and grew distant. But although the cold hue that I lay staring at through the window warmed and changed, the Doctor continued working hard over his patient in the next room. Only a word here and there was distinct; but it was plain from the Virginian's fewer remarks that the sin in his belly was alarming him less. Yes, they made this time long. But it proved, indeed, the last one. And though some sort of catastrophe was bound to fall upon us, it was myself who precipitated the thing that did happen.

Day was wholly come. I looked at my own watch, and it was six. I had been about seven hours in my bed, and the Doctor had been about seven hours out of his. The door opened, and he came in with his book and lamp. He seemed to be shivering a little, and I saw him cast a longing eye at his couch. But the Virginian followed him even as he blew out the now quite superfluous light. They made a noticeable couple in their underclothes: the Virginian with his lean racehorse shanks running to a point at his ankle, and the Doctor with his stomach and his fat sedentary calves.

"You'll be going to breakfast and the ladies, seh, pretty soon," said the Virginian, with a chastened voice. "But I'll worry through the day somehow without yu'. And to-night you can turn your wolf loose on me again."

Once more it was no use. My face was deep in the pillow, but I made sounds as of a hen who has laid an egg. It broke on the Doctor with a total instantaneous smash, quite like an egg.

He tried to speak calmly. "This is a disgrace. An infamous disgrace. Never in my life have I—" Words forsook him, and his face grew redder. "Never in my life—" He stopped again, because at the sight of him being dignified in his red drawers, I was making the noise of a dozen hens. It was suddenly too much for the Virginian. He hastened into his room, and there sank on the floor with his head in his hands. The Doctor immediately slammed the door upon him, and this rendered me easily fit for a lunatic asylum. I cried into my pillow, and wondered if the Doctor would come and kill me. But he took no notice of me whatever. I could hear the Virginian's convulsions through the door, and also the Doctor furiously making his toilet within three feet of my head; and I lay quite still with my face the other way, for I was really afraid to look at him. When I heard him walk to the door in his boots, I ventured to peep; and there he was, going out with his bag in his hand. As I still continued to lie, weak and sore, and with a mind that had ceased all operation, the Virginian's door opened. He was clean and dressed and decent, but the devil still sported in his eye. I have never seen a creature more irresistibly handsome.

Then my mind worked again. "You've gone and done it," said I. "He's packed his valise. He'll not sleep here."

The Virginian looked quickly out of the door. "Why, he's leavin' us!" he exclaimed. "Drivin' away right now in his little old buggy!" He turned to me, and our eyes met solemnly over this large fact. I thought that I perceived the faintest tincture of dismay in the features of Judge Henry's new, responsible trusty foreman. This was the first act of his administration. Once again he looked out at the departing missionary.

"Well," he vindictively stated, "I cert'nly ain't goin' to run afteh him." And he looked at me again.

"Do you suppose the Judge knows?" I inquired.

He shook his head. "The windo' shades is all down still oveh yondeh." He paused. "I don't care," he stated, quite as if he had been ten years old. Then he grinned guiltily. "I was mighty respectful to him all night."

"Oh, yes, respectful! Especially when you invited him to turn his wolf loose."

The Virginian gave a joyous gulp. He now came and sat down on the edge of my bed. "I spoke awful good English to him most of the time," said he. "I can, yu' know, when I cinch my attention tight on to it. Yes, I cert'nly spoke a lot o' good English. I didn't understand some of it myself!"

Poster from *The Virginian*.

ZANE GREY

From *Riders of the Purple Sage*

If Owen Wister's The Virginian *was, in many respects, a novel of manners that happened to be set in the West, few of Zane Grey's dozens of cowboy novels would ever be described as sedate. In the work of this dentist-turned-novelist, good was good, bad was bad, six-guns blazed, and the action was fast and furious as in this rousing chase scene from* Riders of the Purple Sage *(1912), a novel that sold more than a million copies.*

Black Star and Night, answering to spur, swept swiftly westward along the white, slow-rising, sage-bordered trail. Venters heard a mournful howl from Ring, but Whitie was silent. The blacks settled into their fleet, long-striding gallop. The wind sweetly fanned Venters's hot face. From the summit of the first low-swelling ridge he looked back. Lassiter waved his hand; Jane waved her scarf. Venters replied by standing in his stirrups and holding high his sombrero. Then the dip of the ridge hid them. From the height of the next he turned once more. Lassiter, Jane, and the burros had disappeared. They had gone down into the Pass. Venters felt a sensation of irreparable loss.

"Bern—look!" called Bess, pointing up the long slope.

A small, dark, moving dot split the line where purple sage met blue sky. That dot was a band of riders.

"Pull the black, Bess."

They slowed from gallop to canter, then to trot. The fresh and eager horses did not like the check.

"Bern, Black Star has great eyesight."

"I wonder if they're Tull's riders. They might be rustlers. But it's all the same to us."

The black dot grew to a dark patch moving under low dust-clouds. It grew all the time, though very slowly. There were long periods when it was in plain sight, and intervals when it dropped behind the sage. The blacks trotted for half an hour, for another half-hour, and still the moving patch appeared to stay on the horizon line. Gradually, however, as time passed, it began to enlarge, to creep down the slope, to encroach upon the intervening distance.

"Bess, what do you make them out?" asked Venters. "I don't think they're rustlers."

"They're sage-riders," replied Bess. "I see a white horse and several grays. Rustlers seldom ride any horses but bays and blacks."

"That white horse is Tull's. Pull the black, Bess. I'll get down and cinch up. We're in for some riding. Are you afraid?"

"Not now," answered the girl, smiling.

"You needn't be. Bess, you don't weigh enough to make Black Star know you're on him. I won't be able to stay with you. You'll leave Tull and his riders as if they were standing still."

"How about you?"

"Never fear. If I can't stay with you I can still laugh at Tull."

"Look, Bern! They've stopped on that ridge. They see us."

"Yes. But we're too far yet for them to make out who we are. They'll recognize the blacks first. We've passed most of the ridges and the thickest sage. Now, when I give the word, let Black Star go and ride!"

Venters calculated that a mile or more still intervened between them and the riders. They were approaching at a swift canter. Soon Venters recognized Tull's white horse, and concluded that the riders had likewise recognized Black Star and Night. But it would be impossible for Tull yet to see that the blacks were not ridden by Lassiter and Jane. Venters noted that Tull and the line of horsemen, perhaps ten or twelve in number, stopped several times and evidently

DOUGLAS DUER. "Don't Look Back!" From *Riders of the Purple Sage* by Zane Grey. New York, Grosset & Dunlap. Original edition, Harper & Brothers, 1912. Courtesy National Park Service, Zane Grey Museum, Lackawaxen, Pennsylvania.

looked hard down the slope. It must have been a puzzling circumstance for Tull. Venters laughed grimly at the thought of what Tull's rage would be when he finally discovered the trick. Venters meant to sheer out into the sage before Tull could possibly be sure who rode the blacks.

The gap closed to a distance to half a mile. Tull halted. His riders came up and formed a dark group around him. Venters thought he saw him wave his arms, and was certain of it when the riders dashed into the sage, to right and left of the trail. Tull had anticipated just the move held in mind by Venters.

"Now Bess!" shouted Venters. "Strike north. Go round those riders and turn west."

Black Star sailed over the low sage, and in a few leaps got into his stride and was running. Venters spurred Night after him. It was hard going in the sage. The horses could run as well there, but keen eyesight and judgment must constantly be used by the riders in choosing ground. And continuous swerving from aisle to aisle between the brush, and leaping little washes and mounds of the pack-rats, and breaking through sage, made rough riding. When Venters had turned into a long aisle he had time to look up at Tull's riders. They were now strung out into an extended line riding northeast. And, as Venters and Bess were holding due north, this meant, if the horses of Tull and his riders had the speed and the staying power, they would head the blacks and turn them back down the slope. Tull's men were not saving their mounts; they were driving them desperately. Venters feared only an accident to Black Star or Night, and skilful riding would mitigate possibility of that. One glance ahead served to show him that Bess could pick a course through the sage as well as he. She looked neither back nor at the running riders, and bent forward over Black Star's neck and studied the ground ahead.

It struck Venters, presently, after he had glanced up from time to time, that Bess was drawing away from him as he had expected. He had, however, only thought of the light weight Black Star was carrying and of his superior speed; he saw now that the black was being ridden as never before, except when Jerry Card lost the race to Wrangle. How easily, gracefully, naturally, Bess sat her saddle! She could ride! Suddenly Venters remembered she had said she could ride. But he had not dreamed she was capable of such superb horsemanship. Then all at once, flashing over him, thrilling him, came the recollection that Bess was Oldring's Masked Rider.

He forgot Tull—the running riders—the race. He let Night have a free rein and felt him lengthen out to suit himself, knowing he would keep to Black Star's course, knowing that he had been chosen by the best rider now on the upland sage. For Jerry Card was dead. And fame had rivaled him with only one rider, and that was the slender girl who now swung so easily with Black Star's stride. Venters had abhorred her notoriety, but now he took passionate pride in her skill, her daring, her power over a horse. And he delved into his memory, recalling famous rides which he had heard related in the villages and round the camp-fires. Oldring's Masked Rider! Many times this strange rider, at once well known and unknown, had escaped pursuers by matchless riding. He had to run the gauntlet of vigilantes down the main street of Stone Bridge, leaving dead horses and dead rustlers behind. He had jumped his horse over the Gerber Wash, a deep, wide ravine separating the fields of Glaze from the wild sage. He had been surrounded north of Sterling; and he had broken through the line. How often had been told the story of day stampedes, of night raids, of pursuit, and then how the Masked Rider, swift as the wind, was gone in the sage! A fleet, dark horse—a slender, dark form—a black mask—a driving run down the slope—a dot on the purple sage— a shadowy, muffled steed disappearing in the night!

And this Masked Rider of the uplands had been Elizabeth Erne!

The sweet sage wind rushed in Venters's face and sang a song in his ears. He heard the dull, rapid beat of Night's hoofs; he saw Black Star drawing away, farther and farther. He realized both horses were swinging to the west. Then gunshots in the rear reminded him of Tull. Venters looked back. Far to the side, dropping behind, trooped the riders. They were shooting. Venters saw no puffs or dust, heard no whistling bullets. He was out of range. When he looked back again Tull's riders had given up pursuit. The best they could do, no doubt, had been to get near enough to recognize who really rode the blacks. Venters saw Tull drooping in his saddle.

Then Venters pulled Night out of his running stride. Those few miles had scarcely warmed the black, but Venters wished to save him. Bess turned, and, though she was far away, Venters caught the white glint of her waving hand. He held Night to a trot and rode on, seeing Bess and Black Star, and the sloping upward stretch of sage, and from time to time the receding black riders behind. Soon they disappeared behind a ridge, and he turned no more. They would go back to Lassiter's trail and follow it, and follow in vain. So Venters rode on, with the wind growing sweeter to taste and smell, and the purple sage richer and the sky bluer in his sight; and the song in his ears ringing. By and by Bess halted to wait for him, and he knew she had come to the trail. When he reached her it was to smile at sight of her standing with arms round Black Star's neck.

"Oh, Bern! I love him!" she cried. "He's beautiful; he knows; and how he can run! I've had fast horses. But Black Star! . . . Wrangle never beat him!"

"I'm wondering if I didn't dream that. Bess, the blacks are grand. What it must have cost Jane—ah!—well, when we get out of this wild country with Star and Night, back to my old home in Illinois, we'll buy a beautiful farm with meadows and springs and cool shade. There we'll turn the horses free—free to roam and browse and drink—never to feel a spur again—never to be ridden!"

"I would like that," said Bess.

They rested. Then, mounting, they rode side by side up the white trail. The sun rose higher behind them. Far to the left a low line of green marked the site of Cottonwoods. Venters looked once and looked no more. Bess gazed only straight ahead. They put the blacks to the long, swinging rider's canter, and at times pulled them to a trot, and occasionally to a walk. The hours passed, the miles slipped behind, and the wall of rock loomed in the fore. The Notch opened wide. It was a rugged, stony pass, but with level and open trail, and Venters and Bess

DOUGLAS DUER. "Bess, I'll Not Go Again." From *Riders of the Purple Sage* by Zane Grey. New York, Grosset & Dunlap. Original edition, Harper & Brothers, 1912. Courtesy National Park Service, Zane Grey Museum, Lackawaxen, Pennsylvania.

ran the blacks through it. An old trail led off to the right, taking the line of the wall, and this Venters knew to be the trail mentioned by Lassiter.

The little hamlet, Glaze, a white and green patch in the vast waste of purple, lay miles down a slope much like the Cottonwoods slope, only this descended to the west. And miles farther west a faint green spot marked the location of Stone Bridge. All the rest of that world was seemingly smooth, undulating sage, with no ragged lines of cañons to accentuate its wildness.

"Bess, we're safe—we're free!" said Venters. "We're alone on the sage. We're half way to Sterling."

"Ah! I wonder how it is with Lassiter and Miss Withersteen."

"Never fear, Bess. He'll outwit Tull. He'll get away and hide her safely. He might climb into Surprise Valley, but I don't think he'll go so far."

"Bern, will we ever find any place like our beautiful valley?"

"No. But, dear, listen. We'll go back some day, after years—ten years. Then we'll be forgotten. And our valley will be just as we left it."

"What if Balancing Rock falls and closes the outlet to the Pass?"

"I've thought of that. I'll pack in ropes and ropes. And if the outlet's closed we'll climb up the cliffs and over them to the valley and go down on rope ladders. It could be done. I know just where to make the climb, and I'll never forget."

"Oh yes, let us go back!"

"It's something sweet to look forward to. Bess, it's like all the future looks to me."

"Call me—Elizabeth," she said, shyly.

"Elizabeth Erne! It's a beautiful name. But I'll never forget Bess. Do you know—have you thought that very soon—by this time to-morrow—you will be Elizabeth Venters?"

So they rode on down the old trail. And the sun sloped to the west, and a golden sheen lay on the sage. The hours sped now; the afternoon waned. Often they rested the horses. The glisten of a pool of water in a hollow caught Venters's eye, and here he unsaddled the blacks and let them roll and drink and browse. When he and Bess rode up out of the hollow the sun was low, a crimson ball, and the valley seemed veiled in purple fire and smoke. It was that short time when the sun appeared to rest before setting, and silence, like a cloak of invisible life, lay heavy on all that shimmering world of sage.

They watched the sun begin to bury its red curve under the dark horizon.

"We'll ride on till late," he said. "Then you can sleep a little, while I watch and graze the horses. And we'll ride into Sterling early to-morrow. We'll be married! . . . We'll be in time to catch the stage. We'll tie Black Star and Night behind—and then—for a country not wild and terrible like this!"

"Oh, Bern! . . . But look! The sun is setting on the sage—the last time for us till we dare come again to the Utah border. Ten years! Oh, Bern, look, so you will never forget!"

Slumbering, fading purple fire burned over the undulating sage ridges. Long streaks and bars and shafts and spears fringed the far western slope. Drifting, golden veils mingled with low, purple shadows. Colors and shades changed in slow, wondrous transformation.

Larry McMurtry

From *Lonesome Dove*

With the possible exception of Log of a Cowboy, *Larry McMurtry's* Lonesome Dove *(1985) may well be the best cowboy novel ever written. Like other examples of the genre, this work is a romance and cannot be read as history. Nevertheless, the novel reveals some important truths about the frontier—not least among them the relentless savagery which could snuff life out in casual moments of violence. Here is one of them.*

"I'll be glad to get to Dodge," Jake said. "I'd like a bath and a whore. And a good barber to shave me. There's a barber there named Sandy that I fancy, if nobody ain't shot him."

"You'll know tomorrow, I guess," Dan Suggs said. "I've never liked barbers myself."

"Dan don't even like whores," Roy Suggs said. "Dan's hard to please."

Jake was cheered by the thought that Dodge was so close. He was tired of the empty prairie and the sullen Suggses, and was looking forward to jolly company and some good card games. He had every intention of wiggling loose from the Suggses in Dodge. Gambling might be his ticket. He could win a lot of money and tell them he'd had enough of the roving life. They didn't own him, after all.

It was a sunny day, and Jake rode along happily. Sometimes he got a lucky feeling—the feeling that he was meant for riches and beautiful women and that nothing could keep him down for long. The lucky feeling came to him as he rode, and the main part of it was his sense that he was about to get free of the Suggs brothers. They were hard men, and he had made a bad choice in riding with them, but nothing very terrible had come of it, and they were almost to Dodge. It seemed to him he had slid into bad luck in Arkansas the day he accidentally shot the dentist, and now he was about to slide out of it in Kansas and resume the kind of enjoyable life he felt he deserved. Frog Lip was riding just in front of him, and he felt how nice it would be not to have to consort with such a man again. Frog Lip rode along silently, as he had the whole trip, but there was menace in his silence, and Jake was ready for lighter company—a whore, particularly. There was sure to be plenty of them in Dodge.

In the afternoon, though, Dan Suggs, the man who was hard to please, saw something he liked: a herd of about twenty-five horses being driven south by three men. He rode over to a ridge and inspected the horses through his spyglasses. When he came back he had a pleased look on his face. At the sight of it Jake immediately lost his lucky feeling.

"It's old Wilbarger," Dan said. "He's just got two hands with him."

"Why, I've heard of him," Jake said. "We returned some of his horses to him, out of Mexico. Pedro Flores had them. I never met Wilbarger myself."

"I've met him, the son of a bitch," Dan said. "I rode for him once."

"Where's he goin' with them horses, back to Texas?" Roy asked.

"He's probably sold his lead herd in Dodge and has got another bunch or two headed for Denver. He's taking his boys some fresh mounts."

Wilbarger and his horses were soon out of sight, but Dan Suggs made no move to resume the trip to Dodge.

"I guess Dan's feeling bloody," Roy said, observing his brother.

"I thought Wilbarger was rough," little Eddie said.

"He is, but so am I," Dan Suggs said. "I never liked the man. I see no reason why we shouldn't have them horses."

Roy Suggs was not greatly pleased by his brother's behavior. "Have 'em and do what with 'em?" he asked. "We can't sell 'em in Dodge if Wilbarger's just been there."

"Dodge ain't the only town in Kansas," Dan said. "We can sell 'em in Abilene."

With no further discussion, he turned and rode southwest at a slow trot. His brothers followed. Jake sat for a moment, his lucky feeling gone and a sense of dread in its place. He thought maybe the Suggs brothers would forget him and he could ride on to Dodge, but then he saw Frog Lip looking at him. The black man was impassive.

"You coming?" he asked—the first time on the whole trip that he had spoken to Jake directly. There was an insolence in his voice that caused Jake to flare up for a moment despite himself.

"I guess if you watch you'll find out," Jake said, bitter that the man would address him so.

Frog Lip just looked at him, neither smiling nor frowning. The insolence of the look was so great that for a moment Jake contemplated gunplay. He wanted to shoot the look off the black man's face. But instead he touched his horse lightly with the spurs and followed the Suggs brothers across the plain. He felt angry—the barber and the whore he had been looking forward to had been put off. Soon he heard the black man's horse fall in behind him.

Dan Suggs traveled at a leisurely pace; they didn't see Wilbarger or his horses again that day. When they spotted a spring with a few low trees growing by it, Dan even stopped for a nap.

"You don't want to steal horses in the daytime," he remarked when he awoke. "It works better at night. That way you can put it off on Indians, if you're lucky."

"We better pull the shoes off these horses then," Roy Suggs said. "Indians don't use horseshoes much."

"You're a stickler for details, ain't you?" Dan said. "Who's gonna track us?" He lay back in the shade and put his hat over his eyes.

"Wilbarger might, if he's so rough," little Eddie said.

Dan Suggs just chuckled.

"Hell, I thought we come up here to rob banks and regulate settlers," Jake said. "I don't remember hiring on to steal horses. Stealing horses is a hanging crime, as I recall."

"I never seen such a bunch of young ladies," Dan said. "Everything's a hanging crime up here in Kansas. They ain't got around to making too many laws."

"That may be," Jake said. "Horse stealing don't happen to be my line of work."

"You're young, you can learn a new line of work," Dan said, raising up on an elbow. "And if you'd rather not learn, we can leave you here dead on the ground. I won't tolerate a shirker." With that he put his hat back over his face and went to sleep.

Jake knew he was trapped. He could not fight four men. The Suggs brothers all took naps, but Frog Lip sat by the spring all afternoon, cleaning his guns.

Late in the afternoon Dan Suggs got up and took a piss by the spring. Then he lay down on

BILL ANTON. *The Morning Rounds.* 1992. Oil. 24 x 30 in. Courtesy of the artist.

his belly and had a long drink of water. When he got up, he mounted his horse and rode off, without a word to anyone. His brothers quickly mounted and followed him, and Jake had no choice but to do the same. Frog Lip, as usual, brought up the rear.

"Dan's feeling real bloody," little Eddie said.

"Well, he gets that way," Roy said. "I hope you don't expect me to preach him a sermon."

"He don't want them horses," little Eddie said. "He wants to kill that man."

"I doubt he'll turn down free horses, once he has them," Roy said.

Jake felt bitter that the day had turned so bad. It was his bad luck again—he couldn't seem to beat it. If Wilbarger had been traveling even half a mile further west, they would never have seen him and his horses, and they would be in Dodge, enjoying the comforts of the town. On that vast plain, spotting three men and some horses was a mere accident—as much a matter of luck as the bullet that killed Benny Johnson. Yet both had happened. It was enough to make a man a pessimist, that such things had started occurring regularly.

They soon struck Wilbarger's trail and followed it west through the sunset and the long dusk. The trail led northwest toward the Arkansas, easy to follow even in the twilight. Dan Suggs never slowed. They struck the river and swam it by moonlight. Jake hated to ride sopping wet, but was offered no choice, for Dan Suggs didn't pause. Nobody said a word when they came to the river; nobody said one afterward. The moon was well over in the west before Dan Suggs drew rein.

"Go find them, Frog," he said. "I doubt they're far."

"Do I shoot or not?" the black man asked.

"Hell, no, don't shoot," Dan said. "Do you think I'd ride all this way and swim a river just to miss the fun? Come on back when you find 'em."

Frog Lip was back in a few minutes.

"We nearly rode into them," he said. "They're close."

Dan Suggs had been smoking, but he quickly put his smoke out and dismounted.

"You hold the horses," he said to little Eddie. "Come on once you hear the shooting."

"I can shoot as good as Roy," little Eddie protested.

"Hell, Roy couldn't hit his foot if it was nailed to a tree," Dan said. "Anyway, we're gonna let Jake shoot them—he's the man with the reputation."

He took the rifle and walked off. Jake and the others followed. There was no sign of a campfire, no sign of anything but plains and darkness. Though Frog Lip had said the men were close, it seemed to Jake they walked a long time. He didn't see the horses until he almost bumped into one. For a moment he thought of trying to grab a horse and run away bareback. The commotion would warn Wilbarger, and maybe one or two of the Suggs boys would get shot. But the horse quickly stepped away from him and the moment passed. He drew his pistol, not knowing what else to do. They had found the horses, but he didn't know where the camp was. Frog Lip was near him, watching, Jake supposed.

When the first shot came, he didn't know who fired it, though he saw a flash from a rifle barrel. It seemed so far away that he almost felt it must be another battle. Then gunfire flared just in front of him, too much to be produced by three men, it seemed. So much shooting panicked him for a second and he fired twice into the darkness, with no idea of what he might be shooting at. He heard gunfire behind him—it was Frog Lip shooting. He began to sense running figures, although it was not clear to him who they were. Then there were five or six shots close together, like sudden thunder, and the sound of a running horse. Jake could see almost nothing—once in a while he would think he saw a man, but he couldn't be sure.

"Frog, did you get him?" he heard Dan Suggs ask.

"No, he got me, damn him," he heard the black man say.

"I swear I put three into him but he made it to that horse anyway," Dan said. "You alive, Roy?"

"I'm alive," Roy Suggs said, from back near the horse herd.

"Well, what are you doing over there?" Dan wanted to know. "The damn fight was over here."

"We want the horses, don't we?" Roy asked, anger in his voice.

"I wanted that goddamn Wilbarger worse," Dan said. "What about you, Spoon?"

"Not hurt," Jake said.

"Hell, you and Roy might as well have stayed in Dodge, for all the good you are in the dark," Dan said.

Jake didn't answer. He was just glad he had not been forced to shoot anybody. It seemed ridiculous, attacking men in the dark. Even Indians waited until sunup. He took some hope from the fact that Frog Lip claimed to have been hit, though how anybody knew where to shoot was a mystery to him.

"Where's that goddamn kid?" Dan asked. "I told him to bring them horses. Old Wilbarger's getting away. Where'd you get hit, Frog?"

Frog Lip didn't answer.

"Goddamn the old son of a bitch," Dan said. "I guess he's killed Frog. Go get Eddie, Roy."

"You told him to come, I guess he'll come," Roy said.

"You best to get him unless you think you're bulletproof," Dan said in a deadly voice.

"I ain't going if Wilbarger's out there," Roy said. "You won't shoot me neither—I'm your brother."

There were two more shots, so close that Jake jumped.

"Did I get you?" Dan asked.

"No, and don't shoot no more," Roy said, in a surprised voice. "Why would you shoot at me?"

"There ain't nobody else around to shoot at except Jake, and you know his reputation," Dan said sarcastically.

They heard horses coming. "Boys?" little Eddie called out.

"No, mostly girls here tonight," Dan said. "Are you waiting for election day or what? Bring the goddamn horses."

Little Eddie brought them. The dawn was behind him, very faint but coming. Soon it was possible to make out the results of the battle. Wilbarger's two men were dead, still in their blankets. One was Chick, the little weasel Jake remembered seeing the morning they brought the horses in from Mexico. He had been hit in the neck by a rifle bullet, Frog Lip's, Dan said. The bullet had practically torn his head loose from his body—the corpse reminded Jake of a dead rabbit, perhaps because Chick had rabbitlike teeth, exposed now in a stiff grimace.

The other dead man was just a boy, probably Wilbarger's wrangler.

Of Wilbarger himself, there was no sign.

"I know I put three into him," Dan Suggs said. "He must have slept with the damn reins in his hand or he'd have never got to his horse."

Frog Lip lay on the ground, still gripping his rifle. His eyes were wide open and he was breathing as heavily as a horse after a long run. His wound was in the groin—his pants were wet with blood. The rising sun shone in his face, which was beaded with sweat.

"Who shot Frog?" little Eddie asked in surprise.

"Why, that damn Wilbarger, who else?" Dan said. He had no more than glanced at Frog Lip—he was scanning the plains with his spyglass, hoping to catch a glimpse of the cowman. But the plains were empty.

"I never thought anybody would get Frog," little Eddie said, unnerved by what he saw.

Dan Suggs was snarling with frustration. He glared at his brothers as if they were solely responsible for Wilbarger's escape.

"You boys ought to go home and teach school," he said. "It's all you're good for."

"What did you expect me to do?" Roy asked. "I can't see in the dark."

Dan walked over and looked down at Frog Lip. He ignored his brothers. He knelt down and pulled the Negro's bloodstained shirt loose from his pants, exposing the wound. After a second he stood up.

"Frog, I guess this was your unlucky day," he said. "I guess we better just shoot you."

Frog Lip didn't answer. He didn't move or even blink his eyes.

"Shoot him and let's go," Dan said, looking at little Eddie.

"Shoot Frog?" little Eddie said, as if he had not heard quite right.

"Yes, Frog's the one with the slug in his gut," Dan said. "He's the one that needs to finish up dying. Shoot him and let's ride."

"I hate to shoot Frog," little Eddie said in a dazed tone.

"I guess we'll just leave him for the buzzards then, if you're so squeamish," Dan said. He removed the rifle from the Negro's hand and took the big pistol out of his belt.

"Ain't you gonna let him keep his guns?" Roy asked.

"Nope," Dan said. "He won't need 'em, but we might."

With that he mounted and rode over to look at the horse herd they had captured.

"You shoot him, Roy," little Eddie said. "I hate to."

"No, Dan's mad at me anyway," Roy said. "If I do something he ordered you to do, I'll be the one shot."

With that he mounted and rode off too. Jake walked over to his horse, feeling that it had been a black day when he met the Suggses.

"Would you like to shoot him, Jake?" little Eddie asked. "I've known him all my life."

"I wouldn't care to," Jake said. He remembered how insolent Frog Lip had been only the day before, and how he had wanted to shoot him then. It had been a rapid turnabout. The man lay on the ground, dying of a cruel wound, and none of the men he rode with even wanted to put him out of his misery.

"Well, damn," little Eddie said. "Nobody's much help."

He shrugged, drew his gun, and without another word walked over and shot Frog Lip in the head. The body jerked, and that was that.

"Get his money," Dan Suggs yelled. "I forgot to."

Little Eddie went through the dead man's bloody pockets before he mounted.

Jake had supposed they might try to go after Wilbarger, since he was wounded, but Dan Suggs turned the horse herd north.

"Ain't we going after that man?" Roy asked.

"I couldn't track an elephant and neither could you," Dan said. "Frog was our tracker. I shot Wilbarger three times, I expect he'll die."

"I thought we was going to Abilene," little Eddie said. "Abilene ain't this way."

Dan sneered at his brother. "I wish Wilbarger had shot you instead of Frog," he said. "Frog was a damn sight better hand."

Jake thought maybe he had seen the last of the killing. He felt it could be worse. The shooting had all been in pitch-darkness. Wilbarger hadn't seen him. He couldn't be connected with the raid. It was luck, of a sort. If he could just get free of the Suggses, he wouldn't be in such hopeless trouble.

As he rode along, trailing the twenty-five horses, he decided the best thing for him would be to leave the west. He could travel over to St. Louis and catch a boat down to New Orleans, or even go east to New York. Both of them were fine towns for gamblers, or so he had heard. In either one he could be safe and could pursue the kind of life he enjoyed. Looking back on it, it seemed to him that he had been remarkably lucky to survive as long as he had in such a rough place, where killing was an everyday affair. No man's luck lasted forever, and the very fact that he had fallen in with the Suggses suggested that his was about exhausted.

He resolved to bend his wits to getting out while the getting was possible. The death of Frog Lip made the task easier, for, as Dan said, Frog Lip was the only tracker in the crowd. If he could just manage to get a good jump, somehow, he might get away. And if he did he wouldn't stop until he hit the Mississippi.

With his mind made up, he felt cheerful—it always gave a man a lift to escape death. It was a beautiful sunny day and he was alive to see it. With any luck at all, he had seen the end of the trouble.

His good mood lasted two hours, and then something occurred which turned it sour. It seemed as if the world was deserted except for them and the horses, and then to his surprise he saw a tent. It was staked under a single tree, directly ahead of them. Near the tent, two men were plowing with four mules. Dan Suggs was riding ahead of the horse herd, and Jake saw him lope off toward the settlers. He didn't think much about it—he was watching the tent to see if any women were around. Then he heard the faint pop of a shot and looked up to see one of the settlers fall. The other man was standing there, no gun in his hand, nothing. He stood as if paralyzed, and in a second Dan Suggs shot him too. Then he trotted over to the tent, got off his horse and went inside.

Jake hardly knew what to think. He had just seen two men shot in the space of seconds. He had no idea why. By the time he got near the tent Dan Suggs had drug a little trunk outside and was rifling it. He pitched the clothes which were in the trunk out on the grass. His brothers rode over to join the fun, and were soon holding up various garments, to see if they fit. Jake rode over too, feeling nervous. Dan Suggs was clearly in a killing mood. Both farmers lay dead on the grass near their mule team, which was quietly grazing. Both had bullet holes in their foreheads. Dan had shot them at point-blank range.

"Well, they didn't have much but a watch," Dan said, holding up a fine-looking silver pocket watch. "I guess I'll take the watch."

His brothers found nothing of comparable value, although they searched the tent thoroughly. While they were looking, Dan started a fire with some coal oil he had found and made some coffee.

"I tell you, let's hang 'em," he said, strolling over to look at the dead men. Both were in their forties, and both had scraggly beards.

Roy Suggs looked puzzled. "Why would you want to hang them?" he asked. "They're already dead."

"I know, but it's a shame to waste that tree," Dan said. "It's the only tree around. What's a tree good for if not to hang somebody from?"

The thought made little Eddie giggle, a nervous giggle.

"Dan, you beat all," he said. "I never heard of hanging dead men."

Nonetheless Dan meant it. He put ropes around both the dead men's necks and had his brothers drag them to the tree and hoist them up. It was not a large tree, and the dead men's feet were only a few inches off the ground. Jake was not called on to help, and he didn't.

When the men were hung, twisting at the end of the ropes, Dan Suggs stood back to study the effect, and evidently didn't like it. His brothers were watching him nervously—it was plain from his face that he was still in an angry mood.

"These goddamn sodbusters," he said. "I hate their guts and livers."

"Well, that's fine, Dan," Roy said. "They're dead enough."

ILA MAE MCAFEE.
Longhorns Watering on Cattle Drive. Oil on canvas. From the Collection of Gilcrease Museum, Tulsa, Oklahoma.

"No, they ain't," Dan said. "A goddamn sodbuster can never be dead enough to suit me."

With that he went over and got the can of coal oil he had used to start the fire. He began to splash it on the hanged men's clothes.

"What's that for?" little Eddie asked. "You've already shot 'em and hung 'em."

"Yes, and now I intend to burn them," Dan said. "Any objections from you schoolteachers?" He looked at all three of them, challenge in his angry eyes. No one said a word. Jake felt sickened by what was happening, but he didn't try and stop it. Dan Suggs was crazy, there was no doubt of that, but his craziness didn't affect his aim. The only way to stop him would be to kill him, a risky business in broad daylight.

Little Eddie giggled his nervous giggle again as he watched his brother set the dead men's clothes on fire. Even with the coal oil it wasn't easy—Dan had to splash them several times before he got their clothes wet enough to blaze. But finally he did, and the clothes flared up. It was a terrible sight. Jake thought he wouldn't look, but despite himself he did. The men's sweaty clothes were burned right off them, and their scraggly beards seared. A few rags of clothes fell off beneath their feet. The men's pants burned off, leaving their belts and a few shreds of cloth around their waists.

"Dan, you beat all," little Eddie repeated several times. He giggled often—he was unnerved. Roy Suggs methodically tore the tent apart and poked through all the men's meager belongings, hoping to find valuables.

"They didn't have nothing," he said. "I don't know why you even bothered to kill them."

"It was their unlucky day, same as it was Frog's," Dan said. "We'll miss Frog, the man could shoot. I wish I had that damn Wilbarger here, I'd cook him good."

After drinking some more coffee, Dan Suggs mounted up. The two farmers, the trunks of their bodies blackened, still hung from the tree.

"Don't you intend to bury them?" Jake asked. "Somebody's gonna find them, you know, and it could be the law."

Dan Suggs just laughed. "I'd like to see the law that could take me," he said. "No man in Kansas could manage it, and anyway I fancy seeing Nebraska."

He turned to his brothers, who were dispiritedly raking through the settlers' clothes, still hoping to find something worth taking.

"Get them mules, boys," Dan said. "No sense in leaving good mules."

With that he rode off.

"He's bloody today," Roy said, going over to the mules. "If we run into any more sod-busters, it's too bad for them."

Jake's happy mood was gone, though the day was as sunny as ever. It was clear to him that his only hope was to escape the Suggses as soon as possible. Dan Suggs could wake up feeling bloody any day, and the next time there might be no sodbusters around to absorb his fury, in which case things could turn really grim. He trotted along all day, well back from the horse herd, trying to forget the two blackened bodies, whose shoes had still been smoldering when they left.

Theodore Roosevelt

From *Ranch Life and the Hunting-Trail*
"Winter Weather"

By the 1880s, so many cattle had been driven north to fatten on the rich grasslands of Montana, Wyoming, and the Dakotas that the land already was overgrazed when drought hit in the summer of 1886, leaving hundreds of thousands of cattle undernourished. In Ranch Life and the Hunting-Trail *(1911), Theodore Roosevelt described the consequences to his own and other western ranches when drought was followed by a terrible winter. The event is still called "The Big Die-Up."*

When the days have dwindled to their shortest, and the nights seem never ending, then all the great northern plains are changed into an abode of iron desolation. Sometimes furious gales blow out of the north, driving before them the clouds of blinding snow-dust, wrapping the mantle of death round every unsheltered being that faces their unshackled anger. They roar in a thunderous bass as they sweep across the prairie or whirl through the naked cañons; they shiver the great brittle cottonwoods, and beneath their rough touch the icy limbs of the pines that cluster in the gorges sing like the chords of an Æolian harp. Again, in the coldest midwinter weather, not a breath of wind may stir; and then the still, merciless, terrible cold that broods over the earth like the shadow of silent death seems even more dreadful in its gloomy rigor than is the lawless madness of the storms. All the land is like granite; the great rivers stand still in their beds, as if turned to frosted steel. In the long nights there is no sound to break the lifeless silence. Under the ceaseless, shifting play of the Northern Lights, or lighted only by the wintry brilliance of the stars, the snow-clad plains stretch out into dead and endless wastes of glimmering white.

Then the great fire-place of the ranch house is choked with blazing logs, and at night we have to sleep under so many blankets that the weight is fairly oppressive. Outside, the shaggy ponies huddle together in the corral, while long icicles hang from their lips, and the hoar-frost whitens the hollow backs of the cattle. For the ranchman the winter is occasionally a pleasant holiday, but more often an irksome period of enforced rest and gloomy foreboding.

* * *

The winters vary greatly in severity with us. During some seasons men can go lightly clad even in January and February, and the cattle hardly suffer at all; during others there will be spells of bitter weather, accompanied by furious blizzards, which render it impossible for days and weeks at a time for men to stir out-of-doors at all, save at the risk of their lives. Then line rider, ranchman, hunter, and teamster alike all have to keep within doors. I have known of several cases of men freezing to death when caught in shelterless places by such a blizzard, a

COLORPLATE 68

W. H. D. KOERNER. *Madonna of the Prairie.* 1921. Oil on canvas. 42 ¹/8 x 36 ³/8 in. Buffalo Bill Historical Center, Cody, Wyoming. *This painting for the serialized version of Emerson Hough's hugely popular novel,* The Covered Wagon, *served as the cover illustration for the April 1, 1922 issue of* The Saturday Evening Post.

COLORPLATE 69

MAYNARD DIXON. *Open Range*. 1942. Oil on canvas. 34 ¹/₂ x 39 in. Museum of Western Art, Denver, Colorado.

COLORPLATE 70

JOHN SLOAN. *Chama Running Red*. 1925. Oil on canvas. 30 x 40 in. Courtesy of The Anschutz Collection, Denver, Colorado.

COLORPLATE 71

DAVID HALBACH. *Headin' Out.* c. 1993. Watercolor. 18 x 29 ¹/₂ in. Private collection. Photograph courtesy of the artist.

213

COLORPLATE 72

HAROLD VON SCHMIDT. *Rustlers at Work.* 1934. Oil on canvas. 29 ½ x 49 ½ in. The Rockwell Museum, Corning, New York.

COLORPLATE 73

FLETCHER MARTIN. *July 4th, 5th and 6th.* 1940. Oil on canvas. 40 x 55 in. Courtesy of The Anschutz Collection, Denver, Colorado.

COLORPLATE 74

CHARLES CHRISTIAN NAHL and FREDERICK AUGUST WENDEROTH. *Miners in the Sierras*. 1851–1852. Oil on canvas. 54 ¹/₄ x 67 in. National Museum of American Art, Washington, D.C. Gift of The Fred Heilbron Collection. *Charles Nahl made a career out of romanticizing California's past, especially the brief period when* rancheros *ruled the state as an early autonomous province of Mexico. His Mother Lode scenes from the years of the Gold Rush—which he knew from first-hand observation—are a little more realistic than his imagined scenes of* vaqueros *trifling with "the cattle on a thousand hills," as one American described the pastoral society of the* Californios. *Still, too much reality would not have done, and in the collaborative painting above one gets little sense of the terrible diet, homesickness, illness, frustration, and depression that comprised the average goldseeker's burden.*

Teddy Roosevelt in western dress.
c. 1911. Photograph.

strange fact being that in about half of them the doomed man had evidently gone mad before dying, and had stripped himself of most of his clothes, the body when found being nearly naked. On our ranch we have never had any bad accidents, although every winter some of us get more or less frost-bitten. My last experience in this line was while returning by moonlight from a successful hunt after mountain sheep. The thermometer was 26° below zero, and we had had no food for twelve hours. I became numbed, and before I was aware of it had frozen my face, one foot, both knees, and one hand. Luckily, I reached the ranch before serious damage was done.

About once every six or seven years we have a season when these storms follow one another almost without interval throughout the winter months, and then the loss among the stock is frightful. One such winter occurred in 1880–81. This was when there were very few ranchmen in the country. The grass was so good that the old range stock escaped pretty well; but the trail herds were almost destroyed. The next severe winter was that of 1886–87, when the rush of incoming herds had overstocked the ranges, and the loss was in consequence fairly appalling, especially to the outfits that had just put on cattle.

The snow-fall was unprecedented, both for its depth and for the way it lasted; and it was this, and not the cold, that caused the loss. About the middle of November the storms began. Day after day the snow came down, thawing and then freezing and piling itself higher and higher. By January the drifts had filled the ravines and coulées almost level. The snow lay in great masses on the plateaus and river bottoms; and this lasted until the end of February. The preceding summer we had been visited by a prolonged drought, so that the short, scanty grass was already well cropped down; the snow covered what pasturage there was to the depth of several feet, and the cattle could not get at it at all, and could hardly move round. It was all but impossible to travel on horseback—except on a few well-beaten trails. It was dangerous to attempt to penetrate the Bad Lands, whose shape had been completely altered by the great white mounds and drifts. The starving cattle died by scores of thousands before their helpless

Cattle drive. 1907. Photograph. Courtesy of The Wilderness Society.

owners' eyes. The bulls, the cows who were suckling calves, or who were heavy with calf, the weak cattle that had just been driven up on the trail, and the late calves suffered most; the old range animals did better, and the steers best of all; but the best was bad enough. Even many of the horses died. An outfit near me lost half its saddle-band, the animals having been worked so hard that they were very thin when fall came.

In the thick brush the stock got some shelter and sustenance. They gnawed every twig and bough they could get at. They browsed the bitter sage brush down to where the branches were the thickness of a man's finger. When near a ranch they crowded into the outhouses and sheds to die, and fences had to be built around the windows to keep the wild-eyed, desperate beasts from thrusting their heads through the glass panes. In most cases it was impossible either to drive them to the haystacks or to haul the hay out to them. The deer even were so weak as to be easily run down; and on one or two of the plateaus where there were bands of antelope, these wary creatures grew so numbed and feeble that they could have been slaughtered like rabbits. But the hunters could hardly get out, and could bring home neither hide nor meat, so the game went unharmed.

The way in which the cattle got through the winter depended largely on the different localities in which the bands were caught when the first heavy snows came. A group of animals in a bare valley, without underbrush and with steepish sides, would all die, weak and strong alike; they could get no food and no shelter, and so there would not be a hoof left. On the other hand, hundreds wintered on the great thickly wooded bottoms near my ranch house with little more than ordinary loss, though a skinny sorry-looking crew by the time the snow melted. In intermediate places the strong survived and the weak perished.

It would be impossible to imagine any sight more dreary and melancholy than that offered by the ranges when the snow went off in March. The land was a mere barren waste; not a green thing could be seen; the dead grass eaten off till the country looked as if it had been shaved with a razor. Occasionally among the desolate hills a rider would come across a band of gaunt, hollow-flanked cattle feebly cropping the sparse, dry pasturage, too listless to move out of the way; and the blackened carcasses lay in the sheltered spots, some stretched out, others in as natural a position as if the animals had merely lain down to rest. It was small wonder that cheerful stockmen were rare objects that spring.

Our only comfort was that we did not, as usual, suffer a heavy loss from weak cattle getting mired down in the springs and mud-holes when the ice broke up—for all the weak animals were dead already. The truth is, ours is a primitive industry, and we suffer the reverses as well as enjoy the successes only known to primitive peoples. A hard winter is to us in the north what a dry summer is to Texas or Australia—what seasons of famine once were to all peoples. We still live in an iron age that the old civilized world has long passed by. The men of the border reckon upon stern and unending struggles with their iron-bound surroundings; against the grim harshness of their existence they set the strength and the abounding vitality that come with it. They run risks to life and limb that are unknown to the dwellers in cities; and what the men freely brave, the beasts that they own must also sometimes suffer.

Don Russell

From "Cody, Kings, and Coronets"
"Buffalo Bill's Wild West"

The U.S. Bureau of the Census declared in 1890 that the "frontier line of settlement" had come to an end. Perhaps, but the romance of the frontier lived on in song, story, and, not least, theatrical extravaganzas like "Buffalo Bill's Wild West." In an adaptation from his book, The Wild West: A History of the Wild West Shows *(1970), historian Don Russell tells of an entertainment form that presaged the "oaters" of both movies and television.*

Buffalo Bill, sometimes known more formally as William Frederick Cody, but not yet dubbed Colonel, came home to North Platte, Nebraska, in the early summer of 1882 at the close of his tenth season in stage melodrama. According to the late William McDonald, who was there at the time, Cody came into Charles J. Foley's store. Charles F. Ormsby, onetime mayor of North Platte, and other leading citizens were already there. Cody asked what had been planned for celebrating the Fourth of July. When told that nothing was scheduled, "Cody mumbled something to the effect that he was surprised, then went up the street to the saloon, but he hardly stayed long enough to get a drink. He wasn't one to take a drink just to get his mouth wet. He came back, protesting that it was not patriotic not to have a Fourth of July celebration. Ormsby and Foley said, 'OK, Bill, you are chairman to get up a celebration.'"

So Buffalo Bill set about planning North Platte's "Old Glory Blow Out." There are those who have doubted his energy and his managerial ability, but he manifested both this time. The arena was a race track with a fence around it. Buffalo Bill proposed to give a demonstration of his methods of killing buffalo, using steers and blank ammunition. McDonald recalled that M. C. Keefe had a small herd of buffalo that might be borrowed. Cody persuaded businessmen to offer prizes for roping, shooting, riding, and bronco-breaking events; five thousand handbills were sent out. Cody estimated he might get one hundred cowboy entrants; he actually got one thousand. It has been said that no similar event ever had so many able competitors. The unprecedented and unexpected success gave Cody an idea.

That Fourth of July, 1882, in North Platte marks the beginning of both the Wild West show and the rodeo. It was not, however, the "first" for either. Rodeo historians are sound in tracing their sport to the byplay and show-off of early cattle roundups. Captain Mayne Reid, author of *The Scalp Hunters* and *The Rifle Rangers,* wrote from Santa Fe in 1847: "This roundup is a great time for the cowhands, a Donnybrook fair it is indeed. They contest with each other for the best roping and throwing, and there are horse races and whiskey and wines."

The Wild West was brought to New York as early as 1843 by way of Boston, where a herd of yearling buffalo had been exhibited at the celebration dedicating Bunker Hill monument. P. T. Barnum bought the herd and announced a one-day "Grand Buffalo Hunt," free to the public in Hoboken—after he had chartered the ferryboats for the day. His hunter roped a calf or two, and a free band concert helped the crowd enjoy being humbugged, according to Barnum.

Many of the elements that made up Buffalo Bill's Wild West, then, were already in existence when William F. Cody got his idea for a new type of outdoor entertainment. What was different about it was this combination in a formula that spelled success.

* * *

The Wild West, Hon. W. F. Cody and Dr. W. F. Carver's Rocky Mountain and Prairie Exhibition, opened at the Omaha Fair Grounds, May 19, 1883. Besides the attack on the Deadwood stagecoach, the show included many acts that were to become standard: the Pony Express, bucking broncos in "Cow-Boys' Fun," roping and riding wild Texas steers, much shooting, and many races. The closing spectacle was "A Grand Hunt on the Plains," with buffalo, elk, deer, mountain sheep, wild horses, and longhorns.

Carver had an off day in his shooting, perhaps because of too much celebrating prior to the opening, so Cody tried his hand at some glass balls as targets. His performance was so successful that his act became a regular part of the show. The show had no tentage and no lighting. An attempt at a night show with bonfires, flares, and rockets flopped, so the show settled for afternoon engagements at fairgrounds and similar arenas during its first season's tour. It played Springfield, Illinois, and Chicago, then went to Boston, Newport, and Coney Island. The Hartford *Courant* declared it "the best open-air show ever seen. . . . The real sight of the whole thing is, after all, Buffalo Bill. . . . Cody was an extraordinary figure and sits on a horse as if he were born to the saddle. His feats of shooting are perfectly wonderful. . . . He has, in this exhibition, out-Barnumed Barnum."

Just how successful Cody and Carver were during the first season of the Wild West is unclear. Cody wrote his sister Julia that he had not made much money but that he had spent freely for advertising and facilities for the following season. Nate Salsbury, who was shortly to become a partner, said Cody told him in Chicago in October that he would not go through another season with Carver. The break came when Carver proposed a winter tour. Cody refused, and the two men divided their assets when the show closed at Omaha.

John Peter Altgeld, later a famed liberal governor of Illinois, drew up the contract under which Cody, Bogardus, and Salsbury carried on the show to be known as "Buffalo Bill's Wild West—America's National Entertainment." Salsbury, just two days younger than Cody, had run away from home at fifteen to join the Union Army in the Civil War. He was captured and imprisoned in Andersonville, started the study of law after the war, but was detoured to the stage by way of amateur theatricals. After an apprenticeship in stock companies, he organized his own company, the "Troubadours," with which he toured for twelve years, including a trip to Australia. He stayed with this troupe during the season of 1884 to keep the pot boiling for the Wild West.

However, when Salsbury visited the lot in the spring, he found Cody "surrounded by a lot of harpies called old-timers who were getting as drunk as he at his expense." He left a letter for Cody to read when he sobered up. There is persistent legendry that Nate limited Bill to one, or ten, or twelve drinks a day, which Bill took in the largest available glassware. The fact is that Cody promised, "This drinking surely ends today and your pard will be himself, and on deck all the time." The evidence indicates that Cody hewed to the line and that he never missed a performance because of being drunk—nor did he hesitate to notify Nate that "when the show is laid up for winter, I am going to get on a drunk that is a drunk."

Over the next several years, the Cody-Salsbury partnership developed Buffalo Bill's Wild West into one of the leading entertainment spectacles of its time, taking the show to most of the major cities in the eastern United States and on a major tour of Canada.

During this time they also added to the cast such crowd-pleasing luminaries as Sitting Bull, who joined in 1885 for a few months; "Doc" Middleton, the renowned Nebraska bandit; and the redoubtable Annie Oakley—"Little Sure Shot." These were viewed by other notables from the stands—General Sherman, Mark Twain, P. T. Barnum, Thomas A. Edison, and Mrs. George Armstrong Custer, widow of the general slain at the Little Big Horn. All had words of praise for the show, and they were not alone; in one July week the attendance totaled 193,960.

Both Cody and Salsbury had long been ambitious to show the Wild West in Europe. The opportunity came with an offer to take part in the American Exhibition planned for Queen Victoria's Golden Jubilee in 1887 in London. The State Line steamship *State of Nebraska* was engaged, and the on-board count of the "company of more than two hundred" totaled 83 saloon passengers, 38 steerage passengers, and 37 Indians. Livestock included 180 horses, 18 buffalo, ten elk, ten mules, five Texas steers, four donkeys, and two deer. After unloading at Gravesend, three trains took the show to Earl's Court, London, where camp was set up. Notables of stage and politics, Henry Irving, Ellen Terry, Mary Anderson, Justin McCarthy, and William E. Gladstone visited the camp, and on May 5, four days before the opening, a special performance was given for Albert Edward, Prince of Wales (who became King Edward VII), and his royal party. This resulted in a command performance for Queen Victoria, her first appearance at a public entertainment since the death of her consort, Prince Albert.

Another command performance was given June 20 for the Jubilee guests, and it was on this occasion that the Deadwood coach carried four kings in addition to the Prince of Wales, with Buffalo Bill as driver. The kings were Leopold II of Belgium, Christian IX of Denmark, George I of Greece, and Albert of Saxony. Said the Prince of Wales, an experienced poker player:

"Colonel, you never held four kings like this before."

"I've held four kings," said Cody, "but four kings and the Prince of Wales makes a royal flush such as no man ever held before."

ROSA BONHEUR. *Col. William F. Cody.* 1889. Oil on canvas. 18 1/2 x 15 1/4 in. Buffalo Bill Historical Center, Cody, Wyoming. Given in memory of William R. Coe and Mai Rogers Coe.

DREAMS OF PERMANENCE

Richard F. Burton

From *The City of the Saints*

On Plurality

Settling in the valley of the Great Salt Lake in 1847, the Mormons, or Latter-Day Saints, established the most successful cooperative community in American history. As with most other "gentiles," however, what fascinated British visitor Richard F. Burton about the Mormons was less their success as a community than their peculiar marital habits, which he scrutinizes closely in this excerpt from The City of the Saints and Across the Rocky Mountains to California *(1862).*

It will, I suppose, be necessary to supply a popular view of the "peculiar institution," at once the bane and blessing of Mormonism—plurality. I approach the subject with a feeling of despair, so conflicting are opinions concerning it, and so difficult is it to naturalise in Europe the customs of Asia, Africa, and America, or to reconcile the habits of the 19th century A.D. with those of 1900 B.C. A return to the patriarchal ages, we have seen, has its disadvantages.

There is a prevailing idea, especially in England, and even the educated are labouring under it, that the Mormons are Communists or Socialists of Plato's, Cicero's, Mr. Owen's and M. Cabet's school; that wives are in public, and that a woman can have as many husbands as the husband can have wives—in fact, to speak colloquially, that they "all pig together." The contrary is notably the case. The man who, like Messrs. Hamilton and Howard Egan, murders, in cold blood, his wife's lover, is invariably acquitted, the jury declaring that civil damages mark the rottenness of other governments, and that "the principle, the only one that beats and throbs through the heart of the *entire inhabitants* (!) of this Territory, is simply this: *The man who seduces his neighbour's wife must die, and her nearest relation must kill him.*" Men, like Dr. Vaughan and Mr. Monroe, slain for the mortal sin, perish for their salvation; the Prophet, were they to lay their lives at his feet, would, because unable to hang or behead them, counsel them to seek certain death in a righteous cause as an expiatory sacrifice; which may save their souls alive. Their two mortal sins are: 1. Adultery; 2. Shedding innocent blood.

This severity of punishing an offence, which modern and civilized society looks upon rather in the light of a sin than of a crime, is clearly based upon the Mosaic code. It is also, *lex loci,* the "common mountain law," a "religious and social custom," and a point of personal honour. Another idea underlies it: the Mormons hold, like the Hebrews of old, "children of shame" in extreme dishonour. They quote the command of God, (Deuteronomy xxiii. 2), "a mamzer shall not enter into the Church of the Lord, till the tenth generation," and ask when the order was repealed. They would expel all impurity from the Camp of Zion, and they adopt every method of preventing what they consider a tremendous evil, viz. the violation of God's temple in their own bodies.

The marriage ceremony is performed in the temple, or, that being impossible, in Mr.

Brigham Young's office, properly speaking by the Prophet, who can, however, depute any follower, as Mr. Heber Kimball, a simple apostle, or even an elder, to act for him. When mutual consent is given, the parties are pronounced man and wife, in the name of Jesus Christ, prayers follow, and there is a patriarchal feast of joy in the evening.

The first wife, as among polygamists generally, is *the* wife, and assumes the husband's name and title. Her "plurality-" partners are called sisters—such as sister Anne or sister Blanche—and are the aunts of her children. The first wife is married for time, the others are sealed for eternity. Hence, according to the Mormons, arose the Gentile calumny concerning spiritual wifedom, which they distinctly deny. Girls rarely remain single past sixteen—in England the average marrying age is thirty—and they would be the pity of the community, if they were doomed to a waste of youth so unnatural.

Divorce is rarely obtained by the man who is ashamed to own that he cannot keep his house in order; some, such as the President, would grant it only in case of adultery; wives, however, are allowed to claim it for cruelty, desertion, or neglect. Of late years, Mormon women married to Gentiles are cut off from the society of the Saints, and without uncharitableness men suspect a sound previous reason. The widows of the Prophet are married to his successor, as David took unto himself the wives of Saul; being generally aged, they occupy the position of matron rather than wife, and the same is the case when a man espouses a mother and her daughter.

It is needless to remark how important a part matrimony plays in the history of an individual, and of that aggregate of individuals, a people; or how various and conflicting has been Christian practice concerning it, from the double marriage, civil and religious, the former temporary, the latter permanent, of the Coptic or Abyssinian church, to the exaggerated purity of Mistress Anne Lee, the mother of the Shakers, who exacted complete continence in a state established according to the first commandment, *crescite et multiplicamini.* The literalism with which the Mormons have interpreted Scripture has led them directly to polygamy. The texts promising to Abraham a progeny numerous as the stars above or the sands below, and that "in his seed (a polygamist) all the families of the earth shall be blessed," induce them, his descendants, to seek a similar blessing. The theory announcing that "the man is not without the woman, nor the woman without the man," is by them interpreted into an absolute command that both sexes should marry, and that a woman cannot enter the heavenly kingdom without a husband to introduce her. A virgin's end is annihilation or absorption, *nox est perpetua una dormienda;* and as baptism for the dead—an old rite, revived and founded upon the writings of

St. Paul quoted in the last chapter,—has been made a part of practice, vicarious marriage for the departed also enters into the Mormon scheme. Like certain British dissenters of the royal burgh of Dundee, who in our day petitioned parliament for permission to bigamise, the Mormons, with Bossuet and others, see in the New Testament no order against plurality; and in the Old dispensation they find the practice sanctioned in a family, ever the friends of God, and out of which the Redeemer sprang. Finally, they find throughout the nations of the earth, three polygamists in theory to one monogame.

The "chaste and plural marriage" being once legalised, finds a multitude of supporters. The anti-Mormons declare that it is at once fornication and adultery—a sin which absorbs all others. The Mormons point triumphantly to the austere morals of their community, their superior freedom from maladive influences, and the absence of that uncleanness and licentiousness which distinguish the cities of the civilized world. They boast that if it be an evil they have at least chosen the lesser evil, that they practise openly as a virtue what others do secretly as a sin—how full is society of these latent Mormons!—that their plurality has abolished the necessity of concubinage, cryptogamy, contubernium, celibacy, *mariages du treizième arrondissement,* with their terrible consequences, infanticide, and so forth; that they have removed their ways from those "whose end is bitter as wormwood, and sharp as a two-edged sword." Like its sister institution Slavery, the birth and growth of a similar age, Polygamy acquires *vim* by abuse and detraction; the more turpitude is heaped upon it, the brighter and more glorious it appears to its votaries.

There are rules and regulations of Mormonism—I cannot say whether they date before or after the heavenly command to pluralise—which disprove the popular statement that such marriages are made to gratify licentiousness, and which render polygamy a positive necessity. All sensuality in the married state is strictly forbidden beyond the requisite for ensuring progeny,—the practice, in fact, of Adam and Abraham. During the gestation and nursing of children, the strictest continence on the part of the mother is required—rather for a hygienic than for a religious reason.

*   *   *

The other motive for polygamy in Utah is economy. Servants are rare and costly; it is cheaper and more comfortable to marry them. Many converts are attracted by the prospect of becoming wives, especially from places where, like Clifton, there are sixty-four females to thirty-six males. The old maid is, as she ought to be, an unknown entity. Life in the wilds of Western America is a course of severe toil: a single woman cannot perform the manifold duties of housekeeping, cooking, scrubbing, washing, darning, child-bearing, and nursing a family. A division of labour is necessary, and she finds it by acquiring a sisterhood. Throughout the States whenever a woman is seen at manual or outdoor work, one is certain that she is Irish, German, or Scandinavian. The delicacy and fragility of the Anglo-American female nature is at once the cause and the effect of this exemption from toil.

The moral influence diffused over social relations by the presence of polygyny will be intelligible only to those who have studied the workings of the system in lands where seclusion is practised in its modified form, as amongst the Syrian Christians. In America society splits into two parts—man and woman—even more readily than in England, each sex is freer and happier in the company of its congeners. At Gt. S. L. City there is a gloom, like that which the late Professor H. H. Wilson described as being cast by the invading Moslem over the innocent gaiety of the primitive Hindu. The choice egotism of the heart called Love, that is to say, the propensity elevated by sentiment, and not undirected by reason, subsides into a calm and unimpassioned domestic attachment: romance and reverence are transferred, with the true Mormon concentration, from Love and Liberty to Religion and the Church. The consent of the first wife to a rival is seldom refused, and a *ménage à trois,* in the Mormon sense of the phrase, is fatal to the development of that tender tie which must be confined to two. In its stead there is household comfort, affection, circumspect friendship, and domestic discipline. Womanhood is not petted and spoiled as in the Eastern States; the inevitable cyclical revolution, indeed, has rather placed her below par, where, however, I believe her to be happier than when set upon an uncomfortable and unnatural eminence.

ALMA TRALLER COMPTON. *The Joseph Henry Byington Family, "A Mormon Family."* c.1870. Denver Public Library, Western History Department..

It will be asked what view does the softer sex take of polygyny? A few, mostly from the old country, lament that Mr. Joseph Smith ever asked of the Creator that question which was answered in the affirmative. A very few, like the Curia Electa, Emma, the first wife of Mr. Joseph Smith—who said of her, by-the-bye, that she could not be contented in heaven without rule—apostatise, and become Mrs. Bidamon. The many are, as might be expected of the easily moulded weaker vessel, which proves its inferior position by the delicate flattery of imitation, more in favour of polygyny than the stronger.

For the attachment of the women of the Saints to the doctrine of plurality there are many reasons. The Mormon prophets have expended all their arts upon this end, well knowing that without the hearty co-operation of mothers and wives, sisters and daughters, no institution can live long. They have bribed them with promises of Paradise—they have subjugated them with threats of annihilation. With them once a Mormon always a Mormon. I have said that a modified reaction respecting the community of Saints has set in throughout the States; people no longer wonder that their missionaries do not show horns and cloven feet, and the Federal officer, the itinerant politician, the platform orator, and the place-seeking demagogue, can no longer make political capital by bullying, oppressing, and abusing them. The tide has turned, and will turn yet more. But the individual still suffers: the apostate Mormon is looked upon by other people as a scamp or a knave, and the woman worse than a prostitute. Again, all the fervour of a new faith burns in their bosoms, with a heat which we can little appreciate, and the revelation of Mr. Joseph Smith is considered on this point as superior to the Christian as the latter is in others to the Mosaic Dispensation. Polygamy is a positive command from heaven: if the flesh is mortified by it *tant mieux*—"no Cross, no Crown;" "blessed are they that mourn." I have heard these words from the lips of a well-educated Mormon woman who, in the presence of a Gentile sister, urged her husband to take unto himself a second wife. The Mormon household has been described by its enemies as a hell of envy, hatred, and malice—a den of murder and suicide. The same has been said of the Moslem harem. Both, I believe, suffer from the assertions of prejudice or ignorance. The temper of the new is so far superior to that of the old country, that, incredible as the statement may appear, rival wives do dwell together in amity; and do quote the proverb "the more the merrier." Moreover, they look with horror at the position of the "slavery" of a pauper mechanic, at being required to "nigger it" upon love and starvation, and at the necessity of a numerous family. They know that nine-tenths of the miseries of the poor in large cities arise from early and imprudent marriages, and they would rather be the fiftieth "sealing" of Dives than the toilsome single wife of Lazarus. The French saying concerning motherhood—*"le premier embellit, le second détruit, le troisième gâte tout,"* is true in the Western World. The first child is welcomed, the second is tolerated, the third is the cause of tears and reproaches, and the fourth, if not prevented by gold pills, or some similar monstrosity, causes temper, spleen, and melancholy, with disgust and hatred of the cause. What the Napoleonic abolition of the law of primogeniture, combined with centralisation of the peasant class in towns and cities, has effected on this side of the Channel, the terrors of maternity, aggravated by a highly nervous temperament, small cerebellum, constitutional frigidity, and extreme delicacy of fibre have brought to pass in the older parts of the Union.

Another curious effect of fervent belief may be noticed in the married state. When a man has four or five wives with reasonable families by each, he is fixed for life: his interests, if not his affections, bind him irrevocably to his New Faith. But the bachelor, as well as the monogamic youth, is prone to backsliding. Apostacy is apparently so common that many of the new Saints form a mere floating population. He is proved by a mission before being permitted to marry, and even then women, dreading a possible renegade with the terrible consequences of a heavenless future to themselves, are shy of saying yes. Thus it happens that male celibacy is mixed up in a curious way with polygyny; and that also in a Faith whose interpreter advises youth not to remain single after sixteen, nor girls after fourteen. The celibacy also is absolute; any infraction of it would be dangerous to life. Either then the first propensity of the phrenologist is poorly developed in these lands—this has been positively stated of the ruder sex in California—or its action is to be regulated by habit to a greater degree than is usually believed.

I am conscious that my narrative savours of incredibility: the fault is in the subject, not in the narrator.

EMMA MITCHELL NEW

"Years Came Along One After the Other . . ."

"Homesteaders" were farm families who tried to scrape out a living on the semi-arid plains with the aid of government grants of land. For most of these brave souls, insufficient water, grasshoppers, various forms of blight, winter storms, deteriorating health, and fluctuating markets made the job impossible. Others stuck in spite of it all. One such was Emma Mitchell New, whose starkly simple memoir, a testament to raw determination, was dictated near the end of her life.

We landed in Russell [on the prairie of central Kansas] forepart of December, 1877, with our car-load of goods, consisting of a few household goods, team of horses, a few chickens, a wagon and plow, enough lumber to build a small house, and a fairly good supply of provisions. We boarded at a hotel for two weeks and by that time the house was finished enough that we could move in out on a claim two miles northwest of Russell. Many a homesick day I saw, many a tear was shed. I couldn't bear to go to the window and look out. All I could see everywhere was prairie and not a house to be seen. We had been there about three months when my two little children, a boy and a girl, came rushing into the house so excited, for they saw a woman coming over the hill toward the house. It proved to be a neighbor that lived a mile and a half from us. The hill between us had obscured their little dugout. We felt so happy to know that we had a neighbor. I called on them one day, and they insisted on bringing me home with an ox team and buckboard.

Springtime came, my husband broke a piece of ground for a garden, took the sod off and built a fence around the garden, and then replowed the soil. I thought I was going to have a good garden, but the rain failed to come and we got nothing. In the meantime we were hunting water and hauling it in barrels. We dug a deep well and got nothing. Many a time I walked a

Ada McColl on the Prairie near Lakin, Kansas. 1893. Photograph. The Kansas State Historical Society, Topeka.

quarter of a mile down into a deep draw with pails and carried water to wash with. Also used to walk to town and back, making four miles, to get a little sewing to do from the hotel girls I got acquainted with.

My husband broke prairie as fast as he could with the old team. One time he broke a fire guard around some grass that was quite tall and then set fire to it. The wind carried the sparks across the guards and set the prairie on fire. We worked hard to put it out to save our home and buildings, until we were completely exhausted. And many a time afterward I fought fires until I was all in, for we had so many in those days from the quarter [their claim].

Years came along one after the other and also droughts. Times looked perilous to us. We finally got a cow, which helped us to live. Then there came along the Indian scare. All the people around about flocked to town for safety except me. I was all alone with my two children and knew nothing of it, as my husband was a good many miles from home trying to earn a little something. He worked out many a day for fifty cents and was glad to get it. Grasshoppers were very plentiful in those days. At times, swarms of them would shade the sun.

Our house was very poor, so my husband in a few spare minutes would saw soft rocks into bricks and lay them between the studding to make it firm, as the Kansas wind rocked it so bad. I helped carry all the bricks. And when he was sawing I would take the team and go to the field and walk behind a drag all the time I could get from my house work. Finally a baby boy came to us and we toiled along for almost a year. We picked up and burned "cow chips" for fuel.

A neighbor ranchman decided to leave, so we went on his place, took care of the stock, and made better on shares. We were doing fairly well when in two years he came back and wanted his place again. So we moved back on the claim. We stayed there a while with no water and lived on corn meal for nearly a year. My husband got a chance to put papers on a discarded timber claim, so we went ahead again with hearts brave and true to make another home. Traded our first claim for a one-room house and sort of a summer kitchen. This we moved out to our claim. We had a fair-sized granary on our first claim. We moved it out and put them together, making quite a home for us. The granary was made into a living room and two bedrooms. This claim was down in a big draw and we put the buildings beside a small stream where there were nice springs of water. We toiled on, not losing heart, and soon got us some milk cows and started a dairy.

Hardships and trials came along in their turn. Got a young team to deliver our milk to town. A baby girl came to us, making the second that came to us in Kansas without doctor or nurses and practically no help except the two older children.

We got along very well when a terrible storm and cloudburst came upon us and we lost almost everything, except the cows and an old team in the pasture. It came on the twenty-third of July. We had a nice cow barn put up and that day they put up a stack of millet the whole length of the barn. It commenced to rain in the afternoon, but in due time we started the children to town with the milk. It was a general downpour and the creeks were commencing to rise. So my husband started out to meet the children and get them home in safety. My husband said to the children, "We will be good to the ponies tonight and put them in the cow barn and give them some nice millet." They hadn't been in the house very long before we discovered our cellar was full of water from the outside door, and the well curb and toilet were gone.

The creek was up to the house and still pouring down. My husband investigated and found that the underpinning of the house was going and that we had to get out. We took a lantern and matches and some blankets, and started for the side hills. When we opened the door to get out, the water came up to our necks. We had a struggle to get out and I can't tell to this day how we ever made it, but the Lord must have been with us. My husband carried the baby girl in his arms as high as his head. We soon got out of the deepest water, as there was a turn in the creek. We went by way of the horse stable and found we would be safe in it. Still the water was up and it was pitch dark. The matches were wet, so we couldn't light the lantern.

We stayed there until the storm abated and the water went down. Then we started out to see if we had a home left and to our delight, even in such a mess, we found it still standing. It was still dark and we couldn't see what havoc the storm had made for us. We found some dry matches and lit the lamp. Such a deplorable sight words can't express. We couldn't shut the door when we left the house, so the kitchen was full of rubbish and everything had been swimming in the high water. Many things were upside down. The water didn't get into the other rooms so badly, but when the water went down there was an inch of mud all over the carpets and floors.

When daylight came it was a sad sight to behold. Our cow barn and ponies were swept away, also our stack of millet. Practically everything we had was gone or ruined: machinery, wagons, and nice garden. Back of the house was a nice patch of potatoes, but it washed them out clean and the soil as far as was ever plowed. Our ponies washed down stream about sixteen miles to the Saline River before lodging. When they were found, they were still tied to the same ridge pole. We did not have much to eat for breakfast, as all our food and groceries were

The Harvey Andrews Family at the grave of their child, Willie, on their farm near New Helena and Victoria Creek, Nebraska. Photograph. Nebraska State Historical Society, Lincoln. Solomon D. Butcher Collection.

in a cupboard in the kitchen and everything was ruined in the cellar. Even the water was not fit to drink. One of our good neighbors rallied to our relief and by night had us another team of ponies and harness ready to deliver milk when we could get things together again. Two years afterward some of our harnesses were found in the bottom of the creek. This is only a partial list of the flood disasters.

We finally got started again in the dairy business and got more cows. My husband thought if we could get nearer the town with our daily work it would be easier for us. So we rented a pasture close by town and built us a house in the suburbs with the assistance of the Building and Loan Association. We still held our timber claim and raised feed for the dairy.

Thus, we got along very well until our milk business wasn't so profitable, as the price of cows went down and so many bought cows, some only paying fifteen dollars for one. I worked so hard to get along. I did my share of the milking, took in washing, and did everything I could to earn a cent. Hard work brought us a seven-months baby boy, who lived only fourteen days. Still we toiled on. I worked from five in the morning until ten at night without ceasing.

After two years another baby boy came to us. About this time my husband got a chance to go out on a big ranch as foreman, so we decided to rent our house and sell part of the cows. We got along very well and after eighteen months another baby boy came to us. I nearly lost my life then but the Good Father spared me to do farther work in the new country and arise by my children. Toiled on for some time and then my husband got a bigger raise in his salary from another ranchman still farther away, so we decided to move again. He was to take charge the first of April, so he engaged teams to move all at once.

The day came to move and a big snow storm was raging, so only one team came. We loaded our stove and just enough things to carry us over the night, intending to move the rest the next day. It cleared off in the night and the teams came, but there was nothing to move, as the house was burned down and, as one would suppose, everything in it. It was a great loss to us, for we had got a fairly good start again. We lost everything in the cellar, meat, lard, potatoes, fruit, and all of our milk fixtures, as we still had cows. Most of our clothing and all of our best things went. We never understood how the fire started but it wasn't any carelessness of ours.

It seemed luck was against us but we had faith and pushed ahead. My husband and oldest son and daughter worked at everything they could find to do, dug deep wells, etc., I as usual doing my part with a big family to earn a few cents. Two years more and another baby boy came to us, making six boys and two girls. We worked on for another year and then decided to move back to the old timber claim, which we still held. We had a few cows yet to start with and how happy I was to get back there once again, resolving I would never move again unless retiring.

It would be almost impossible to tell you of the hardships we went through with a big family. My oldest girl got married soon after moving. Farming had commenced to get better, as the country was more improved. Got into stock and more cows, made lots of butter, getting fifteen cents a pound. We still burnt cow chips to help along. As the children grew older I went out nursing, getting one dollar a day and doing the housework besides.

Our two oldest boys got married, leaving us with the three younger. We bought some more land and kept on so doing until we owned nearly a section. When our baby boy was within a few days of eighteen he was taken from us. Heartbroken, we kept on. In two years our other daughter was married, leaving us with two boys. The following year one of the boys decided to get married, so we let him have the ranch to work and we retired, moving back to town in our little house. The one boy left made his home with us. My aged mother came to live with us. In three years my husband was stricken with heart trouble and died instantly in December. The following month Mother passed away, and in March the last son got married and I was left all alone.

These sad events covered forty years of pioneer life. As I am writing this, ten years later, I am within a few days of seventy-seven years, a very feeble old woman, yet thankful for all the blessings I have had.

HAMLIN GARLAND

From *A Son of the Middle Border*
"Our First Winter on the Prairie"

The homesteader's life was marked by everlasting work and long periods of solitude. But necessary trips to the nearest town for supplies, wintertime school for the children, and the occasional revival meeting did manage to provide at least some sense of community. All of this was brilliantly condensed into a single chapter, excerpted here, from Hamlin Garland's account of his own life in Dakota Territory, A Son of the Middle Border *(1914).*

One night as we were all seated around the kerosene lamp my father said, "Well, Belle, I suppose we'll have to take these young ones down to town and fit 'em out for school." These words so calmly uttered filled our minds with visions of new boots, new caps and new books, and though we went obediently to bed we hardly slept, so excited were we, and at breakfast next morning not one of us could think of food. All our desires converged upon the wondrous expedition—our first visit to town.

Our only carriage was still the lumber wagon but it had now two spring seats, one for father, mother and Jessie, and one for Harriet, Frank and myself. No one else had anything better, hence we had no sense of being poorly out-fitted. We drove away across the frosty prairie toward Osage—moderately comfortable and perfectly happy.

Osage was only a little town, a village of perhaps twelve hundred inhabitants, but to me as we drove down its Main Street, it was almost as impressive as LaCrosse had been. Frank clung close to father, and mother led Jessie, leaving Harriet and me to stumble over nail-kegs and dodge whiffle trees what time our eyes absorbed jars of pink and white candy, and sought out boots and buckskin mittens. Whenever Harriet spoke she whispered, and we pointed at each shining object with cautious care.—Oh! the marvelous exotic smells! Odors of salt codfish and spices, calico and kerosene, apples and ginger-snaps mingle in my mind as I write.

Each of us soon carried a candy marble in his or her cheek (as a chipmunk carries a nut) and Frank and I stood like sturdy hitching posts whilst the storekeeper with heavy hands screwed cotton-plush caps upon our heads,—but the most exciting moment, the crowning joy of the day, came with the buying of our new boots.—If only father had not insisted on our taking those which were a size too large for us!

They were real boots. No one but a Congressman wore "gaiters" in those days. War fashions still dominated the shoe-shops, and high-topped cavalry boots were all but universal. They were kept in boxes under the counter or ranged in rows on a shelf and were of all weights and degrees of fineness. The ones I selected had red tops with a golden moon in the center but my brother's taste ran to blue tops decorated with a golden flag. Oh! that deliciously oily *new* smell. My heart glowed every time I looked at mine. I was especially pleased because they did *not* have copper toes. Copper toes belonged to little boys. A youth who had plowed seventy acres of land could not reasonably be expected to dress like a child.—How smooth and delightfully stiff they felt on my feet.

Then came our new books, a McGuffey reader, a Mitchell geography, a Ray's arithmetic, and a slate. The books had a delightful new smell also, and there was singular charm in the smooth surface of the unmarked slates. I was eager to carve my name in the frame. At last with our treasures under the seat (so near that we could feel them), with our slates and books in our laps we jolted home, dreaming of school and snow. To wade in the drifts with our fine high-topped boots was now our desire.

It is strange but I cannot recall how my mother looked on this trip. Even my father's image is faint and vague (I remember only his keen eagle-gray terrifying eyes), but I can see every acre of that rented farm. I can tell you exactly how the house looked. It was an unpainted square cottage and stood bare on the sod at the edge of Dry Run ravine. It had a small lean-to on the eastern side and a sitting room and bedroom below. Overhead was a low unplastered chamber in which we children slept. As it grew too cold to use the summer kitchen we cooked, ate and lived in the square room which occupied the entire front of the two story upright, and which was, I suppose, sixteen feet square. As our attic was warmed only by the stove-pipe, we older children of a frosty morning made extremely simple and hurried toilets. On very cold days we hurried down stairs to dress beside the kitchen fire.

Our furniture was of the rudest sort. I cannot recall a single piece in our house or in our neighbors' houses that had either beauty or distinction. It was all cheap and worn, for this was the middle border, and nearly all our neighbors had moved as we had done in covered wagons. Farms were new, houses were mere shanties, and money was scarce. "War times" and "war prices" were only just beginning to change. Our clothing was all cheap and ill fitting. The women and children wore home-made "cotton flannel" underclothing for the most part, and the men wore rough, ready-made suits over which they drew brown denim blouses or overalls to keep them clean.

Father owned a fine buffalo overcoat (so much of his song's promise was redeemed) and we possessed two buffalo robes for use in our winter sleigh, but mother had only a sad coat and a woolen shawl. How she kept warm I cannot now understand—I think she stayed at home on cold days.

All of the boys wore long trousers, and even my eight year old brother looked like a miniature man with his full-length overalls, high-topped boots and real suspenders. As for me I carried a bandanna in my hip pocket and walked with determined masculine stride.

My mother, like all her brothers and sisters, was musical and played the violin—or fiddle, as we called it,—and I have many dear remembrances of her playing. *Napoleon's March, Money Musk, The Devil's Dream* and half-a-dozen other simple tunes made up her repertoire. It was very crude music of course but it added to the love and admiration in which her children always held her. Also in some way we had fallen heir to a Prince melodeon—one that had belonged to the McClintocks, but only my sister played on that.

Once at a dance in neighbor Button's house, mother took the "dare" of the fiddler and with shy smile played *The Fisher's Hornpipe* or some other simple melody and was mightily cheered at the close of it, a brief performance which she refused to repeat. Afterward she and my father danced and this seemed a very wonderful performance, for to us they were "old"— far past such frolicking, although he was but forty and she thirty-one!

At this dance I heard, for the first time, the local professional fiddler, old Daddy Fairbanks, as quaint a character as ever entered fiction, for he was not only butcher and horse doctor but a renowned musician as well. Tall, gaunt and sandy, with enormous nose and sparse projecting teeth, he was to me the most enthralling figure at this dance and his queer "Calls" and his "York State" accent filled us all with delight. "*Ally* man left," "Chassay *by* your pardners," "Dozy-*do*" were some of the phrases he used as he played *Honest John* and *Haste to the Wedding*. At times he sang his calls in high nasal chant, "*First* lady lead to the *right,* deedle, deedle dum-dum—*gent* foller after—dally-deedle-do-do—*three* hands round"—and everybody laughed with frank enjoyment of his words and action.

It was a joy to watch him "start the set." With fiddle under his chin he took his seat in a big chair on the kitchen table in order to command the floor. "Farm on, farm on!" he called disgustedly. "Lively now!" and then, when all the couples were in position, with one mighty No. 14 boot uplifted, with bow laid to strings he snarled, "Already—GELANG!" and with a thundering crash his foot came down, "Honors TEW your pardners—right and left FOUR!" And the dance was on!

I suspect his fiddlin' was not even "middlin'," but he beat time fairly well and kept the dancers somewhere near to rhythm, and so when his ragged old cap went round he often got a handful of quarters for his toil. He always ate two suppers, one at the beginning of the party and another at the end. He had a high respect for the skill of my Uncle David and was grateful to him and other better musicians for their noninterference with his professional engagements.

CHARLES REDMOND.
Frontier Classroom.
Photograph. Denver
Public Library. Western
History Department.

The school-house which was to be the center of our social life stood on the bare prairie about a mile to the southwest and like thousands of other similar buildings in the west, had not a leaf to shade it in summer nor a branch to break the winds of savage winter. "There's been a good deal of talk about setting out a wind-break," neighbor Button explained to us, "but nothing has as yet been done." It was merely a square pine box painted a glaring white on the outside and a desolate drab within; at least drab was the original color, but the benches were mainly so greasy and hacked that original intentions were obscured. It had two doors on the eastern end and three windows on each side.

A long square stove (standing on slender legs in a puddle of bricks), a wooden chair, and a rude table in one corner, for the use of the teacher, completed the movable furniture. The walls were roughly plastered and the windows had no curtains.

It was a barren temple of the arts even to the residents of Dry Run, and Harriet and I, stealing across the prairie one Sunday morning to look in, came away vaguely depressed. We were fond of school and never missed a day if we could help it, but this neighborhood center seemed small and bleak and poor.

With what fear, what excitement we approached the door on that first day, I can only faintly indicate. All the scholars were strange to me except Albert and Cyrus Button, and I was prepared for rough treatment. However, the experience was not so harsh as I had feared. True, Rangely Field did throw me down and wash my face in snow, and Jack Sweet tripped me up once or twice, but I bore these indignities with such grace and could command, and soon made a place for myself among the boys.

Burton Babcock was my seat-mate, and at once became my chum. You will hear much of him in this chronicle. He was two years older than I and though pale and slim was unusually swift and strong for his age. He was a silent lad, curiously timid in his classes and not at ease with his teachers.

I cannot recover much of that first winter of school. It was not an experience to remember for its charm. Not one line of grace, not one touch of color relieved the room's bare walls or softened its harsh windows. Perhaps this very barrenness gave to the poetry in our readers an appeal that seems magical, certainly it threw over the faces of Frances Babcock and Mary

COLORPLATE 75

HENRY KELLER. *Pueblo Stop*. Oil on canvas. 22 x 27 in. The Harmsen Collection.

COLORPLATE 78

JAMES BAMA. *Bill Smith—Number One*. 1974. Oil on canvas. 23 ¹/₂ x 24 in. National Cowboy Hall of Fame and Western Heritage Center, Oklahoma City, Oklahoma. © James Bama/VAGA, New York 1994.

COLORPLATE 76 (top, opposite page)

TOM PALMORE. *Texas Jack*. Acrylic on canvas. 72 x 108 in. Courtesy Elaine Horwitch Galleries, Scottsdale, Arizona.

COLORPLATE 77 (bottom, opposite page)

TOM PALMORE. *Great American Buffalo*. 1980. Acrylic on canvas. 72 x 96 in. Courtesy Elaine Horwitch Galleries, Scottsdale, Arizona.

COLORPLATE 79 (following spread)

BILL ANTON. *Crossing Sun Canyon Wash*. 1992. Oil on masonite. 24 x 36 in. Private collection. Courtesy of the artist.

COLORPLATE 81

HUBERT SHUPTRINE. *Old Texan II*. 1984. Egg tempera on panel. 24 x 18 in. Courtesy of the artist.

COLORPLATE 80 (opposite page)

ROBERT HENRI. *Portrait of Dieguito Roybal of San Ildefonso, New Mexico*. 1916. Oil on canvas. 65 3/8 x 40 7/16 in. Collection of the Museum of Fine Arts, Museum of New Mexico, Santa Fe. Gift of the artist, 1916.

COLORPLATE 82

ANDREW DASBURG. *Portrait of a Cowboy*. 1928. Oil on canvas. 30 x 25 in. Courtesy of The Anschutz Collection, Denver, Colorado.

Abbie Gammons a lovelier halo.—They were "the big girls" of the school, that is to say, they were seventeen or eighteen years old,—and Frances was the special terror of the teacher, a pale and studious pigeon-toed young man who was preparing for college.

In spite of the cold, the boys played open air games all winter. "Dog and Deer," "Dare Gool" and "Fox and Geese" were our favorite diversions, and the wonder is that we did not all die of pneumonia, for we battled so furiously during each recess that we often came in wet with perspiration and coughing so hard that for several minutes recitations were quite impossible.—But we were a hardy lot and none of us seemed the worse for our colds.

There was not much chivalry in the school—quite the contrary, for it was dominated by two or three big rough boys and the rest of us took our tone from them. To protect a girl, to shield her from remark or indignity required a good deal of bravery and few of us were strong enough to do it. Girls were foolish, ridiculous creatures, set apart to be laughed at or preyed upon at will. To shame them was a great joke.—How far I shared in these barbarities I cannot say but that I did share in them I know, for I had very little to do with my sister Harriet after crossing the school-house yard. She kept to her tribe as I to mine.

This winter was made memorable also by a "revival" which came over the district with sudden fury. It began late in the winter—fortunately, for it ended all dancing and merry-making for the time. It silenced Daddy Fairbanks' fiddle and subdued my mother's glorious voice to a wail. A cloud of puritanical gloom settled upon almost every household. Youth and love became furtive and hypocritic.

The evangelist, one of the old-fashioned shouting, hysterical, ungrammatical, gasping sort, took charge of the services, and in his exhortations phrases descriptive of lakes of burning brimstone and ages of endless torment abounded. Some of the figures of speech and violent gestures of the man still linger in my mind, but I will not set them down on paper. They are too dreadful to perpetuate. At times he roared with such power that he could have been heard for half a mile.

And yet we went, night by night, mother, father, Jessie, all of us. It was our theater. Some of the roughest characters in the neighborhood rose and professed repentance, for a season, even old Barton, the profanest man in the township, experienced a "change of heart."

We all enjoyed the singing, and joined most lustily in the tunes. Even little Jessie learned to sing *Heavenly Wings, There is a Fountain filled with Blood,* and *Old Hundred.*

As I peer back into that crowded little school-room, smothering hot and reeking with lamp smoke, and recall the half-lit, familiar faces of the congregation, it all has the quality of a vision, something experienced in another world. The preacher, leaping, sweating, roaring till the windows rattle, the mothers with sleeping babes in their arms, the sweet, strained faces of the girls, the immobile wondering men, are spectral shadows, figures encountered in the phantasmagoria of disordered sleep.

WILLA CATHER

From *O Pioneers!*

Dark Days

In the following vignette from O Pioneers! *(1913), Willa Cather's classic novel of farming life in the endless flat sweep of Nebraska before the turn of the century, three of the central characters begin the return home after the weekly trip to town. With brevity and grace, Cather evokes both the immensity of the land and the lonely courage it took to survive in it.*

Widvey Farm, North of Round Valley in Canyon, Custer County, Nebraska. c. 1887–91. Photograph. Nebraska State Historical Society, Lincoln. Solomon D. Butcher Collection.

Although it was only four o'clock, the winter day was fading. The road led southwest, toward the streak of pale, watery light that glimmered in the leaden sky. The light fell upon the two sad young faces that were turned mutely toward it: upon the eyes of the girl, who seemed to be looking with such anguished perplexity into the future; upon the sombre eyes of the boy, who seemed already to be looking into the past. The little town behind them had vanished as if it had never been, had fallen behind the swell of the prairie, and the stern frozen country received them into its bosom. The homesteads were few and far apart; here and there a windmill gaunt against the sky, a sod house crouching in a hollow. But the great fact was the land itself, which seemed to overwhelm the little beginnings of human society that struggled in its sombre wastes. It was from facing this vast hardness that the boy's mouth had become so bitter; because he felt that men were too weak to make any mark here, that the land wanted to be let alone, to preserve its own fierce strength, its peculiar, savage kind of beauty, its uninterrupted mournfulness.

The wagon jolted along over the frozen road. The two friends had less to say to each other than usual, as if the cold had somehow penetrated to their hearts.

"Did Lou and Oscar go to the Blue to cut wood to-day?" Carl asked.

"Yes. I'm almost sorry I let them go, it's turned so cold. But mother frets if the wood gets low." She stopped and put her hand to her forehead, brushing back her hair. "I don't know what is to become of us, Carl, if father has to die. I don't dare to think about it. I wish we could all go with him and let the grass grow back over everything."

Carl made no reply. Just ahead of them was the Norwegian graveyard, where the grass had, indeed, grown back over everything, shaggy and red, hiding even the wire fence. Carl realized that he was not a very helpful companion, but there was nothing he could say.

"Of course," Alexandra went on, steadying her voice a little, "the boys are strong and work hard, but we've always depended so on father that I don't see how we can go ahead. I almost feel as if there were nothing to go ahead for."

"Does your father know?"

"Yes, I think he does. He lies and counts on his fingers all day. I think he is trying to count up what he is leaving for us. It's a comfort to him that my chickens are laying right on through the cold weather and bringing in a little money. I wish we could keep his mind off such things, but I don't have much time to be with him now."

"I wonder if he'd like to have me bring my magic lantern over some evening?"

Alexandra turned her face toward him. "Oh, Carl! Have you got it?"

"Yes. It's back there in the straw. Didn't you notice the box I was carrying? I tried it all morning in the drug-store cellar, and it worked ever so well, makes fine big pictures."

"What are they about?"

"Oh, hunting pictures in Germany, and Robinson Crusoe and funny pictures about cannibals. I'm going to paint some slides for it on glass, out of the Hans Anderson book."

Alexandra seemed actually cheered. There is often a good deal of the child left in people who have had to grow up too soon. "Do bring it over, Carl. I can hardly wait to see it, and I'm sure it will please father. Are the pictures colored? Then I know he'll like them. He likes the calendars I get him in town. I wish I could get more. You must leave me here, must n't you? It's been nice to have company."

Carl stopped the horses and looked dubiously up at the black sky. "It's pretty dark. Of course the horses will take you home, but I think I'd better light your lantern, in case you should need it."

He gave her the reins and climbed back into the wagon-box, where he crouched down and made a tent of his overcoat. After a dozen trials he succeeded in lighting the lantern, which he placed in front of Alexandra, half covering it with a blanket so that the light would not shine in her eyes. "Now, wait until I find my box. Yes, here it is. Good-night, Alexandra. Try not to worry." Carl sprang to the ground and ran off across the fields toward the Linstrum homestead. "Hoo, hoo-o-o-o!" he called back as he disappeared over a ridge and dropped into a sand gully. The wind answered him like an echo, "Hoo, hoo-o-o-o-o-o!" Alexandra drove off alone. The rattle of her wagon was lost in the howling of the wind, but her lantern, held firmly between her feet, made a moving point of light along the highway, going deeper and deeper into the dark country.

Mari Sandoz

From *Old Jules*

"Snakebite"

Extraordinary things were demanded of children on the homesteader's frontier. Work, always, often work that no child should have been required to perform, but much else, too, including levels of bravery and fortitude that would have challenged the strongest adult. Consider this tale from Old Jules *(1935), Mari Sandoz's powerful memoir of her father and the raw necessities of life along the Niobrara River in Nebraska.*

When the first fires of autumn ran yellow through the low places, Marie gripped the unaccustomed lines over the temperamental buckskins, while Jules swung the leather-lashed willow whip. With a jerk of the wagon they were off into the hills, the land of deep-grassed valleys, blue lakes: home to Jules; the habitation of gray wolves, cattlemen, and rattlesnakes to the girl.

All forenoon heat waves and low chophills undulated and blurred into a rhythmic pattern of mauve and tans before them. Not even a saddle horse stirred the ragweed dust of the trail. Game was scarce. They saw panting gray lizards, a rabbit or two, a grouse against the whitish sky far away, a rattlesnake slide into a prairie-dog hole. That was all.

At the gates Marie climbed over the wheel and strained at the stick or jumped on the wires to loosen them. Between fences Jules smoked and sang and talked of the first time he saw the country, of the deer and the antelope he shot in the buckbrush patching the last endings of the long, dry valleys, and of that happy time before his leg was broken. Then for a mile or two he was silent and there was only the whir of grasshoppers in the limp sunflowers along the trail,

Old Jules. (Jules Sandoz). Photograph. Nebraska State Historical Society, Omaha.

the creak of harness, and the grind of sand in the wheels. Finally he talked again—of the man and the Winchester.

"Now I got a better gun—more improved." He spit emphatically into the sand, but to-day even that masculine bolster of confidence failed him. "I got a fine rifle, but it don't make a show like his," he admitted.

Marie slapped the lines, not daring to answer.

They passed an occasional dugout against a hill, a little soddy or an old cattleman claim shack, dull gray and alone, tawny grass growing in the doorway and about the piece of pipe sticking up where Jules said there was no water, only a few feet of rusty iron driven into the ground. A fraud.

And often his long fingers pointed across the prairie and obediently Marie pulled the buckskins towards two dim, yellowish streaks or through a pass where there was no track at all in the rippled sand. They stopped at one of the Modisett mills, at the foot of Deer Hill. Marie slipped the bits from the horses' mouths and let them graze while they ate from the leather-hinged grub box and drank the clear cold water gushing night and day from the two-inch pipe into the low stock tanks. Then they went on. The hills grew higher; the valleys harder, resounding under the ponies' hoofs. Soddies were more frequent, with here and there a long strip of gray breaking, a few anæmic sunflowers pushing up between the sods.

Jules had kept his filing from Mary as long as he could, but it slipped out one evening when he was particularly pleased with his supper—quail, with potatoes fried into golden sticks, the last cauliflower of the winter creamed and specked with nutmeg, watercress salad, muffins, plum jam, coffee, and canned cherries with juice bright as deer's blood on fresh snow. By golly, it was fine. And it would be even finer on the new place.

Mary threw up her knotted hands and rolled her faded blue eyes back. Now, at last, he had gone crazy. The children drew away into the shadows, their voices buzzing softly. Got to live in the sandhills—where the gray wolves lived, and the cattlemen, the rattlesnakes.

But Jules recovered in a minute and went on planning his new community grandly as in 1884. During the summer he helped circulate a petition for a school district, one of the many cut from the cattle range, and called a preliminary meeting for the middle of September. "Let Marie go with you this time, instead of the boys," Mary suggested. They could stay overnight with Pete, Jules's cousin, married to Elise, Ferdinand's first wife. "Look good and see how it is for fuel and a garden place," Mary instructed her. "And don't get a headache from Papa's scolding." The girl shook her head. He told her many fine stories when the others were n't around.

By the time they got to the half-soddy, half-frame house on Pete's Kinkaid it was filled with prairie-gaunted, sun-bronzed Kinkaiders. Several slightly gray girl-women—"Boston old maids," Jules dubbed them — sat primly on improvised benches, squeezed in between women nursing babies and men chewing tobacco. Few of the men carried guns, although Pete had a rifle hung against the wall. Someone told about a celebration given at the Spade ranch, with everything free for the settlers, including ice cream.

"They shore steps around like an old Indian pony tangled in bob wire since the government's took a hand," a squint-eyed boomer from Oklahoma said.

The meeting went well. Five months of school in a work-donated soddy. Jules refused the directorship. Too damn busy.

The next morning they drove to the new claim, bumping over trackless bunch-grass knolls and finally rattling down a steep hill into a high valley with a tiny yellow pine shack leaning against the slope. "Your papa's new home," Jules said grandly, as though it were the mansion of a cattle king.

The buckskins snorted and fidgeted about approaching. "Hold the ponies; I'll walk over. I just want to see what the settlers stole from me now."

Before Marie had the nervous team quieted he came running back, bobbing grotesquely in his limp, his mouth to the back of his hand.

"Bit by a rattler under the house where I hide my hammer."

The words came in jerks between spittings of clear saliva. Groping frantically in his pocket, Jules pushed his knife into the girl's hands, jerked it away almost before she could open it, and slashed at the purplish swelling rising about two pinpricks. The dull blade sank into the flesh, puffy as dough, but it did not even cut the skin. With a groan he flung the knife from him and sucked fiercely.

Then his eyes turned habitually to his companions in danger — his weapons. He grasped the pump gun by the barrel. "Hold the team!" he commanded, slapping his palm down on the rim of the hind wheel, the muzzle against the swelling, holding the gun steady between his body and the wagon bed. A shot echoed from the hills. The buckskins plunged forward. The girl fell off the seat, but clung to the lines. Bracing her feet against the dashboard, she pulled and jerked until the ponies slowed to a short lope, to a trot. When she finally turned them, Jules was limping toward her, shaking great clots of black blood from the back of his hand.

Tying the lines about her waist, Marie ripped the blue shirt sleeve and made a handkerchief tourniquet just below the shoulder. Then, gray-faced, Jules lay down in the wagon bed.

"Drive for Pete's, and drive like hell!"

Too terrified to ask the direction, the girl swung the whip over the ponies, giving them their heads. They sprang out; her sunbonnet flew off; the board seat went next, and behind her the father bounced like a heavy bedroll as the wheels bumped over the bunch grass.

Foam from the ponies' mouths hit cold against the girl's cheek. With her feet wide apart she clung to the lines as they tore down a long hill and across a vacant valley. No house, no road, not even an animal. Another valley, and still nothing. Marie was sure she was lost.

Then the low house of Pete's swung around a hill towards her and a man came running out to stop what he considered just another of the buckskins' runaways.

With his wife he helped Jules into the house and ran to the corral for a horse and was gone to John Strasburger's homestead for whiskey. Marie stood inside the door and looked at her father's swelling arm, the black-crusted wound on the purple hand. He was still; his face like plaster, his breath rasping. She twisted her hand into her apron and remembered that John

Jules Sandoz and his wife Mary on the Sandoz Ranch, 1926. Photograph. Nebraska State Historical Society, Omaha.

Strasburger was temperance. He wouldn't have anything. Anyway, she had heard of a sheepherder who died from snakebite while dead drunk. This was September, the worst month.

By the time Pete came back with about an inch of brown liquid in a tall bottle, Jules's arm was purple to the shoulder. He drank all the whiskey, choking, and sank back. "It's not enough," he mumbled, hopelessly. "Get me home, Marie, I want to die on the Running Water."

Obediently she ran to the buckskins, but her legs were like dead water. She didn't remember the road; the gates were hard; the ponies would run away. Suddenly she couldn't stand it and, pushing her face between the spokes of a wheel, she cried as she had never cried before. The buckskin mare looked back, pricking her ears sharp. Then she went to sleep again in the harness.

In a moment Pete swung his buggy up to the door, called to Marie to hold the restive horses while he brought Jules out. Then he dropped her into the buggy bed at her father's feet, they shot through the yard gate, and were on their way home.

After four or five miles of sand the wild young team slowed, their lathered sides heaving. Jules's face was sunken into his beard, his eyes closed. Now and then he mumbled — of the sheepmen, the cattlemen, all who had worked against him. They ran through his head like dark waves of cattle sweeping down the lane from the Flats to the river. Then he seemed to sleep a little, talking as from a dream of Neuchâtel and Zurich and Rosalie. And as he dozed he swayed with the shaking buggy.

Marie reached her arm around his knees and held to the seat to keep him from sliding forward. Once he looked down on her.

"Swelling's spreading into the lungs," he panted, thickly. Pete whipped the jaded team into an unbelievably slow run.

"If he kills his team getting me home tell Mama to pay for them."

Marie pulled her skirt up to her face. "Your mama's a good woman," he went on, the breath wheezing from his beard. "You'll get like her. Marry a farmer and help build up the country."

The girl began to cry aloud. Pete touched her shoulder.

"Steady. We may need you to drive before this day is gone."

Biting the gingham of her skirt, she calmed herself. After all, they had faced bad times before, the time John Peters almost got shot. Jules deep in the hills when Baby Flora was born. The day when the killer stopped before the door.

And still the wheels spun yellow sand. Jules didn't answer any more. Pete stopped at two claim shacks, but no one had anything. No whiskey, no potassium permanganate. Nothing. Frightened faces looked after them as they hurried on; women clutched their children to their flat chests.

They stopped a moment at Surbers' to say good-bye. Henri was not there. It was too bad, his old friend . . .

Then at last they were in sight of the blue ribbon of the Niobrara. Pete whipped up the thin-flanked, lathered team and in a weary, flapping trot they stumbled into the home yard.

"Ah, now, you let the horses run away!" Mary scolded as she ran out. But when she understood she sent Marie flying on cramped legs into the house for a cup of whiskey, a big cup. Jules shot it into his mouth. Before they had him in the house she was on her way to Charley Sears's, for of course the fence-line telephone was out of order. She could make the mile trip in less time than Pete's horses, already down in the harness in the yard.

Dropping into a dogtrot previous emergencies had taught her she could hold for the mile, she finally reached the man's door, gasped out her need to the kindly bachelor, and was sick over his doorstep while he called Hay Springs.

Long after dark she was awakened by the boys. They were lined up beside her bed, poking her and whispering, "The doctor's come — in a red automobile!"

A funny, short man came in, chased the boys out and pushed her back. Old Jules would be all right, — cast-iron constitution, — but he'd have been gone long before this from the deadly September venom if he hadn't shot it off.

In a week Jules, still pale, limped through the orchard admiring his plum trees, but it was months before he could use the two middle fingers of his left hand. Tendons heal slowly.

MILTON SHATRAW

From *Thrashin' Time*

There was little that one would choose to call romantic about wheat-ranching on the High Plains of Montana before World War I, but every year October brought a measure of high drama. This moment belonged to a great machine of the era—the horse-powered thresher— and its excitement is recalled in this selection from Milton Shatraw's Thrashin' Time: Memories of a Montana Boyhood *(1970).*

Against my father's orders, my sister Iris and I had been swinging each other on the big pole-gate that opened into the ranch yard. We were sitting now on the top bar of the gate, resting.

"Look! Look!" Iris was pointing. Sure enough there was a little single-seated, high-wheeled car gingerly working its way along the deep-rutted road leading down from the bench across the valley.

"It's Gene Leach's automobile."

"Naw. Can't you see it's red? Leach's is blue. I bet it's the J.I.C. man."

In northwest Montana automobiles and our 1908 brand of roads had as little as possible to do with each other. So when a car approached, it was a source of great excitement for young and old alike.

"If it *is* the J.I.C. man," Iris said, "he'll stay all night, and we can sit up late and listen to them talk."

But my mind was on the car. "He'll give us a ride," I said, "like the last time. Come on. Let's go tell Ma."

We tumbled off the gate and ran to the house, screaming loud enough for all Teton County to hear, "There's an automobile coming! The J.I.C. man's coming!"

The J.I.C. man was the service representative of the J.I. Case Threshing Machine Company. He came every summer to check over our machine. Last year he had abandoned his usual hired livery rig and appeared in a brand new four-cylinder Reo painted a blinding red, and he had given everyone a breath-taking twenty-mile-an-hour ride down the long lane to the bend in the road and back. Even better than that was the fun of tagging him and my father around all day and listening to them talk "machine." Any kind of machinery had a fascination for me but especially the huge threshing machine, which my father drove from ranch to ranch during two months of the early fall, threshing the ranchers' grain crops.

A couple of weeks ago a large wooden crate of repair parts had arrived by freight from the Case factory. Now Mr. Shaeffer had come to replace the worn parts and check and adjust the whole rig. As they worked, my father, patiently trying to keep me out of the way, invented numerous errands for me to run and finally in desperation turned me loose with a long-spouted oil can and a pail of very black grease. "Oil these bearings here," he directed. "Then put some grease on that big gear." And as a vague afterthought, "Don't get any on your clothes, now."

It was a blissful afternoon. When I tramped into the house with the men for supper, my mother gave me one look and wailed, "My God, Ed! How could you do it? It'll take me a week to clean that kid up."

My father soothed her with his easy laugh and said, winking broadly at Mr. Shaeffer, "He's been a real help, Peg. I don't think we could have finished today without him." Mr. Shaeffer agreed heartily. "Never saw so much grease and oil squirted around in one day in my whole life."

I ate supper in a happy daze.

Before dark we each had our ride. The car, with its soft springs and rubber-shod wheels, carried us along like a magic carpet. Then the men pulled the buggy from the wagon shed and the car took its place because, as Mr. Shaeffer said, "If it gets rained on tonight, it'll take me half the day tomorrow to get it started."

After that, we sat around on the porch listening while the grown folks talked about "back East," where Mr. Shaeffer came from. He told about the St. Louis fair, about cities where automobiles were almost as common as horses (which I could hardly believe), about houses lighted by gas, and people riding around in electric trolley cars. He gave us news of the coming elections, the latest reports on grain and beef prices, and told how Teddy Roosevelt was digging a huge ditch a mile wide and forty miles long across Panama, wherever that was. How I wished that day would never end! I wouldn't have traded it for the Fourth of July, Christmas, and the last day of school—all rolled into one.

Lying just in front of our log house was a forty-acre pasture where we kept the working horses, a few ailing cattle, and our lone milk cow. In the angle where the barbed wire pasture fence met the big roping and branding corral stood the threshing machine. Except for the tarp that covered the cylinder head and gearbox, it stood there exposed to the weather ten months of the year.

Its bright red paint had faded to a dull brick color. In winter the wind-whipped snow drifted deep around it, sifting into its innermost working parts. The spring rains seeped in also, starting pockets of rust and rot. Later still, the blazing summer sun took over and got in its dirty work of flaking the paint, warping the wood, drying up the grease and oil. But when threshing time came, it always worked. Crouching between the high conical grain stacks, gulping down the sheaves with a great roaring and shaking, sending out clouds of dust and chaff, it filled the big sacks with silvery oats and tawny wheat, and piled the clean yellow straw higher and higher. It was a major source of income to my father; for me it provided endless hours of entertainment and pleasure.

Standing bent-kneed on its towering back, I would—with loud cries and man-sized swear words—pretend to drive the four-horse team out through the lane gate and down the valley. Sometimes I would stand on the platform of the power unit, urging on my teams by means of a long whip borrowed without permission from the whipsocket of the buggy. Even on rainy days I could see it from the kitchen window, standing in its bleak surroundings and mud puddles, and I would dream of the excitement of the coming "thrashin'."

The next few weeks after Mr. Shaeffer's visit were mighty busy ones for everybody. My father had to get things in shape before he left on his threshing rounds. The last of the hay crop was cut and stacked, harness and threshing gear put into shape, the range cattle brought up and put on the home ranch. My mother had meat and vegetables to can, new school dresses to make for my sisters, and new shirts for me. Also, there was a horrible amount of housecleaning and clothes-washing to be done before my mother was satisfied. Horrible for me at any rate, for it seemed to me that the grownups spent all their waking hours dreaming up errands and jobs that only an eight-year-old boy could do.

I could hardly wait until the time came when I'd *really* be old enough to join the crew and maybe take Johnny Pfeiffer's place up there cracking the whip over the six teams, getting up each morning to water and feed them, making the last rounds at night. Then, digging a hole in the side of a newly made straw stack and wrapping my blanket around me, I would slide in and pull the straw snug about me and sleep warm and content, the thousand-acre prairie for a bedroom.

*   *   *

By the time the sun had cleared the prairie's rim that Saturday morning, everyone was hard at work. A team of horses dragged the thresher to its place between the grain stacks. The power unit was lined up on a spot carefully measured from the separator so that the sections of the drive shaft would come out just right when the two parts of the machine were joined. Johnny and Joe watered and fed the horses. Carl and my father uncovered the cylinder and set up the feeding tables ready to start. As usual I tried to be everywhere at once and succeeded in getting stepped on and bumped into continually. But all were in good humor, for the sky was clear and the sun was bright. It would be a good threshing day.

We hurried through our workday breakfast of hot oatmeal and cream, ham and eggs with fried potatoes, and platters of biscuit dough fried like pancakes, which my father liked so much he called them "dough gods." Just as we were finishing, the neighbors started to arrive—Uncle George and his hired man, each with a team and hay wagon, followed by Aunt Minnie and their kids in the spring wagon. From the opposite direction came my cousins George and Lily and their gang. Several other neighbors arrived in hay wagons and on horseback. Finally came Torval Johannsen, a middle-aged bachelor who was already a persistent admirer of the new teacher and who spoke a wild jargon of broken English. He drove in with thundering wagon and flying hair, and skidded to a halt in an obvious attempt to attract Grace's attention. Seeing her on the porch, he waved and grinned, showing his huge mouthful of tobacco-stained teeth.

Then he turned to the rest of his audience and asked, "Vell, vy iss ve vaiting? Torval iss come."

"Hi! Hup!" Johnny's voice, competing with a series of loud whipcracks, announced the beginning of the day's work. Eight tons of horseflesh strained again the heavy sweeps, and the big cylinder began slowly, silently to revolve. Then, as the teams stepped up to a faster pace, its silence turned into a low growl, and from there it went up through the scale until it became a steady, singing roar. The sprocket wheels along the sides of the separator eased into motion and picked up speed, their chains tightening, glinting like water in the sun. Deep in the big machine's belly, the sieves began to shiver and shake, and the slats on the straw-carrier rattled and banged. The threshing machine had come to life. When the horses' pace and the whine of the cylinder satisfied my father's critical eye and ear, he nodded his head to the men on the grain stacks, and they began tossing the sheaves to the feeding tables. Here the bandcutters slashed the heavy twine, loosening the stalks that slid off and were gulped down by the ravenous monster.

I watched the whole operation intently, desperately wanting to have some part of it. True, my father had told me to keep the water pails full, and once Carl had allowed me to cut the hank of heavy cord to proper lengths for sewing the filled grain sacks. But mostly it was, "Keep away from the team, Mick, the off horse kicks." And, "Don't fool around that tumbling rod, boy. You'll get your overh'alls caught in a coupling and that'll be the end of you." Everyone was too busy with his own job to find one for me.

Dinner was a welcome break. The men washed up with much snorting and blowing at the wash bench outside the kitchen door, then combed their soaking wet hair with the metal comb hanging by a string beside the mirror nailed to the log wall. With a great deal of joking and scraping of chairs, the places around the kitchen table were quickly filled.

Feeding the "thrashin'" crew had a special significance in those times. A sort of county fair atmosphere prevailed, for it was an opportunity for the women to prove their reputations as cooks. Nothing fancy, just good, well-cooked food and lots of it. Of course, any cook with an ounce of pride belittled her efforts at least enough to ensure a few handsome compliments. My mother, who baked bread fit for the gods, always remarked as she passed the platter that "it hadn't raised just right this time," or that the mouth-watering coconut layer cake she was cutting had "fallen just a bit when one of the kids had slammed the kitchen door." Everyone knew that they were perfection itself—and so did she.

I was sure I would die of hunger before those at the first table were finished. It wasn't hard to persuade the younger men (also dying of hunger) to wait for the second table, for that was the one the schoolteacher presided over. As many of us older kids as there was room for also ate then. The women and smaller fry straggled along behind at a third and final table.

After dinner the men gathered in groups on the porch and down by the bunkhouse, discussing the price of wool and beef on the Chicago market and how much wheat and barley were bringing at the Conrad elevators. By one o'clock everyone was hard at work again.

But the festive atmosphere among the workers was gone now. A biting wind had blown up out of the north, and the sun had disappeared behind darkening clouds. The men cast apprehensive glances at the sky, making doleful predictions of snow before morning, and they increased their efforts. All too soon for me, the last load of grain went through the machine, the neighbors gathered up their families and effects, said their good-byes and left for their homes to batten down for the expected storm; and we were alone again. Another harvest was over.

After supper we all sat in the kitchen talking over the happenings of the day. My father had almost disappeared into a thick cloud of smoke from his favorite calabash pipe. Frank and Leo were puffing contentedly on fresh-rolled Bull Durham cigarettes. I had propositioned each of them hopefully for "just one puff," but my father's disapproving gaze discouraged that, and I retreated to my favorite perch on the freshly filled woodbox. I sat there in the shadows thinking about the day and how splendid it must be to be grown up and actually taking part in the "thrashin'." Finally, seeing the relaxed expression on my father's face, I blurted out, "Pa, next year can't I help *some* on the machine?"

He answered, a bit shortly, "You're too young, Mick. And it's too dangerous."

I persisted, close to tears. "But how'm I ever going to know how to run a thrashin' machine if you *never* let me do anything?"

His eyes softened, and he laid his pipe on the table beside him. "Come here, Mick," he said.

I slid off the woodbox and walked slowly over to him. His strong arm crooked around my shoulders.

"Look," he said, "just as soon as you're old enough I'll let you start doing things. Right now you're learning how. One way to learn anything is to watch. Someday you'll be the best damn thrashin' machine man in the whole state of Montana. Only it's going to be a different kind of machine."

He reached up to the mantel shelf and pulled down a catalog. Opening it, he pointed to a picture of a huge steam traction engine.

"That's what we'll have pretty soon instead of the old horsepower rig," he said proudly. "How'll you like to run that?"

I stared at the brightly colored picture in disbelief. It looked so huge, so complicated, so fascinating—almost too much to grasp.

"Gosh, Pa. You mean it?" Then I remembered. "How soon you going to get it? Won't I ever get to drive the horses?"

He laughed, "Don't worry, Mick. We haven't got it yet."

Later that night I went blissfully off to bed, already feeling my hand on the throttle as I steered the gleaming new rig across the prairie. I could picture myself sitting up there beneath its green metal canopy, its huge red wheels rolling along crushing down the heavy sod, its emblem of a bald eagle on top of the world painted boldly on its side, proclaiming to all that this was a genuine J. I. Case steam engine.

C. C. Blue Thresher Group near Lowell, Nebraska. 1910. Photograph. Nebraska State Historical Society, Lincoln. Solomon D. Butcher Collection.

Helen Ellsberg

"Meanie: The Life and Good Times of a Roman-Nosed Mare"

The stories that westerners tell about their horses tend to be fairly mawkish tales having to do with beauty, nobility, bravery, near-human intelligence, and exemplary loyalty. The relationship was not always sublime, however, as this uproarious memoir demonstrates.

The air was blue for miles around the day Meanie arrived at our Oregon farm and my dad got his first look at her.

Meanie was a buckskin cayuse, and if there ever had been a prize offered for the world's homeliest horse, she'd have won, hoofs down. Her wispy black mane hung irregularly on her ewe neck like a week's wash on a sagging clothesline. She was Roman-nosed, swaybacked, and her tail resembled a moth-eaten whiskbroom.

Pa had traded a mule to Uncle Fletcher for Meanie, sight unseen. He and Fletch had been enemies for years, but they had recently buried the hatchet. It seemed to be buried in a shallow grave, however, for we heard Pa chuckling to himself over what Fletch would say when he discovered some of the mule's less endearing habits. But it seemed now that Fletcher might be doing a little chuckling himself.

"That crook!" Pa stormed. "Saying this horse would outwork anything on the farm. Work! Hah!" he laughed derisively. "That old crowbait."

The horse had endured all Pa's insults with stony indifference, but being called an old crowbait was evidently too much. She suddenly laid back her ears. There was a snap like a closing bear trap as her large, yellow teeth came together so close to Pa's head that he gingerly felt the side of his head to make sure his ear was still there. Then he *was* mad!

"Take that equine monstrosity out of my sight before I get the shotgun!" he bellowed.

My brother and I obediently picked up the buckskin's lead rope and started for the barn. Pa was still rubbing the ear he had almost lost, and as she went by, he delivered a smart kick to her ribs. Swift as a snake, she swung her artillery into position. From long association with horses, Pa instinctively ducked—just in time to miss getting a smart kick in *his* ribs.

The feud was on, and from that day forward, these two carried on a barnyard version of the Hatfields and McCoys.

"Wow!" exclaimed my brother. "She sure is a *meanie*." And that became her name.

One day Pa had to return a sack of oats he had borrowed from a neighbor. The only available horse was Meanie. He grumbled that it would take all day with that old nag, but he hitched her to the spring wagon, loaded the oats, and climbed in. As he picked up the lines, my mother handed him a jar of pickles for the neighbors.

"You be back by noon?" she asked.

Pa shrugged. "No telling how long it will take with this critter. Don't look for me till you see me. Just keep my dinner warm." He picked up the buggy whip. "Git up!" he said, and brought the whip down sharply on Meanie's angular rump.

From a standing start, Meanie exploded into a dead run. Pa's heels flew up as he was thrown against the back of the seat. His hat fell off, and he had no chance to rescue it as he clung to the lines. He disappeared up the road in a cloud of dust to the sound of thudding hoofs and rattling wheels.

Ma clutched the corner of her apron and stared after them. "Those pickles will get broken, sure," she said.

"Pa's apt to get his neck broke!" said my brother who never cared much for pickles.

Mattie Lucas. 1886. Photograph. Nebraska State Historical Society, Lincoln. Solomon D. Butcher Collection.

About eleven-thirty they were back. Pa wiped his dusty face with his big, red handkerchief and said, "Well, Fletch was right about her having plenty of pep. Danged if she didn't gallop most of the way there and back. I thought I'd wear her down, but she's not even winded."

There was grudging admiration in his voice. He gave her a half-friendly slap on the neck. This was the nearest either of them ever came to a truce. Meanie laid back her ears and bared her teeth. Pa moved hastily, remembering yesterday. "Unhitch the ill-tempered beast before I lose my temper," he snapped. "I'll take your mother this cake Mrs. Warner sent over, if it ain't all shook to crumbs."

The next day Pa had to go to town. He said he supposed the quickest way to get there was to drive Meanie. So he hitched her up, pulled his hat on tight, and climbed gingerly into the wagon. He braced his feet, picked up the lines, and we kids backed up to keep out of the dust.

"Git up!" he said, and slapped the lines across Meanie's back.

Nothing happened. Pa looked puzzled. He slapped the lines and "giddapped" again. Meanie stood like a statue.

Pa braced himself and smacked her with the buggy whip. Meanie's hide rippled slightly, as if she'd been bitten by a fly, but her four hoofs remained firmly planted.

"Here," said my brother, "I'll lead her a ways." He took her by the bridle. He pulled and tugged. Pa applied persuasion from the rear. Meanie refused to budge.

Pa was controlling his temper pretty well. "There's always one thing to do," he said, "when you can't make a balky horse move any other way. Build a fire under 'em. Fetch me some kindling wood."

So Pa piled sticks under Meanie's belly, and whittled some shavings so it would burn quicker. Now all she had to do was start walking when she began to get too warm.

Once more Pa got in and braced himself. "Light the fire," he said. "She'll probably take off like she did yesterday when it gets hot."

My brother lit the shavings. As they flared up, Meanie switched her tail and laid back her ears. But as it grew hotter, she hastily moved ahead. She was no fool. Pa grinned triumphantly, but the grin soon faded. She walked ahead all right—just enough so the fire was directly beneath the wagon.

"Pa," I shouted, jumping up and down, "the wagon's on fire!" The flames from the dry shavings had leaped up and spread to the straw that stuck between the cracks in the bottom of the wagon. Pa, who had visions of his spring wagon going up in smoke, vaulted across the back of the seat and began stamping on the straw as he shouted to us kids to get water and put out the blaze beneath the wagon.

Meanie was never one to miss a cue. Now that there was no one to hold the lines, away she went, while Pa did a fine impersonation of a movie stunt man trying to get back into the seat. He had stamped the fire out, but the straw was still smoking, and the smoke billowed out behind the wagon, giving a very dramatic effect as they disappeared over the hill.

Mustangs—or cayuses, as we used to call them—are known as the toughest of horses; and Meanie was a worthy descendant of ancestors who had carried the Indians over endless miles of prairie on hunt and warpath, surviving blizzards, drought, and overwork. It was unbelievable the amount of energy that was stored in that dilapidated-looking frame.

It was a problem to find another horse to work with Meanie in a team. She either balked or went so fast she wore any other horse out within a few hours.

Meanie couldn't get along with any of the other horses. Perhaps she was sensitive about her looks. Anyway, she fought all the others until none of them would go near her. On a hot Sunday afternoon when the horses were standing around the pasture in groups, switching each other's flies, Meanie would be off by herself looking sulkily indifferent—or lonely.

But all that was before we got Blackie. He was a sleek gelding, black as midnight, with a star on his face and four white feet—the exact opposite of Meanie in looks and, apparently, in temperament. When Pa first hitched him up, it seemed a more docile, well-behaved horse would have been hard to find.

The first time we turned Blackie out to pasture, my brother warned him, "Look out for Meanie. She'll make mincemeat out of a pretty boy like you." But an hour later, when we went down in the pasture, there were Meanie and Blackie, standing side by side, Blackie nibbling affectionately at Meanie's neck.

"Well, I'll be—!" said Pa. "Meanie's got a boy friend. I wonder if she could work with him without wearing him out?" So Pa hitched the two of them to the corn planter to see what would happen.

For the information of the uninitiated, a corn planter runs along a wire that is stretched from one end of a row to the other. On this wire are little knobs spaced at the same intervals as the hills of corn. As the planter moves along the wire it strikes each knob, opens, and deposits the proper number of grains of corn in the hill. There is a steady "click, click, click" as the horses move the planter down the wire.

The day Pa tried out Meanie and Blackie as a team, I was stationed at the end of the field to move the wire over to the next row each time the planter reached me. I liked the job because it gave me time to daydream. But there was to be no daydreaming today. As soon as Meanie and Blackie were hitched up, they started off down the corn row at a gallop. Instead of the usual monotonous "click, click," the planter sounded like a machine-gun. Pa clung to the lines and braced his feet as the horses went clattering down the field. I had barely time to move the wire over to the next row before they were off again.

"They'll slow down by the next row," Pa shouted as they tore away toward the far end of the field. But they didn't. Almost before I knew it, they were charging toward me again. For some reason, it didn't make Pa sore. He was sitting there on the careening planter, grinning from ear to ear. "Looks like Meanie's got somebody that can keep up with her," he yelled as they turned.

Two neighbors going down the road, paused in astonishment.

"Great balls of fire," exclaimed one, "lookit them horses go!"

"Listen to that corn planter poppin'," said the other. "He'll have the whole field planted by noon at that rate."

"Row's mighty crooked," observed the first.

"Oh, well, you can grow more corn in a crooked row," laughed the other.

It was funny about Meanie and Blackie. By himself or with any other horses, Blackie was always the perfect gentleman, but Meanie seemed to bring out the gypsy in him. All she had to do was give the signal, and he was game for anything. They could get more work done than any other horses on the farm, and would behave well for weeks on end, but every so often they had to run away.

The time I remember best was when they were hitched to the hack to take a crate of Ma's prize Brahma chickens to town.

I had been sent ahead to open the gate at the top of the hill, and was picking wild flowers, waiting for them to reach the top. I thought that when they came in sight, there would still be plenty of time for me to open the gate.

But I hadn't figured on a runaway. Suddenly I heard the familiar clatter of hoofs accompanied by Pa's cussing, and I looked up to see them bearing down on me with the speed of a young tornado. I dropped my flowers and ran for the gate, but I was too late. The horses got there first, and sailed grandly over it. The front wheels of the hack cleared the gate, but that was all. There was a sound of splintering wood as the doubletree broke loose from the tongue. Pa let go of the lines, and Meanie and Blackie went pounding on down the road, leaving the hack hanging on the gate with Pa still in the seat, so mad I could almost see the steam coming out his ears. The crate of chickens fell out, and squawking Brahmas fled in every direction. At the time, I saw no humor in the situation, for I had to catch every one of those feather-footed fowls and put them back in the crate.

My brother always vowed that Meanie could think ahead. She never bothered Pa when she was tied in a stall, because obviously if she took a nip or a kick at him, she would get soundly wallowed for it, and there was nothing she could do but stand there and take it. But one day Pa unhitched the horses, and while they were drinking at the watering trough, he went into the barn. Meanie came in and went to her stall, and he slipped her harness off without tying her up. Meanie, finding herself free and unfettered, and Pa unarmed, laid back her ears and made for him. Pa jumped into a manger and headed up the ladder to the haymow where we kids were playing hide-and-seek, but he was seconds too late. There was a ripping sound, and by the time Pa arrived in the loft beside us, he was minus the seat of his pants.

With murder in his eye, he grabbed a pitchfork and started back down the ladder. But Meanie knew when to attack and when to retreat. She ran out into the barnyard with Pa right behind her. We kids peeked through a crack in the barn, and held our hands over our mouths so he wouldn't hear us laughing. Round and round the barnyard they went, Meanie with her tail derisively in the air, and Pa using language that should have blistered the paint off the barn. All the while the seat of his long underwear, its buttons ripped from their moorings during his flight to the haymow, flapped like an unlatched cellar door in a cyclone. Meanie evidently decided he was getting too close for comfort. She jumped the gate and went barreling off down the pasture, while Pa stood shaking the pitchfork after her and swearing he'd sell her to the glue factory the very next day.

Whenever Pa turned the horses into the lower pasture, the first place they headed for was a patch of alfalfa at the far end. Meanie had a favorite way of reaching this patch ahead of the others. She would take a narrow path that lay along the top of a cliff above Coon Creek. This path was so narrow that all the other horses refused to walk on it, but she was sure-footed as a mountain goat, and the dizzy height of the trail bothered her not in the least.

One day after it had been raining for about a week, Pa turned the horses into the lower pasture, and as usual, Meanie started down her favorite path toward the alfalfa patch. But as she reached the narrowest part, the bank, softened by the prolonged rain, gave way, and she plunged thirty feet into the shallow waters of the creek, breaking her neck instantly.

My brother and I found her, and went to tell Pa. "He'll probably be just as glad she's dead," said my brother, "she was always causing him so much trouble."

But Pa didn't seem pleased. He looked downright sad. "Poor old Meanie," he said. "Homeliest, orneriest horse I ever saw in all my born days, but she had more brains and spunk than a lot of people I know. The place won't seem the same without her."

And we knew just what he meant.

WALLACE STEGNER

From *Wolf Willow*

A Sense of Place

Wallace Stegner, who died at the age of eighty-four in 1993, was perhaps the last remaining great American writer who had grown up on what could still be described as a frontier—on the Montana–Saskatchewan border. In this excerpt from Wolf Willow: A History, a Story, and Memory *(1962), he tells us what it was like to return to this place after a long absence—and in a single, profoundly moving epiphany, of the power of memory itself.*

It is with me all at once, what I came hoping to re-establish, an ancient, unbearable recognition, and it comes partly from the children and the footbridge, and the river's quiet curve, but much more from the smell. For here, pungent and pervasive, is the smell that has always meant my childhood. I have never smelled it anywhere else, and it is as evocative as Proust's madeleine and tea.

But what is it? Somehow I have always associated it with the bath house, with wet bathing suits and damp board benches, heaps of clothing, perhaps even the seldom rinsed corners where desperate boys had made water. I go into the men's bath house, and the smell is there, but it does not seem to come from any single thing. The whole air smells of it, outside as well as in. Perhaps it is the river water, or the mud, or something about the float and footbridge. It is the way the old burlap-tipped diving board used to smell; it used to remain in the head after a sinus-flooding dive.

I pick up a handful of mud and sniff it. I step over the little girls and bend my nose to the wet rail of the bridge. I stand above the water and sniff. On the other side I strip leaves off wild rose and dogwood. Nothing doing. And yet all around me is that odor that I have not smelled since I was eleven, but have never forgotten—have *dreamed,* more than once. Then I pull myself up the bank by a gray-leafed bush, and I have it. The tantalizing and ambiguous and wholly native smell is no more than the shrub we called wolf willow, now blooming with small yellow flowers.

It is wolf willow, and not the town or anyone in it, that brings me home. For a few minutes, with a handful of leaves to my nose, I look across at the clay bank and the hills beyond where the river loops back on itself, enclosing the old sports and picnic ground, and the present and all the years between are shed like a boy's clothes dumped on the bath-house bench. The perspective is what it used to be, the dimensions are restored, the senses are as clear as if they had not been battered with sensation for forty alien years. And the queer adult compulsion to return to one's beginnings is assuaged. A contact has been made, a mystery touched. For the moment, reality is made exactly equivalent with memory, and a hunger is satisfied. The sensuous little savage that I once was is still intact inside me.

Later, looking from the North Bench hills across my restored town, I can see the river where it shallows and crawls southeastward across the prairie toward the Milk, the Missouri, and the Gulf, and I toy with the notion that a man is like the river or the clouds, that he can be constant-

COLORPLATE 83

MAYNARD DIXON. *Earth Knower*. 1931, 1932, 1935. Oil on canvas. 40 x 50 in. Collection of the Oakland Museum.
Bequest of Abilio Reis. *Maynard Dixon, who enjoyed his greatest success as a magazine and book illustrator in the
1930s and 1940s, was especially tuned to the very largeness of the western landscape. And more. "For him," Dixon's
friend Ansel Adams once wrote, "there was something truly sacred in the primitive simplicity of the American Indian
way of life and art. It was in close harmony with the primal realities—sun, sky, earth, and space." In* Earth Knower
all four elements blend with the human figure that is only barely distinguishable from the earth itself.

COLORPLATE 84

MARSDEN HARTLEY. *El Santo.* 1919. Oil on canvas. 36 x 32 in. Collection of the Museum of Fine Arts, Museum of New Mexico, Santa Fe.

COLORPLATE 85

WILLIAM PENHALLOW-HENDERSON. *Holy Week in New Mexico (Penitente Procession)*. c. 1918. Oil on panel. 32 x 40 in.
Museum of Fine Arts, Museum of New Mexico, Santa Fe. Gift of Mrs. Edgar L. Rossin, daughter of the artist.
*The beginnings of what is now called "Santa Fe style" go back to the years before World War I, when more and more
artists discovered an unearthly light and wondrously evocative people and landscapes in the Southwest. From then until
the present—when Southwestern Art has become an international business—the region bordered by Taos on the north
and Santa Fe on the south has boasted probably more artists per square mile than any comparable place on earth.
Superior artists, many of them, including at one time or another John Sloan, Peter Hurd, Georgia O'Keeffe, Edward
Hopper, George Bellows, Maynard Dixon, and Marsden Hartley, whose* El Santo *(COLORPLATE 84) puts a modernist twist
on one of the oldest folk art forms in the Southwest. In the painting above, William Penhallow-Henderson turns to
another kind of folk art—the annual reenactment of the agony of the Cross during Easter Week. Each year, until fairly
recent times, the members of the ancient (and officially unapproved) Penitente sect scourged themselves in an attempt to
share Christ's experience and chose one of their own to be roped (and sometimes nailed) to a cross and left to hang
there until he fainted from pain and exhaustion.*

COLORPLATE 86

WALTER UFER. *Oferta para San Esquipula*. 1918. Oil on canvas. 25 x 30 in. Courtesy of The Anschutz Collection, Denver, Colorado.

COLORPLATE 87

GEORGE BELLOWS. *Pueblo, Tesuque, Number One*. 1917. Oil on canvas. 34 x 44 in. Courtesy of The Anschutz Collection, Denver, Colorado.

COLORPLATE 88

Marsden Hartley. *Landscape, New Mexico*. 1923. Oil on canvas. 21 3/4 x 35 3/4 in. Collection, The Equitable Life Assurance Society of the United States, New York City. © The Equitable Life Assurance Society of the United States.

COLORPLATE 89

RAYMOND JONSON. *Pueblo, Acoma.* 1927. Oil. 37 x 44 in. The Harmsen Collection.

COLORPLATE 90

STUART DAVIS. *New Mexico Landscape*. 1923. Oil on canvas. 15 x 24 in. Courtesy of The Anschutz Collection, Denver, Colorado. © Estate of Stuart Davis/VAGA, New York 1994.

ly moving and yet steadily renewed. The sensuous little savage, at any rate, has not been rubbed away or dissolved; he is as solid a part of me as my skeleton.

And he has a fixed and suitably arrogant relationship with his universe, a relationship geometrical and symbolic. From his center of sensation and question and memory and challenge, the circle of the world is measured, and in that respect the years of experience I have loaded upon my savage have not altered him. Lying on a hillside where I once sprawled among the crocuses, watching the town herd and snaring May's emerging gophers, I feel how the world still reduces me to a point and then measures itself from me. Perhaps the meadowlark singing from a fence post—a meadowlark whose dialect I recognize—feels the same way. All points on the circumference are equidistant from him; in him all radii begin; all diameters run through him; if he moves, a new geometry creates itself around him.

No wonder he sings. It is a good country that can make anyone feel so.

And it is a fact that once I have, so to speak, recovered myself as I used to be, I can look at the town, whose childhood was exactly contemporary with my own, with more understanding. It turns out to have been a special sort of town—special not only to me, in that it provided the indispensable sanctuary to match the prairie's exposure, but special in its belated concentration of Plains history. The successive stages of the Plains frontier flowed like a pageant through these Hills, and there are men still alive who remember almost the whole of it. My own recollections cover only a fragment; and yet it strikes me that this is *my* history. My disjunct, uprooted, cellular family was more typical than otherwise on the frontier. But more than we knew, we had our place in a human movement. What this town and its surrounding prairie grew from, and what they grew into, is the record of my tribe. If I am native to anything, I am native to this.

JOHN SMART. *The Madison River near Cameron (Montana).* 1987. Photograph. © John Smart.

IVAN DOIG

From *This House of Sky*
Hoofed Catastrophes

Among its many other virtues, Ivan Doig's evocative memoir of his own childhood in Montana,
This House of Sky: Landscapes of a Western Mind *(1978), brings to glowing life his father,*
Charles Campbell Doig, one of the most purely appealing characters in all of Western
American literature. In the following selection, Doig sketches the outlines of his tough little
father's peripatetic evolution from hardworking drifter to settled-down manager—more or less.

But the deep ingredient of my father's adventuring in those years of his early twenties was
horses. It was a time when a man still did much of his day's work atop a saddle pony, and the
liveliest of his recreation as well. And with every hour in the saddle, the odds built that there
was hoofed catastrophe ahead. Built, as Dad's stories lessened into me, until the most casual
swing into the stirrups could almost cost your life: *I'll tell ye a time. I was breakin' this horse,*
and I'd rode the thing for a couple of weeks, got him pretty gentle—a big nice tall brown horse
with a stripe in his face. I'd been huntin' elk up in the Castles, and I'd rode that horse all day
long. Comin' home, I was just there in the Basin below the Christison place, and got off to
open a gate. My rifle was on the saddle there, with the butt back toward the horse's hip, and
it'd rubbed a sore there and I didn't notice the rubbin'. When I went to get back on, took hold
of the saddle horn to pull myself up, ye know, the rifle scraped across that sore. Boy, he ducked
out from under me and I went clear over him. I caught my opposite foot in the stirrup as I went
over, and away he went, draggin' me. He just kicked the daylights out of me as we went. It was
in a plowed field, and I managed to turn over and get my face like this—cradling his arms in
front of his face, to my rapt watching—*but he kept kickin' me in the back of the head here,*
until he had knots comin' on me big as your fist. And he broke my collarbone. Finally my boot
came off, or he'd of dragged me around until he kicked my head off, I guess.

The accident of flailing along the earth with a horse's rear hooves thunking your skull was
one thing. Courting such breakage was another, and it was in my father not to miss that chance,
either. Most summer Sundays, the best riders in the county would gather at a ranch and try to
ride every bucking horse they had been able to round up out of the hills. It was the kind of hell-
bending contest young Charlie Doig was good at, and he passed up few opportunities to show
it.

The hill broncs which would be hazed in somewhere for this weekend rodeoing—the Doig
homestead had a big stout notched-pole corral which was just right—were not scruffy little
mustangs. They were half again bigger and a lot less rideable than that: herds grown from
ranch stock turned out to pasture, with all the heft of workhorses added to their new wildness.
Eventually there came to be a couple of thousand such renegades roaming the grassed hills
around the valley. Some would weigh more than three-quarters of a ton and measure almost as
tall at the shoulder as the height of a big man. A rider would come away from a summer of
those massive hill broncs with one experience or another shaken into his bones and brain, and
Dad's turn came up when the last two horses were whooped into the Doig corral at dusk one of
those Sunday afternoons.

Five or six of us were ridin', all had our girls there and were showin' off, ye know. Neither
of the last horses looked worth the trouble of climbing on—a huge club-hoofed bay, and a
homely low-slung black gelding. Someone yelled out, *That black one looks like a damned milk*
cow! Dad called across the corral to the other rider, *Which one of those do you want, Frankie,*
the big one or that black thing? The bay was saddled, and thudded around the corral harmless-

FREDERIC REMINGTON.
Turn Him Loose, Bill.
1892. Oil on canvas.
25 x 33 in. Courtesy of
The Anschutz Collection,
Denver, Colorado.

ly on its club hooves. Then the corral crew roped the black for Dad and began to discover that this one was several times more horse than it looked. *Oh, he was a bearcat, I'm here to tell you.*

The gelding was so feisty they had to flop him flat and hold him down to cinch the saddle on, the last resort for a saddling crew that took any pride in itself. Dad swung into the stirrups while the horse was uncoiling up out of the dirt. When the bronc had all four feet under him, he sunfished for the corral poles and went high into them as intentionally as if he were a suicide plunging off a cliff. Horse and rider crashed back off the timbers, then the bronc staggered away into another quick running start and slammed the fence again. And then again.

He like to have beat my brains out on that corral fence. Then, worse: He threw me off over his head upside down and slammed me against that log fence again, and still he kept a-buckin'. I jumped up and got out of his way and tried to climb the fence. Dad had made it onto the top of the fence when the battering caught up with his body. Blacking out, he pitched off the corral backwards, into the path of the gelding as it rampaged past. The horse ran over him full length, full speed. *One hoof hit me in the ribs here, and the other hit me in the side of the head here, and just shoved all the skin down off the side of my face in a bunch.* The gelding would have hollowed him out like a trough if the corral crew hadn't managed to snake Dad out under the fence before the horse could get himself turned. By then, someone already was sprinting for a car for the forty-five-mile ride to a doctor. *I was laid up six weeks that time, before I could even get on crutches.*

That was his third stalking by death; Dad himself had invited most of the risk that time, although in the homely black gelding it came by the sneakiest of means. But the next near-killing hit him as randomly as a lightning bolt exploding a snag. It began with the yip of coyote pups on a mountainside above the Basin. *I was workin' for Bert Plymale, and we lambed a bunch of sheep over there near the D.L. place.* Coyotes, sheep killers that they were, were hated as nothing else in that country, especially on the lean foothill ranches where any loss of livestock hurt like a wound. *They were eatin' the lambs just about as fast as we could turn 'em out. And we could hear these coyotes in a park up on the side of the mountain, yippin' up there early morning and evening. So I had a young kid workin' with me, and we decided we'd go up there and find that den.*

When they reined up in a clearing in the timber where the yips were coming from, Dad stepped off his horse and walked ahead a few steps to look for the den. *I was carryin' the pick and the kid was carryin' the shovel—in case we found the den, we could dig it out. I'd stepped off of this bay horse, dropped the lines and walked several feet in front of him, clear away from him. That sap of a kid, he dropped that shovel right at the horse's heels. And instead of kickin' at the shovel like a normal horse would, ye know, he jumped ahead and whirled and kicked me right in the middle of the back. Drove two ribs into my lungs.*

Dad hunched on the ground like a shot animal. *I couldn't get any breath atall when I'd try straighten up. When I was down on all fours, I could get enough breath to get by on. The kid, he was gonna leave me there and take off to find everybody in the country to come get me with a stretcher. I said no, by God, I was gonna get out of there somehow.* Spraddled on hands and knees in a red fog of pain, he gasped out to the youngster to lead his horse beneath a small cliff nearby. Dad crawled to the cliff, climbed off the ledge into the saddle. Then, crumpled like a dead man tied into the stirrups, he rode the endless mile and a half to the ranch. *That was one long ride, I'm-here-to-tell-you.*

Getting there only began a new spell of pain—the pounding car ride across rutted roads to town and the doctor. By then, Dad's breathing had gone so ragged and bloody that the doctor set off with him for the hospital in Bozeman. Two gasping hours more in a car. At last, by evening, he lay flat in a hospital bed. *But I always healed fast, anyway,* and a few weeks later, he climbed stiffly onto a horse again.

He wouldn't have thought, when he was being battered around from one near-death to the next, that he was heading all the while into the ranch job he would do for many of the rest of his years. But the valley, which could always be counted on to be fickle, now was going to let him find out in a hurry what he could do best. Sometime in 1925, when he was twenty-four years old, Dad said his goodbyes at the Basin homestead another time, saddled up, and rode to the far end of the Smith River Valley to ask for a job at the Dogie ranch.

More than any other ranch, the Dogie had been set up—which is to say, pieced together of bought-out homesteads and other small holdings—to use the valley's advantages and work around its drawbacks. Wild hay could be cut by the mile from its prime bottomland meadows; a crew of three dozen men would begin haying each mid-June and build the loaflike stacks by the hundreds. Cattle and sheep—like many Montana ranches of the time, the Dogie raised both—could be grazed over its tens of thousands of acres of bunchgrass slopes along and above the north fork of the Smith River, and sheltered from winter blizzards in the willow thickets cloaking the streambed. And the trump card of it all: hard years could be evened out with the wealth of the Seattle shipping family who owned the enterprise and ran it in a fond vague style.

The Dogie readily put Dad on its payroll, but that was the most that could be said for the job. He was made choreboy, back again at the hated round of milking cows and feeding chickens and hogs and fetching stovewood for the cook. But he had come to the Dogie and was biding time there because the owners were signing into a partnership with a sheep rancher from near Sixteenmile Creek. The "Jasper" at the front of his name long since crimped down to "Jap" by someone's hurried tongue, Jap Stewart had arrived out of Missouri some twenty years before, leaving behind the sight in one eye due to a knife fight in a St. Joe saloon, but bringing just the kind of elbowing ambition to make a success in the wide-open benchlands he found a few miles east of the Basin. Drinker, scrapper, sharp dealer and all the rest, Jap also was a ranchman to the marrow, and he prospered in the Sixteen country as no one before or since. Now he was quilting onto the Dogie holdings his own five thousand head of sheep and the allotted pasture in the national forest for every last woolly one of them. He also moved in to kick loose anything that didn't work, such as most of the Dogie's crew.

Jap began by giving them a Missouri growling at—*most of you sonsabitches've worked here so goddamn long all you know any more is how to hide out in the goddamn brush*—and ended up sacking every man on the ranch except Dad and a handful of others. While Jap's new men streamed in past the old crew on the road to town, Dad, at the age of 25, was made sheep boss, in charge of the Dogie's nine bands grazing across two wide ends of the county. *In another six months, I was foreman of the whole damn shebang.*

Frank Waters

From *The Colorado*

The Men Who Built Boulder Dam

Although John Wesley Powell had warned forty years before that there would never be enough water in the Colorado River to meet the public's demands, the federal government began the river's first major dam (then called Boulder, now called Hoover) in 1928. In the best book ever written about the river, The Colorado *(1946), novelist and historian Frank Waters illuminates the financial frenzy that preceded the construction of this gargantuan plug.*

Boulder Dam is the Great Pyramid of the American Desert, the Ninth Symphony of our day, and the key to the future of the whole Colorado River basin.

No other single piece of man's handiwork in this vast wilderness hinterland has epitomized so well during its construction all the strange and complex ramifications of our American Way—all its democratic faults and virtues, the political interlocking of local, state and federal governments, the meshed and rival economies of public and private enterprise, the conflicting needs of urban, agrarian and industrial groups. Finished, it stands in its desert gorge like a fabulous, unearthly dream. A visual symphony written in steel and concrete—the terms of our mathematical and machine-age culture—it is inexpressibly beautiful of line and texture, magnificently original, strong, simple and majestic as the greatest works of art of all times and all peoples, and as eloquently expressive of our own as anything ever achieved. Yet wholly utilitarian and built to endure, it is the greatest single work yet undertaken to control a natural resource dominating an area of nearly a quarter million square miles. . . .

Boulder Dam, the biggest dam on the face of the earth and the first major work in the Colorado River Project. Already the blue chips were down. The United States Reclamation Service had finished the specifications. Government lawyers had condemned 150,000 acres above the site. The secretary of the interior had planned the route of the little construction railway running from Las Vegas, Nevada, and on July 7, 1930, the traditional silver spike had been driven.

It was now nearly eight months later, and in two days bids for the construction of the dam were due. Yet no one knew if there was a man or company in the country big enough to ask for the job.

No one but a small group of men in the St. Francis Hospital, San Francisco. They were gathered about the deathbed of an old man of seventy-two. A muffled knock on the door broke the silence. Into the room came a younger man of forty-eight wheeling a strange contraption. The eyes of the old man lighted up as it was placed beside his bed. It was a scale model of Boulder Dam. The younger man had made it just as he was to construct it full size later. He knew it. All the others felt it in his voice as carefully now he went over its every detail. At last he finished. For a moment there was silence. The old man on his deathbed waved his hand in approval.

"One last thing," another spoke up. "What'll we add to the cost for profit?"

"Profit? Twenty-five per cent! Tidy up the estimates and get the bid in."

"Right!" Quietly the men shook hands and left. W. H. Wattis sank back content into his pillows. He had seen the crowning achievement of his life work as clearly as if it already stood across the turbulent Colorado.

Behind it lay a story almost as fabulous as the dam itself—his own and that of his companions who were to build it.

Eighty years before, an Englishman had joined the California gold rush. He got no farther than Utah. His two sons, W. H. Wattis and E. O. Wattis, became Mormons and contractors, helping to build the old Colorado Midland Railroad that ran through the mountains from Colorado Springs to Ogden. Here at its western terminus the two Wattis brothers founded the Utah Construction Company which built the Hetch Hetchy dam that impounded San Francisco's water supply. E. O. Wattis was now approaching the age of seventy-six; W. H. Wattis, seventy-two and ailing; and they had made as president of the company their 60-year-old cousin, Lester S. Corey. But Boulder Dam was due and they determined to build it.

The project was too big for the Utah Construction Company to handle alone. They decided to appeal to the Morrison-Knudsen Company, Inc., of Boise, Idaho. This company had been formed in 1912 by Harry Morrison and Morris Knudsen, who in 1925 had taken into the firm Frank T. Crowe. Crowe had spent most of his forty-eight years in river bottoms. With Morrison-Knudsen he had just finished building the Guernsey dam in Wyoming and the Deadwood dam in Idaho. Previous to this he had been general superintendent of the United States Bureau of Reclamation and in 1919 had made one of its first rough estimates of Boulder Dam.

The two firms got together. Boulder Dam, they figured, would cost from 40 to 50 million dollars. At least $5,000,000 working capital would be needed to start it. The two old Wattis brothers offered to put up $1,000,000 for the Utah Construction Company. Morrison-Knudsen agreed to chip in $500,000. Together they approached a third company.

The J. F. Shea Company, Inc., of Los Angeles had been founded in 1914 by a plumber and his son, Charles A. Shea. The son soon became one of the best sewer and tunnel experts on the Pacific coast, and the firm secured contracts for laying the water-supply lines for San Francisco, Oakland and Berkeley. The Shea Company now jumped at the chance to get in on Boulder, agreed to ante $500,000, and suggested that the Pacific Bridge Company of Portland be called in.

This fourth company was famous for its underwater work. It had driven the piers for the first bridge across the Willamette River at Portland, and working with Shea had laid the water line across the Mokelumne River. Heading the company was W. Gorrill Swigert, an Oregonian. He too agreed to put up $500,000.

Colorado River flood waters pouring over the Hoover Dam spillways. 1983. Photograph.

A total of $2,500,000 had now been secured—just half of the $5,000,000 required, when W. H. Wattis took to bed. It was found he had developed a cancer of the hip. Nevertheless, he decided to stay by his proposal and urged his associates to find another company to finance the remainder.

The fifth company picked was MacDonald and Kahn, Inc., of San Francisco. No stranger pair of partners could have been found. One of them, Felix Kahn, was a quiet, shrewd, 61-year-old Jew born in Detroit, the son of a rabbi. The other, Alan MacDonald, was a fiery and impetuous Scot who had been fired from fifteen consecutive jobs before teaming up with Kahn. From the start they got along, building the Mark Hopkins Hotel of San Francisco and some of the largest office buildings on the West Coast, totaling some $75,000,000 in construction. They were already interested in Boulder Dam and agreed to add another million dollars to the pool.

It was still $1,500,000 short; time was slipping by. Meanwhile another group of men had become just as interested in the biggest dam in the world.

Two of these were W. A. Bechtel, founder of the construction firm W. A. Bechtel Company of San Francisco in 1900, and his son, S. D. Bechtel.

Another was Henry J. Kaiser of Oakland, 61-year-old head of the firm bearing his name. Years before, Kaiser as a young man from Upper New York State had gone to California hunting construction work. "Dad" Bechtel, "a tall beefy man with a bull-like roar" took him in and pushed him up the ladder to success. Kaiser was a rapid climber. He soon established his own company, and became national president of the Association of General Contractors. At the present time he was working on a subcontract secured from Warren Brothers, a construction company of Cambridge, Massachusetts, for building a 20-million dollar highway in Cuba.

In 1930 Kaiser was in Cuba finishing the job when Bechtel arrived to propose Boulder Dam as their next joint project. Kaiser agreed, but suggested they talk it over with John Dearborn, chairman of the board of Warren Brothers.

As representatives of their three companies they all met to discuss their own plans, and to consider those of the Wattis-Morrison group about which they had learned. Obviously the two groups could not be rivals; the dam was bigger than both of them. Accordingly the Bechtel, Kaiser and Warren firms teamed up with the preceding five firms as the sixth company, adding the remaining $1,500,000 split between them.

For the new combine Kahn suggested the appropriate name of Six Companies, Inc., called after the famous tribunal to which the Chinese tongs in San Francisco had submitted their differences in preference to warring with hatchet men.

In February, 1931, it was so incorporated in Delaware. W. H. Wattis on his deathbed in San Francisco was selected president; Dad Bechtel and E. O. Wattis, first and second vice-presidents; Shea, secretary; and Kahn, treasurer. Crowe worked out all the details and made his own scale model from his blueprints.

Approved in Wattis's hospital room, the last preliminaries were then agreed upon. Next night in the Cosmopolitan Hotel, Denver, Crowe made up the final bid of $48,890,000 from three separate estimates. The following day, March 4, 1931, it was submitted.

The weeks dragged by until a decision was rendered. Few of the men waiting so patiently could guess even then how it was to shape their entire future. Four of them were to die without seeing the dam finished: W. H. Wattis, in his hospital bed six months after it was bid; E. O. Wattis, soon after; Dad Bechtel, in 1933 while on a trip to examine Russia's subway system; and Alan MacDonald, in 1935.

The rest of the group was to stay together as the Six Companies and gain world renown. After some quarreling, Shea was placed in charge of field construction; Kahn in charge of finances, legal affairs and housing; the younger Bechtel of purchasing, administration and transportation; and Kaiser, having a knack for making them cooperate, was made chairman of the board. Finishing Boulder Dam with a profit of $10,400,000, they sank the piers for the Golden Gate Bridge; worked on the Bay Bridge; built Bonneville Dam and finished the Grand Coulee Dam on the Columbia River. Today they are finishing a length of the Alaska Military Highway; have built underground storage tanks for Pacific Navy air bases; have helped to raise warships sunk at Pearl Harbor.

Frank Crowe, who as superintendent of construction did more than any other single man to build Boulder Dam, made his fame and fortune of nearly $300,000 from his modest salary and 2.5 per cent of the gross profit.

Henry J. Kaiser from Boulder, the world's highest dam, climbed swiftly to world eminence. Almost "psychopathetically" power-mad and bluff as his old boss, he first built Permanente, the world's biggest cement plant, to break the cement combine. Foreseeing the war crisis he next built with $106,000,000 of RFC funds a new steel mill at Fontana, near Los Angeles, establishing himself in the steel industry. Finally with the war and his own knack for obtaining publicity, he rose to his present fame as the world's fastest shipbuilder. On his first 120-million-dollar order for 60 ships, he built the first one in 196 days. This time was then cut to 25 days, and Kaiser finally was launching a new Liberty ship every 10 hours. The great postwar reconstruction period offers still greater opportunities to him and his companions of the Six Companies.

But as yet they were all still chewing their nails over the outcome of their bid for their first big job. It was not long in coming. There had been only two other bids on Boulder Dam. One was $5,000,000 and the other $10,000,000 higher; the Six Companies' bid was taken. Wattis and Morrison had hit the nail on the head in figuring the minimum working capital that would be required. For the surety companies, which first demanded $8,000,000 for underwriting the job, now agreed to accept the $5,000,000. And on April 20, 1931, the Six Companies received notice to begin. Work with dollars and decimal points was over; it was time to pick up shovels.

STANLEY VESTAL

From *Short Grass Country*

"Oklahoma Rain"

Nature demonstrated the consequences of abuse with precision during "The Big Die-Up" of the 1880s, and again in the 1930s. Overgrazing, bad farming habits, and drought created an enormous "Dust Bowl" from west Texas to the Canada line. Tens of thousands were driven off the land, fleeing to California. Many more stayed, however, and in this excerpt from Short Grass Country *(1941), Stanley Vestal celebrates the perseverance of those who stuck it out.*

Feeding the family was a hard job, and at first it seemed as if everybody would starve to death. Food was no sooner placed on the table than it was covered with what seemed a layer of fine black salt. Every morsel was grit between the teeth at the first bite, and then mud on the tongue. Hungry children, tired men, could not down such food, and quickly gave up trying. Milk and coffee were liquid mud, and added to disgust was the fear of infection.

But as storm after storm followed, smart housewives found ingenious ways of preparing food with a minimum of dust. Liquids they put into Mason jars with screw tops and rubber collars. They learned to mix dough in a bureau drawer—almost closed—thrusting their arms through two holes cut in a cloth covering the opening. They baked nearly everything in the oven of the range, and fried meat on a hot stove, so that the warm air, rising from the pan, carried the dust upward. All food was kept in covered containers, and those women who had ice-boxes and electric refrigerators sealed tight against the outer air counted themselves lucky, and thanked God for American ingenuity. As soon as food was cooked, it was served from the stove piping hot, and every plate was immediately covered by a cloth. Milk and coffee were drunk through straws from bottles.

The moment the first sign of a coming dust cloud appeared, everyone hurried to fill every available container with drinking water to last through the ordeal. At that, the only person who got his ration clean was the baby at his mother's breast.

People learned not to leave the house during a storm, and if caught driving, would stop and park the car to wait until the storm was over, though it lasted half a day. Men on foot clung to some shrub, or tree, or followed a wire fence hand over hand until they reached shelter. It was a perfect blackout.

As for sleeping—how could anyone sleep with his bedding and clothing thick with dust? To leave the window open or the door ajar was intolerable. Yet to keep them closed on a warm night was suffocating. Everyone was coughing and wheezing, and a man who could spit at all, spat mud. The only way one could sleep was with a wet cloth masking the face, and young children were in danger of their lives because they threw off their masks. No one could watch them, for no one could see to watch. Houses in the Southern country are not so tightly built as they are in the North, and the dry winds had a way of warping wood, or finding crevices around windows and doors, even of stone or brick buildings. Nothing, it seemed, would keep out the dust. You could not see a person across the room. At school, with the lights on, the teacher could not see the pupils in the second row. The dust seemed able to pass through the very walls and windowpanes.

Sometimes the dust storm was followed by thunder, lightning, hail, and rain. People rushed out when the rain began—only to find, as the drops fell through the dusty air, that these had turned to pellets. Their clothing was ruined. It was raining mud.

Travel was dangerous, for no driver could see the ditch, or make out his radiator cap in such a fog. Headlights helped hardly at all, and cars bumped into each other fore and aft, went into the ditch, or swung crossways of the road. The road itself was so blocked with drifted sand that it was often impassable. Worst of all, dust got into the motors and stalled—or ruined—them in a few minutes' time.

Those who drove horses or mules were "just as bad off." The eyes of the animals soon filled with dust, mud would form from the tears, and the lids stuck together and remained sealed as the mud dried and locked the eyelashes together. For, if the people suffered, the livestock suffered more. Dust clogged the noses of the helpless creatures, soon turning to mud and hardening there, so that all were choked and suffocated. When the farmer swilled his hogs, or poured milk in the trough for his calves, the stuff turned to mud before it could be swallowed. Forage was blown away while the bawling, blinded cattle drifted with the wind and cut themselves up on barbed-wire fences. Horses went frantic with the dust, coughing and snorting. And chickens smothered—even in the snuggest henhouses.

No sooner had the dust stopped blowing than people began to laugh and joke about their troubles.

It was reported that dust had been found in the vault at the bank, that a banana crate used as a waste-paper basket by the local editor was full and running over with dust. One man claimed that gravel had come through his windowpane and wakened him during the night. Another, finding his car stalled by the grit in the engine, opened the door and shot ground squirrels overhead which were tunneling upward for air! A local paper reported finding gold nuggets in the street which had been blown from the mines in New Mexico. The county farmer advised his clients that it would be unnecessary to rotate crops in the future, since the wind was rotating soils. One of the natives proposed a test for wind velocity: "Fasten one end of a logchain to the top of a fence-post. If the wind does not blow the chain straight out from the post, the breeze is moderate. You have a calm day."

Allergy in its various forms became so common that, it was said, even the snakes had learned to sneeze; in the night you could tell when a duster was coming by the sneezing of the rattlesnakes on the prairie. Everyone jestingly referred to a dust storm as an "Oklahoma rain." A man caught some huge bullfrogs, so he said, and put them in his watertank to multiply; but, he said, the poor things all drowned immediately. It hadn't rained for so long that they had never had a chance to learn to swim.

A housewife claimed that she scoured her pans by holding them up to a keyhole. The sand coming through in a stream polished them better than she could by the usual method. One old lady, on hearing a man compare the climate to that of hell, put her chin up and declared that if the good Lord sent *her* to hell, he'd have to give her a constitution to stand it.

They laughed about the Black Snow which covered their fields. One farmer said he was going to leave Texas and move to Kansas to pay taxes—"There's where my farm is now."

Another said he could not keep up with his farm, which had taken a trip north. "But next week she'll be back," he said. "I can plow then."

One leather-faced dry farmer said, "I hope it'll rain before the kids grow up. They ain't never seen none."

Those dust storms were magnificent and terrifying, huge walls of tawny cloud, or black, sweeping in ominously to black out the world, sky-high, swift, horrible. But the Short Grass folks laughed them off.

People talk about the horrors of bombed London—and no doubt they are bad enough. But vital statistics show that the death rate on the Plains was as high as that in bombed London at its worst. Nobody lauded the Dust Bowl heroes, for nobody wanted to fight their war. What's more, none of them asked anybody to fight it. The Men of the Short Grass are a hardy breed. And their humor, their gameness, is every whit as admirable as any shown anywhere. A hero is without honor in his own country.

Most of the people who live on the High Plains live there from choice, for most of them could find homes elsewhere where it would be easier to make a living. When the drouth was at its height in the 1930's, a farmer proposed to give his wife a holiday and take her back to Georgia where her parents lived.

"Molly," he said, "we have been out here forty years. You have worked hard and deserve a vacation. We can afford it now. Let's go back where your folks live for a visit. It will do you good."

His wife, brown as a berry, looked at him, startled into alarm.

"Why, Jim," she protested, "do you think I'd go back there where they have all that water and rain all the time? Not me. It ain't healthy."

In the days of this dry cycle it is often forgotten that not so long ago, before the grass had been grazed off and while the water table was only a few yards below the surface of the earth, the great plague on the Plains was malaria. Nowadays malaria is almost unknown there.

The man who knows he may not make a crop for five, or even seven, years is not going to be cast down by any temporary difficulty or minor disaster. He plants and cultivates, and loses his crop. The next year he repeats, with the same result. Again he tries and fails. This discipline forces him to take the long view, to hope and work and wait—and then do it all over again. Like the Indian hunter, who might have plenty of fat buffalo one moon and be starving the next, the farmer on the Short Grass was neither discouraged nor ashamed when the drouth or the grasshoppers destroyed his crops. He knew that it would rain again sometime; when it did, he would pay off the debt, make a fresh start. He stuck.

For seven lean years there was no crop. He stuck. He had faith, he had hope, and he had charity for the fellow less well off than himself. He was what Short Grass folks call "friendly." His labor was his prayer, and in the long run it got results. Such prayers are strong.

When, finally, the dust storms robbed him of the very soil under his feet, he still stuck—if it was humanly possible. The tune of the migrants to the Coast is always the same: "I'd rather be back in Oklahoma, if I could make it go." Those who left the Plains generally did so unwillingly, and, in the midst of their disaster, with a joke on their lips: "Well, the wind blew the dirt away. But we haven't lost everything. We still got the mortgage!"

JOSEPHINE JOHNSON

From *Now in November*

"The Long Drouth"

Among western farmers nothing—not floods, tornadoes, even locusts—was more desperately feared than drought, and there were few droughts more relentless than those of the early 1930s. In an excerpt from her bleak but wonderfully moving autobiographical novel, Now in November *(1935), the author shows us how the very soul could be shaken by the devastation of suddenly dashed hope.*

The drouth went on. Trees withered, the grass turned hay, even the weeds dried into ashes, even the great trees with their roots fifty years under ground. Burdock and cockle were green near the empty creekbed, but the giant elms began to die. The limas died, lice on their blossoms, convolvulus strangling the string-bean bushes, and the carrots so bound in earth that nothing could budge them from the ground.

I walked some nights in the hay fields hoping to find a cooler air, and the desire for rain came to be almost a physical hurt. I could not feel any more the immensity of night and space, that littleness we speak of feeling before the stretching of fields and stars. I felt always too big and clumsy and achingly present. I could not shrink.

And then one noon when it seemed that we could not stand it any longer, that we should dry and crack open like the earth, there was a sudden blast of cold air and in the north we saw an

enormous bank of rising clouds. The air had been hot and still, storm-quiet and dark; but for a week clouds ominous and storm-surfed had been covering the sky and dissolving into nothing. The sunsets were clear and crystal as after a great rain, but not one drop had fallen. Now we saw the clouds tower up and reach forward like great waves, and there was the bull-mumbling of thunder. It had come up fast and still, no warning except the quiet, and we stood there staring like blocks of stone. Then Merle shouted, "It's here!" and ran out fast like a crazy person, and we saw stabs of lightning all through the black upboiling mass. Dad looked at Mother, and I saw the awful unmasking of his face, as if all the underground terror and despair were brought to the surface by his hope, and I felt a jab of pity and love for him stronger than I'd ever known before. Mother snatched up a bucket and put it out on the stones, half-wild to think that a drop might escape or go where it wasn't needed. We dragged out buckets and saucepans, even grabbed up bowls and put them out on the window-sill, and Merle pulled Grant's drinking-cup down from the nail. It got darker and a fierce wind whipped our clothes, and Merle was wild with excitement and the cold rushing of air. We saw Kerrin running up from the barn, lashed back and forth like a willow switch, and the sheep poured down along the road in a lumpy flood, baaing and crying toward the barn. I wanted to run and shriek, get wings and flap like the swooping crows. Grant looked ten years younger, shouted and called like a boy. We all looked at each other and felt burst free, poured out like rain. "Bring up the tubs," Father shouted. "She's coming, all right! She's here, I tell you!" He ran toward the cellar steps just as the first drops fell, hard-splashing and wide apart. He staggered back up with the wash-tubs, and the drops struck down like a noise of hammers on hollow tin. There was a wonderful brightness on Mother's face, a sort of light shining from it, almost a rapt and mystic look as she stood there with flower-pots dangling from her hand.

Those first drops scattered a few dead leaves on the vine and sank out of sight in earth. In the north a rift of blue widened and spread with terrible swiftness. The storm clouds loomed high and went on south. No more drops fell, and a long pole of sunlight came down through the clouds. A burnt and ragged hole in the clouds with the sun's eye coming through. We could feel the wind dying already, leaving only a cooler air. No rain.

Father's knees seemed to crumple up under him and he sat down heavy on the steps.

"God's will be done!" Kerrin said, and burst out laughing. "What're the barrels for, Grant?"

"Tubs to catch sunlight in," he answered her, "—storing up sweet light for the dark!" He looked fierce and haggard, sweat dry on his face from the wind, and a wire-cut ragged across his cheek like a lightning mark. Kerrin started to laugh again and threw up her arms. She looked queer and ridiculous, and I saw how thin she'd gotten, her neck like a twist of wire, and the wind seemed to blow through her bones. It made my heart sick to look at her. Grant turned away and shaded his eyes toward the sun. "Damned old Cyclopean eye!" he muttered. Stared up hating and helpless at the sky.

The clouds moved out and apart. Enormous stretches of sky were clean as glass. The thunder sounded a long way off, almost unheard. . . . Nothing was changed at all.

WOODY GUTHRIE

The New Deal dams of the 1930s brought both water and electrical power to much of the interior West. They also perpetuated land monopoly and factory-like farms harvested by migrant workers, part of an anonymous army of laborers—including refugees from the Dust Bowl—who wandered the West in the years of the Great Depression. Troubadour Woody Guthrie memorialized the joys and sorrows of these people in prose and in the lyrics of hundreds of songs that have become part of the national inheritance. The prose here is from his memoir, Bound for Glory *(1943); the lyrics are from "Pastures of Plenty" (1937), which many believe to be his greatest song. It was written, interestingly enough, as one of twenty-six he completed in twenty-six days while working for the government in an effort to publicize the virtues of Grand Coulee Dam.*

From *Bound for Glory*

I followed the trail out over the hill through the sun and the weeds. The camp was bigger than the town itself. People had dragged old car fenders up from the dumps, wired them from the limbs of oak trees a few feet off of the ground and this was a roof for some of them. Others had taken old canvas sacks or wagon sheets, stretched the canvas over little limbs cut so the forks braced each other, and that was a house for those folks. I heard two brothers standing back looking at their house saying, "I ain't lost my hand as a carpenter, yet." "My old eyes can still see to hit a nail." They'd carried buckets and tin cans out of the heap, flattened them on the ground, then nailed the tin onto crooked boards, and that was a mansion for them. Lots of people, families mostly, had some bedclothes with them, and I could see the old stinky, gummy quilts and blankets hung up like tents, and two or three kids of all ages playing around underneath. There was scatterings of cardboard shacks, where the people had lugged cartons, cases, packing boxes out from town and tacked them into a house. They was easy to build, but the first rain that hit them, they was goners.

Then about every few feet down the jungle hill you'd walk past a shack just sort of made out of everything in general—old strips of asphalt tar paper, double gunny sacks, an old dress, shirt, pair of overhalls, stretched up to cover half a side of a wall; bumpy corrugated iron, cement sacks, orange and apple crates took apart and nailed together with old rusty burnt nails from the cinder piles. Through a little square window on the side of a house, I'd hear bedsprings creaking and people talking. Men played cards, whittled, and women talked about work they'd struck and work they were hunting for. Dirt was on the floor of the house, and all kinds and colors of crawling and flying bugs come and went like they were getting paid for it. There were the big green blow-flies, the noisy little street flies, manure and lot flies, caterpillars

DOROTHEA LANGE. *Migrant worker on California highway.* 1935. Photograph. Bancroft Library, University of California, Berkeley.

and gnats from other dam jobs, bed bugs, fleas, and ticks sucking blood, while mosquitoes of all army and navy types, hummers, bombers, fighters, sung some good mosquito songs. In most cases, though, the families didn't even have a roof or shelter, but just got together once or twice every day and, squatting sort of Indian fashion around their fire, spaded a few bites of thickened flour gravy, old bread, or a thin watery stew. Gunny sacks, old clothes, hay and straw, fermenting bedclothes, are usually piled full of kids playing, or grown-ups resting and waiting for the word "work" to come.

The sun's shining through lots of places, other patches pretty shady, and right here at my elbow a couple of families are squatting down on an old slick piece of canvas; three or four quiet men, whittling, breaking grass stems, poking holes in leaves, digging into the hard ground; and the women rocking back and forth laughing out at something somebody'd said. A little baby sucks at a wind-burnt breast that nursed the four other kids that crawl about the fire. Cold rusty cans are their china cups and aluminum ware, and the hot still bucket of river water is as warm and clear as the air around. I watch a lot of little circles waving out from the middle of the water where a measuring worm has dropped from the limb of a tree and flips and flops for his very life. And I see a man with a forked stick reach the forks over into the bucket, smile, and go on talking about the work he's done; and in a moment, when the little worm clamps his feet around the forks of the stick, the man will lift him out, pull him up close to his face and look him over, then tap the stick over the rim of the bucket. When the little worm flips to the ground and goes humping away through the twigs and ashes, the whole bunch of people will smile and say, "Pretty close shave, mister worm. What do you think you are, a parshoot jumper?"

You've seen a million people like this already. Maybe you saw them down on the crowded side of your big city; the back side, that's jammed and packed, the hard section to drive through. Maybe you wondered where so many of them come from, how they eat, stay alive, what good they do, what makes them live like this? These people have had a house and a home just about like your own, settled down and had a job of work just about like you. Then something hit them and they lost all of that. They've been pushed out into the high lonesome highway, and they've gone down it, from coast to coast, from Canada to Mexico, looking for that home again. Now they're looking, for a while, in your town. Ain't much difference between you and them. If you was to walk out into this big tangled jungle camp and stand there with the other two thousand, somebody would just walk up and shake hands with you and ask you, What kind of work do you do, pardner?

Then maybe, farther out on the ragged edge of your town you've seen these people, after they've hit the road: the people that are called strangers, the people that follow the sun and the seasons to your country, follow the buds and the early leaves and come when the fruit and crops are ready to gather, and leave when the work is done. What kind of crops? Oil fields, power dams, pipe lines, canals, highways and hard-rock tunnels, skyscrapers, ships, are their crops. These are migrants now. They don't just set along in the sun—they go by the sun, and it lights up the country that they know is theirs.

*   *   *

When night come down, everything got a little stiller, and you could walk around from one bunch of people to the other one and talk about the weather. Although the weather wasn't such an ace-high subject to talk about, because around Redding for nine months hand running the weather don't change (it's hot and dry, hot and dry, and tomorrow it's still going to be hot and dry), you can hear little bunches of folks getting acquainted with each other, saying, "Really hot, ain't it?" "Yeah, dry too." "Mighty dry."

I run onto a few young people of twelve to twenty-five, mostly kids with their families, who picked the banjo or guitar, and sung songs. Two of these people drew quite a bunch every evening along toward sundown and it always took place just about the same way. An old bed was under a tree in their yard, and a baby boy romped around on it when the shade got cool, because in the early parts of the day the flies and bugs nearly packed him off. So this was his ripping and romping time, and it was the job of his two sisters, one around twelve and the other one around fourteen, to watch him and keep him from falling off onto the ground. Their dad parked his self back on an old car cushion. He threwed his eyes out over the rims of some two-bit specks just about every line or two on his reading matter, and run his Adam's apple up and down; and his wife nearby was singing what all the Lord had done for her, while the right young baby stood up for his first time, and jumped up and down, bouncing toward the edge of the mattress. The old man puckered up his face and sprayed a tree with tobacco juice, and said, "Girls. You girls. Go in the house and get your music box, and set there on the bed and play with the baby, so's he won't fall off."

One of the sisters tuned a string or two, then chorded a little. People walked from all over the camp and gathered, and the kid, mama, and dad, and all of the visitors, kept as still as daylight while the girls sang:

> *Takes a worried man to sing a worried song*
> *Takes a worried man to sing a worried song*
> *Takes a worried man to sing a worried song*
> *I'm worried nowwww*
> *But I won't be worried long.*

I heard these two girls from a-ways away where I was leaning back up against an old watering trough. I could hear their words just as plain as day, floating all around in the trees and down across the low places. I hung my guitar up on a stub of a limb, went down and stretched myself out on some dry grass, and listened to the girls for a long time. The baby kicked and bucked like a regular army mule whenever they'd quit their singing; but, as quick as they struck their first note or two on the next song, the kid would throw his wrist in his mouth, the slobbers would drip down onto his sister's lap, and the baby would kick both feet, but easy, keeping pretty good time to the guitar.

I don't know why I didn't tell them I had a guitar up yonder hanging on that tree. I just reared back and soaked in every note and every word of their singing. It was so clear and hon-

Dorothea Lange. *Migrant family.* c. 1935. Photograph. Library of Congress.

est sounding, no Hollywood put-on, no fake wiggling. It was better to me than the loud squalling and bawling you've got to do to make yourself heard in the old mobbed saloons. And, instead of getting you all riled up mentally, morally and sexually—no, it done something a lot better, something that's harder to do, something you need ten times more. It cleared your head up, that's what it done, caused you to fall back and let your draggy bones rest and your muscles go limber like a cat's.

Two little girls were making two thousand working people feel like I felt, rest like I rested. And when I say two thousand, take a look down off across these three little hills. You'll see a hat or two bobbing up above the brush. Somebody is going, somebody is coming, somebody is kneeling down drinking from the spring of water trickling out of the west hill. Five men are shaving before the same crooked hunk of old looking-glass, using tin cans for their water. A woman right up close to you wrings out a tough work shirt, saves the water for four more. You skim your eye out around the south hill, and not less than a hundred women are doing the same thing, washing, wringing, hanging out shirts, taking them down dry to iron. Not a one of them is talking above a whisper, and the one that is whispering almost feels guilty because she knows that ninety-nine out of every hundred are tired, weary, have felt sad, joked and laughed to keep from crying. But these two little girls are telling about all of that trouble, and everybody knows it's helping. These songs say something about our hard traveling, something about our hard luck, our hard get-by, but the songs say we'll come through all of these in pretty good shape, and we'll be all right, we'll work, make ourself useful, if only the telegram to build the dam would come in from Washington.

COLORPLATE 91

VICTOR HIGGINS. *Pueblo of Taos*. Before 1927. Oil on canvas. 52 x 56 in. Courtesy of The Anschutz Collection, Denver, Colorado.

COLORPLATE 92

OSCAR BERNINGHAUS. *A Showery Day, Grand Canyon*. 1915. Oil on canvas. 30 x 40 in. The Santa Fe Railway Collection of Southwestern Art, Schaumburg, Illinois.

COLORPLATE 93

FREMONT ELLIS. *New Mexico Spring*. c. 1950. Oil on canvas. 36 x 30 in. Courtesy of The Anschutz Collection, Denver, Colorado. © 1983 Fremont Ellis.

COLORPLATE 94

Leon Kroll. *Santa Fe Hills.* 1917. Oil on canvas. 26 1/4 x 32 1/4 in. Courtesy of The Anschutz Collection, Denver, Colorado.

COLORPLATE 95

ERNEST L. BLUMENSCHEIN. *Sangre De Cristo Mountains.* 1925. Oil on canvas. 50 x 60 in. Courtesy of The Anschutz Collection, Denver, Colorado.

COLORPLATE 96

EDWARD HOPPER. *Shoshone Cliffs*. 1941. Watercolor. 20 x 25 in. Butler Institute of American Art, Youngstown, Ohio.

COLORPLATE 97

Kenneth Miller Adams. *New Mexico Landscape*. Oil on canvas. 40 ¹/₈ x 36 ¹/₈ in.
Stark Museum of Art, Orange, Texas.

COLORPLATE 98

JOHN MARIN. *Storm over Taos*. 1930. Watercolor over graphite. 15 $^1/_{16}$ x 20 $^{15}/_{16}$ in. National Gallery of Art, Washington D.C. Alfred Stieglitz Collection.

"Pastures of Plenty"

It's a mighty hard row that my poor hands have hoed
My poor feet have traveled a hot dusty road
Out of your dustbowl and westward we rolled,
And your desert was hot and your mountains were cold.

I worked in your orchards of peaches and prunes,
Slept on the ground in the light of your moon;
On the edge of your city you've seen us and then
We come with the dust and we go with the wind.

California and Arizona, I make all your crops,
And it's north up to Oregon to gather your hops;
Dig the beets from your ground, cut the grapes from your vines
To set on your table your light sparkling wine.

Green Pastures of Plenty from dry desert ground,
From that Grand Coulee Dam where the water runs down;
Every state in this union us migrants have been
We work in this fight and we'll fight till we win.

Well, it's always we ramble, that river and I,
All along your green valley I'll work till I die;
My land I'll defend with my life if it be,
'Cause my Pastures of Plenty must always be free.

JOHN STEINBECK

"The Leader of the People"

As a movement, of course, the frontier experience was limited by its geography. But the westward movement was as much psychological as it was physical, and its ending inspired elegies. None was more moving than this well-loved short story from John Steinbeck's The Long Valley *(1938), in which an old man who stares at the sea embraces within his own vision an entire generation whose dreams and experiences can never be replicated.*

On Saturday afternoon Billy Buck, the ranch-hand, raked together the last of the old year's haystack and pitched small forkfuls over the wire fence to a few mildly interested cattle. High in the air small clouds like puffs of cannon smoke were driven eastward by the March wind. The wind could be heard whishing in the brush on the ridge crests, but no breath of it penetrated down into the ranch-cup.

The little boy, Jody, emerged from the house eating a thick piece of buttered bread. He saw Billy working on the last of the haystack. Jody tramped down scuffing his shoes in a way he had been told was destructive to good shoe-leather. A flock of white pigeons flew out of the black cypress tree as Jody passed, and circled the tree and landed again. A half-grown tortoise-shell cat leaped from the bunkhouse porch, galloped on stiff legs across the road, whirled and

BILL ANTON. *Basic Training*. c. 1988. Pencil. 20 x 30 in. Courtesy of the artist.

galloped back again. Jody picked up a stone to help the game along, but he was too late, for the cat was under the porch before the stone could be discharged. He threw the stone into the cypress tree and started the white pigeons on another whirling flight.

Arriving at the used-up haystack, the boy leaned against the barbed wire fence. "Will that be all of it, do you think?" he asked.

The middle-aged ranch-hand stopped his careful raking and stuck his fork into the ground. He took off his black hat and smoothed down his hair. "Nothing left of it that isn't soggy from ground moisture," he said. He replaced his hat and rubbed his dry leathery hands together.

"Ought to be plenty mice," Jody suggested.

"Lousy with them," said Billy. "Just crawling with mice."

"Well, maybe, when you get all through, I could call the dogs and hunt the mice."

"Sure, I guess you could," said Billy Buck. He lifted a forkful of the damp ground-hay and threw it into the air. Instantly three mice leaped out and burrowed frantically under the hay again.

Jody sighed with satisfaction. Those plump, sleek, arrogant mice were doomed. For eight months they had lived and multiplied in the haystack. They had been immune from cats, from traps, from poison and from Jody. They had grown smug in their security, overbearing and fat. Now the time of disaster had come; they would not survive another day.

Billy looked up at the top of the hills that surrounded the ranch. "Maybe you better ask your father before you do it," he suggested.

"Well, where is he? I'll ask him now."

"He rode up to the ridge ranch after dinner. He'll be back pretty soon."

Jody slumped against the fence post. "I don't think he'd care."

As Billy went back to his work he said ominously, "You'd better ask him anyway. You know how he is."

Jody did know. His father, Carl Tiflin, insisted upon giving permission for anything that was done on the ranch, whether it was important or not. Jody sagged farther against the post until he was sitting on the ground. He looked up at the little puffs of wind-driven cloud. "Is it like to rain, Billy?"

"It might. The wind's good for it, but not strong enough."

"Well, I hope it don't rain until after I kill those damn mice." He looked over his shoulder to see whether Billy had noticed the mature profanity. Billy worked on without comment.

Jody turned back and looked at the side-hill where the road from the outside world came down. The hill was washed with lean March sunshine. Silver thistles, blue lupins and a few poppies bloomed among the sage bushes. Halfway up the hill Jody could see Doubletree Mutt, the black dog, digging in a squirrel hole. He paddled for a while and then paused to kick bursts of dirt out between his hind legs, and he dug with an earnestness which belied the knowledge he must have had that no dog had ever caught a squirrel by digging in a hole.

Suddenly, while Jody watched, the black dog stiffened, and backed out of the hole and looked up the hill toward the cleft in the ridge where the road came through. Jody looked up too. For a moment Carl Tiflin on horseback stood out against the pale sky and then he moved down the road toward the house. He carried something white in his hand.

The boy started to his feet. "He's got a letter," Jody cried. He trotted away toward the ranch house, for the letter would probably be read aloud and he wanted to be there. He reached the house before his father did, and ran in. He heard Carl dismount from his creaking saddle and slap the horse on the side to send it to the barn where Billy would unsaddle it and turn it out.

Jody ran into the kitchen. "We got a letter!" he cried.

His mother looked up from a pan of beans. "Who has?"

"Father has. I saw it in his hand."

Carl strode into the kitchen then, and Jody's mother asked, "Who's the letter from, Carl?"

He frowned quickly. "How did you know there was a letter?"

She nodded her head in the boy's direction. "Big Britches Jody told me."

Jody was embarrassed.

His father looked down at him contemptuously. "He *is* getting to be a Big-Britches," Carl said. "He's minding everybody's business but his own. Got his big nose into everything."

Mrs. Tiflin relented a little. "Well, he hasn't enough to keep him busy. Who's the letter from?"

Carl still frowned on Jody. "I'll keep him busy if he isn't careful." He held out a sealed letter. "I guess it's from your father."

Mrs. Tiflin took a hairpin from her head and slit open the flap. Her lips pursed judiciously. Jody saw her eyes snap back and forth over the lines. "He says," she translated, "he says he's going to drive out Saturday to stay for a little while. Why, this is Saturday. The letter must have been delayed." She looked at the postmark. "This was mailed day before yesterday. It should have been here yesterday." She looked up questioningly at her husband, and then her face darkened angrily. "Now what have you got that look on you for? He doesn't come often."

Carl turned his eyes away from her anger. He could be stern with her most of the time, but when occasionally her temper arose, he could not combat it.

"What's the matter with you?" she demanded again.

In his explanation there was a tone of apology Jody himself might have used. "It's just that he talks," Carl said lamely. "Just talks."

"Well, what of it? You talk yourself."

"Sure I do. But your father only talks about one thing."

"Indians!" Jody broke in excitedly. "Indians and crossing the plains!"

Carl turned fiercely on him. "You get out, Mr. Big-Britches! Go on, now! Get out!"

Jody went miserably out the back door and closed the screen with elaborate quietness. Under the kitchen window his shamed, downcast eyes fell upon a curiously shaped stone, a stone of such fascination that he squatted down and picked it up and turned it over in his hands.

The voices came clearly to him through the open kitchen window. "Jody's damn well right," he heard his father say. "Just Indians and crossing the plains. I've heard that story about how the horses got driven off about a thousand times. He just goes on and on, and he never changes a word in the things he tells."

When Mrs. Tiflin answered her tone was so changed that Jody, outside the window, looked up from his study of the stone. Her voice had become soft and explanatory. Jody knew how her face would have changed to match the tone. She said quietly, "Look at it this way, Carl. That was the big thing in my father's life. He led a wagon train clear across the plains to the coast, and when it was finished, his life was done. It was a big thing to do, but it didn't last long enough. Look!" she continued, "it's as though he was born to do that, and after he finished it, there wasn't anything more for him to do but think about it and talk about it. If there'd been any farther west to go, he'd have gone. He's told me so himself. But at last there was the ocean. He lives right by the ocean where he had to stop."

She had caught Carl, caught him and entangled him in her soft tone.

"I've seen him," he agreed quietly. "He goes down and stares off west over the ocean." His voice sharpened a little. "And then he goes up to the Horseshoe Club in Pacific Grove, and he tells people how the Indians drove off the horses."

She tried to catch him again. "Well, it's everything to him. You might be patient with him and pretend to listen."

Carl turned impatiently away. "Well, if it gets too bad, I can always go down to the bunkhouse and sit with Billy," he said irritably. He walked through the house and slammed the front door after him.

Jody ran to his chores. He dumped the grain to the chickens without chasing any of them. He gathered the eggs from the nests. He trotted into the house with the wood and interlaced it so carefully in the wood-box that two armloads seemed to fill it to overflowing.

His mother had finished the beans by now. She stirred up the fire and brushed off the stove-top with a turkey wing. Jody peered cautiously at her to see whether any rancor toward him remained. "Is he coming today?" Jody asked.

"That's what his letter said."

"Maybe I better walk up the road to meet him."

Mrs. Tiflin clanged the stove-lid shut. "That would be nice," she said. "He'd probably like to be met."

"I guess I'll just do it then."

Outside, Jody whistled shrilly to the dogs. "Come on up the hill," he commanded. The two dogs waved their tails and ran ahead. Along the roadside the sage had tender new tips. Jody tore off some pieces and rubbed them on his hands until the air was filled with the sharp wild smell. With a rush the dogs leaped from the road and yapped into the brush after a rabbit. That was the last Jody saw of them, for when they failed to catch the rabbit, they went back home.

Jody plodded on up the hill toward the ridge top. When he reached the little cleft where the road came through, the afternoon wind struck him and blew up his hair and ruffled his shirt. He looked down on the little hills and ridges below and then out at the huge green Salinas Valley. He could see the white town of Salinas far out in the flat and the flash of its windows under the waning sun. Directly below him, in an oak tree, a crow congress had convened. The tree was black with crows all cawing at once.

Then Jody's eyes followed the wagon road down from the ridge where he stood, and lost it behind a hill, and picked it up again on the other side. On that distant stretch he saw a cart slowly pulled by a bay horse. It disappeared behind the hill. Jody sat down on the ground and watched the place where the cart would reappear again. The wind sang on the hilltops and the puff-ball clouds hurried eastward.

Then the cart came into sight and stopped. A man dressed in black dismounted from the seat and walked to the horse's head. Although it was so far away, Jody knew he had unhooked the check-rein, for the horse's head dropped forward. The horse moved on, and the man walked slowly up the hill beside it. Jody gave a glad cry and ran down the road toward them. The squirrels bumped along off the road, and a road-runner flirted its tail and raced over the edge of the hill and sailed out like a glider.

Jody tried to leap into the middle of his shadow at every step. A stone rolled under his foot and he went down. Around a little bend he raced, and there, a short distance ahead, were his grandfather and the cart. The boy dropped from his unseemly running and approached at a dignified walk.

The horse plodded stumble-footedly up the hill and the old man walked beside it. In the lowering sun their giant shadows flickered darkly behind them. The grandfather was dressed in a black broadcloth suit and he wore kid congress gaiters and a black tie on a short, hard collar. He carried his black slouch hat in his hand. His white beard was cropped close and his white eyebrows overhung his eyes like moustaches. The blue eyes were sternly merry. About the whole face and figure there was a granite dignity, so that every motion seemed an impossible thing. Once at rest, it seemed the old man would be stone, would never move again. His steps

SAMUEL COLMAN. *The Oregon Trail.* Courtesy Paulus Leeser.

were slow and certain. Once made, no step could ever be retraced; once headed in a direction, the path would never bend nor the pace increase nor slow.

When Jody appeared around the bend, Grandfather waved his hat slowly in welcome, and he called, "Why, Jody! Come down to meet me, have you?"

Jody sidled near and turned and matched his step to the old man's step and stiffened his body and dragged his heels a little. "Yes, sir," he said. "We got your letter only today."

"Should have been here yesterday," said Grandfather. "It certainly should. How are all the folks?"

"They're fine, sir." He hesitated and then suggested shyly, "Would you like to come on a mouse hunt tomorrow, sir?"

"Mouse hunt, Jody?" Grandfather chuckled. "Have the people of this generation come down to hunting mice? They aren't very strong, the new people, but I hardly thought mice would be game for them."

"No, sir. It's just play. The haystack's gone. I'm going to drive out the mice to the dogs. And you can watch, or even beat the hay a little."

The stern, merry eyes turned down on him. "I see. You don't eat them, then. You haven't come to that yet."

Jody explained, "The dogs eat them, sir. It wouldn't be much like hunting Indians, I guess."

"No, not much—but then later, when the troops were hunting Indians and shooting children and burning teepees, it wasn't much different from your mouse hunt."

They topped the rise and started down into the ranch cup, and they lost the sun from their shoulders. "You've grown," Grandfather said. "Nearly an inch, I should say."

"More," Jody boasted. "Where they mark me on the door, I'm up more than an inch since Thanksgiving even."

Grandfather's rich throaty voice said, "Maybe you're getting too much water and turning to pith and stalk. Wait until you head out, and then we'll see."

Jody looked quickly into the old man's face to see whether his feelings should be hurt, but there was no will to injure, no punishing nor putting-in-your-place light in the keen blue eyes. "We might kill a pig," Jody suggested.

"Oh, no! I couldn't let you do that. You're just humoring me. It isn't the time and you know it."

"You know Riley, the big boar, sir?"

"Yes. I remember Riley well."

"Well, Riley ate a hole into that same haystack, and it fell down on him and smothered him."

"Pigs do that when they can," said Grandfather.

"Riley was a nice pig, for a boar, sir. I rode him sometimes, and he didn't mind."

A door slammed at the house below them, and they saw Jody's mother standing on the porch waving her apron in welcome. And they saw Carl Tiflin walking up from the barn to be at the house for the arrival.

The sun had disappeared from the hills by now. The blue smoke from the house chimney hung in flat layers in the purpling ranch-cup. The puff-ball clouds, dropped by the falling wind, hung listlessly in the sky.

Billy Buck came out of the bunkhouse and flung a wash basin of soapy water on the ground. He had been shaving in mid-week, for Billy held Grandfather in reverence, and Grandfather said that Billy was one of the few men of the new generation who had not gone soft. Although Billy was in middle age, Grandfather considered him a boy. Now Billy was hurrying toward the house too.

When Jody and Grandfather arrived, the three were waiting for them in front of the yard gate.

Carl said, "Hello, sir. We've been looking for you."

Mrs. Tiflin kissed Grandfather on the side of his beard, and stood still while his big hand patted her shoulder. Billy shook hands solemnly, grinning under his straw moustache. "I'll put up your horse," said Billy, and he led the rig away.

Grandfather watched him go, and then, turning back to the group, he said as he had said a hundred times before, "There's a good boy. I knew his father, old Mule-tail Buck. I never knew why they called him Mule-tail except he packed mules."

Mrs. Tiflin turned and led the way into the house. "How long are you going to stay, Father? Your letter didn't say."

"Well, I don't know. I thought I'd stay about two weeks. But I never stay as long as I think I'm going to."

In a short while they were sitting at the white oilcloth table eating their supper. The lamp with the tin reflector hung over the table. Outside the dining-room windows the big moths battered softly against the glass.

Grandfather cut his steak into tiny pieces and chewed slowly. "I'm hungry," he said. "Driving out here got my appetite up. It's like when we were crossing. We all got so hungry every night we could hardly wait to let the meat get done. I could eat about five pounds of buffalo meat every night."

"It's moving around does it," said Billy. "My father was a government packer. I helped him when I was a kid. Just the two of us could about clean up a deer's ham."

"I knew your father, Billy," said Grandfather. "A fine man he was. They called him Mule-tail Buck. I don't know why except he packed mules."

"That was it," Billy agreed. "He packed mules."

Grandfather put down his knife and fork and looked around the table. "I remember one time we ran out of meat—" His voice dropped to a curious low sing-song, dropped into a tonal groove the story had worn for itself. "There was no buffalo, no antelope, not even rabbits. The hunters couldn't even shoot a coyote. That was the time for the leader to be on the watch. I was the leader, and I kept my eyes open. Know why? Well, just the minute the people began to get hungry they'd start slaughtering the team oxen. Do you believe that? I've heard of parties that just ate up their draft cattle. Started from the middle and worked toward the ends. Finally they'd eat the lead pair, and then the wheelers. The leader of a party had to keep them from doing that."

In some manner a big moth got into the room and circled the hanging kerosene lamp. Billy got up and tried to clap it between his hands. Carl struck with a cupped palm and caught the moth and broke it. He walked to the window and dropped it out.

"As I was saying," Grandfather began again, but Carl interrupted him. "You'd better eat some more meat. All the rest of us are ready for our pudding."

Jody saw a flash of anger in his mother's eyes. Grandfather picked up his knife and fork. "I'm pretty hungry, all right," he said. "I'll tell you about that later."

When supper was over, when the family and Billy Buck sat in front of the fireplace in the other room, Jody anxiously watched Grandfather. He saw the signs he knew. The bearded head leaned forward; the eyes lost their sternness and looked wonderingly into the fire; the big lean fingers laced themselves on the black knees. "I wonder," he began, "I just wonder whether I ever told you how those thieving Piutes drove off thirty-five of our horses."

"I think you did," Carl interrupted. "Wasn't it just before you went up into the Tahoe country?"

Grandfather turned quickly toward his son-in-law. "That's right. I guess I must have told you that story."

"Lots of times," Carl said cruelly, and he avoided his wife's eyes. But he felt the angry eyes on him, and he said, " 'Course I'd like to hear it again."

Grandfather looked back at the fire. His fingers unlaced and laced again. Jody knew how he felt, how his insides were collapsed and empty. Hadn't Jody been called a Big-Britches that very afternoon? He arose to heroism and opened himself to the term Big-Britches again. "Tell about Indians," he said softly.

Grandfather's eyes grew stern again. "Boys always want to hear about Indians. It was a job for men, but boys want to hear about it. Well, let's see. Did I ever tell you how I wanted each wagon to carry a long iron plate?"

Everyone but Jody remained silent. Jody said, "No. You didn't."

"Well, when the Indians attacked, we always put the wagons in a circle and fought from between the wheels. I thought that if every wagon carried a long plate with rifle holes, the men could stand the plates on the outside of the wheels when the wagons were in the circle and they would be protected. It would save lives and that would make up for the extra weight of the iron. But of course the party wouldn't do it. No party had done it before and they couldn't see why they should go to the expense. They lived to regret it, too."

Jody looked at his mother, and knew from her expression that she was not listening at all. Carl picked at a callus on his thumb and Billy Buck watched a spider crawling up the wall.

Grandfather's tone dropped into its narrative groove again. Jody knew in advance exactly what words would fall. The story droned on, speeded up for the attack, grew sad over the wounds, struck a dirge at the burials on the great plains. Jody sat quietly watching Grandfather. The stern blue eyes were detached. He looked as though he were not very interested in the story himself.

When it was finished, when the pause had been politely respected as the frontier of the story, Billy Buck stood up and stretched and hitched his trousers. "I guess I'll turn in," he said. Then he faced Grandfather. "I've got an old powder horn and a cap and ball pistol down to the bunkhouse. Did I ever show them to you?"

Grandfather nodded slowly. "Yes, I think you did, Billy. Reminds me of a pistol I had when I was leading the people across." Billy stood politely until the little story was done, and then he said, "Good night," and went out of the house.

Carl Tiflin tried to turn the conversation then. "How's the country between here and Monterey? I've heard it's pretty dry."

"It is dry," said Grandfather. "There's not a drop of water in the Laguna Seca. But it's a long pull from '87. The whole country was powder then, and in '61 I believe all the coyotes starved to death. We had fifteen inches of rain this year."

"Yes, but it all came too early. We could do with some now." Carl's eye fell on Jody. "Hadn't you better be getting to bed?"

Jody stood up obediently. "Can I kill the mice in the old haystack, sir?"

"Mice? Oh! Sure, kill them all off. Billy said there isn't any good hay left."

Jody exchanged a secret and satisfying look with Grandfather. "I'll kill every one tomorrow," he promised.

Jody lay in his bed and thought of the impossible world of Indians and buffaloes, a world that had ceased to be forever. He wished he could have been living in the heroic time, but he knew he was not of heroic timber. No one living now, save possibly Billy Buck, was worthy to do the things that had been done. A race of giants had lived then, fearless men, men of a staunchness unknown in this day. Jody thought of the wide plains and of the wagons moving across like centipedes. He thought of Grandfather on a huge white horse, marshaling the people. Across his mind marched the great phantoms, and they marched off the earth and they were gone.

He came back to the ranch for a moment, then. He heard the dull rushing sound that space and silence make. He heard one of the dogs, out in the doghouse, scratching a flea and bumping his elbow against the floor with every stroke. Then the wind arose again and the black cypress groaned and Jody went to sleep.

He was up half an hour before the triangle sounded for breakfast. His mother was rattling the stove to make the flames roar when Jody went through the kitchen. "You're up early," she said. "Where are you going?"

"Out to get a good stick. We're going to kill the mice today."

"Who is 'we'?"

"Why, Grandfather and I."

"So you've got him in it. You always like to have someone in with you in case there's blame to share."

"I'll be right back," said Jody. "I just want to have a good stick ready for after breakfast."

He closed the screen door after him and went out into the cool blue morning. The birds were noisy in the dawn and the ranch cats came down from the hill like blunt snakes. They had been hunting gophers in the dark, and although the four cats were full of gopher meat, they sat in a semicircle at the back door and mewed piteously for milk. Doubletree Mutt and Smasher moved sniffing along the edge of the brush, performing the duty with rigid ceremony, but when Jody whistled, their heads jerked up and their tails waved. They plunged down to him, wriggling their skins and yawning. Jody patted their heads seriously, and moved on to the weathered scrap pile. He selected an old broom handle and a short piece of inch-square scrap wood. From his pocket he took a shoelace and tied the ends of the stick loosely together to make a flail. He whistled his new weapon through the air and struck the ground experimentally, while the dogs leaped aside and whined with apprehension.

Jody turned and started down past the house toward the old haystack ground to look over the field of slaughter, but Billy Buck, sitting patiently on the back steps, called to him, "You better come back. It's only a couple of minutes till breakfast."

Jody changed his course and moved toward the house. He leaned his flail against the steps. "That's to drive the mice out," he said. "I'll bet they're fat. I'll bet they don't know what's going to happen to them today."

"No, nor you either," Billy remarked philosophically, "nor me, nor anyone."

Jody was staggered by this thought. He knew it was true. His imagination twitched away from the mouse hunt. Then his mother came out on the back porch and struck the triangle, and all thoughts fell in a heap.

Grandfather hadn't appeared at the table when they sat down. Billy nodded at his empty chair. "He's all right? He isn't sick?"

"He takes a long time to dress," said Mrs. Tiflin. "He combs his whiskers and rubs up his shoes and brushes his clothes."

Carl scattered sugar on his mush. "A man that's led a wagon train across the plains has got to be pretty careful how he dresses."

Mrs. Tiflin turned on him. "Don't do that, Carl! Please don't!" There was more of threat than of request in her tone. And the threat irritated Carl.

"Well, how many times do I have to listen to the story of the iron plates, and the thirty-five horses? That time's done. Why can't he forget it, now it's done?" He grew angrier while he talked, and his voice rose. "Why does he have to tell them over and over? He came across the plains. All right! Now it's finished. Nobody wants to hear about it over and over."

The door into the kitchen closed softly. The four at the table sat frozen. Carl laid his mush spoon on the table and touched his chin with his fingers.

RANDALL DAVEY. *Western Man.* Oil.
24 x 20 in. The Harmsen Collection.

Then the kitchen door opened and Grandfather walked in. His mouth smiled tightly and his eyes were squinted. "Good morning," he said, and he sat down and looked at his mush dish.

Carl could not leave it there. "Did—did you hear what I said?"

Grandfather jerked a little nod.

"I don't know what got into me, sir. I didn't mean it. I was just being funny."

Jody glanced in shame at his mother, and he saw that she was looking at Carl, and that she wasn't breathing. It was an awful thing that he was doing. He was tearing himself to pieces to talk like that. It was a terrible thing to him to retract a word, but to retract it in shame was infinitely worse.

Grandfather looked sidewise. "I'm trying to get right side up," he said gently. "I'm not being mad. I don't mind what you said, but it might be true, and I would mind that."

"It isn't true," said Carl. "I'm not feeling well this morning. I'm sorry I said it."

"Don't be sorry, Carl. An old man doesn't see things sometimes. Maybe you're right. The crossing is finished. Maybe it should be forgotten, now it's done."

Carl got up from the table. "I've had enough to eat. I'm going to work. Take your time, Billy!" He walked quickly out of the dining-room. Billy gulped the rest of his food and followed soon after. But Jody could not leave his chair.

"Won't you tell any more stories?" Jody asked.

"Why, sure I'll tell them, but only when—I'm sure people want to hear them."

"I like to hear them, sir."

"Oh! Of course you do, but you're a little boy. It was a job for men, but only little boys like to hear about it."

Jody got up from his place. "I'll wait outside for you, sir. I've got a good stick for those mice."

He waited by the gate until the old man came out on the porch. "Let's go down and kill the mice now," Jody called.

"I think I'll just sit in the sun, Jody. You go kill the mice."

"You can use my stick if you like."

"No, I'll just sit here a while."

Jody turned disconsolately away, and walked down toward the old haystack. He tried to whip up his enthusiasm with thoughts of the fat juicy mice. He beat the ground with his flail. The dogs coaxed and whined about him, but he could not go. Back at the house he could see Grandfather sitting on the porch, looking small and thin and black.

Jody gave up and went to sit on the steps at the old man's feet.

"Back already? Did you kill the mice?"

"No, sir. I'll kill them some other day."

The morning flies buzzed close to the ground and the ants dashed about in front of the steps. The heavy smell of sage slipped down the hill. The porch boards grew warm in the sunshine.

Jody hardly knew when Grandfather started to talk. "I shouldn't stay here, feeling the way I do." He examined his strong old hands. "I feel as though the crossing wasn't worth doing." His eyes moved up the side-hill and stopped on a motionless hawk perched on a dead limb. "I tell those old stories, but they're not what I want to tell. I only know how I want people to feel when I tell them.

"It wasn't Indians that were important, nor adventures nor even getting out here. It was a whole bunch of people made into one big crawling beast. And I was the head. It was westering and westering. Every man wanted something for himself, but the big beast that was all of them wanted only westering. I was the leader, but if I hadn't been there, someone else would have been the head. The thing had to have a head.

"Under the little bushes the shadows were black at white noonday. When we saw the mountains at last, we cried—all of us. But it wasn't getting here that mattered, it was movement and westering.

"We carried life out here and set it down the way those ants carry eggs. And I was the leader. The westering was as big as God, and the slow steps that made the movement piled up and piled up until the continent was crossed.

"Then we came down to the sea, and it was done." He stopped and wiped his eyes until the rims were red. "That's what I should be telling instead of stories."

When Jody spoke, Grandfather started and looked down at him. "Maybe I could lead the people some day," Jody said.

The old man smiled. "There's no place to go. There's the ocean to stop you. There's a line of old men along the shore hating the ocean because it stopped them."

"In boats I might, sir."

"No place to go, Jody. Every place is taken. But that's not the worst—no, not the worst. Westering has died out of the people. Westering isn't a hunger any more. It's all done. Your father is right. It is finished." He laced his fingers on his knee and looked at them.

Jody felt very sad. "If you'd like a glass of lemonade I could make it for you."

Grandfather was about to refuse, and then he saw Jody's face. "That would be nice," he said. "Yes, it would be nice to drink a lemonade."

Jody ran into the kitchen where his mother was wiping the last of the breakfast dishes. "Can I have a lemon to make a lemonade for Grandfather?"

His mother mimicked—"And another lemon to make a lemonade for you."

"No, ma'am. I don't want one."

"Jody! You're sick!" Then she stopped suddenly. "Take a lemon out of the cooler," she said softly. "Here, I'll reach the squeezer down to you."

SCENES OF WONDER AND CURIOSITY

N. P. LANGFORD

From "The Wonders of the Yellowstone"

The West had always been perceived as a place where scenes of wonder and curiosity could be discovered—and none were more wondrous or curious than those of the Yellowstone region. N.P. Langford joined an expedition up the Yellowstone River in 1870 to satisfy his own curiosity. His description of what he and his companions found, published in the May 1871 issue of Scribner's Monthly, *helped persuade Congress to establish Yellowstone as America's first national park in 1872.*

We made a circuit round the head of the inlet to the springs we had seen. . . . They were widely different from any we had visited before. In all they numbered 150, and were scattered along the lake shore about a mile, at a distance of 100 yards from the beach. Those farthest inland resembled boiling mud of various degrees of consistency, some not thicker than paint, others so dense that as they boiled over, the contents piled into heaps, which gradually spread over the ground, forming an extensive vitrified surface. This sediment varies in color—that flowing from some of the apertures being white as chalk, that from others of a delicate lavender hue, and from others, of a brilliant pink color. . . .

In close proximity to these springs are others of pure, odorless water. Near the shore were several boiling springs, around which the sedimentary increment had formed into mounds of various sizes and heights. The deposit around one of these springs resembles a miniature forest of pines.

The most remarkable springs in this group, six or seven in number, are of pure ultramarine hue—very large, and wonderfully transparent. The largest is forty feet wide by seventy feet long. The sides are funnel-shaped, converging regularly to the depth of forty feet, where they present a dark and apparently unfathomable chasm. From the surface to this opening the sides of the funnel are furrowed and sinuous, coated with a white sediment, which contrasts vividly with the dark orifice at its base.

This group of springs exhibit in their deposits a great variety of shades and colors—no two of them being alike. Their constant overflow has fashioned a concrete bank of commingled tufa, eight feet in height and a quarter of a mile in length, on the margin of the lake. The waves have worn this bank into large caverns, which respond in hollow murmurs to their fierce assaults. Between the springs are numerous vents and craters, from which heated vapor is constantly rising. Along the edge of the water, and ten or twenty feet from shore, many springs are bubbling, none of which seem to be strongly impregnated with sulphur. The beach, for a mile or more, is strewn with fragments of sinter of various colors, which have been worn by the waves into many fantastic forms.

* * *

We bade adieu to Yellowstone Lake, surfeited with the wonders we had seen, and in the belief that the interesting portion of our journey was over. The desire for home had superseded

WILLIAM HENRY JACKSON. *Old Faithful in eruption in Yellowstone National Park.* 1872. Photograph. Courtesy Museum of New Mexico, Santa Fe.

all thought of further exploration. We had seen the greatest wonders on the continent, and were convinced that there was not on the globe another region where, within the same limits, nature had crowded so much of grandeur and majesty, with so much of novelty and wonder. Our only care was to return home as rapidly as possible. Three days of active travel from the head-waters of the Madison, would find us among the settlers in the beautiful lower valley of that picturesque river, and within twelve miles of Virginia City, where we hoped to meet with Mr. Everts, and realize afresh that "all is well that ends well."

Judge, then, what must have been our astonishment, as we entered the basin at midafternoon of our second day's travel, to see in the clear sunlight, at no great distance, an immense volume of clear, sparkling water projected into the air to the height of one hundred and twenty-five feet. "Geysers! geysers!" exclaimed one of our company, and, spurring our jaded horses, we soon gathered around this wonderful phenomenon. It was indeed a perfect geyser. The aperture through which the jet was projected was an irregular oval, three feet by seven in diameter. The margin of sinter was curiously piled up, and the exterior crust was filled with little hollows full of water, in which were small globules of sediment, some having gathered around bits of wood and other nuclei. This geyser is elevated thirty feet above the level of the surrounding plain, and the crater rises five or six feet above the mound. It spouted at regular intervals nine times during our stay, the columns of boiling water being thrown from ninety to one hundred and twenty-five feet at each discharge, which lasted from fifteen to twenty minutes. We gave it the name of "Old Faithful."

CLARENCE E. DUTTON

From *Tertiary History of the Grand Cañon District*
Grand Landscapes

The Grand Canyon (designated a national park in 1908) is perhaps the prime example of the outlandishly beautiful geography that gives the western landscape much of its appeal. When the Spanish encountered the chasm in 1540, they were terrified by its unfamiliar terrain. But geologist Clarence E. Dutton was so fascinated by it that his account in Tertiary History of the Grand Cañon District *(1882) achieved levels of poetic description not usually seen in government reports.*

The observer who, unfamiliar with plateau scenery, stands for the first time upon the brink of the inner gorge, is almost sure to view his surroundings with commingled feelings of disappointment and perplexity. The fame of the chasm of the Colorado is great; but so indefinite and meager have been the descriptions of it that the imagination is left to its own devices in framing a mental conception of it. And such subjective pictures are of course wide of the truth. When he first visits it the preconceived notion is at once dissipated and the mind is slow to receive a new one. The creations of his own fancy no doubt are clothed with a vague grandeur and beauty, but not with the grandeur and beauty of Nature. When the reality is before him the impression bears some analogy to that produced upon the visitor who for the first time enters St. Peter's Church at Rome. He expected to be profoundly awe-struck by the unexampled dimensions, and to feel exalted by the beauty of its proportions and decoration. He forgets that the human mind itself is of small capacity and receives its impressions slowly, by labored processes of comparison. So, too, at the brink of the chasm, there comes at first a feeling of disappointment; it does not seem so grand as we expected. At length we strive to make comparisons. The river is clearly defined below, but it looks about large enough to turn a village gristmill; yet we know it is a stream three or four hundred feet wide. Its surface looks as motionless as a lake seen from a distant mountain-top. We know it is a rushing torrent. The ear is strained to hear the roar of its waters and catches it faintly at intervals as the eddying breezes waft it upwards; but the sound seems exhausted by the distance. We perceive dimly a mottling of light and shadow upon the surface of the stream, and the flecks move with a barely perceptible cloud-like motion. They are the fields of white foam lashed up at the foot of some cataract and sailing swiftly onward.

Perhaps the first notion of the reality is gained when we look across the abyss to the opposite crest-line. It seems as if a strong, nervous arm could hurl a stone against the opposing wallface; but in a moment we catch sight of vegetation growing upon the very brink. There are trees in scattered groves which we might at first have mistaken for wage or desert furze. Here at length we have a stadium or standard of comparison which serves for the mind much the same purpose as a man standing at the base of one of the sequoias of the Mariposa grove. And now the real magnitudes begin to unfold themselves, and as the attention is held firmly the mind grows restive under the increasing burden. Every time the eye ranges up or down its face it seems more distant and more vast. At length we recoil, overburdened with the perceptions already attained and yet half vexed at the inadequacy of our faculties to comprehend more.

The magnitude of the chasm, however, is by no means the most impressive element of its character; nor is the inner gorge the most impressive of its constituent parts. The thoughtful mind is far more deeply moved by the splendor and grace of Nature's architecture. Forms so new to the culture of civilized races and so strongly contrasted with those which have been the ideals of thirty generations of white men cannot indeed be appreciated after the study of a sin-

JOHN K. HILLERS. *Grand Canyon, Colorado River, Arizona.* 1871–79. Photograph. U.S. Geological Survey.

gle hour or day. The first conception of them may not be a pleasing one. They may seem merely abnormal, curious, and even grotesque. But he who fancies that Nature has exhausted her wealth of beauty in other lands strangely underestimates her versatility and power. In this far-off desert are forms which surprise us by their unaccustomed character. We find at first no place for them in the range of our conventional notions. But as they become familiar we find them appealing to the aesthetic sense as powerfully as any scenery that ever invited the pencil of Claude or of Turner.

JOHN MUIR

From "Explorations in the Great Tuolumne Cañon"

John Muir, founder of the Sierra Club (1892) and the Great Ancestor of American conservation, first saw the Sierra Nevada of California in 1868 and nearly swooned. From then on, he wrote about these mountains—particularly what became, largely through his efforts, Yosemite National Park (1890)—with greater passion and precision than anyone before or since, as this excerpt from an article first published in the Overland Monthly *of 1873 demonstrates.*

By the time the glaciers were melted from my mind, the sun was nearing the horizon. Looking once more at the Tuolumne glistening far beneath, I was seized with an invincible determination to descend the cañon wall to the bottom. Unable to discover any way that I cared to try, from where I stood, I ran back along the ridge by which I approached the valley, then westward about a mile, and clambered out upon another point that stood boldly forward into the cañon. From here I had a commanding view of a small side-cañon on my left, running down at a steep angle; which I judged, from the character of the opposite wall, might possibly be practicable all the way. Then I hastened back among the latest sun-shadows to my camp in the spruce trees, resolved to make an attempt to penetrate the heart of the Great Cañon next day. I awoke early, breakfasted, and waited for the dawn. The thin air was frosty, but, knowing that I would be warm in climbing, I tightened my belt, and set out in my shirt-sleeves, limb-loose as a pugilist.

Below, the cañon becomes narrow and smooth, the smoothness being due to the action of snow avalanches that sweep down from the mountains above and pour through this steep and narrow portion like torrents of water. I had now accomplished a descent of nearly 2,500 feet from the top, and there remained about 2,000 feet to be accomplished before I reached the river. As I descended this smooth portion, I found that its bottom became more and more steeply inclined, and I halted to scan it closely, hoping to discover some way of avoiding it altogether, by passing around on either of the sides. But this I quickly decided to be impossible, the sides being apparently as bare and seamless as the bottom. I then began to creep down the smooth incline, depending mostly upon my hands, wetting them with my tongue and striking them flatly upon the rock to make them stick by atmospheric pressure. In this way I very nearly reached a point where a seam comes down to the bottom in an easy slope, which would enable me to escape to a portion of the main wall that I knew must be climbable from the number of live-oak bushes growing upon it. But after cautiously measuring the steepness — scrutinizing it again and again, and trying my wet hands upon it — both mind and limbs declared it unsafe, for the least slip would insure a tumble of hundreds of feet. I was, therefore, compelled to retrace my devious slides and leaps up the cañon, making a vertical rise of about 500 feet, in order that I might reach a point where I could climb out to the main cañon-wall, my only hope of reaching the bottom that day being by picking my way down its face. I knew from my observations of the previous day that this portion of the cañon was crossed by well-developed planes of cleavage, that prevented the formation of smooth vertical precipices of more than a few hundred feet in height, and the same in width. These may usually be passed without much difficulty.

After two or three hours more of hard scrambling, I at length stood among cool shadows on the river-bank, in the heart of the great unexplored cañon, having made a descent of about 4,500 feet, the bottom of this portion of the cañon above the level of the sea being quite 4,600 feet. The cañon is here fully 200 yards wide (about twice the size of the Merced at Yosemite), and timbered richly with libocedrus and pine. A beautiful reach stretches away from where I sat resting, its border-trees leaning toward each other, making a long arched lane, down which the joyous waters sung in foaming rapids. Stepping out of the river grove to a small sandy flat, I obtained a general view of the cañon-walls, rising to a height of from 4,000 to 5,000 feet, composed of rocks of every form of which Yosemites are made. About a mile up the cañon, on the south side, there is a most imposing rock, nearly related in form to the Yosemite Half Dome. About a mile farther down the cañon, I came to the mouth of a tributary that enters the trunk cañon on the north. Its glacier must have been of immense size, for it eroded its channel down to a level with the bottom of the main cañon. The rocks of both this tributary and of the main cañon present traces of all kinds of ice-action—moraines, polished and striated surfaces, and rocks of special forms. Among these mighty cliffs and domes there is no word of chaos, or of desolation; every rock is as elaborately and thoughtfully carved and finished as a crystal or shell.

The life of a mountaineer is favorable to the development of soul-life as well as limb-life, each receiving abundance of exercise and abundance of food. We little suspect the great capacity that our flesh has for knowledge. Oftentimes in climbing cañon-walls I have come to polished slopes near the heads of precipices that seemed to be too steep to be ventured upon. After scrutinizing them and carefully noting every dint and scratch that might give hope for a foothold, I have decided that they were unsafe. Yet my limbs, possessing a separate sense, would be of a different opinion, after they also had examined the descent, and confidently have

EDWARD HUGHES. *John Muir*. Photograph. Library of Congress.

set out to cross the condemned slopes against the remonstrances of my other will. My legs sometimes transport me to camp, in the darkness, over cliffs and through bogs and forests that are inaccessible to city legs during the day, even when piloted by the mind which owns them. In like manner the soul sets forth at times upon rambles of its own. Brooding over some vast mountain landscape, or among the spiritual countenances of mountain flowers, our bodies disappear, our mortal coils come off without any shuffling, and we blend into the rest of Nature, utterly blind to the boundaries that measure human quantities into separate individuals.

The next morning after my raid in the Tuolumne country, I passed back over the border to Merced, glad that I had seen so much, and glad that so much was so little of the whole. The grand rocks, I said, of this Tuolumne Yosemite are books never yet opened; and, after studying the mountains of the Merced Basin, I shall go to them as to a library, where all kinds of rock-structure and rock-formation will be explained, and I shall yet discover a thousand waterfalls.

MARY AUSTIN

From *The Land of Little Rain*

"The Streets of the Mountains"

Mary Austin—novelist, journalist, and mystic—wrote nearly three dozen books of fiction and nonfiction during her long and productive career. For her, like John Muir, the Sierra Nevada range was the central geographic fact in much of her life, and inspired some of her most vivid work, like this excerpt from The Land of Little Rain *(1903).*

COLORPLATE 99

LEN JENSHEL. *The Cholla Garden, Joshua Tree National Monument, California.* 1986. Photograph. © 1986 Len Jenshel. *As Len Jenshel's work suggests, art in the modern West includes photography as often as it does the plastic arts, and artists like Ansel Adams, Edward Weston, Eliot Porter, William Clift, David Plowden, Joel Sternfeld, Richard Misrach, and Robert Adams, among scores of others, have provided their own visions of western landscapes and peoples.*

COLORPLATE 100

BEN SHAHN. *Years of Dust.* 1936. Poster. Photo-offset color printing. 38 x 27 7/8 in. Library of Congress.

COLORPLATE 101

THOMAS HART BENTON. *Boom Town.* 1928. Oil on canvas. 45 x 54 in. Memorial Art Gallery of the University of
Rochester, Rochester, New York. Marion Stratton Gould Fund. © T. H. Benton and R. P. Benton Testamentary
Trust/VAGA, New York 1994. *There was more to the twentieth-century West than the compelling landscapes and people
of the Southwest. There was, for example, the spectacular eruption of oil discoveries in California, Oklahoma, and
Texas, where the "boom and bust" economic patterns endemic to the West were replicated on a grand scale in the 1920s.
The definitive "bust"—in the West as elsewhere—of course, was the Great Depression of the 1930s, and the worst part
of that, at least in the states of the Great Plains, was drought followed by dust storms that drove tens of thousands from
their farms. President Franklin Roosevelt's New Dealers tried to do something about it and hired such artists as Ben
Shahn (opposite) to advertise programs like the Resettlement Administration. Shahn later served as a photographer for
the Farm Security Administration.*

COLORPLATE 102 (following spread)

DAVID HOCKNEY. *Pearblossom Hwy., 11–18th April, 1986.* 1986. Photographic collage . 78 x 111 in. © David Hockney.
*The montages of British artist David Hockney give photography a surreal character that transcends any notion of
simple realism. Still, anyone who has ever been privileged to drive along Highway 138, the old desert road that pierces
the Antelope Valley between Cajon Pass in the San Bernardino Range and Tejon Pass in the Tehachapi Range of southern
California, will appreciate the heightened reality of Hockney's wonderful interpretation.*

COLORPLATE 103

LEN JENSHEL. *The Mittens, Monument Valley Navajo Tribal Park, Arizona*. 1985. Photograph. © 1985 Len Jenshel.

COLORPLATE 104

WILLARD MIDGETTE. *"Sitting Bull Returns" at the Drive-In*. 1976. Oil on canvas. 108 ¼ x 134 ⅛ in. National Museum of American Art, Washington, D.C. Gift of Donald B. Anderson. *Irony and humor abound in some of the most idiosyncratic examples of western art over the past two or three decades, from Willard Midgette's wry commentary on the strands of memory that still link modern Indians to their troubled but prideful history (above) to the explosive comedy of Red Grooms (COLORPLATE 118) or the sharp-edged frivolity of Marisol's triumphant wooden "John Wayne" (COLORPLATE 117). Perhaps it is all a reflection of the confused and sometimes contentious mix of traditional cultures, hidebound myths, modern technology, changing economic patterns, burgeoning population growth, environmental awareness, and political volatility that marks the modern West.*

COLORPLATE 105

RICHARD MISRACH. *Waiting, Edwards Air Force Base*. 1983. Photograph. © Richard Misrach. From: *Desert Cantos,* University of New Mexico Press, 1987.

Who shall say what another will find most to his liking in the streets of the mountains. As for me, once set above the country of the silver firs, I must go on until I find white columbine. Around the amphitheatres of the lake regions and above them to the limit of perennial drifts they gather flock-wise in splintered rock wastes. The crowds of them, the airy spread of sepals, the pale purity of the petal spurs, the quivering swing of bloom, obsesses the sense. One must learn to spare a little of the pang of inexpressible beauty, not to spend all one's purse in one shop. There is always another year, and another.

Lingering on in the alpine regions until the first full snow, which is often before the cessation of bloom, one goes down in good company. First snows are soft and clogging and make laborious paths. Then it is the roving inhabitants range down to the edge of the wood, below the limit of early storms. Early winter and early spring one may have sight or track of deer and bear and bighorn, cougar and bobcat, about the thickets of buckthorn on open slopes between the black pines. But when the ice crust is firm above the twenty foot drifts, they range far and forage where they will. Often in midwinter will come, now and then, a long fall of soft snow piling three or four feet above the ice crust, and work a real hardship for the dwellers of these streets. When such a storm portends the weather-wise black-tail will go down across the valley and up to the pastures of Waban where no more snow falls than suffices to nourish the sparsely growing pines. But the bighorn, the wild sheep, able to bear the bitterest storms with no signs of stress, cannot cope with the loose shifty snow. Never such a storm goes over the mountains that the Indians do not catch them floundering belly deep among the lower rifts. I have a pair of horns, inconceivably heavy, that were borne as late as a year ago by a very monarch of the flock whom death overtook at the mouth of Oak Creek after a week of wet snow. He met it as a king should, with no vain effort or trembling, and it was wholly kind to take him so with four of his following rather than that the night prowlers should find him.

There is always more life abroad in the winter hills than one looks to find, and much more in evidence than in summer weather. Light feet of hare that make no print on the forest litter leave a wondrously plain track in the snow. We used to look and look at the beginning of winter for the birds to come down from the pine lands; looked in the orchard and stubble; looked north and south on the mesa for their migratory passing, and wondered that they never came. Busy little grosbeaks picked about the kitchen doors, and woodpeckers tapped the eaves of the farm buildings, but we saw hardly any other of the frequenters of the summer cañons. After a while when we grew bold to tempt the snow borders we found them in the street of the mountains. In the thick pine woods where the overlapping boughs hung with snow-wreaths make wind-proof shelter tents, in a very community of dwelling, winter the bird-folk who get their living from the persisting cones and the larvæ harboring bark. Ground inhabiting species seek the dim snow chambers of the chaparral. Consider how it must be in a hill-slope overgrown with stout-twigged, partly evergreen shrubs, more than man high, and as thick as a hedge. Not all the cañon's sifting of snow can fill the intricate spaces of the hill tangles. Here and there an over-hanging rock, or a stiff arch of buckthorn, makes an opening to communicating rooms and run-ways deep under the snow.

The light filtering through the snow walls is blue and ghostly, but serves to show seeds of shrubs and grass, and berries, and the wind-built walls are warm against the wind. It seems that live plants, especially if they are evergreen and growing, give off heat; the snow wall melts earliest from within and hollows to thinness before there is a hint of spring in the air. But you think of these things afterward. Up in the street it has the effect of being done consciously; the buckthorns lean to each other and the drift to them, the little birds run in and out of their appointed ways with the greatest cheerfulness. They give almost no tokens of distress, and even if the winter tries them too much you are not to pity them. You of the house habit can hardly understand the sense of the hills. No doubt the labor of being comfortable gives you an exaggerated opinion of yourself, an exaggerated pain to be set aside. Whether the wild things understand it or not they adapt themselves to its processes with the greater ease. The business that goes on in the street of the mountain is tremendous, world-formative. Here go birds, squirrels, and red deer, children crying small wares and playing in the street, but they do not obstruct its affairs. Summer is their holiday; "Come now," says the lord of the street, "I have need of a great work and no more playing."

But they are left borders and breathing-space out of pure kindness. They are not pushed out except by the exigencies of the nobler plan which they accept with a dignity the rest of us have not yet learned.

LAURA GILPIN. *Rain Drops on Lupin Leaves.* c. 1931. Platinum print. Amon Carter Museum, Fort Worth, Texas. © 1981 Amon Carter Museum.

EDWARD ABBEY

From *Desert Solitaire*

"Water"

Edward Abbey's rambunctious 1976 novel, The Monkey-Wrench Gang, *earned him a not entirely undeserved (nor unwelcomed) reputation as a western Luddite devoted to the obliteration of most of humankind's works in the West. In this excerpt from* Desert Solitaire *(1968), a somewhat more sedate account of his brief career as supervisor of Arches National Park in Utah, Abbey provides some neatly-drawn paragraphs on the anatomy of water in the West.*

"This would be good country," a tourist says to me, "if only you had some water."

He's from Cleveland, Ohio.

"If we had water here," I reply, "this country would not be what it is. It would be like Ohio, wet and humid and hydrological, all covered with cabbage farms and golf courses. Instead of this lovely barren desert we would have only another blooming garden state, like New Jersey. You see what I mean?"

"If you had more water more people could live here."

"Yes sir. And where then would people go when they wanted to see something besides people?"

"I see what you mean. Still, I wouldn't want to live here. So dry and desolate. Nice for pictures but my God I'm glad I don't have to live here."

"I'm glad too, sir. We're in perfect agreement. You wouldn't want to live here, I wouldn't want to live in Cleveland. We're both satisfied with the arrangement as it is. Why change it?"

"Agreed."

We shake hands and the tourist from Ohio goes away pleased, as I am pleased, each of us thinking he has taught the other something new.

The air is so dry here I can hardly shave in the mornings. The water and soap dry on my face as I reach for the razor: aridity. It is the driest season of a dry country. In the afternoons of July and August we may get thundershowers but an hour after the storms pass the surface of the desert is again bone dry.

It seldom rains. The geography books credit this part of Utah with an annual precipitation of five to nine inches but that is merely a statistical average. Low enough, to be sure. And in fact the rainfall and snowfall vary widely from year to year and from place to place even within the Arches region. When a cloud bursts open above the Devil's Garden the sun is blazing down on my ramada. And wherever it rains in this land of unclothed rock the runoff is rapid down cliff and dome through the canyons to the Colorado.

Sometimes it rains and still fails to moisten the desert—the falling water evaporates halfway down between cloud and earth. Then you see curtains of blue rain dangling out of reach in the sky while the living things wither below for want of water. Torture by tantalizing, hope without fulfillment. And the clouds disperse and dissipate into nothingness.

Streambeds are usually dry. The dry wash, dry gulch, *arroyo seco*. Only after a storm do they carry water and then but briefly—a few minutes, a couple of hours. The spring-fed perennial stream is a rarity. In this area we have only two of them, Salt Creek and Onion Creek, the first too salty to drink and the second laced with arsenic and sulfur.

Permanent springs or waterholes are likewise few and far between though not so rare as the streams. They are secret places deep in the canyons, known only to the deer and the coyotes and the dragonflies and a few others. Water rises slowly from these springs and flows in little rills over bare rock, over and under sand, into miniature fens of wire grass, rushes, willow and tamarisk. The water does not flow very far before disappearing into the air and under the ground. The flow may reappear farther down the canyon, surfacing briefly for a second time, a third time, diminishing in force until it vanishes completely and for good.

Another type of spring may be found on canyon walls where water seeps out between horizontal formations through cracks thinner than paper to support small hanging gardens of orchids, monkeyflower, maidenhair fern, and ivy. In most of these places the water is so sparingly measured that it never reaches the canyon floor at all but is taken up entirely by the thirsty plant life and transformed into living tissue.

Long enough in the desert a man like other animals can learn to smell water. Can learn, at least, the smell of things associated with water—the unique and heartening odor of the cottonwood tree, for example, which in the canyonlands is the tree of life. In this wilderness of naked rock burnt to auburn or buff or red by ancient fires there is no vision more pleasing to the eyes and more gratifying to the heart than the translucent acid green (bright gold in autumn) of this venerable tree. It signifies water, and not only water but also shade, in a country where shelter from the sun is sometimes almost as precious as water.

Signifies water, which may or may not be on the surface, visible and available. If you have what is called a survival problem and try to dig for this water during the heat of the day the effort may cost you more in sweat than you will find to drink. A bad deal. Better to wait for nightfall when the cottonwoods and other plants along the streambed will release some of the water which they have absorbed during the day, perhaps enough to allow a potable trickle to rise to the surface of the sand. If the water still does not appear you may then wish to attempt to

MARK KLETT. *Ed Abbey Taking Notes in Turkey Pen Ruins, Grand Gulch, Utah.* 1988. Photograph. Courtesy of Etherton Gallery, Tucson, Arizona. © 1988 Mark Klett.

dig for it. Or you might do better by marching farther up the canyon. Sooner or later you should find a spring or at least a little seep on the canyon wall. On the other hand you could possibly find no water at all, anywhere. The desert is a land of surprises, some of them terrible surprises. Terrible is derived from terror.

When out for a walk carry water; not less than a gallon a day per person.

More surprises. In places you will find clear-flowing streams, such as Salt Creek near Turnbow Cabin, where the water looks beautifully drinkable but tastes like brine.

You might think, beginning to die of thirst, that any water however salty would be better than none at all. Not true. Small doses will not keep you going or alive and a deep drink will force your body to expend water in getting rid of the excess salt. This results in a net loss of bodily moisture and a hastening of the process of dehydration. Dehydration first enervates, then prostrates, then kills.

Nor is blood, your own or a companion's, any adequate substitute for water; blood is too salty. The same is true of urine.

If it's your truck or car which has failed you, you'd be advised to tap the radiator, unless it's full of Prestone. If this resource is not available and water cannot be found in the rocks or under the sand and you find yourself too tired and discouraged to go on, crawl into the shade and wait for help to find you. If no one is looking for you write your will in the sand and let the wind carry your last words and signature east to the borders of Colorado and south to the pillars of Monument Valley—someday, never fear, your bare elegant bones will be discovered and wondered and marveled at.

*　　*　　*

There are rumors that when dying of the thirst you can save your soul *and* body by extracting water from the barrel cactus. This is a dubious proposition and I don't know anyone who has made the experiment. It might be possible in the Sonoran desert where the barrel cactus grows tall as a man and fat as a keg of beer. In Utah, however, its nearest relative stands no more than a foot high and bristles with needles curved like fishhooks. To get even close to this devilish vegetable you need leather gloves and a machete. Slice off the top and you find inside not water but only the green pulpy core of the living plant. Carving the core into manageable chunks you might be able to wring a few drops of bitter liquid into your cup. The labor and the exasperation will make you sweat, will cost you dearly.

When you reach this point you are doomed. Far better to have stayed at home with the TV and a case of beer. If the happy thought arrives too late, crawl into the shade and contemplate the lonely sky. See those big black scrawny wings far above, waiting? Comfort yourself with the reflection that within a few hours, if all goes as planned, your human flesh will be working its way through the gizzard of a buzzard, your essence transfigured into the fierce greedy eyes and unimaginable consciousness of a turkey vulture. Whereupon you, too, will soar on motionless wings high over the ruck and rack of human suffering. For most of us a promotion in grade, for some the realization of an ideal.

*   *   *

Water, water, water. . . . There is no shortage of water in the desert but exactly the right amount, a perfect ratio of water to rock, of water to sand, insuring that wide, free, open, generous spacing among plants and animals, homes and towns and cities, which makes the arid West so different from any other part of the nation. There is no lack of water here, unless you try to establish a city where no city should be.

The Developers, of course—the politicians, businessmen, bankers, administrators, engineers—they see it somewhat otherwise and complain most bitterly and interminably of a desperate water shortage, especially in the Southwest. They propose schemes of inspiring proportions for diverting water by the damful from the Columbia River, or even from the Yukon River, and channeling it overland down into Utah, Colorado, Arizona and New Mexico.

What for? "In anticipation of future needs, in order to provide for the continued industrial and population growth of the Southwest." And in such an answer we see that it's only the old numbers game again, the monomania of small and very simple minds in the grip of an obsession. They cannot see that growth for the sake of growth is a cancerous madness, that Phoenix and Albuquerque will not be better cities to live in when their populations are doubled again and again. They would never understand that an economic system which can only expand or expire must be false to all that is human.

So much by way of futile digression: the pattern is fixed and protest alone will not halt the iron glacier moving upon us.

No matter, it's of slight importance. Time and the winds will sooner or later bury the Seven Cities of Cibola, Phoenix, Tucson, Albuquerque, all of them, under dunes of glowing sand, over which blue-eyed Navajo bedouin will herd their sheep and horses, following the river in winter, the mountains in summer, and sometimes striking off across the desert toward the red canyons of Utah where great waterfalls plunge over silt-filled, ancient, mysterious dams.

Only the boldest among them, seeking visions, will camp for long in the strange country of the standing rock, far out where the spadefoot toads bellow madly in the moonlight on the edge of doomed rainpools, where the arsenic-selenium spring waits for the thirst-crazed wanderer, where the thunderstorms blast the pinnacles and cliffs, where the rustbrown floods roll down the barren washes, and where the community of the quiet deer walk at evening up glens of sandstone through tamarisk and sage toward the hidden springs of sweet, cool, still, clear, unfailing water.

Joseph Wood Krutch

From *The Desert Year*

Devil's Garden in Bloom

Deserts encourage soothsayers, a statement no less true for the deserts of the American West than for those of the Middle East. One such was Joseph Wood Krutch, an editor of The Nation *and one of the country's leading critics of drama and literature, who fled the intellectual warrens of Manhattan in 1952 and reinvented his reputation by becoming one of the Sonoran Desert's most perceptive interpreters. Here, he vignettes spring in* The Desert Year *(1952).*

Now that mid-May has arrived, there is not likely to be even in the mountains, any more winter, and here below spring has passed into summer. The omnipresent prickly pears, which grew thin and discouraged during the seven-month drought, grew plump again after the first real shower and are covered with the large, lemon-colored flowers which will presently give way to luscious-looking, purple fruits in incredible numbers. These the Indians used to eat and in eastern cities one sometimes sees them exposed for sale in the more luxurious fruit stores. But they look, I must confess, more luscious than they taste—as I discovered last summer when on an idle afternoon I collected a bushel from one plant and turned them into a beautiful red syrup to be added to cool drinks. It was as good as grenadine in taste as well as in color; but that is such mild praise that on the whole I considered my experiment in smoking the common wild tobacco of the region rather more successful.

Other, smaller cacti are also blooming, and so are the giant saguaros, at the ends of whose grotesquely curving arms there appear little circlets of creamy white flowers. The effect is modestly pretty but seems a little inadequate for so gigantic a plant; and it suggests the odd fact that in the cactus family there seems to be a strange lack of proportion between the size of the various species and the size of the blossoms they bear. The saguaro flower is smaller than that of the prickly pear; even more remarkable, many a five- or six-inch variety, half-hidden under a shrub or a stone, bears flowers as large or larger than either. One hardly notices these plants until they bloom; and one would hardly notice the bloom on the saguaro had not the forty- or fifty-foot trunk long been the most conspicuous thing in the landscape.

These monsters are almost the trade-mark of Arizona and their blossoms are its official "state flower." That is understandable enough, both because the giants are absolutely unique in the vegetable world and also because they are, practically speaking, Arizona's exclusive possession since, except for a few negligible stands in California, they grow nowhere else north of the border. Nevertheless, if I had to choose one plant to express the spirit of the Sonoran Desert—one which combines oddness of form and habit with the courage to flourish under seemingly impossible conditions, and which combines also the defensive fierceness of thorns with the spectacular, unexpected beauty of brilliant flowers—I think I should choose the ocotillo.

This spectacular shrub, sometimes appropriately called slimwood and coachwhip, is officially *Fouquieria splendens* and is the only representative of its genus and family in the United States. Its unbranched, almost straight stems, sometimes as many as fifteen or twenty of them, radiate from the common center at ground level and often reach ten or twelve feet into the air. Standing a few feet apart, they frequently dominate many acres of their preferred desert slopes, which they have claimed so successfully that one is aware of little else. The long wands, an inch or more thick and colored a soft gray faintly tinged with green, are composed of wood so dense, so hard, and so tough that the Papago Indians still use them for palisades; yet in the light breeze they nod just sufficiently to avoid any suggestion of stiffness as they stand, most of the time bare of leaves, waiting patiently for their moments. Yet only the very unobservant would think them dead. Even in the stillest air of the hottest midday a certain springiness or resilience which is the very essence of life somehow expresses itself clearly.

After any substantial shower which happens to fall at almost any time of the year, hundreds of very small leaves spring directly from the wands along their entire lengths and clothe them in a sort of layer of green too thin to obscure their outline. For a week or two these leaves go actively about their business of turning carbon dioxide into the carbohydrate of plant tissues; then, when the soil has ceased to supply the moisture which the plant cannot afford any longer to lose by evaporation, the leaves drop off to appear again a few months later, so that, in the course of a year, the ocotillo may enjoy not one but four or five separate springs and autumns.

Nevertheless, it knows somehow when the one authentic spring has come and, whether it be at the moment leafy or leafless, a tapering cluster of buds forms at the very tip of nearly every branch and soon expands into a four- or five-inch cone of waxy scarlet blossoms. Over many a bare slope otherwise almost completely destitute of bright color, hundreds of these little flames are waved gently back and forth in the breeze until it is hard not to believe, literally, the inevitable description—hundreds of torches mysteriously burning across the desert as far as

MARK KLETT. *Cactus Carved by Gunfire, Tucson.* 1990. Photograph. Courtesy of Etherton Gallery, Tucson, Arizona. © 1990 Mark Klett.

sight can reach. Seen as one often sees them, the tips against the deep blue of an Arizona sky, the effect is as surprising and as festive as anything in nature.

Ever since midwinter I have had my eye on a wonderful stretch of desert tucked away in a valley among the lowest foothills of a mountain range; when I judged that the ocotillos would be in full flame I sought it out again. Except for the cabin of a forest ranger a mile or two away, there was no human habitation less than four or five miles distant; except for my one companion and the lizards which scampered about everywhere, I had the whole torch lighted world to myself, and that included a great deal more than the dominant torches themselves. It was near summer by now; we had had our delayed showers and every living thing had responded. Though the prickly pear, also in yellow bloom, was the only other large plant seriously to dispute with the ocotillos for possession of the land, there were scores of humbler organisms able to find their niches. Tucked away between stones, the little echinocereus cacti were shaded under the absurd opulence of their large purple flowers, and, by way of variety, there was an area of desert floor a few hundred yards away which looked just as dry as the rest but which must have been somehow more favorably situated in some respect since it was covered by a bright, variegated carpet of tiny plants.

Many of them were annuals and most looked like the little alpines of some cultivated rock garden. Within an area of a few square yards I counted some fifteen different species, all in bloom. Most had almost no foliage and seemed to consist almost exclusively of blossoms.

Such vegetative parts as they had were either threadlike, or fuzzy, or dry, for they were all determined to waste no moisture. Yet many of the blossoms are recognizable as desert cousins of familiar flowers. This delicately pale yellow one is, by its form and structure, obviously related to the blue, rankly growing wild lettuce of the East, though the stem is only a few inches instead of several feet high. That tiny pink one is unmistakably a houstonia or bluet; even more evidently, this other is a dwarf delphinium. Most of the annuals will be dead within a few weeks, after having rushed from dormant seed to dormant seed again before the scanty moisture is all gone. A few of the perennials may bloom again after the summer rains; the others will have left seeds to lie inactive for perhaps nine months before they germinate in their turn. Since this was an unusually dry spring I probably saw none except the least demanding sorts, but I know that there are some which will tolerate only the wetter seasons and whose seeds, therefore, sometimes lie in the ground for several years until a relatively rainy spring comes around again.

On postcards and in travel magazines such scenes as this are usually labeled "Devil's Garden." But I see nothing infernal about it. Even the sentimental admit that every rose has its thorn, and they should be willing to admit that here every thorn is accompanied by its rose. Persistent legends notwithstanding, the cholla is not a "jumping cactus," and its joints do not detach themselves from the plant to leap at inoffensive passers-by. He who finds thorns in his arm or leg has certainly been, however inadvertently, the aggressor. The rudeness of the cactus, like that of Dr. Johnson, is a defensive rudeness. Its motto is only the motto of South Carolina: "Do not tread upon me."

When a wild animal is described as vicious, it usually means only that if you try to kill him he will sometimes defend himself. Those of us who do not consider this evidence of notable wickedness should not find it difficult to understand a cactus. When ranch visitors amuse themselves by lassoing the saguaros and pull over a giant which has been a century and a half in growing, that is merely another illustration of the fact that of all living creatures man is the most dangerous—to everything else that lives, as well as to himself.

Perhaps I am still a little bit romantic about the desert and therefore like best of all these "devil's gardens" because they represent the desert way of life in its most characteristic and most successful form. I have noticed, nevertheless, that even those permanent residents who love this country are inclined to form little oases about their houses and to pamper with the water from their wells some of the lusher forms of vegetation. Perhaps, after a time, the natural desert comes to seem too strenuous and too difficult for human nature's daily food, something to be contemplated for stimulation rather than lived with in one's more relaxed moments. It may be that in time I should come to feel the same way. But for the present I still find a cactus or an ocotillo very good company. I respect their virtues and they are indifferent to my weaknesses.

Ann Zwinger

From *The Mysterious Lands*

Desert Rhythms

No one has written about the natural world of the western deserts with quite the loving attention to detail that Ann Zwinger, as accomplished a field artist as she is a writer, routinely has. Here is such a precisely observed moment from The Mysterious Lands *(1989).*

G. Pearson from a drawing by F. W. Keyl or E. Smith. *A Prairie Dog Town*. Wood engraving. From *Homes without Hands* by John George Wood. Harper & Brothers, 1866. General Research Division. New York Public Library, Astor, Lenox and Tilden Foundations.

Three concerns haunted me before I came on this bighorn sheep count: that I would be uneasy alone, that time would hang heavy, that I could not endure the heat. Instead I have felt at home, there have not been enough hours in the day, and the heat has become a bearable if not always welcome companion. The words of Joseph Wood Krutch, also writing about the Sonoran Desert, came to mind: "Not to have known—as most men have not—either the mountain or the desert is not to have known one's self. Not to have known one's self is to have known no one."

At noontime I am concentrating so hard on taking notes that when a cicada lets off a five-second burst like a bandsaw going through metal I jump. When there has been no activity at the tank for over an hour I opt for a can of tuna sprinkled with the juice of half a lemon.

No sooner do I open the can and get my fork out than all the birds explode from the rocks on which they've congregated. A red-tailed hawk bullets straight toward me, talons extended, tail spread. No sound, no screaming. It breaks off, rises with no rodent in its talons, wheels, spirals upward, and swoops again. Again no luck. It makes no third try. Its disappearance is followed by a great shocked silence. Half an hour passes before the doves venture, one by one, back to their sentinel rock.

I see only this one hawk stoop. The only time redtails are quiet is on the attack. Otherwise I hear their eerie *KEEEeeeeer KEEEeeer* that ricochets off the sky itself long before they come in to water. One afternoon a redtail sits on the steep cliff to the right; a couple of feet below it perch some house finches; a black-throated sparrow searches the bush beside it; a pair of ash-throated flycatchers rest above it; and across the tank, a batch of doves roost peacefully on their rock. All birds must be vulnerable to attack at the water hole and many avoid too much exposure by being able to drink very quickly, or coming in early and late when raptors are not hunting. Yet there are also these moments when the lion and the lamb lie down together.

I put aside my field glasses and lift my fork. This time a turkey vulture alights on the big rock. The rock is nearly vertical on the side overlooking the tank and this is where it chooses to descend to water. It gets about a quarter of the way down, contorted in an awkward position, big feet splayed out on the rock, tail pushed up behind at a painful angle, as it looks intently down at the water, a hilarious study in reluctance. Gingerly it inches down (vultures have no claw-grasping capability as birds of prey like eagles and hawks do) until it can hold no longer and crash-lands so ridiculously onto the apron to drink that I laugh out loud. The closeness of the rocks around the pool impedes the bird's maneuvering space because of its broad wingspan, and so it edges as close as it can to ensure dropping upon the only place where it can stand and drink.

Four species of this misanthropic-looking bird existed in the Pleistocene, and this creature looks like one of the originals. On the ground, vultures are hunched and awkward bundles of feathers, but in the air, where I watch them during much of the day, they are magnificent, graceful soarers. They ascend with the updrafts coming off the hot desert floor, floating and lifting to cooler air, where visibility is superb; at five hundred feet the visible horizon is twenty-seven miles away, and at two thousand feet, fifty-five miles. Such big raptors generally get as much water as they need from the carrion they consume.

One more try on the tuna fish. A Harris' antelope squirrel scuttles down the wash to nibble on saguaro seeds. Tail held high over its back for shade, a single white stripe on each flank, it has quick, jerky movements typical of the ever-watchful. It stands slightly hunkered up on its hind legs to eat, but its rear end never touches the hot sand. It spends little time feeding and soon tucks back into the brush near the blind, where it undoubtedly has a burrow. There it spread-eagles on the cool soil and unloads its body heat, before taking on the desert again. Still, it withstands unusually high heat loads because of a lower basal metabolism.

The next day, emboldened, it hops up on the iceless ice chest in the blind and puts its head in my empty plastic cup, which tips over with a clatter, sending the squirrel flying.

I eat lunch at a fashionable three o'clock. By four o'clock, shadows cover the tank and the blind is in sun. A cloud cover that has kept the temperature relatively low all day has disappeared and the sun has an unobstructed shot at my back. Until the sun drops behind the ridge, it is the most miserable time of the day.

The resident robber fly alights in front of me, makes a slapdash attempt at a wandering fly, misses, and returns to watching. Flies are widely dispersed in the desert, more prevalent than any other insect order, and of these, bee flies and robber flies are the most numerous. The huge eyes of robber flies give them peripheral vision; with streamlined stilletolike bodies that allow swift flight, and needlelike beaks, they are efficient predators on the desert wafters and drifters. I've watched this one impale a smaller fly in flight, almost too quickly for the eye to follow, then alight to suck out the juices. Today it seems scarcely to care.

In the evening a caterwauling of Gambel's quail issues from the mesquite trees, where they perch in the branches. Their fussing is interspersed with a short soapsudsy cluck, embellished by a silvery *tink* at the end. The first night I was here they scolded and fumed about the stranger in their midst. The second night they gossiped and fussed, and the third night I awoke to find them within a few feet of the cot.

They visit the big mesquites only in the evening, always after sunset, and they are always noisy. I would think a predator could hear them a mile off. Their drinking patterns have evolved to avoid predators: they commonly come in to water twice a day, one period beginning at dawn, the other ending at dusk. Birds of prey tend to arrive around noon, so the quail's watering time does not overlap.

Quail have been termed "annual" birds because of their variable yearly populations. In the Sonoran Desert, the number of young quail per adult found in the fall correlates to rainfall during the previous December to April; in the Mojave, the same high correlation exists between young and October-to-March precipitation (a relationship that exists in other desert animals, among them bighorn sheep). Their reproductive activity begins before green vegetation becomes a part of their diet, the amount of which would give them clues to the amount of nourishment available, and hence the clutch size that could survive. Although quail do not breed at all in exceptionally dry years, they are one of the most prolific of birds.

They remind me of charming windup toys, painted wooden birds bustling about with staccato movements, officiously giving each other directions as they bustle among the creosote bushes. As I watch them, I remember the Kawaiisu Indian story about the tear marks on Quail's face because her young died, one after the other, when she made her cradles out of sandbar willow—a wood that the Indians therefore do not use for cradles.

The day dims and I stretch out to count the stars framed in a triangle of mesquite branches. Content, I realize I have reached, as Sigurd Olsen wrote, "the point where days are governed by daylight and dark, rather than by schedules, where one eats if hungry and sleeps when tired, and becomes completely immersed in the ancient rhythms, then one begins to live."

Yes.

ALDO LEOPOLD

From *A Sand County Almanac*

By the 1940s, many were questioning the thoughtless exploitation of the West's natural resources and the continuing blind slaughter of its wild things. Aldo Leopold, forester, game management specialist, wilderness philosopher, and cofounder of The Wilderness Society (1935), began to think that something had gone terribly wrong when he was still a young forester in Arizona. He tells the story in "Thinking Like a Mountain" from A Sand County Almanac *(1949).*

A deep chesty bawl echoes from rimrock to rimrock, rolls down the mountain, and fades into the far blackness of the night. It is an outburst of wild defiant sorrow, and of contempt for all the adversities of the world.

FREDERIC REMINGTON. *Moonlight, Wolf.* c. 1909. Oil on canvas. 20 $^1/_{16}$ x 26 in. © Addison Gallery of American Art, Phillips Academy, Andover, Massachusetts. Gift of the Members of the Board of Trustees, Phillips Academy. All Rights Reserved.

Every living thing (and perhaps many a dead one as well) pays heed to that call. To the deer it is a reminder of the way of all flesh, to the pine a forecast of midnight scuffles and of blood upon the snow, to the coyote a promise of gleanings to come, to the cowman a threat of red ink at the bank, to the hunter a challenge of fang against bullet. Yet behind these obvious and immediate hopes and fears there lies a deeper meaning, known only to the mountain itself. Only the mountain has lived long enough to listen objectively to the howl of a wolf.

Those unable to decipher the hidden meaning know nevertheless that it is there, for it is felt in all wolf country, and distinguishes that country from all other land. It tingles in the spine of all who hear wolves by night, or who scan their tracks by day. Even without sight or sound of wolf, it is implicit in a hundred small events: the midnight whinny of a pack horse, the rattle of rolling rocks, the bound of a fleeing deer, the way shadows lie under the spruces. Only the ineducable tyro can fail to sense the presence or absence of wolves, or the fact that mountains have a secret opinion about them.

My own conviction on this score dates from the day I saw a wolf die. We were eating lunch on a high rimrock, at the foot of which a turbulent river elbowed its way. We saw what we thought was a doe fording the torrent, her breast awash in white water. When she climbed the bank toward us and shook out her tail, we realized our error: it was a wolf. A half-dozen others, evidently grown pups, sprang from the willows and all joined in a welcoming mêlée of wagging tails and playful maulings. What was literally a pile of wolves writhed and tumbled in the center of an open flat at the foot of our rimrock.

In those days we had never heard of passing up a chance to kill a wolf. In a second we were pumping lead into the pack, but with more excitement than accuracy: how to aim a steep downhill shot is always confusing. When our rifles were empty, the old wolf was down, and a pup was dragging a leg into impassable slide-rocks.

We reached the old wolf in time to watch a fierce green fire dying in her eyes. I realize then, and have known ever since, that there was something new to me in those eyes—something known only to her and to the mountain. I was young then, and full of trigger-itch; I thought that because fewer wolves meant more deer, that no wolves would mean hunters' paradise. But after seeing the green fire die, I sensed that neither the wolf nor the mountain agreed with such a view.

*   *   *

Since then I have lived to see state after state extirpate its wolves. I have watched the face of many a newly wolfless mountain, and seen the south-facing slopes wrinkle with a maze of new deer trails. I have seen every edible bush and seedling browsed, first to anaemic desuetude, and then to death. I have seen every edible tree defoliated to the height of a saddlehorn. Such a mountain looks as if someone had given God a new pruning shears, and forbbidden Him all other exercise. In the end the starved bones of the hoped-for deer herd, dead of its own too-much, bleach with the bones of the dead sage, or molder under the high-lined junipers.

I now suspect that just as a deer herd lives in mortal fear of its wolves, so does a mountain live in mortal fear of its deer. And perhaps with better cause, for while a buck pulled down by wolves can be replaced in two or three years, a range pulled down by too many deer may fail of replacement in as many decades.

So also with cows. The cowman who cleans his range of wolves does not realize that he is taking over the wolf's job of trimming the herd to fit the range. He has not learned to think like a mountain. Hence we have dustbowls, and rivers washing the future into the sea.

T. H. Watkins
"Little Deaths"

In spite of the eloquence of Aldo Leopold and others, most westerners, when they think of wild creatures at all, still treat them with a carelessness that borders on pathology—a tradition that lies at the heart of this cautionary tale from the April 1974 issue of The Sierra Club Bulletin.

It has been more than ten years since the day my cousin let me walk his traplines with him. We never see each other now. Our worlds, never very close, have grown even farther apart. He left California several years ago to become a trapping supervisor somewhere in Nevada, while I have joined the ranks of those who would cheerfully eliminate his way of life. He would, rightly enough, consider me one of his natural enemies, and it is not likely that we would have much to say if we did meet. Still, I am grateful to him for giving me a glimpse into the reality of a world normally hidden from us, a dark little world where death is the only commonplace.

At the time, my cousin was a lowly field trapper at the beck and call of any rancher or farmer who made an official complaint to the trapping service about varmint troubles — coyotes or wildcats getting after newborn lambs, foxes sneaking into chicken coops, that sort of thing. His current assignment was to trap out the varmint population of some ranchland high in the Diablo Hills southeast of Oakland, a country of rolling grassland, scrub oak, and chaparral dominated by the 3,000-foot upthrust of Mount Diablo. His base was a house trailer planted on

JOHN WOODHOUSE AUDUBON. *Raccoon*. From *The Quadrupeds*, 1849. Rare Books and Manuscripts Division. New York Public Library, Astor, Lenox and Tilden Foundations. Arents Collection.

the edge of one of the ranches he was servicing near Livermore, although he got into Oakland quite a lot for weekend visits to a lady of his acquaintance. I lived in Oakland at the time, and he usually made a point of stopping by to see my children, of whom he was particularly fond.

I was then a practicing student of western history and thoroughly intrigued by the glittering adventure that pervaded my reading — especially in the stories of the mountain men, those grizzled, anarchic beings with a lust for far places and far things, stubborn individualists who had lived freer than any Indian and had followed their quest for beaver pelts into nearly all the mysterious blanks of the American West, from Taos, New Mexico, to Puget Sound, from the Marys River of the northern Rockies to the Colorado River of the Southwest; hopelessly romantic creatures with a predilection for Indian women, a talent for profanity, and a thirst for liquor profound enough to melt rivets. And here was my cousin, the literary — if not lineal — descendant of the mountain man. True, he was neither grizzled nor given much to profanity, nor had he, so far as I knew, ever offered his blanket to an Indian woman. Still, he was a *trapper,* beGod, and when on one of his visits he invited me to accompany him on his rounds, I was entranced with the notion.

Late one spring afternoon I bundled wife and children into the car and drove down to Livermore and out to the ranch where he was staying. After a dinner cooked in the trailer's tiny kitchen, my wife and the children bedded down in the trailer's two little bunks. "When we get back tomorrow afternoon," my cousin told the children, "I'll take you out and show you some spring lambs. You'd like that, right?" he added, giving them a pinch and tickle that set them to giggling in delight. He and I bundled up in sleeping bags on the ground outside.

It was pitch black when he woke me the next morning at five o'clock. After shocking ourselves out of sleep by bathing our faces in water from the outside faucet, we got into his pickup and drove off for breakfast at an all-night diner on the road. Dawn was insinuating itself over the dark hills by the time we finished breakfast, and had laid a neon streak across the sky when we finally turned off the highway and began climbing a rutted dirt road that led to the first trapline (we would be walking two traplines, my cousin explained, one on the western side of the hills, one on the eastern; these were two of the six he had scattered over the whole range, each of them containing between 15 and 20 traps and each checked out and reset or moved to a new location every ten days or so). As we bumped and rattled up the road, daylight slowly illu-

JOHN WOODHOUSE AUDUBON. *Coyote or Prairie Wolf.* c. 1843. Oil. 22 x 25 3/8 in. American Museum of Natural History, New York. Courtesy Department of Library Services (Neg./Trans. no. 322985).

minated the hills. For two or three months in the spring, before the summer sun turns them warm and brown, these hills look as if they had been transplanted whole from Ireland or Wales. They are a celebration of green, all shades of green, from the black-green of manzanita leaves to the bright, pool-table green of the grasses. Isolated bundles of cows and sheep stood almost motionless, like ornaments, added for the effect of contrast, and morning mist crept around the base of trees and shrouded dark hollows with the ghost of its presence. Through all this, the exposed earth of the road cut like a red scar, and the sounds of the pickup's engine and the country-western music yammering out of its radio intruded themselves on the earth's silence gracelessly.

We talked of my cousin's father, whom he worshipped and emulated. My cousin was, in fact, almost literally following in his father's footsteps, for "the old man" had been a state trapper himself and was now a trapping supervisor. Before that, back in the deep of the Depression, he had been a lion hunter for the state, when a mountain lion's ears were as good as money, and before that he had "cowboyed some," as he put it; at one time, according to family tradition, his grandfather's ranch had encompassed much of what became the town of San Bernardino in Southern California. At one point in his life, he had led jaguar-hunting trips to the jungles of northwestern Mexico, and he was still a noteworthy hunter, though now he confined himself principally to an occasional deer, antelope, or bear. My cousin had grown up in a house where skins of various types served as rugs and couch-throws, where stuffed heads glared unblinkingly from the walls, where sleek hounds were always in-and-out, where hunting magazines dominated the tables, hunting talk dominated the conversations, and everywhere was the peculiarly masculine smell of newly oiled guns, all kinds of guns — pistols (including an old Colt once used by my cousin's great-grandfather, legend had it, to kill a man), rifles, shotguns. It was a family that had been killing things for a long time, sometimes for meat, sometimes for a living, sometimes for what was called the sport of it, and one of my cousin's consuming ambitions was to bag a bighorn sheep, something his father had never managed to do.

I had never killed anything in my life except fish, and since fish neither scream, grunt, squeal, nor moan when done in, it had never seemed like killing at all. In any case, I was by no means prepared for the first sight of what it was my cousin did to earn his bread. I don't know what I had expected with my romantic notions of the trapper's life, but surely it was something other than what I learned when we crawled up the road through increasingly heavy underbrush and stopped to check out the first of my cousin's traps.

We got out of the truck and beat our way through the brush to a spot perhaps 30 feet from the road. I did not see the animal until we were nearly on top of it. It was a raccoon, the first raccoon I had ever seen in person, and at that moment I wished that I never had seen one. It was dead, had been dead for several days, my cousin informed me. "Hunger, thirst, and shock is what kills them, mostly," he said in response to my question. "That, and exhaustion, I reckon." The animal seemed ridiculously tiny in death. It lay on its side, its small mouth, crawling with ants, open in a bared-tooth grin, and its right rear leg in the clutch of the steel trap. It was easy to see how the animal had exhausted itself; it had been at its leg. A strip of flesh perhaps three inches in width had been gnawed away, leaving the white of bone and a length of tendon exposed. Tiny flies sang about the ragged wound and over the pool of dried blood beneath the leg. There was a stink in the air, and it suddenly seemed very, very warm to me there in the morning shadows of the brush.

"Once in a while," my cousin said, prying open the curved jaws of the trap, "one of them will chew his way loose, and if he doesn't lose too much blood he can live. I caught a three-legged coyote once. Too stupid to learn, I guess."

"Do you ever find one of them still alive?" I asked.

"Sometimes."

"What do you do with them?"

He looked up at me. "Do with them? I shoot them," he said, patting the holstered pistol at his waist. He lifted the freed raccoon by the hind legs and swung it off into the brush. "Buzzard meat," he said. He then grabbed the steel stake to which the trap was attached by a chain and worked it out of the ground. "I've had this line going for over a month, now. The area's just about trapped out." He carried the trap back to the road, threw it in the back of the pickup, and we drove up the increasingly rough road to the next trap. It was empty, as was the one after it. I was beginning to hope they would all be empty, but the fourth one contained a small skunk, a black-and-white pussycat of a creature that had managed to get three of its feet in the trap at once and lay huddled in death like a child's stuffed toy. It, too, was disengaged and tossed into the brush. A little further up the ridge, and we found a fox, to my cousin's visible relief. "Great," he said. "That has to be the mate to the one I got a couple of weeks ago. Pregnant, too. There won't be any little foxes running around this year." Into the brush the animal went.

By the time we reached the top of the long ridge on which my cousin had set his traps, the morning had slipped toward noon and our count had risen to seven animals: three raccoons, three skunks, and the pregnant fox. There was only one trap left now, but it was occupied by the prize of the morning, a bobcat. "I'll be damned," my cousin said, "I've been after that bugger all month. Just about give up hope." The bobcat had not died well, but in anger. The marks of its rage and anguish were laid out in a torn circle of earth described by the length of the chain that had linked the animal to its death. Even the brush had been ripped and clawed at, leaves and twigs stripped from branches, leaving sweeping scars. Yellow tufts of the animal's fur lay scattered on the ground, as if the bobcat had torn at its own body for betraying it, and its death-mask was a silent howl of outrage. My cousin took it out of the trap and heaved it down the side of the hill. Buzzard meat.

We had to go back down the hills and around the range in order to come up the eastern slopes and check out the second trapline, and on the way we stopped at a small roadhouse in Clayton for a hamburger and a beer. I found I could eat, which surprised me a little, and I certainly had a thirst for the beer. We sat side-by-side at the bar, not saying much. Something Wallace Stegner had once written kept flashing through my mind. "Like most of my contemporaries," he had said, "I grew up careless. I grew up killing things." I wondered if my cousin would know what Stegner had been talking about, and decided it would be best not to bring it up. I could have canceled out right there, I suppose, asking him to take me back to his camp, explaining that I had seen enough, too much, of the trapper's life. I could always plead exhaustion. After all, the day's hiking had been more real exercise than I had had in months, and I was, in fact, tired. A stubborn kernel of pride would not let me do it. I would see the day through to the end.

So the ritual continued. We climbed back up into the hills on the east side of the range in the oven-heat of a strong spring sun. The day's count rose even more as the pickup bounced its way up the ragged weedgrown road: two more skunks, another fox, two more raccoons. The work went more slowly than the morning's run, for this was a new line, and each trap had to be reset. My cousin performed this task with an efficient swiftness and the kind of quiet pride any craftsman takes in his skill, snapping and locking the jaws of the traps, covering them with a thin scattering of earth and twigs, sprinkling the ground about with dog urine from a plastic squeeze bottle to cover up the man-smell. By the time we were ready to approach the last three traps of the line, it was well after three o'clock. We were very high by then, well up on the slopes of Mount Diablo itself, and we had to abandon the pickup to hike the rest of the way on foot. We broke out of the brush and walked along a spur of the hills. About 1,500 feet below us and some miles to the east, we could see the towns of Pittsburg and Martinez sending an urban haze into the air. Ahead of me, my cousin suddenly stopped.

"Wait a minute. Listen," he said.

A distant thrashing and rattling sound came from the slope below us. "That's where the trap is," he said. "Might be a bobcat, but I didn't expect to get him so soon. Come on."

The slope was very steep, and we slid much of the way down to the trap on our bottoms, slapped at and tangled by brush. The animal was not a bobcat. It was a dog, a large, dirty-white mongrel whose foreleg was gripped in the trap. The dog snarled at us as we approached it. Saliva had gathered at its lips and there was wildness in its eyes.

"*Dammit*," my cousin said. He had owned dogs all his life. "A wild dog. Probably abandoned by somebody. They do it all the time. Dogs turn wild and start running in packs. Some people ought to be shot."

I didn't know what he wanted to do. He hadn't pulled out his gun. "Can we turn him loose?

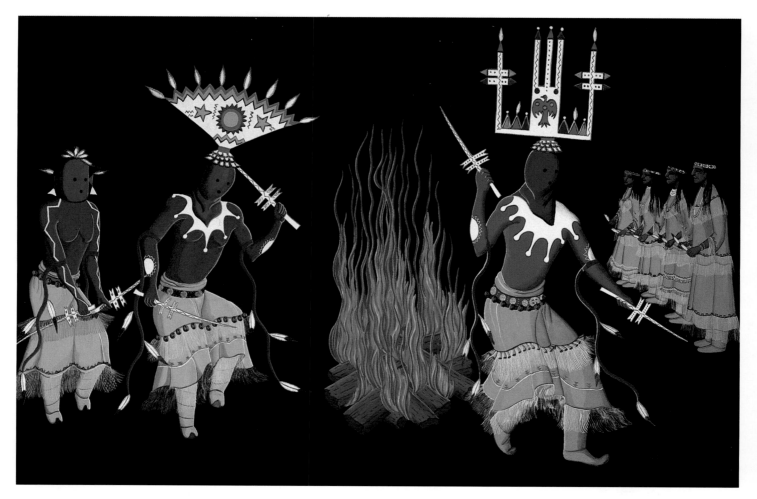

COLORPLATE 111

Pablita Velarde. (Santa Clara Pueblo, New Mexico). *Apache Devil Dancers*. c. 1955. Watercolor on paper. 19 ¹/₄ x 30 ¹/₂ in. Courtesy of The Amerind Foundation, Inc., Dragoon, Arizona.

COLORPLATE 112 (following page)

Jan Matulka. *Indian Dancers*. 1918. Oil on canvas. 26 x 16 in. Courtesy of The Anschutz Collection, Denver, Colorado.

COLORPLATE 113

Ada Suina. (Cochiti Pueblo, New Mexico). *Storyteller Doll*. 1988. Clay. 9 x 5 in. Courtesy of The Amerind Foundation, Inc., Dragoon, Arizona.

Maybe he isn't wild. Maybe he just wandered up here on his own."

My cousin looked at me. "Maybe. There's a noose-pole in the back of the truck — a kind of long stick with a loop of rope at the end. Why don't you get it?"

I scrambled back up the slope and made my way back to the pickup, where I found the noose-pole. As thick as a broomhandle and about five feet in length, it looked like a primitive fishing-pole. When I got back down to the trap, the dog was still snarling viciously. My cousin took the pole from me, opened the loop at the end, and extended it toward the dog. "If I can hook him," he said, "I'll hold his head down while you open the trap. You've seen how I do it."

It was useless. The dog fought at the loop frantically in a madness of pain and fear. After perhaps 15 minutes, my cousin laid the pole down. "He just isn't going to take it."

"What'll we do?" I asked, though I'm sure I knew.

He shrugged. "Can't just leave him here to die." He unsnapped his holster and pulled out the gun. He duck-walked to within a couple of feet of the animal, which watched him suspiciously. "I'll try to do it with one shot," he said. The gun's discharge slammed into the silence of the mountain. The dog howled once, a long, penetrating song of despair that rang in echoes down the hill. My cousin nudged the animal with his boot. It was dead. He opened the trap, freed the leg, and heaved the body down the slope. The crashing of its fall seemed to go on for a long time. My cousin reset the trap. "Come on," he said. "It's getting late."

The last trap of the day held a dead raccoon.

My cousin was pleased with the day's work. "If it keeps up like this," he said as we rattled down the highway toward his trailer, "I could be out of here in a month."

"What's the hurry?"

He indicated a small housing development by the side of the road. "Too much civilization around here for me. Too many people. I need to get back up into the mountains."

There was plenty of light left when we got back, and true to his promise, my cousin took the children out into the fields to see a newborn lamb. While its mother bleated in protest, he ran one down and brought it to my children so they could pet it. I watched his face as he held the little creature. There was no hint in it of all the death we had harvested that day, no hint of the half-eaten legs we had seen, no hint of the fearful thrashing agony the animals had endured before dying. No hint, even, of the death-howl of the dirty white dog that may or may not have been wild. There was neither irony nor cynicism in him. He held the lamb with open, honest delight at the wonder my children found in touching this small, warm, live thing.

My cousin is not an evil man. We are none of us evil men.

Attributed to FRANK S. NICHOLSON. *Wild Life*.
28 x 22 in. Poster. Library of Congress.

WALLACE STEGNER

From *The Sound of Mountain Water*
"Wilderness Letter"

In 1956 American conservationists rallied around an attempt to establish a system of permanently protected wildlands in the national parks, forests, wildlife refuges, and other federal lands in the United States—most of them in the West. One of those who most vigorously supported the cause was novelist and historian Wallace Stegner, whose 1960 letter to David Pesonen still stands as the single most eloquent argument for wilderness preservation.

Los Altos, Calif.
Dec. 3, 1960

David E. Pesonen
Wildland Research Center
Agricultural Experiment Station
243 Mulford Hall
University of California
Berkeley 4, Calif.

Dear Mr. Pesonen:

I believe that you are working on the wilderness portion of the Outdoor Recreation Resources Review Commission's report. If I may, I should like to urge some arguments for wilderness preservation that involve recreation, as it is ordinarily conceived, hardly at all. Hunting, fishing, hiking, mountain-climbing, camping, photography, and the enjoyment of natural scenery will all, surely, figure in your report. So will the wilderness as a genetic reserve, a scientific yardstick by which we may measure the world in its natural balance against the world in its man-made imbalance. What I want to speak for is not so much the wilderness uses, valuable as those are, but the wilderness *idea,* which is a resource in itself. Being an intangible and spiritual resource, it will seem mystical to the practical-minded—but then anything that cannot be moved by a bulldozer is likely to seem mystical to them.

I want to speak for the wilderness idea as something that has helped form our character and that has certainly shaped our history as a people. It has no more to do with recreation than churches have to do with recreation, or than the strenuousness and optimism and expansiveness of what historians call the "American Dream" have to do with recreation. Nevertheless, since it is only in this recreation survey that the values of wilderness are being compiled, I hope you will permit me to insert this idea between the leaves, as it were, of the recreation report.

Something will have gone out of us as a people if we ever let the remaining wilderness be destroyed; if we permit the last virgin forests to be turned into comic books and plastic cigarette cases; if we drive the few remaining members of the wild species into zoos or to extinction; if we pollute the last clear air and dirty the last clean streams and push our paved roads through the last of the silence, so that never again will Americans be free in their own country from the noise, the exhausts, the stinks of human and automotive waste. And so that never again can we have the chance to see ourselves single, separate, vertical and individual in the world, part of the environment of trees and rocks and soil, brother to the other animals, part of the natural world and competent to belong in it. Without any remaining wilderness we are

committed wholly, without chance for even momentary reflection and rest, to a headlong drive into our technological termite-life, the Brave New World of a completely man-controlled environment. We need wilderness preserved—as much of it as is still left, and as many kinds—because it was the challenge against which our character as a people was formed. The reminder and the reassurance that it is still there is good for our spiritual health even if we never once in ten years set foot in it. It is good for us when we are young, because of the incomparable sanity it can bring briefly, as vacation and rest, into our insane lives. It is important to us when we are old simply because it is there—important, that is, simply as idea.

We are a wild species, as Darwin pointed out. Nobody ever tamed or domesticated or scientifically bred us. But for at least three millennia we have been engaged in a cumulative and ambitious race to modify and gain control of our environment, and in the process we have come close to domesticating ourselves. Not many people are likely, any more, to look upon what we call "progress" as an unmixed blessing. Just as surely as it has brought us increased comfort and more material goods, it has brought us spiritual losses, and it threatens now to become the Frankenstein that will destroy us. One means of sanity is to retain a hold on the natural world, to remain, insofar as we can, good animals. Americans still have that chance, more than many peoples; for while we were demonstrating ourselves the most efficient and ruthless environment-busters in history, and slashing and burning and cutting our way through a wilderness continent, the wilderness was working on us. It remains in us as surely as Indian names remain on the land. If the abstract dream of human liberty and human dignity became, in America, something more than an abstract dream, mark it down at least partially to the fact that we were in subtle ways subdued by what we conquered.

The Connecticut Yankee, sending likely candidates from King Arthur's unjust kingdom to his Man Factory for rehabilitation, was over-optimistic, as he later admitted. These things cannot be forced, they have to grow. To make such a man, such a democrat, such a believer in human individual dignity, as Mark Twain himself, the frontier was necessary, Hannibal and the Mississippi and Virginia City, and reaching out from those the wilderness; the wilderness as opportunity and as idea, the thing that has helped to make an American different from and, until we forget it in the roar of our industrial cities, more fortunate than other men. For an American, insofar as he is new and different at all, is a civilized man who has renewed himself in the wild. The American experience has been the confrontation by old peoples and cultures of a world as new as if it had just risen from the sea. That gave us our hope and our excitement, and the hope and excitement can be passed on to newer Americans, Americans who never saw any phase of the frontier. But only so long as we keep the remainder of our wild as a reserve and a promise—a sort of wilderness bank.

As a novelist, I may perhaps be forgiven for taking literature as a reflection, indirect but profoundly true, of our national consciousness. And our literature, as perhaps you are aware, is sick, embittered, losing its mind, losing its faith. Our novelists are the declared enemies of their society. There has hardly been a serious or important novel in this century that did not repudiate in part or in whole American technological culture for its commercialism, its vulgarity, and the way in which it has dirtied a clean continent and a clean dream. I do not expect that the preservation of our remaining wilderness is going to cure this condition. But the mere example that we can as a nation apply some other criteria than commercial and exploitative considerations would be heartening to many Americans, novelists or otherwise. We need to demonstrate our acceptance of the natural world, including ourselves; we need the spiritual refreshment that being natural can produce. And one of the best places for us to get that is in the wilderness where the fun houses, the bulldozers, and the pavements of our civilization are shut out.

Sherwood Anderson, in a letter to Waldo Frank in the 1920's, said it better than I can. "Is it not likely that when the country was new and men were often alone in the fields and the forest they got a sense of bigness outside themselves that has now in some way been lost . . . Mystery whispered in the grass, played in the branches of trees overhead, was caught up and blown across the American line in clouds of dust at evening on the prairies . . . I am old enough to remember tales that strengthen my belief in a deep semi-religious influence that was formerly at work among our people. The flavor of it hangs over the best work of Mark Twain . . . I can remember old fellows in my home town speaking feelingly of an evening spent on the big empty plains. It had taken the shrillness out of them. They had learned the trick of quiet . . ."

We could learn it too, even yet; even our children and grandchildren could learn it. But only if we save, for just such absolutely non-recreational, impractical, and mystical uses as this, all the wild that still remains to us.

It seems to me significant that the distinct downturn in our literature from hope to bitterness took place almost at the precise time when the frontier officially came to an end, in 1890, and when the American way of life had begun to turn strongly urban and industrial. The more urban it has become, and the more frantic with technological change, the sicker and more embittered our literature, and I believe our people, have become. For myself, I grew up on the empty plains of Saskatchewan and Montana and in the mountains of Utah, and I put a very high valuation on what those places gave me. And if I had not been able periodically to renew myself in the mountains and deserts of western America I would be very nearly bughouse. Even when I can't get to the back country, the thought of the colored deserts of southern Utah, or the reassurance that there are still stretches of prairie where the world can be instantaneously perceived as disk and bowl, and where the little but intensely important human being is exposed to the five directions and the thirty-six winds, is a positive consolation. The idea alone can sustain me. But as the wilderness areas are progressively exploited or "improved," as the jeeps and bulldozers of uranium prospectors scar up the deserts and the roads are cut into the alpine timberlands, and as the remnants of the unspoiled and natural world are progressively eroded, every such loss is a little death in me. In us.

I am not moved by the argument that those wilderness areas which have already been exposed to grazing or mining are already deflowered, and so might as well be "harvested." For mining I cannot say much good except that its operations are generally short-lived. The extractable wealth is taken and the shafts, the tailings, and the ruins left, and in a dry country such as the American West the wounds men make in the earth do not quickly heal. Still, they are only wounds; they aren't absolutely mortal. Better a wounded wilderness than none at all. And as for grazing, if it is strictly controlled so that it does not destroy the ground cover, damage the ecology, or compete with the wildlife it is in itself nothing that need conflict with the wilderness feeling or the validity of the wilderness experience. I have known enough range cattle to recognize them as wild animals; and the people who herd them have, in the wilderness context, the dignity of rareness; they belong on the frontier, moreover, and have a look of rightness. The invasion they make on the virgin country is a sort of invasion that is as old as Neolithic man, and they can, in moderation, even emphasize a man's feeling of belonging to the natural world. Under surveillance, they can belong; under control, they need not deface or mar. I do not believe that in wilderness areas where grazing has never been permitted, it should be permitted; but I do not believe either that an otherwise untouched wilderness should be eliminated from the preservation plan because of limited existing uses such as grazing which are in consonance with the frontier condition and image.

Let me say something on the subject of the kinds of wilderness worth preserving. Most of those areas contemplated are in the national forests and in high mountain country. For all the usual recreational purposes, the alpine and forest wildernesses are obviously the most important, both as genetic banks and as beauty spots. But for the spiritual renewal, the recognition of identity, the birth of awe, other kinds will serve every bit as well. Perhaps, because they are less friendly to life, more abstractly non-human, they will serve even better. On our Saskatchewan prairie, the nearest neighbor was four miles away, and at night we saw only two lights on all the dark rounding earth. The earth was full of animals—field mice, ground squirrels, weasels, ferrets, badgers, coyotes, burrowing owls, snakes. I knew them as my little brothers, as fellow creatures, and I have never been able to look upon animals in any other way since. The sky in that country came clear down to the ground on every side, and it was full of great weathers, and clouds, and winds, and hawks. I hope I learned something from knowing intimately the creatures of the earth; I hope I learned something from looking a long way, from looking up, from being much alone. A prairie like that, one big enough to carry the eye clear to the sinking, rounding horizon, can be as lonely and grand and simple in its forms as the sea. It is as good a place as any for the wilderness experience to happen; the vanishing prairie is as worth preserving for the wilderness idea as the alpine forests.

So are great reaches of our western deserts, scarred somewhat by prospectors but otherwise open, beautiful, waiting, close to whatever God you want to see in them. Just as a sample, let me suggest the Robbers' Roost country in Wayne County, Utah, near the Capitol Reef National Monument. In that desert climate the dozer and jeep tracks will not soon melt back into the earth, but the country has a way of making the scars insignificant. It is a lovely and terrible wilderness, such a wilderness as Christ and the prophets went out into; harshly and beautifully colored, broken and worn until its bones are exposed, its great sky without a smudge or taint from Technocracy, and in hidden corners and pockets under its cliffs the sudden poetry of springs. Save a piece of country like that intact, and it does not matter in the slightest that only a few people every year will go into it. That is precisely its value. Roads would be a desecration, crowds would ruin it. But those who haven't the strength or youth to go into it and live can simply sit and look. They can look two hundred miles, clear into Colorado; and looking down over the cliffs and canyons of the San Rafael Swell and the Robbers' Roost they can also look as deeply into themselves as anywhere I know. And if they can't even get to the places on the Aquarius Plateau where the present roads will carry them, they can simply contemplate the *idea,* take pleasure in the fact that such a timeless and uncontrolled part of earth is still there.

These are some of the things wilderness can do for us. That is the reason we need to put into effect, for its preservation, some other principle than the principles of exploitation or "usefulness" or even recreation. We simply need that wild country available to us, even if we never do more than drive to its edge and look in. For it can be a means of reassuring ourselves of our sanity as creatures, a part of the geography of hope.

Very sincerely yours,

Wallace Stegner

Preamble to the Wilderness Act of 1964

After eight years of deliberation, Congress passed and President Lyndon B. Johnson signed the Wilderness Act of 1964, one of the most important conservation measures in our history. Most of the act was written (then rewritten no less than sixty-six times) by The Wilderness Society's Howard Zahniser, a former editor for the U. S. Biological Survey, who gave to the act's brief preamble a singular grace of language.

In order to assure that an increasing population, accompanied by expanding settlement and growing mechanization, does not occupy and modify all areas within the United States and its possessions, leaving no lands designated for preservation and protection in their natural condition, it is hereby declared to be the policy of the Congress to secure for the American people of present and future generations the benefits of an enduring resource of wilderness. For this purpose there is hereby established a National Wilderness Preservation System to be composed of federally owned areas designated by Congress as "wilderness areas," and these shall be administered for the use and enjoyment of the American people in such manner as will leave them unimpaired for future use and enjoyment as wilderness. . . .

A wilderness, in contrast with those areas where man and his own works dominate the landscape, is hereby recognized as an area where the earth and its community of life are untrammeled by man, where man himself is a visitor who does not remain. . . .

LIVING IN THE NEW WEST

RICHARD SHELTON

From *Going Back to Bisbee*

For most westerners, history—of their region, of themselves—is never very far away. Until recent times, the mining town of Bisbee, Arizona, throbbed with industry. Now it sits more quietly amid its tiny, twisting canyons, harboring a clutch of artists and other nonindustrial types, memorializing its past, pondering its future. In his prize-winning Going Back to Bisbee *(1992), poet Richard Shelton gives a personal glimpse of the new-old life of the place.*

I drive past Lowell School in the growing dusk, and it's almost dark when I pull up in front of Ida's house in Warren. While I'm parking the van, she comes out on the front porch to greet me. Each time I see her again I am reminded by the way she dresses that she is an artist with an eye for color and texture. During the day she often wears bright, true purples and magentas. Tonight it's lustrous black with a subtle pattern of deep orange and gold, dark and rich like the features on her mother's hat in the photo. She stands there as if perched on one foot, her head to the side, carriage jaunty, and eyes laughing, happy to see me. The years have been much kinder to her than they have been to me. What a privilege it is to walk up on the porch and put my arms around this good and beautiful woman. For a moment I am holding Bisbee in my arms, and it has survived. But the bones are light and fragile like the bones of a bird. A couple of lines by E. E. Cummings pop into my head and make me sad and happy all at once: "the power of your intense fragility; whose texture/compels me with the colour of its countries."

Suddenly I realize that Bisbee was always fragile, even while I lived here, while Lavender Pit was a maelstrom of activity and the whistle blew every day, and while on my way to work I could watch long lines of grim-looking men filing onto open elevator platforms which dropped them hundreds of feet into the earth. Bisbee has always been fragile, and never more so than now. I wonder if the people who live here realize how fragile it is, a kind of Shangri-La in the Mule Mountains, a timeless space attacked from without and within, an attitude threatened by the forces of greed. Bisbee was born of greed, but it has outlived its parents. For many, Bisbee has become an idea, a way to live simply, even in poverty according to some standards, but well. Such an idea will always be a threat to the forces of greed, which assume that everyone is as greedy as they are and can't bear it when they find that some are not.

But I can't stand here on Ida's front porch thinking about all this while Ida hops around me, talking in her rapid-fire way. She's all energy, bottled up and ready to take on the world. I feel old by comparison, and I sense that Bisbee is young again and that Ida's energy reflects the town's energy. It is much younger than it was when I lived here. Young and fresh and eager, although the buildings are old. I was wrong to refer to Bisbee as "old girl" this afternoon. Bisbee has grown younger while I have grown older. And all at once I know why I had to come back. I had to touch youth again, my own past youth and the renewed youth of a town where I lived in ignorance and audacity, as only the young can live. I thought towns had to grow old, but Bisbee has grown young, and seeing this eighty-year-old woman with her laughing eyes and young spirit has finally made me understand it.

* * *

But it's time to ask Ida the big question, the sixty-four-dollar question I've been wanting to ask her all evening. How does she feel about the news that Phelps Dodge might be coming back to Bisbee, just as the new Bisbee is beginning to show signs that it can make it on its own, and even grow? For several years Phelps Dodge has been drilling and testing on the hills immediately across the highway from Sacramento Pit between Old Bisbee and all that is left of Lowell. Recently, the company held meetings with the people of Bisbee to explain what its managers had in mind, although everything seems to depend on the future price of copper.

Phelps Dodge has never relinquished its ownership to most of the land in the Warren Mining District, nor its ownership to the mineral rights beneath the land it does not own outright. In a sense, the mining industry operates on the same principles that modern archaeologists do. When archaeologists have excavated the site of a center of prehistoric culture and learned all they can from it, they often backfill it and wait for the development of new technology that will make it possible for them to return to the site and learn even more. When it pulled out in the mid-1970s, Phelps Dodge did not fill in the enormous pits it had created nor clear away the tons of tailings that scar the landscape, but it has been waiting while new mining technology has developed, technology that will make it possible to process, at a profit, ore of a lower grade than was previously worthwhile. That technology has now been developed.

Phelps Dodge plans to strip-mine a new section of the Mule Mountains just across the highway from Sacramento Pit, creating a new pit, and to process the ore by means of a recently improved electrolytic method. They would then dump the waste material and tons of overburden into Lavender Pit. The company is not specific as to when this process will begin, but there is little doubt in the minds of most Bisbee residents that it will occur, and probably soon. Because it will be a highly technical operation depending on huge earth-moving machines and a very sophisticated processing plant, it will employ relatively few people, possibly as few as one hundred and no more than two hundred. Don Fry says that the addition of even one hundred workers and their families would revolutionize the Bisbee economy. "There isn't a merchant here that isn't hanging on by his fingernails," Fry says. The reactions of Bisbee residents to the Phelps Dodge plan range from wild enthusiasm to horror. The possibility of renewed paternalism, like a spectre, now walks the streets of Bisbee, feared by some and welcomed by others.

But what does Ida think about all this? She has had time to weigh the pros and cons and estimate the impact on the town and the landscape she loves. In answer to my question, she raises her head and gives me a long, cool look which reminds me of her mother's look in the photograph I so much admire. "I would be pleased," she says very quietly and very deliberately, "to see Phelps Dodge return."

Again I am reminded of what Don Fry said. "A mining town with culture." Maybe he and Ida are not so far apart in their dreams after all. But is it possible to have a town of Bisbee's size that includes both a high level of artistic culture and a large, active copper mine? It's possible, I suppose, but difficult to imagine, and so many questions pop up. Would the artists accept the miners and their families? Would the miners drive the artists out? Would the people who have worked so hard to make Bisbee a good town to live in slide back into the complacency that comes with paternalism? What would become of Bisbee's rapidly growing tourism? Would water seeping through thousands of tons of debris in Lavender Pit pollute the water supply as it does at abandoned mine sites in Colorado?

Ida seems satisfied that it will all work out for the best. "It's good to get these new people with new ideas in," she says, referring to all kinds of people. "My theory is that I like people and I don't get torn apart with arguments. I do what I can. Gradually, some of the newer people will take over." I think about what she says, remembering that it comes from a woman who has been walking through a social and political mine field for the last twenty years and has come through in excellent shape. Some good angel has been watching over her, and it isn't the angel of ignorance. Ida knows what she is doing, and she does it with care and precision.

As I am driving her home, we are both quiet, pensive. I don't know what Ida is thinking about, but I'm thinking about Sacramento Hill, which exists only in photographs, where it stands as the most prominent feature of the horizon southeast of Old Bisbee. I'm wondering how many of the neighboring hills will soon be gone as well, and how much of the Mule Mountains will be transformed into enormous pits? How do you put a dollar value on a mountain? How do you weigh a mountain's survival against the survival of a town? It's just landscape, I keep telling myself, and look at what has happened to the surrounding landscape. Gone, destroyed, ravaged. And it's only two or three more hills. What are two or three more hills as compared with what all that money will do for the town?

It's easy for me to say that I like Bisbee as it is and wouldn't want to change it. Easy because I live in Tucson and have a steady income. But how would I feel if I lived in Bisbee and had to scramble every day to make a rather meager living? So much for picturesque! Things look different when you have children to feed and no bank account. And yet . . . the hills . . . the tawny hills . . . the way they throw off amber light in the late afternoon, turning Bisbee into a magic place as seen in a sepia print. Why must the mountains be sacrificed for economic progress that will be temporary at best?

I don't know the answers to any of the questions. I am not as old or wise as Ida, but I don't think I agree with her on this matter, and it makes me sad. She has given her life and her labor for the people of Bisbee, and now she must sacrifice even the mountains she loves. I think of her beautiful collages of the mountains fading into blue distances. Somehow it isn't right, it isn't fair. Not for Ida or the other artists in Bisbee, and not for the mountains.

I say good-night to Ida on her front porch and tell her that I probably won't see her again on this trip. I'm going hiking tomorrow, and then I will probably drive back to Tucson tomorrow night or the next morning. But I will be back in a few months, and then we can have the elegant dinner I had planned, maybe at the Copper Queen or the Courtyard. I'll call her and warn her that I am coming.

"If you don't get me the first time," she says, "keep trying. I'm gone a lot during the day. Meetings and things."

"I'll catch you one way or the other," I say as I wave good-bye and get into Blue Boy. Yes, I'll catch her. I'll call city hall or the Arts Commission or Central School or the Women's Club or the county courthouse or the historical museum. I'll catch her in midflight somewhere. And I wonder where they will catch me when I'm eighty. Probably not on the wing.

Driving back to the Copper Queen Hotel, I come around the traffic circle and see Lowell

Sacramento Pit—435 feet deep, covers 35 acres, which yielded 20, 843, 667 tons of ore between 1917 and 1991. Bisbee, Arizona. Photograph. Arizona Historical Society, Tucson.

School, all locked up and dark under a blazing full moon and a sky full of stars. The clouds have blown away until tomorrow afternoon, when they will probably reappear for the usual late afternoon storm. Arizona moon and Arizona stars, I think. Bigger and brighter than anywhere else. I will never get used to them or take them for granted. Maybe I will come back to Lowell School in the morning and poke around some. School won't be in session, but there will probably be a secretary or an assistant principal or somebody around to let me in. There won't be anybody who will remember me, but that's O.K. I was the youngest of the crew. Paul Rose is dead now. Molly Bendixon is in a rest home in Phoenix. Carol Mosely and Bill Taylor have retired. Marguerite Knowles lives somewhere in California, surrounded by grandchildren. But I want to see my classroom again, with its high ceilings, dark woodwork, and bank of tall windows. I want to see if it has been changed, and I want to look at the auditorium where my choral speaking groups performed, like the troopers they were, for wildly enthusiastic audiences. It's hard to imagine that those students are all in their mid forties now, the ones who have survived.

So maybe I'll come back in the morning and have a look around. Then I'll amble through Old Bisbee and hike up Brewery Gulch all the way to the top of the ridge of hills that circles the town like the arm of a sleeping giant. From up there, I will be able to get a better perspective on Bisbee and its current problems. I will see it below like a little toy town, with toy houses ranging up the hills and miniature church steeples and silly Italian cypresses sticking up in formal rows. I will not be able to hear any sounds from down there except a dog barking once in awhile or a particularly loud truck as it climbs the high road on the other side of Tombstone Canyon. Bisbee will look very peaceful from there, like a painting by some artist who paints only what is picturesque. I'll sit on the ridge and look down at it, as I have many times in the past.

I'll have a chance to think about the changes, and how the town has grown younger while I haven't. And I'll realize more fully, as I am beginning to realize now, that my trip has been pure nostalgia-time and I can never really go back to Bisbee. My trips to Bisbee will always be visits, brief raids on the past that will retreat before me and remain just out of reach. Whatever

I came here to find is part of the past and will have to remain part of the past—part of the old Bisbee that doesn't exist anymore. I'll come to realize, in spite of the old cliche, that home is the only place I can go back to if I plan to stay, and my home is in the Tucson Mountains, in a house that is getting old now, as I am. Bisbee and I have both been busy surviving for the past thirty years, and we've both been successful at it.

Then, when I've figured it all out, I'll come zigzagging and sliding down the steep hill behind the Copper Queen, get into Blue Boy, and drive the one hundred miles back to Tucson while monsoon clouds rise behind me and lightning dances through the darkening sky above the Mule Mountains. Going home.

John Daniel

From *The Trail Home*

"The Impoverishment of Sightseeing"

The spectacular scenery of the West—its wide open spaces, sapphire skies, upthrust mountain ranges, spires and hoodoos, slickrock canyons, rivers—is what brings most of us to it who were not born to it. We take our photographs—"Back up a little bit, Harry"—we stand and look, we go "Oooh," and we go "Ahhh." But, poet John Daniel wonders in this lively essay from The Trail Home *(1992), how much do we really see?*

Rock climbing and mountaineering are unnecessary, artificial activities, invented by a privileged leisure class. Yet the act of climbing can yield an engagement with the natural world that is anything but artificial. That, I believe, is the reason it arose among the European well-to-do of the nineteenth century—it answered a need for reconnection to the wild nature from which they had so successfully separated themselves. Other kinds of outdoor activities answer the same need for many who pursue them—backpacking, birding, hunting, fishing, white-water rafting. They offer in common the opportunity to be actively involved with nature instead of passively receiving it. Climbers and fishermen may not be at one with nature, but they are immersed in it, interact with it, and in that sense they are part of their surroundings. They experience a sense of place in nature, or at least that experience is potentially available to them. Those who come to sightsee, on the other hand, are not part of the place they look at. They are observers, subjects seeking an object, passing through.

I don't mean that the population can be divided into two groups, the doers and the lookers. I am both, at different times. All of us at various moments are the man on the bus gazing out and murmuring, "Isn't that a sight." Nor do I believe that that man was completely disconnected from what he saw; he was impressed, perhaps even moved, by the spectacle of Yosemite's walls. But he wasn't moved in any way that energized him much, that evoked any sign of elation or fear or awe. Like me at the time, he wasn't in the *presence* of those soaring faces. And as I watched him and others clicking photographs later, I couldn't help thinking that by recording what they saw they were trying to verify that it was real, and that they were actually there.

I've experienced that odd feeling myself. The first time I saw the Tetons I was a teenager sightseeing with my family. We sat at an outdoor chuckwagon breakfast place, eating pancakes and staring at the most dramatic mountains I had ever seen, so dramatic my eyes didn't quite believe them. They seemed to have no depth, hardly any substance—I kept thinking they looked like cut-outs someone had propped up on the other side of the lake. Part of my trouble, I'm sure, was due to the fact that an eastern kid was seeing his first western mountains. But I

ANSEL ADAMS. *Grand Teton, View from River Valley toward Snow-Covered Mountains*. Photograph. National Archives.

think there was more. I was expecting to experience those mountains, to perceive their full reality, simply by looking at them from a distance. They seemed to lack substance because I was reducing them to an image on the screen of my vision.

*   *   *

Appreciation of nature in our society takes two forms above all others. The prevailing form, the cult of utility, shapes and perpetuates our sense of land as something from which to extract uses and materials. The other, the cult of beauty, values land for its own sake, but chiefly for its visual appearance. The cult of beauty has had important positive consequences—most of our national and state parks were set aside because of their scenic splendor—but it also works hand-in-hand with the cult of utility. Our working assumption as a people has been that except for a scattering of parks and designated wilderness areas, many of them in alpine regions difficult of commercial access anyway, all other land is subject to utility first and other considerations second. On public lands, the much-voiced concept of multiple-use says that scenery and recreation are equal in importance to the land's utilitarian value; but in practice, multiple-use in our national forests means logging first and other uses where logging permits. And in the desert West, which even in the eyes of many nature lovers still lies outside the category of the beautiful, mining, oil and gas drilling, and the wholesale stripping of forest to create range for cows all proceed with practically no restraint.

When those who oppose such "improvements" invoke in its defense only (or mainly) the land's beauty, they are dismissed as sentimental and unrealistic. And there is a certain justice in the dismissal, because at bottom the cult of beauty shares with the cult of utility the same flaw: it views nature as an object separate from the human subject. The timber or mineral executive reduces nature to a commodity, something to be taken out. The tourist seeking scenic beauty reduces nature to pleasing images, enjoyed and taken home on film. Neither recognizes nature as a living system of which our human lives are part, on which our lives and all lives depend, and which places strict limits upon us even as it sustains us.

That is an ecological view, and though most of us have some familiarity with the ideas of ecology, ecology remains *only* ideas, abstract and forceless in our lives, so long as we perceive nature merely as a collection of objects, however lovely. It takes not just looking at nature but getting into it—into some of its unloveliness as well as its splendor—for ideas to begin to bear the fruit of understanding. The rattlesnakes beneath the boulders instructed me, in a way no book could have, that the natural world did not exist entirely for my comfort and pleasure;

indeed, that it did not particularly care whether my small human life continued to exist at all. Being terribly thirsty on Sentinel Rock helped me understand in my body what my mind already knew, or thought it knew—how moisture both makes life possible and sets unequivocal limits on where it can exist. And once I had spent some time in old-growth forests, the profusion of dead trees that had daunted me at first began to elicit an appreciation of how death and life dance to a single music, how a healthy natural community carefully conserves and recycles its living wealth, and so sustains itself through time.

Such perceptions, in their rudimentary way, point toward an ecological understanding of the natural world. Clearly, to fully realize this understanding, we as a people need to follow the lead of the ecological sciences and learn to live by the principles they discover. We need to heal the injuries we have caused in the biosphere. But even as we scientifically study the inner workings of nature and the ways we have disrupted it, we also need to experience it again, to apprehend it in its fullness. As Edward Abbey told us many times, we can't experience the outdoors through a car window. We must take the time to enter the natural world, to engage it, not just to run our eyes along its surfaces but to place ourselves among its things and weathers—to let it exert, at least for intervals in our lives, the ancient influences that once surrounded and formed us.

Enough time under those influences can teach us to use our eyes actively again, as something more than receptacles. They seek a route through trees, across a creek, over a ridge, working in concert with body and mind. They follow the darts and veers of a hummingbird, a lizard skimming across stones, the quick glint of a trout. Things much smaller than El Capitan or the Tetons, things easy to miss, begin to reveal themselves—tiny white flowers of saxifrage, the quarter-sized, web-lined shaft of a tarantula's den, a six-inch screech owl flicking limb to limb in the dusk.

And when later in the evening the owl sounds its soft, tremulous call, and small snaps and rustlings reveal the presence of other lives, the eyes have reached their proper limit. The sense we rely on above all others can never completely know the natural world, for nature's being is only partly what it shows. Its greater part, and greater beauty, is always past what human eyes can understand. When I started hiking desert canyons a few years ago, I kept hearing the song of a bird I couldn't see, a long descending series of sharply whistled notes. It was a canyon wren, I learned from the books, but what I learned from the bird was more important. It sang as I woke up, as brilliant sun spread down the great red walls, and it sang as I started farther up the twisting canyon, sloshing through pools and scrambling up dry water chutes, higher and deeper into the carving of time. And what I remember most vividly from those early hikes is no particular thing I saw, no one fern grotto or sandstone spire, no cottonwood or cactus garden. I remember a bird I couldn't see that called from around the next bend, from over the brink of a dry waterfall where the upper walls held the blaze of sky, where even as it steadily opened itself to sight, the canyon receded further and further into the depth of its mystery.

Pam Houston

From *Cowboys are My Weakness*

For generations, the West as literary fodder was the almost exclusive property of male writers, with such rare exceptions as Mari Sandoz or Willa Cather. No longer. Today's Western American literature is distinguished by a generous number of women writers who are doing some of the best work around anywhere. One of them is Pam Houston, whose collection of short stories, Cowboys are My Weakness, *was published to much acclaim in 1992. Here is an excerpt from the title story.*

HOWARD POST. *Red Riding Shoot*. c. 1990. Oil. 32 x 50 in. Courtesy Suzanne Brown Gallery, Scottsdale, Arizona.

I have a picture in my mind of a tiny ranch on the edge of a stand of pine trees with some horses in the yard. There's a woman standing in the doorway in cutoffs and a blue chambray work shirt and she's just kissed her tall, bearded, and soft-spoken husband goodbye. There's laundry hanging outside and the morning sun is filtering through the tree branches like spiderwebs. It's the morning after a full moon, and behind the house the deer have eaten everything that was left in the garden.

If I were a painter, I'd paint that picture just to see if the girl in the doorway would turn out to be me. I've been out west ten years now, long enough to call it my home, long enough to know I'll be here forever, but I still don't know where that ranch is. And even though I've had plenty of men here, some of them tall and nearly all of them bearded, I still haven't met the man who has just walked out of the painting, who has just started his pickup truck, whose tire marks I can still see in the sandy soil of the drive.

The west isn't a place that gives itself up easily. Newcomers have to sink into it slowly, to descend through its layers, and I'm still descending. Like most easterners, I started out in the transitional zones, the big cities and the ski towns that outsiders have set up for their own comfort, the places so often referred to as "the best of both worlds." But I was bound to work my way back, through the land, into the small towns and beyond them. That's half the reason I wound up on a ranch near Grass Range, Montana; the other half is Homer.

I've always had this thing about cowboys, maybe because I was born in New Jersey. But a real cowboy is hard to find these days, even in the west. I thought I'd found one on several occasions, I even at one time thought Homer was a cowboy, and though I loved him like crazy for a while and in some ways always will, somewhere along the line I had to face the fact that even though Homer looked like a cowboy, he was just a capitalist with a Texas accent who owned a horse.

Homer's a wildlife specialist in charge of a whitetail deer management project on the ranch. He goes there every year to observe the deer from the start of the mating season in late October until its peak in mid-November. It's the time when the deer are most visible, when the bucks get so lusty they lose their normal caution, when the does run around in the middle of the day with their white tails in the air. When Homer talked me into coming with him, he said I'd love the ranch, and I did. It was sixty miles from the nearest paved road. All of the buildings were whitewashed and plain. One of them had been ordered from a 1916 Sears catalogue. The ranch hands still rode horses, and when the late-afternoon light swept the grainfields across from headquarters, I would watch them move the cattle in rows that looked like waves. There was a peace about the ranch that was uncanny and might have been complete if not for the eight or nine hungry barn cats that crawled up your legs if you even smelled like food, and the exotic chickens of almost every color that fought all day in their pens.

Homer has gone to the ranch every year for the last six, and he has a long history of stirring up trouble there. The ranch hands watch him sit on the hillside and hate him for the money he makes. He's slept with more than one or two of their wives and girlfriends. There was even some talk that he was the reason the ranch owner got divorced.

When he asked me to come with him I knew it would be me or somebody else and I'd heard good things about Montana so I went. There was a time when I was sure Homer was the man who belonged in my painting and I would have sold my soul to be his wife, or even his only girlfriend. I'd come close, in the spring, to losing my mind because of it, but I had finally learned that Homer would always be separate, even from himself, and by the time we got to Montana I was almost immune to him.

*   *   *

Five o'clock the next morning was the first time I saw the real cowboy. He was sitting in the cookhouse eating cereal and I couldn't make myself sleep next to Homer so I'd been up all night wandering around.

He was tall and thin and bearded. His hat was white and ratty and you could tell by looking at his stampeded strap that it had been made around a campfire after lots of Jack Daniel's. I'd had my fingers in my hair for twelve hours and my face was breaking out from too much stress and too little sleep and I felt like such a greaseball that I didn't say hello. I poured myself some orange juice, drank it, rinsed the glass, and put it in the dish drainer. I took one more look at the cowboy, and walked back out the door, and went to find Homer in the field.

Homer's truck was parked by a culvert on the South Fork road, which meant he was walking the brush line below the cliffs that used to be the Blackfeet buffalo jumps. It was a boneyard down there, the place where hundreds of buffalo, chased by the Indians, had jumped five hundred feet to their death, and the soil was extremely fertile. The grass was thicker and sweeter there than anywhere on the ranch, and Homer said the deer sucked calcium out of the buffalo bones. I saw Homer crouched at the edge of a meadow I couldn't get to without being seen, so I went back and fell asleep in the bed of his truck.

It was hunting season, and later that morning Homer and I found a deer by the side of the road that had been poached but not taken. The poacher must have seen headlights or heard a truck engine and gotten scared.

I lifted the back end of the animal into the truck while Homer picked up the antlers. It was a young buck, two and a half at the oldest, but it would have been a monster in a few years, and I knew Homer was taking the loss pretty hard.

We took it down to the performance center, where they weigh the organic calves. Homer attached a meat hook to its antlers and hauled it into the air above the pickup.

"Try and keep it from swinging," he said. And I did my best, considering I wasn't quite tall enough to get a good hold, and its blood was bubbling out of the bullet hole and dripping down on me.

That's when the tall cowboy, the one from that morning, walked out of the holding pen behind me, took a long slow look at me trying to steady the back end of the dead deer, and settled himself against the fence across the driveway. I stepped back from the deer and pushed the hair out of my eyes. He raised one finger to call me over. I walked slow and didn't look back at Homer.

"Nice buck," he said. "Did you shoot it?"

"It's a baby," I said. "I don't shoot animals. A poacher got it last night."

"Who was the poacher?" he said, and tipped his hat just past my shoulder toward Homer.

"You're wrong," I said. "You can say a lot of things about him, but he wouldn't poach a deer."

"My name's Montrose T. Coty," he said. "Everyone calls me Monte."

I shook his hand. "Everyone calls you Homer's girlfriend," he said, "but I bet that's not your name."

"You're right," I said, "it's not."

I turned to look at Homer. He was taking measurements off the hanging deer: antler length, body length, width at its girth.

"Tonight's the Stockgrowers' Ball in Grass Range," Monte said. "I thought you might want to go with me."

Homer was looking into the deer's hardened eyeballs. He had its mouth open, and was pulling on its tongue.

"I have to cook dinner for Homer and David," I said. "I'm sorry. It sounds like fun."

In the car on the way back to the cabin, Homer said, "What was that all about?"

I said, "Nothing," and then I said, "Monte asked me to the Stockgrowers' Ball."

"The Stockgrowers' Ball?" he said. "Sounds like a great time. What do stockgrowers do at a ball?" he said. "Do they dance?"

I almost laughed with him until I remembered how much I loved to dance. I'd been with Homer chasing whitetail so long that I'd forgotten that dancing, like holidays, was something I loved. And I started to wonder just then what else being with Homer had made me forget. Hadn't I, at one time, spent whole days listening to music? Wasn't there a time when I wanted, more than anything, to buy a sailboat? And didn't I love to be able to go outdoors and walk anywhere I wanted, and to make, if I wanted, all kinds of noise?

I wanted to blame Homer, but I realized then it was more my fault than his. Because even though I'd never let the woman in the chambray work shirt out of my mind I'd let her, in the last few years, become someone different, and she wasn't living, anymore, in my painting. The painting she was living in, I saw, belonged to somebody else.

"So what did you tell him?" Homer said.

"I told him I'd see if you'd cook dinner," I said.

I tried to talk to Homer before I left. First I told him that it wasn't a real date, that I didn't even know Monte, and really I was only going because I didn't know if I'd ever have another chance to go to a Stockgrowers' Ball. When he didn't answer at all I worked up to saying that maybe it was a good idea for me to start seeing other people. That maybe we'd had two different ideas all along and we needed to find two other people who would better meet our needs. I told him that if he had any opinions I wished he'd express them to me, and he thought for a few minutes and then he said,

"Well, I guess we have Jimmy Carter to thank for all the trouble in Panama."

I spent the rest of the day getting ready for the Stockgrowers' Ball. All I'd brought with me was some of Homer's camouflage and blue jeans, so I wound up borrowing a skirt that David's ex-wife had left behind, some of the chicken woman's dress shoes that looked ridiculous and made my feet huge, and a vest that David's grandfather had been shot at in by the Plains Indians.

Monte had to go into town early to pick up ranch supplies, so I rode in with his friends Buck and Dawn, who spent the whole drive telling me what a great guy Monte was, how he quit the rodeo circuit to make a decent living for himself and his wife, how she'd left without saying goodbye not six months before.

They told me that he'd made two thousand dollars in one afternoon doing a Wrangler commercial. That he'd been in a laundromat on his day off and the director had seen him through the window, had gone in and said, "Hey, cowboy, you got an hour? You want to make two thousand bucks?"

"Ole Monte," Buck said. "He's the real thing."

After an hour and a half of washboard road we pulled into the dance hall just on our edge of town. I had debated about wearing the cowboy hat I'd bought especially for my trip to Montana, and was thankful I'd decided against it. It was clear, once inside, that only the men wore hats, and only dress hats at that. The women wore high heels and stockings and in almost every case hair curled away from their faces in great airy rolls.

We found Monte at a table in the corner, and the first thing he did was give me a corsage, a pink one, mostly roses that couldn't have clashed more with my rust-colored blouse. Dawn pinned it on me, and I blushed, I suppose, over my first corsage in ten years, and a little old woman in spike heels leaned over and said, "Somebody loves you!" just loud enough for Monte and Buck and Dawn to hear.

During dinner they showed a movie about a cattle drive. After dinner a young enthusiastic couple danced and sang for over an hour about cattle and ranch life and the Big Sky, a phrase which since I'd been in Montana had seemed perpetually on the tip of everybody's tongue.

After dinner the dancing started, and Monte asked me if I knew how to do the Montana two-step. He was more than a foot taller than me, and his hat added another several inches to that. When we stood on the dance floor my eyes came right to the place where his silk scarf disappeared into the shirt buttons on his chest. His big hands were strangely light on me and my feet went the right direction even though my mind couldn't remember the two-step's simple form.

"That's it," he said into the part in my hair. "Don't think. Just let yourself move with me."

And we were moving together, in turns that got tighter and tighter each time we circled the dance floor. The songs got faster and so did our motion until there wasn't time for anything but the picking up and putting down of feet, for the swirling colors of Carmen's ugly skit, for breath and sweat and rhythm.

I was farther west than I'd ever imagined, and in the strange, nearly flawless synchronization on the dance floor I knew I could be a Montana ranch woman, and I knew I could make Monte my man. It had taken me ten years, and an incredible sequence of accidents, but that night I thought I'd finally gotten where I'd set out to go.

The band played till two and we danced till three to the jukebox. Then there was nothing left to do but get in the car and begin the two-hour drive home.

First we talked about our horses. It was the logical choice, the only thing we really had in common, but it only lasted twenty minutes.

I tried to get his opinion on music and sailing, but just like a cowboy, he was too polite for me to tell anything for sure.

Then we talked about the hole in my vest that the Indians shot, which I was counting on, and half the reason I wore it.

The rest of the time we just looked at the stars.

I had spent a good portion of the night worrying about what I was going to say when Monte asked me to go to bed with him. When he pulled up between our two cabins he looked at me sideways and said,

"I'd love to give you a great big kiss, but I've got a mouthful of chew."

I could hear Homer snoring before I got past the kitchen.

Partly because I didn't like the way Monte and Homer eyed each other, but mostly because I couldn't bear to spend Thanksgiving watching does in heat, I loaded my gear in my truck and got ready to go back to Colorado.

On the morning I left, Homer told me that he had decided that I was the woman he wanted to spend the rest of his life with after all, and that he planned to go to town and buy a ring just as soon as the rut ended.

He was sweet on my last morning on the ranch, generous and attentive in a way I'd never seen. He packed me a sack lunch of chicken salad he mixed himself, and he went out to my car and dusted off the inch of snow that had fallen in our first brush with winter, overnight. He told me to call when I got to Fort Collins, he even said to call collect, but I suppose one of life's big tricks is to give us precisely the thing we want, two weeks after we've stopped wanting it, and I couldn't take Homer seriously, even when I tried.

When I went to say goodbye to David he hugged me hard, said I was welcome back on the ranch anytime. He said he enjoyed my company and appreciated my insight. Then he said he liked my perfume and I wondered where my taste in men had come from, I wondered whoever taught me to be so stupid about men.

I knew Monte was out riding the range, so I left a note on his car thanking him again for the

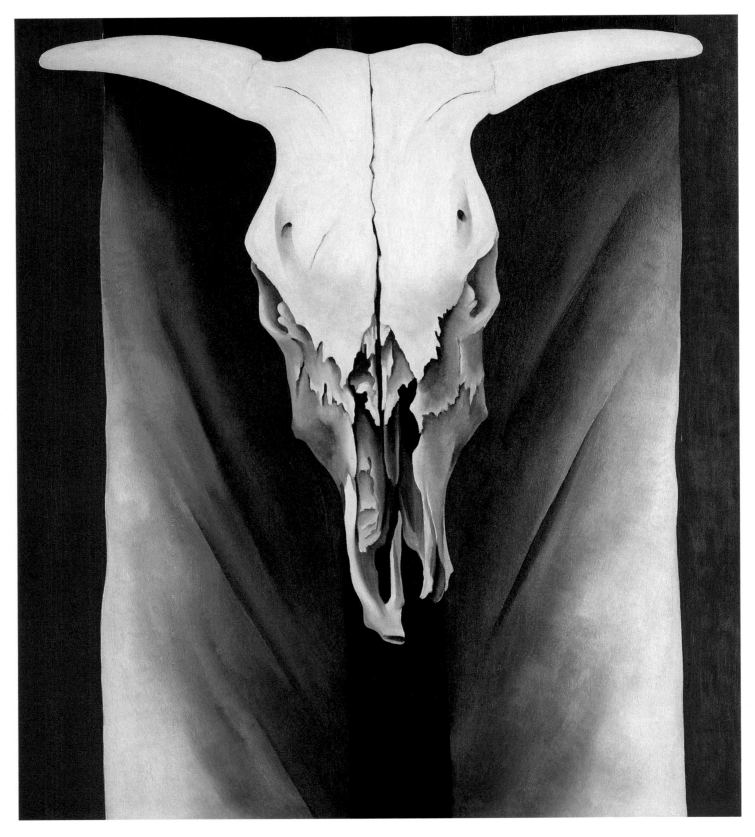

COLORPLATE 114

GEORGIA O'KEEFFE. *Cow's Skull: Red, White, and Blue.* 1931. Oil on canvas. 39 7/8 x 35 7/8 in. The Metropolitan Museum of Art, New York. The Alfred Stieglitz Collection, 1952.

COLORPLATE 115

GEORGIA O'KEEFFE. *From the Faraway Nearby.* 1937. Oil on canvas. 36 x 40 ¹/8 in. The Metropolitan Museum of Art, New York. The Alfred Stieglitz Collection, 1959. © 1994 The Georgia O'Keeffe Foundation/Artists Rights Society, New York.

COLORPLATE 116

HUBERT SHUPTRINE. *Death Dream*. Dry brush. 1984. 20 3/8 x 16 7/8 in. Courtesy of the artist.

COLORPLATE 117

MARISOL (Escobar). *John Wayne*. 1963. Wood, mixed media. 104 x 96 x 15 in. Collection of the Taylor Museum for Southwestern Studies of the Colorado Springs Fine Arts Center, Colorado Springs. © Marisol/VAGA, New York 1994.

COLORPLATE 118

RED GROOMS. *Wheeler Opera House*. 1984. Color 3-D lithograph, Edition 30. 17 ¹/₂ x 20 x 4 ¹/₂ in.
© 1994 Red Grooms/Artists Rights Society (ARS) and Shark's Inc., Boulder, Colorado.

COLORPLATE 120

WAYNE THIEBAUD. *Cliffs*. 1968. Acrylic on canvas. 101 ¹/₄ x 88 in. Private collection.
Photograph courtesy Allan Stone Gallery, New York.

COLORPLATE 119 (opposite page)

JOHN HENRY TWACHTMAN. *Waterfall in Yellowstone*. 1895. Oil on canvas. 25 ³/₈ x 16 ¹/₂ in.
Buffalo Bill Historical Center, Cody, Wyoming. Gift of Mr. and Mrs. Cornelius Vanderbilt Whitney.

COLORPLATE 121

ANDY WARHOL. *The American Indian (Russell Means)*. 1976. Silk screen ink on synthetic polymer paint on canvas. 50 x 42 in. The Andy Warhol Foundation for the Visual Arts, New York.

dancing and saying I'd be back one day and we could dance again. I put my hat on, that Monte had never got to see, and rolled out of headquarters. It was the middle of the day, but I saw seven bucks in the first five miles, a couple of them giants, and when I slowed down they just stood and stared at the truck. It was the height of the rut and Homer said that's how they'd be, love-crazed and fearless as bears.

About a mile before the edge of ranch property, I saw something that looked like a lone antelope running across the skyline, but antelope are almost never alone, so I stopped the car to watch. As the figure came closer I saw it was a horse, a big chestnut, and it was carrying a rider at a full gallop, and it was coming right for the car.

I knew it could have been any one of fifty cowboys employed on the ranch, and yet I've learned to expect more from life than that, and so in my heart I knew it was Monte. I got out of the car and waited, pleased that he'd see my hat most of all, wondering what he'd say when I said I was leaving.

He didn't get off his horse, which was sweating and shaking so hard I thought it might die while we talked.

"You on your way?" he said.

I smiled and nodded. His chaps were sweat-soaked, his leather gloves worn white.

"Will you write me a letter?" he said.

"Sure," I said.

"Think you'll be back this way?" he asked.

"If I come back," I said, "will you take me dancing?"

"Damn right," he said, and a smile that seemed like the smile I'd been waiting for my whole life spread wide across his face.

"Then it'll be sooner than later," I said.

He winked and touched the horse's flank with his spurs and it hopped a little on the takeoff and then there was just dirt flying while the high grass swallowed the horse's legs. I leaned against the door of my pickup truck watching my new cowboy riding off toward where the sun was already low in the sky and the grass shimmering like nothing I'd ever seen in the mountains. And for a minute I thought we were living inside my painting, but he was riding away too fast to tell. And I wondered then why I had always imagined my cowboy's truck as it was leaving. I wondered why I hadn't turned the truck around and painted my cowboy coming home.

There's a story—that isn't true—that I tell about myself when I first meet someone, about riding a mechanical bull in a bar. In the story, I stay on through the first eight levels of difficulty, getting thrown on level nine only after dislocating my thumb and winning my boyfriend, who was betting on me, a big pile of money. It was something I said in a bar one night, and I liked the way it sounded so much I kept telling it. I've been telling it for so many years now, and in such scrupulous detail, that it has become a memory and it's hard for me to remember that it isn't true. I can smell the smoke and beer-soaked carpets, I can hear the cheers of all the men. I can see the bar lights blur and spin, and I can feel the cold iron buck between my thighs, the painted saddle slam against my tailbone, the surprise and pain when my thumb extends too far and I let go. It's a good story, a story that holds my listeners' attention, and although I consider myself almost pathologically honest, I have somehow allowed myself this one small lie.

And watching Monte ride off through the long grains, I thought about the way we invent ourselves through our stories, and in a similar way, how the stories we tell put walls around our lives. And I think that may be true about cowboys. That there really isn't much truth in my saying cowboys are my weakness; maybe, after all this time, it's just something I've learned how to say.

I felt the hoofbeats in the ground long after Monte's white shirt and ratty hat melded with the sun. When I couldn't even pretend to feel them anymore, I got in the car and headed for the hard road.

I listened to country music the whole way to Cody, Wyoming. The men in the songs were all either brutal or inexpressive and always sorry later. The women were victims, every one. I started to think about coming back to the ranch to visit Monte, about another night dancing, about another night wanting the impossible love of a country song, and I thought:

This is not my happy ending.

This is not my story.

GRETEL EHRLICH

From *The Solace of Open Spaces*
Rules of the Rodeo

Rodeoing is a male sport, though it always has had its contingent of interested women, some of whom participate, some of whom follow the men, some of whom simply watch—and some of whom illuminate, like Wyoming ranchwoman and writer Gretel Ehrlich in this essay from The Solace of Open Spaces *(1985).*

Rodeo, like baseball, is an American sport and has been around almost as long. While Henry Chadwick was writing his first book of rules for the fledgling ball clubs in 1858, ranch hands were paying $25 a dare to a kid who would ride five outlaw horses from the rough string in a makeshift arena of wagons and cars. The first commercial rodeo in Wyoming was held in Lander in 1895, just nineteen years after the National League was formed. Baseball was just as popular as bucking and roping contests in the West, but no one in Cooperstown, New York, was riding broncs. And that's been part of the problem. After 124 years, rodeo is still misunderstood. Unlike baseball, it's a regional sport (although they do have rodeos in New Jersey, Florida, and other eastern states); it's derived from and stands for the western way of life and the western spirit. It doesn't have the universal appeal of a sport contrived solely for the competition and winning; there is no ball bandied about between opposing players.

Rodeo is the wild child of ranch work and embodies some of what ranching is all about. Horsemanship—not gunslinging—was the pride of western men, and the chivalrous ethics they formulated, known as the western code, became the ground rules for every human game. Two great partnerships are celebrated in this Oklahoma arena: the indispensable one between man and animal that any rancher or cowboy takes on, enduring the joys and punishments of the alliance; and the one between man and man, cowboy and cowboy.

Though rodeo is an individualist's sport, it has everything to do with teamwork. The cowboy who "covers" his bronc (stays on the full eight seconds) has become a team with that animal. The cowboys' competitive feelings amongst each other are so mixed with western tact as to appear ambivalent. When Bruce Ford, the bareback rider, won a go-round he said, "The hardest part of winning this year was taking it away from one of my best friends, Mickey Young, after he'd worked so hard all year." Stan Williamson, who'd just won the steer wrestling, said, "I just drew a better steer. I didn't want Butch to get a bad one. I just got lucky, I guess."

Ranchers, when working together, can be just as diplomatic. They'll apologize if they cut in front of someone while cutting out a calf, and their thanks to each other at the end of the day has a formal sound. Like those westerners who still help each other out during branding and roundup, rodeo cowboys help each other in the chutes. A bull rider will steady the saddle bronc rider's horse, help measure out the rein or set the saddle, and a bareback rider might help the bull rider set his rigging and pull his rope. Ropers lend each other horses, as do barrel racers and steer wrestlers. This isn't a show they put on; they offer their help with the utmost goodwill and good-naturedness. Once, when a bucking horse fell over backward in the chute with my husband, his friend H.A., who rode bulls, jumped into the chute and pulled him out safely.

Another part of the "westernness" rodeo represents is the drifting cowboys do. They're on the road much of their lives the way turn-of-the-century cowboys were on the trail, but these cowboys travel in style if they can—driving pink Lincolns and new pickups with a dozen fresh shirts hanging behind the driver, and the radio on.

Some ranchers look down on the sport of rodeo; they don't want these "drugstore cowboys" getting all the attention and glory. Besides, rodeo seems to have less and less to do with real ranch work. Who ever heard of gathering cows on a bareback horse with no bridle, or climbing on a herd bull? Ranchers are generalists—they have to know how to do many things—from juggling the futures market to overhauling a tractor or curing viral scours (diarrhea) in calves—while rodeo athletes are specialists. Deep down, they probably feel envious of each other: the rancher for the praise and big money; the rodeo cowboy for the stay-at-home life among animals to which their sport only alludes.

People with no ranching background have even more difficulty with the sport. Every ride goes so fast, it's hard to see just what happened, and perhaps because of the Hollywood mythologizing of the West which distorted rather than distilled western rituals, rodeo is often considered corny, anachronistic, and cruel to animals. Quite the opposite is true. Rodeo cowboys are as sophisticated athletically as Bjorn Borg or Fernando Valenzuela. That's why they don't need to be from a ranch anymore, or to have grown up riding horses. And to undo another myth, rodeo is not cruel to animals. Compared to the arduous life of any "using horse" on a cattle or dude ranch, a bucking horse leads the life of Riley. His actual work load for an entire year, i.e., the amount of time he spends in the arena, totals approximately 4.6 minutes, and nothing done to him in the arena or out could in any way be called cruel. These animals aren't bludgeoned into bucking; they love to buck. They're bred to behave this way, they're athletes whose ability has been nurtured and encouraged. Like the cowboys who compete at the National Finals, the best bulls and horses from all the bucking strings in the country are nominated to appear in Oklahoma, winning money along with their riders to pay their own way.

Bucking. Photograph. Buffalo Bill Historical Collection, Cody, Wyoming. Charles Belden Collection.

The National Finals run ten nights. Every contestant rides every night, so it is easy to follow their progress and setbacks. One evening we abandoned our rooftop seats and sat behind the chutes to watch the saddle broncs ride. Behind the chutes two cowboys are rubbing rosin—part of their staying power—behind the saddle swells and on their Easter-egg-colored chaps which are pink, blue, and light green with white fringe. Up above, standing on the chute rungs, the stock contractors direct horse traffic: "Velvet Drums" in chute #3, "Angel Sings" in #5, "Rusty" in #1. Rick Smith, Monty Henson, Bobby Berger, Brad Gjermudson, Mel Coleman, and friends climb the chutes. From where I'm sitting, it looks like a field hospital with five separate operating theaters, the cowboys, like surgeons, bent over their patients with sweaty brows and looks of concern. Horses are being haltered; cowboys are measuring out the long, braided reins, saddles are set: one cowboy pulls up on the swells again and again, repositioning his hornless saddle until it sits just right. When the chute boss nods to him and says, "Pull 'em up, boys," the ground crew tightens front and back cinches on the first horse to go, but very slowly so he won't panic in the chute as the cowboy eases himself down over the saddle, not sitting on it, just hovering there. "Okay, you're on." The chute boss nods to him again. Now he sits on the saddle, taking the rein in one hand, holding the top of the chute with the other. He flips the loose bottoms of his chaps over his shins, puts a foot in each stirrup, takes a breath, and nods. The chute gate swings open releasing a flood—not of water, but of flesh, groans, legs kicking. The horse lunges up and out in the first big jump like a wave breaking whose crest the cowboy rides, "marking out the horse," spurs well above the bronc's shoulders. In that first second under the lights, he finds what will be the rhythm of the ride. Once again he "charges the point," his legs pumping forward, then so far back his heels touch behind the cantle. For a moment he looks as though he were kneeling on air, then he's stretched out again, his whole body taut but released, free hand waving in back of his head like a palm frond, rein-holding hand thrust forward: "*En garde!*" he seems to be saying, but he's airborne; he looks like a wing that has sprouted suddenly from the horse's broad back. Eight seconds. The whistle blows. He's covered the horse. Now two gentlemen dressed in white chaps and satin shirts gallop beside the bucking horse. The cowboy hands the rein to one and grabs the waist of the other— the flank strap on the bronc has been undone, so all three horses move at a run—and the pickup man from whom the cowboy is now dangling slows almost to a stop, letting him slide to his feet on the ground.

Rick Smith from Wyoming rides, looking pale and nervous in his white shirt. He's bucked off and so are the brash Monty "Hawkeye" Henson, and Butch Knowles, and Bud Pauley, but with such grace and aplomb, there is no shame. Bobby Berger, an Oklahoma cowboy, wins the go-round with a score of 83.

By the end of the evening we're tired, but in no way as exhausted as these young men who have ridden night after night. "I've never been so sore and had so much fun in my life," one first-time bull rider exclaims breathlessly. When the performance is over we walk across the street to the chic lobby of a hotel chock full of cowboys. Wives hurry through the crowd with freshly ironed shirts for tomorrow's ride, ropers carry their rope bags with them into the coffee shop, which is now filled with contestants, eating mild midnight suppers of scrambled eggs, their numbers hanging crookedly on their backs, their faces powdered with dust, and looking at this late hour prematurely old.

We drive back to the motel, where, the first night, they'd "never heard of us" even though we'd had reservations for a month. "Hey, it's our honeymoon," I told the night clerk and showed him the white ribbons my mother had tied around our duffel bag. He looked embarrassed, then surrendered another latecomer's room.

The rodeo finals in Oklahoma may be a better place to honeymoon than Paris. All week, we've observed some important rules of the game. A good rodeo, like a good marriage, or a musical instrument when played to the pitch of perfection, becomes more than what it started out to be. It is effort transformed into effortlessness; a balance becomes grace, the way love goes deep into friendship.

In the rough stock events such as the one we watched tonight, there is no victory over the horse or bull. The point of the match is not conquest but communion: the rhythm of two beings becoming one. Rodeo is not a sport of opposition; there is no scrimmage line here. No one bears malice—neither the animals, the stock contractors, nor the contestants; no one wants to get hurt. In this match of equal talents, it is only acceptance, surrender, respect, and spiritedness that make for the midair union of cowboy and horse. Not a bad thought when starting out fresh in a marriage.

RUTH RUDNER

From *Greetings from Wisdom, Montana*
"Polar John's Bar"

In most of the towns of the Old West—certainly its mining towns and cowboy towns—the spiritual character of the community was more often found in its principal saloon than in its biggest church. And that still holds true in many towns—big and small—as Montana writer Ruth Rudner demonstrates in this selection from Greetings from Wisdom, Montana *(1989).*

Polaris, Montana, can be reached from the north via thirty miles of dirt road, or from the south on twenty-nine miles of paved road from Dillon, the Big Hole Valley's major town (population: 3,976), then six miles of dirt road. There are three buildings in Polaris: a large log structure that houses the post office, the general store and an apartment; a small log cabin; and a still smaller, white frame building that is Polar John's Bar. Polar John lives over the post office. His brother-in-law lives in the cabin. If the bar is closed and you want a beer, you knock on Polar

John's door and he comes down and opens the bar.

In 1981 the bar was the focus of a major conflict between the state health authorities and the people of Polaris and surrounding communities, including Dillon. The health department wanted to close Polar John's on the grounds that its plumbing was inadequate, equipped as it was with only one outhouse when separate facilities for men and women are required in public places, and with no hot water to wash the glasses. On May 3, 1981, a march to save Polar John's john was held.

Hundreds marched.

The results of this action was that the local citizens dug, and built, a second outhouse. Each outhouse has an equally good view of the valley. The health department then agreed that Polar John could use plastic, disposable glasses in the bar. Since most Montanans drink beer out of a can anyway, he can keep his overhead low.

The bar is a simple, square room containing an oilcloth-covered round table in one corner, with benches on two sides of it and a couple of ice cream chairs in front of it. A few wooden chairs, a stool and a rocker line up against two walls. There is a potbellied stove near the front door and an old oak bar with a brass rail. The bar comes from Bannack, Montana's first territorial capital and site, in 1863, of Montana's first gold rush. Two years of cold-blooded violence at the hands of a band of road agents, ably led by the Bannack sheriff, made Bannack one of the roughest towns in the West. When the local citizenry finally tired of being robbed and murdered so often, they formed a vigilante committee, pinning its secret sign, "3-7-77," on hanged bandits. *All* bandits were hanged. The vigilantes managed to capture the entire gang. And then some. Those numbers, 3-7-77, appear today on road signs in southwest Montana and on shoulder patches of the Montana State Police throughout the state. No one can explain what they mean.

Five of us had spent several days backpacking in the West Pioneer Range. The paths we walked were far gentler than the miles of dirt road and one-lane, rock-strewn pass we had driven over to reach the bar. Because the lakes in the West Pioneers are heavily used, we had been boiling the water we drank. Aside from the fact that boiled water tastes awful, it is a pain in the neck to boil enough to drink on a hot Montana day, so we drank less than our bodies required.

By the time we reached the bar we were in serious need of beer.

When we entered Polar John's, a dog was sleeping on the floor, two old cowboys were sitting on wooden chairs drinking beer, Polar John was standing behind the bar and a horse was looking in through the open back door. One of the old cowboys said, "Howdy."

Howdy is an interesting word. In my years of backpacking and hiking, every man I have ever passed in wilderness anywhere in America, even in Harriman Park, forty minutes from New York City, has greeted me with "howdy." These men may be stockbrokers or physicians or engineers who dress in suits and ties on weekdays and greet people with "good morning" or "how are you?," but no sooner do they get into the forest or the mountains than they say, "howdy."

No woman I have ever encountered in the wilderness has greeted me with "howdy."

All three men watched us arrange ourselves on bar stools, take in the bar, try not to appear too curious about them, open our beer. The man who had greeted us turned out to be Polar John's brother-in-law, seventy-seven-year-old Walt Melcher, who quickly connected with one of our group, sixty-six-year-old Bill Barnes, a farmer from the Montana plains. Born in the Big Belt Mountains that edge the plains, Bill had now retired to Great Falls.

He had also just returned from a kayak trip of several weeks in Alaska. His keen interest in everything on earth kept him from any semblance of shyness. Of us all, he was the only one to openly explore his environment in the bar. He began a conversation with Polar John. I suspect it may have been the only conversation Polar John has ever had.

Turning square to him, Bill said, "You've been here quite a while, haven't you?"

A few minutes passed. Finally Polar John said, "Yeah." Then he resumed the silence he'd been moved out of by so direct a question.

"He was born here in nineteen-ten," Walt offered. Watching us seemed to amuse him. His eyes laughed. Clearly there was nothing shy about him, either.

Polar John stood behind the bar, tall and slender, straight as a young man. He continued saying nothing.

"I was born in nineteen-eighteen," Bill said.

"You're lucky to be here," Walt said.

"Yeah, that's true," Bill agreed.

"You probably had a pretty good life," the old cowboy added.

"Yeah, that's probably true too," Bill said.

When he realized there would be a conversation, the silent cowboy got up from his chair as if he didn't want to be in the way of it and ambled over to the end of the bar where he joined Polar John in saying nothing. He stood, rolling a cigarette and watching the two old men of the land talk. It was obvious that if it were not for Walt, there never would be a conversation in Polaris.

They had the land in common, the farmer and the cowboy, and although neither of them worked it anymore, it had formed their tenacity and their humor. They found each other the way children discover one another in a gathering of adults, or the way people of the same nationality find one another on foreign soil.

The dog lifted his head. Walt moved to the wooden stool, raised his leg straight out in front of him. The dog jumped over it several times.

"Usually he does this for potato chips," Walt said.

"Does he work cattle?" Bill asked.

"Well, he's awful good when they're well cooked," Walt said.

It was seven forty-five. The light was fading. Walt said, "You should see the Big Hole Valley while you're here."

"I always meant to," Bill said, "but I think I picked the wrong time. I'm supposed to be in Great Falls by eight."

It is a three-hour drive from Polar John's Bar to Great Falls, out there at the edge of the prairie where the great falls of the Missouri gave birth to the town. There are five falls in a ten-mile stretch of river, the highest of which is the farthest upstream and the one which Meriwether Lewis called the Great Falls in his first view of them:

. . . The grandest sight I ever beheld . . . the irregular and somewhat projecting rocks below receives the water in its passage down and brakes it into a perfect white foam which assumes a thousand forms in a moment sometimes flying up in jets of sparkling foam to the height of fifteen or twenty feet and are scarcely formed before large rolling bodies of the same beaten and foaming water is thrown over and conceals them.

The falls now have been harnessed to provide electrical power.

"Well, there's a jet that flies over . . . ," Walt offered as a way to get Bill home on schedule.

The other cowboy spoke for the first time. "Montana is a goddamn big state," he said.

I bought a bag of potato chips for the dog. He jumped back and forth over my leg which I held increasingly higher. Each time he ate his potato chip before jumping back. When the bag of potato chips was empty, he lay down and went to sleep. At eight-fifteen Bill rose from his chair, saying, "I've got to see Polar John's john, then I'm going to Great Falls."

Walt said, "There's a million acres out there. You can use every one of 'em."

At the back door, Bill looked out on the million acres, then turned and asked, "Where is it?"

Walt followed him out, saying, to us or to himself, "I better go show him. Awful hard to hit that little hole."

Now that everyone who talked had left the bar, the bar was silent again. A second horse walked by the back door.

TERESA JORDAN

From *Riding the White Horse Home*

Calving Season

On the ranches of the modern West, calving season is no less exhilarating and hopeful than it was on the ranches of the Old West. This, for the rancher, is still harvest time, the very measure of the future. Mainly, however, it is work—messy, relentless, exhausting, and in the end, satisfying. Teresa Jordan, who learned these truths while on a Wyoming ranch, provides some intensely drawn vignettes of calving time from Riding the White Horse Home: A Western Family Album *(1993).*

———————

There's a rule to calving: just when you're busiest, you run into trouble. Now the temperature drops and the snow stays on the ground for a couple of days. For once, there is no wind. We'd been cursing it for days, but at least it broke up the snow. Without it, the glare is blinding, and a dozen cows sunburn their bags. Sunburn is as painful for a cow as for a human—sunburnt cows won't let their calves suck. We have to put them in the chute and milk them by hand. Range cows aren't used to being milked. It takes a lot of time and patience. Right now, calving seems endless.

April 24: Carol found a dead calf in the Big Meadow this morning, a big black-baldy that looked like it had been born healthy; probably the sack didn't break and it suffocated. The mother was a nice Hereford heifer, and Charlie and I rode out to get her so we could graft an orphan on her. We found her still with her calf, nosing it, licking it, trying to get it up. It would have been futile to try and herd her away from the calf so I put a rope around the calf's back leg and started to drag it toward home. The cow followed, humming and mooing, sniffing first one side of the calf and then trotting around to sniff the other, sure with each bump and jerk that her baby had come back to life. She followed me all the way to the buildings, over two miles. I led her right into the corral and shut the gate; then we took her calf and threw it in the back of the pickup to take to the dead pile. She kept circling the corral, looking for it.

We had a cow in the Second Meadow with bad mastitis and her calf couldn't get enough to eat. We decided to graft the calf onto the heifer. Charlie and I rode to the Second Meadow and Carol followed in the Suburban. We hog-tied the calf and loaded it in the car. Once the mastitis cow realized we had kidnapped her baby, she was brokenhearted. She ran after the Suburban, bellering all the while. As Carol drove off, I noticed that the calf had kicked off its piggin' string and was standing up in the back of the car, peeing in Ryan's diaper bag.

Sunday night the temperature dropped to 5 degrees. We lost two calves in the meadow but had three live ones born on the hill. Carol found a particularly big newborn chilled in the Big Meadow and brought it in for a dose of heat in the warming booth. When it was warm, Charlie and I took it back in the pickup. The back of the truck was filled with fencing equipment so we put the calf in the cab with us. It felt great by that time and was strong and hungry. All it wanted to do was suck. It tried to suck my knee, my wrist, the gear-shift knob, anything. A calf will butt its mother's udder to make her let down her milk and this calf kept butting reflexively. Each time it did, it bashed its head against the dashboard. Charlie drove while I tried to keep the calf from injuring itself. It was bawling all the time, its voice deafening in the closed cab. The calf was so healthy, so hungry, so warm and so strong—and here it was, in the cab of the pickup with us, knocking the truck out of gear and causing the sort of ruckus that made me want to continue doing this—exactly this—forever.

In this business of cattle raising, we exert our will. We take a calf off a poor cow and graft it onto a good one. We hobble a reticent cow until she lets her calf suck. We midwife these calves into existence, we care for them, sometimes we even risk our lives for them, and they are ultimately slated for slaughter. In this fact lies the essential irony of our work. No one forgets that a live calf is money in the bank. And yet a reverence remains. John Bell and Hungry and the calf in the cab of the pickup are not merely units of production; our connection to them is more than economic. Day in and day out we confront the messiness of this business of living; if we live with slaughter, we also live with nurture, with seasons and cycles, with birth and with death.

April 28: The weather has finally turned. Yesterday was sunny and 50 degrees. This morning we woke to hoar frost—all the tree branches, fence wires and grasses sparkled in the sun. And there was lots of sun: it was a beautiful cloudless, windless day.

Charlie and I spent the afternoon dehorning. I ran out of paste so I held the horses while Charlie worked. It was nice to laze and gawk awhile. A blackbird landed on an Angus cow. She switched her tail and the bird hopped further forward on her back. The cow switched again and tossed back her head. This time she knocked the bird off. It landed on the ground beside her; she turned and butted at it as if it were a dog.

Charlie grabbed a big red calf and it started bawling. A couple dozen mother cows came running. They formed a circle, each cow snorting and sniffing, stretching out her neck in an attempt to get close enough to smell the calf. As each one got a sniff and realized the calf wasn't hers, her ears drooped and she lost interest. One cow recognized her calf and moved right in, almost knocking Charlie over. He popped her on the nose with a glove and finished pasting the calf.

Carol drove over in the Suburban. Chris was in school but Tom and Ryan were with her. We watched a baldy have a calf up along the ditch. She laid down and gave birth in about a minute and a half. Then she got back up and started circling her calf, licking all the time, mooing to it softly, humming. Soon, she started licking it harder, as if she were trying to actually lift it with her tongue. It tried to get up a couple of times and didn't make it. Then it succeeded and stood on its wobbly new legs. "That's how you're 'sposed to do it," Tom observed. Sometimes the boys get bored riding around in the Suburban so much but today everyone was in a good mood.

BILL ANTON. *Five A.M.
and Five Below*. 1993.
Oil. 24 x 36 in. Courtesy
of the artist.

The boys are learning, already and as if by osmosis, an ancient husbandry. Ranching for the Farthings is a family affair and has always been so. They recently took on a mortgage to buy several more sections of land, part of the old Hirsig Ranch on their border. Right now they don't need more acreage, but the chance to buy contiguous land is rare. If Chris and Tom and Ryan want to stay on the ranch and raise their own families, they will be able to do so. The debt is for the future, modest enough not to imperil the present.

The Farthing Ranch is the only long-time family ranch left in the Iron Mountain area and one of the few family ranches in the West with a secure future. Part of that security comes from the fact that the Farthings don't run on public grazing land, but a larger part comes from the fact that the ranch has always been managed with an eye to future generations. They have always been in debt, but not dangerously so. They have never been seduced by machinery or modernization. They are hardly backward—they have two big Haymaster tractors, for instance, and the sheds all have electricity and water—but the Farthings have weighed each purchase carefully and resisted extravagant expense. Their pickups are stripped-down vehicles without air-conditioning or FM radios; they still put up hay in loose stacks rather than in bales or loaves that require new and more sophisticated, single-use machinery. Already they are engaged in estate planning in order to assure that the boys can keep the ranch once Carol and Charlie are gone.

If the Farthings were to sell out, they would be wealthy indeed. As it is, they work seven days a week and enjoy a comfortable though modest material life—something comparable to what a reasonably successful small businessman or associate professor might enjoy. They have nice but unassuming homes and they can afford to take vacations—though they seldom do.

April 30: When Charlie and I get to the top of the Big Hill each day, we split and ride separate ridges. We seem to have developed a ritual with a pair of coyotes. As we ride west, they pass us—one on each ridge—going east. Sometimes they pass within fifty or sixty yards of our horses. We have a running conversation with them—"Well, Mr. Coyote, I didn't find any trouble back my way; how are things up ahead?" When the wind was so bad a couple of days ago, Charlie snuck up on his coyote. It was sniffing around a sagebrush and must not have heard him coming. Charlie got to within a few feet of it before it realized he was there. It jerked around and saw him, jumped straight up into the air and then took off. Since then, it has kept a greater distance in its morning rounds.

Pasted a lot of calves today, doctored the diphtheria steer, cleaned a couple of afterbirths, brought in a starved calf and its mother who has a sunburned bag. The ground is dry enough to start feeding cake again and John Bell is grateful. Mostly, we just took care of business. Nothing too strenuous, nothing too exciting. The weather makes everything easy.

It is nearly the end of April now, and calving season is winding down. New calves will trickle in for another couple of weeks, but the bulk of them are already on the ground.

I can read the past month in my hands. The back of my left one has two long, deep scratches from busting through the brush on Sadie Mae, in pursuit of a cow. Another cut runs the length of my thumb—a heifer kicked me when I was milking her out. On the palm is a blood blister from something I don't remember, and two deep holes from slivers that I picked up trying to remove the bars from the door to the cinder-block shed when I hurried to let in an angry cow. On my right hand, I have two more sliver holes, three blisters from dehorning paste, a burn from a pot, a cut from the bag-balm can, a rope burn across the lower pads of my fingers, and a variety of other miscellaneous nicks and scratches. My hands are sore—they hurt whenever I try to grip anything—and the kids have nicknamed me Scar Hand. I remember going through this every summer when I returned from school to work on the ranch. This is the point where my hands start getting tough. This time, they will just become useful and I will leave.

In my life in the city, I work long days. I break up the hours at my desk or in the classroom with long hikes in the woods near my home, with bicycling, with gardening. Physical activity keeps me grounded in my body; time outdoors keeps me aware of the seasons. And yet here, in the country, is the real work, the interweave of man and animal, weather and land, that is as old as appetite. Here, physical exertion matters. It keeps me aware of what it means to be alive, and what it costs.

CHARLES BOWDEN

From *Blue Desert*

Tracking the Beasts of the Desert

If any single western writer can be said to follow closely in the passionately idiosyncratic tradition of Edward Abbey, it is Charles Bowden, who got much of his training as a professional writer while working as a reporter for the Tucson Citizen, *but even there managed to break free of ordinary journalistic restraints. In this selection from* Blue Desert *(1986), he sets out to write about desert tortoises and ends up eviscerating the Sunbelt West.*

I once knew a woman who had a pet tortoise named Fluffy and I think of this fact as I face the action.

The blue air hangs over the room of clacking machines as people pack this casino hugging the banks of the Colorado River and wearily pull the levers on the slots.

I am hungry. I check my backpack with the doorman and rub my fingers across the stubble of my beard. The people are very intent and do not look up or around or at one another. Laughlin, Nevada, strings a half dozen casinos along the tame stream and is only a minute by boat from the Arizona shore. Outside the parking lots are packed with campers, trucks, and vans and every machine has a toy poodle yapping at the window. This is a blue collar Las Vegas.

I want bacon and eggs, but I hesitate on the floor of the casino. The players are men in caps and t-shirts, fat-hipped women in polyester stretch pants, retired folks plunging with dimes and quarters. I am pretty much dirty clothes, clumps of greasy hair, and hung-over eyes. Last night I slept in the hills overlooking the valley. Cottontails grazed around my head and hopped along the sides of my sleeping bag. All night the casino signs splashed color and form into the night sky and then at first light, lines of herons and ducks and geese slowly winged down the ribbon of river to the feeding grounds. In this big room of smoke, booze, and slots, sunrise and sunset count for nothing.

Clocks are kept from sight, the pit blocks all views of the outside and the women peddling drinks to the players, God! Those women in black net stockings, thrusting breasts, fresh young faces, and ancient eyes. Well, the women strut through the blue air denying that time or age or bills or tomorrow exists or matters. I love the women and what they are doing for us all. Just savor them, I tell myself, don't speak to them, don't go home with them, just brush them with your eyes. In here, they are the promise of flesh and fun and smiles and I do not want to know about the two kids, the old man that skidaddled, the small trailer where everytime you turn around you bump into yourself.

I finally cross the casino floor and walk into the restaurant, a barren that is here and there dotted with tired people pumping coffee and reading the sports pages. I sit down, swallow a couple of cups and start nibbling at the pile of scientific papers I carry. I have come here to listen to experts consider the plight of the desert tortoise and the experts have gathered here from the universities, from the Bureau of Land Management, from the fish and game departments, from all the small offices with grey desks and steady checks, because, hell, why not meet in a casino town?

The desert tortoise itself (*Gopherus agassizii*) has skipped this occasion. In the bright lights and big cities of the Sunbelt this small reptile is no big deal. Loving a desert tortoise is a little bit like bonding with a pet rock—scholars estimate that the beast spends 94.9 percent of its time in dormancy, which means just lying there in its burrow. Today they are being wiped out in the desert, and in Sunbelt cities survive mainly as pets and captives (at least twenty thousand in California and thousands in Tucson and Phoenix). Once upon a time they averaged from ten or twenty up to several hundred per square mile. But this is a new time and a new west.

I thumb through this leviathan study, an 838-page draft report being considered by the Desert Tortoise Council, the cabal of experts zeroing in on this casino for a conference. I discover that *Gopherus agassizii* runs six to fourteen inches, tops the scale at maybe ten pounds and hardly pesters anyone. They endure their slow lives for 50 to 100 years, and I am briefly bewitched by the notion that somewhere out there lumber Methuselah tortoises that have seen the whole western movie, all three reels, from Wyatt Earp to Palm Springs.

The eggs and bacon finally arrive and I devour them. This is a nickel-and-dime trip where I figure on skipping room rent by flopping in the desert, jotting notes during all the weighty sessions of tortoise papers, and hopefully, scribbling a story that will pay the rent.

The tortoise looks to be a perfect foil for a quick hit: they are the innocents, the benign nothings who do not attack cattle, sheep, or hikers, the little rascals who pack no venom and fire up all the fantasies of nature that people relish. Scientists tag them as an indicator species, meaning one that suggests the health of the ecosystem as a whole. Almost stationary in their habits, long-lived, low in reproduction rate and quiet, they function as witnesses to the way human beings in the Southwest treat the land and the form of life woven into the land.

In short, tortoises have a high potential to evoke human guilt. Box office.

I have been counseled at length by a friend who for decades has flourished as a free-lance writer of nature stories. He warned me to avoid all colorful references to the casino ("none of those clinking ice cubes in glasses of whiskey," he fumed) and play it straight and be rich in technical information. This is good advice that I find hard to follow. I have yet to meet the casino that cannot seduce me. The pits are so full of human greed and human hope and always there are those little touches—the men in the glass room packing sacks of money and wearing smocks that have no pockets—that make me glad to be a human being. There are few places as honest as the rampant fraud and fantasy of a casino. Here we let down our hair, our pants, our everything and confess to all our secret hungers.

The women working the place are a problem also, busting out of their britches, bending down to pour coffee and slapping my face with deep cleavage. I can think of few things more pleasurable than to sleep on the desert, watch the rabbits bounce around and then at dawn walk into a casino where time has stopped and everything always promises to be juicy.

I pay the bill and move up the stairs to the meeting rooms where plump, contented tortoise experts gather over coffee and doughnuts. I strike up conversations with perfect strangers who are all friendly in this bastion of tortoise love. An elderly couple tells me of their son who is in the grocery business and has a kind of tortoise preserve at his home with eighteen of the beasts thriving on the wilted lettuce he brings home each night. A lady from Phoenix brags on her pet male who taps the patio doors when he wants in the house. The registration table for the conference is a gold mine of tortoise pendants, pens, pins, t-shirts, key chains, wind chimes.

Everyone seems satisfied after an evening of frolicking over steak dinners, trying their luck at blackjack, having a spin in this dab of sin—all at government expense. Finally, the session comes to order and I hunch in my chair busy noting the hard facts of *Gopherus* scholarship.

Being a desert tortoise may not constitute a full-time job. A calendar of the tortoise year, based on a daily time budget (DTB) and annual time budget (ATB), is not full of big events. The animals emerge from their holes in late March to late July when the days begin to be warm. At first, basking (tortoise sunbathing) takes up about 19 percent of the DTB, a figure which declines as the season advances, and only kills 1.5 percent of the ATB. Once out and about tortoises turn to foraging (1.5 percent ATB) and love-making (0.08 percent ATB). Even during the friskiest part of the summer season they go dormant 33 percent of the time.

Tortoises spend only three to six months a year actively feeding and moving, and even during this frisky period they devote most of their hours to snoozing in their burrows. Basically, *Gopherus agassizii* is not a Type A personality and this wonderful calm has prevented tortoise scholars from glimpsing much action.

A few tidbits have been gleaned. When picked up and alarmed they are liable to piss all over people. When two male tortoises met, they bob their heads and often ram each other—the loser being toppled onto his back and left to die in the heat if he cannot right himself. When sprinting they can cover about six yards in a minute but they hardly ever move far from their burrows unless maddened by thirst.

They have very little to say. When disturbed or when mating, they sometimes hiss, grunt, and make pops and poinks. I hesitate in my note-taking and contemplate the ring of a hearty tortoise poink. Dominant males seem to pack a potent punch when they defecate and have been known to send the rest of the boys scurrying from a burrow with one mighty dump.

Sex occurs to a tortoise after reaching the age of fifteen or twenty and the first date begins with the male bobbing his head and then nipping the female a few times on the shell before mounting her. Tortoise women maintain an air of calm and sometimes keep right on eating during copulation. Eggs are laid, buried, and after 100 days, hatch. The young tortoise must face five years of desert life with a soft shell.

Generally, tortoises are homebodies and spend their lives within a few hundred yards of their burrows, wandering off mainly for a little dining, basking, or love-making. Specimens tagged during a study in the late thirties and early forties were found in the same area by scientists in the eighties. They chow down on green herbs, leaves, and blossoms of annuals, succulents, grasses, and cacti.

The papers come one after another and they stand in contrast to the sea of peace that constitutes normal tortoise life. Outside the casino walls in the desert we cannot see well (the meeting room, naturally, has no windows), out there it is holocaust time for tortoises. I look around at conference attendants and see a lot of grim faces.

People, it seems, have been wreaking havoc on tortoises for a long time—they were sold as dog food in Los Angeles during the 1890s—and from this fact has sprung the modern tortoise industry. We shoot them just for the hell of it, hack them to pieces, drive over them with cars, collapse their burrows with off-road vehicles, stomp them to death with our livestock, and starve them to death by running cattle and sheep on their range—beasts which devour all the forage tortoises crave.

Until the 1970s, nobody much cared. Then something new happened—all those federal laws about endangered species and all those new agency mandates demanding environmental impact statements. I take a closer look at the faces in the room and realize I am sitting with the new servants of the desert tortoise. Hacks from the BLM who suddenly must kowtow to a damn reptile because their beloved steers are destroying it. Biologists from game and fish departments who thought they would spend their days keeping tab on deer and antelope and bighorns and elk who now are here fat with statistics about tortoises and management plans for them.

I no longer like the room. I once had a professor who patiently explained to me that I never could stomach any cause once it had become successful. Well, there must be worse sins. I have heartily supported every law, executive order, and petition to salvage the dwindling biological wealth of the earth. But now I see what happens to every decent impulse in my society: they become that ugly thing, government.

I get up and wander out of the meeting. Downstairs time has passed, but mercifully everything has remained the same. I sidle up to the long bar which stares out at the river and sip whiskey as the afternoon sinks toward evening. Others at the bar amuse themselves with electronic poker games and there is an air of deadly serious sport about the place.

The hills bordering the valley bear the traces of Indian trails where tribes of the Colorado once raced north and south for hundreds and hundreds of miles exporting war, magic, and a few hard goods. The ground cover is scant and low and this is not the kind of country most Americans call beautiful. They storm across it in their machines from Phoenix, Tucson, Los Angeles, and more distant parts of the Republic so they, like their fathers before them, can gather at the river. And once here they drink, gamble and feed.

At my back, hunkered over the crap tables, poker tables, and slots, are my fellow citizens hailing from most states in the Union. And none of them are likely to waste much time pondering the plight of a desert tortoise. The couples, ma and pa, tend to wear matching caps and windbreakers. In the gift shop, there is practically nothing to read for sale. The casino seems dedicated to low-level aerobics and no slackers are allowed to pull back and pursue thick books or falter from doing their reps with the slot machines. No pain, no gain.

Denouncing this place would be like coming out against the tooth fairy.

I join the line for the casino cheap feed, a chicken dinner (all you can eat) for a few bucks. Three Indians sit down at my table. Their faces are brown, blank, and immobile. We chomp on the fried birds and slowly words drone from their mouths. They are Navajos working on a stretch of nearby railroad track and they find the casino curious and the food a great bargain. I arrived in the Southwest in 1957 and according to the best reports, my tablemates seized some local turf in the fifteenth century. But we seem to have wound up in the same situation. We ogle the girls, speculate on the thrill of guzzling a few drinks, and say the casino is a real pleasant puzzler.

The Southwest is a place where almost everyone slips their moorings and just drifts. The cities and towns are ugly, the populace footloose, the crime frequent, the marriages disasters, the plans pathetic gestures, the air electric with promise. There is so much space and so much ground that no one can for a single moment doubt the basic American dream that it is possible to make something worthwhile of life. Everything a desert tortoise is—calm, a homebody, long-lived, patient, quiet—the people of the Southwest are not. We don't stay in our burrows much anymore or limit our motion to the cycle of the sun. Just across the road from the casino, a huge powerplant belches smoke into the sky. The facility burns coal mined on Black Mesa in the Navajo and Hopi country of northern Arizona, coal that is piped as a slurry the 278 miles to Laughlin. The electricity generated here is then flashed outward to blaze in the lights of Southern California. Such grids of energy and rivers of energy-flows are the stuff of life in the Southwest and they do not produce a state of mind that cottons to the issue of endangered species. It is not that we are too busy building the empire to tend to details but simply that we are too busy running to ever look back at the ghosts trailing behind us or down at the ground where the writhing beasts shudder with their last convulsion of life. We haven't got time for this nature stuff. We were born to drive, not park.

Poems

For the most part, the character and quality of the western experience past and present has been limned in prose, not poetry—with such notable exceptions as John G. Neihardt. Perhaps the hugeness of both its history and its landscape discouraged poetic expression for much of the postwar era. Two exceptions that test the rule—if rule it is—are Gary Snyder and the late William Stafford.

GARY SNYDER

"Hay for the Horses"

He had driven half the night
From far down San Joaquin
Through Mariposa, up the
Dangerous mountain roads,
And pulled in at eight a.m.
With his big truckload of hay
   behind the barn.
With winch and ropes and hooks
We stacked the bales up clean

Stacking Hay, Ryan Ranch, Uinta County, Wyoming. 1903. Photograph. Wyoming State Museum, Cheyenne. Stimson Collection.

702 Stacking Hay, Ryan Ranch, Uinta Co., Wyo.

To splintery redwood rafters
High in the dark, flecks of alfalfa
Whirling through shingle-cracks of light,
Itch of haydust in the
    sweaty shirt and shoes.
At lunchtime under Black oak
Out in the hot corral,
—The old mare nosing lunchpails,
Grasshoppers crackling in the weeds—
"I'm sixty-eight" he said,
"I first bucked hay when I was seventeen.
I thought, that day I started,
I sure would hate to do this all my life.
And dammit, that's just what
I've gone and done."

PHILIP PEARLSTEIN.
*White House Ruins,
Canyon de Chelly—
Morning.* 1975. Oil on
canvas. 60 x 60 in.
Frumkin/Adams Gallery,
New York.

WILLIAM STAFFORD

"Witness"

This is the hand I dipped in the Missouri
above Council Bluffs and found the springs.
All through the days of my life I escort
this hand. Where would the Missouri
meet a kinder friend?

On top of Fort Rock in the sun I spread
these fingers to hold the world in the wind;
along that cliff, in that old cave
where men used to live, I grubbed in the dirt
for those cool springs again.

Summits in the Rockies received this diplomat.
Brush that concealed the lost children yielded
them to this hand. Even on the last morning
when we all tremble and lose, I will reach
carefully, eagerly through that rain, at the end—

Toward whatever is there, with this loyal hand.

WALLACE STEGNER

From *The American West as Living Space*

Fittingly, we end this compilation with a 1987 selection from the work of the West's dominant literary figure, Wallace Stegner. These quietly trenchant reflections on what is false and transient and what is true and permanent about the legacy of the West will do to take along, as the mountain men used to say.

There are thousands more federal employees in the West than there are cowboys—more bookkeepers, aircraft and electronics workers, auto mechanics, printers, fry cooks. There may be more writers. Nevertheless, when most Americans east of the Missouri hear the word "West" they think "cowboy." Recently a documentary filmmaker asked me to be a consultant on a film that would finally reveal the true West, without romanticizing or adornment. It was to be done by chronicling the life of a single real-life individual. Guess who he was. A cowboy, and a rodeo cowboy at that—a man who had run away from his home in Indiana at the age of seventeen, worked for a year on a Texas ranch, found the work hard, made his way onto the rodeo circuit, and finally retired with a lot of his vertebrae out of line to an Oklahoma town where he made silver-mounted saddles and bridles suitable for the Sheriff's Posse in a Frontier Days parade, and spun yarns for the wide-eyed local young.

Apart from the fantasy involved in it, which is absolutely authentic, that show business life is about as typically western as a bullfighter's is typically Spanish. The critics will probably praise the film for its realism.

See America. Welcome to Montana. Oil on canvas. 28 x 22 in. WPA. © Wheatley Press, Los Angeles, CA.

I spend this much time on a mythic figure who has irritated me all my life because I would obviously like to bury him. But I know I can't. He is a faster gun than I am. He is too attractive to the daydreaming imagination. It gets me nowhere to object to the self-righteous, limited, violent code that governs him, or to disparage the novels of Louis L'Amour because they are mass-produced with interchangeable parts. Mr. L'Amour sells in the millions, and has readers in the White House.

But what one can say, and be sure of, is that even while the cowboy myth romanticizes and falsifies western life, it says something true about western, and hence about American, character.

Western culture and character, hard to define in the first place because they are only half-formed and constantly changing, are further clouded by the mythic stereotype. Why hasn't the stereotype faded away as real cowboys became less and less typical of western life? Because we can't or won't do without it, obviously. But also there is the visible, pervasive fact of western space, which acts as a preservative. Space, itself the product of incorrigible aridity and hence more or less permanent, continues to suggest unrestricted freedom, unlimited opportunity for testings and heroisms, a continuing need for self-reliance and physical competence. The untrammeled individualist persists partly as a residue of the real and romantic frontiers, but also partly because runaways from more restricted regions keep reimporting him. The stereotype continues to affect romantic Westerners and non-Westerners in romantic ways, but if I am right it also affects real Westerners in real ways.

In the West it is impossible to be unconscious of or indifferent to space. At every city's edge it confronts us as federal lands kept open by aridity and the custodial bureaus; out in the boondocks it engulfs us. And it does contribute to individualism, if only because in that much emptiness people have the dignity of rareness and must do much of what they do without help, and because self-reliance becomes a social imperative, part of a code. Witness the crudely violent code that governed a young Westerner like Norman Maclean, as he reported it in the stories of *A River Runs through It*. Witness the way in which space haunts the poetry of such western poets as William Stafford, Richard Hugo, Gary Snyder. Witness the lonely, half-attached childhood of a writer such as Ivan Doig. I feel the childhood reported in his *This House of Sky* because it is so much like my own.

Even in the cities, even among the dispossessed migrants of the factories in the fields, space exerts a diluted influence as illusion and reprieve. Westerners live outdoors more than people elsewhere, because outdoors is mainly what they've got. For clerks and students, factory workers and mechanics, the outdoors is freedom, just as surely as it is for the folkloric and mythic figures. They don't have to own the outdoors, or get permission, or cut fences, in order to use it. It is public land, partly theirs, and that space is a continuing influence on their minds and senses. It encourages a fatal carelessness and destructiveness because it seems so limitless and because what is everybody's is nobody's responsibility. It also encourages, in some, an impassioned protectiveness: the battlegrounds of the environmental movement lie in the western public lands. Finally, it promotes certain needs, tastes, attitudes, skills. It is those tastes, attitudes, and skills, as well as the prevailing destructiveness and its corrective, love of the land, that relate real Westerners to the myth.

David Rains Wallace, in *The Wilder Shore,* has traced the effect of the California landscape—the several California landscapes from the Pacific shore to the inner deserts—on California writers. From Dana to Didion, the influence has been varied and powerful. It is there in John Muir ecstatically riding a storm in the top of a two-hundred-foot sugar pine; in Mary Austin quietly absorbing wisdom from a Paiute basketmaker; in Jack London's Nietzschean supermen pitting themselves not only against society but against the universe; in Frank Norris's atavistic McTeague, shackled to a corpse that he drags through the 130-degree heat of Death Valley; and in Robinson Jeffers on his stone platform between the stars and the sea, falling in love outward toward space. It is also there in the work of western photographers, notably Ansel Adams, whose grand, manless images are full of the awe men feel in the face of majestic nature. Awe is common in that California tradition. Humility is not.

Similar studies could be made, and undoubtedly will be, of the literature of other parts of the West, and of special groups of writers such as Native Americans who are mainly western. The country lives, still holy, in Scott Momaday's *Way to Rainy Mountain*. It is there like a half-forgotten promise in Leslie Marmon Silko's *Ceremony,* and like a homeland lost to invaders in James Welch's *Winter in the Blood* and Louise Erdrich's *Love Medicine*. It is a dominating presence, as I have already said, in the work of Northwest writers.

Western writing turns out, not surprisingly, to be largely about things that happen outdoors. It often involves characters who show a family resemblance of energetic individualism, great physical competence, stoicism, determination, recklessness, endurance, toughness, rebelliousness, resistance to control. It has, that is, residual qualities of the heroic, as the country in which it takes place has residual qualities of the wilderness frontier.

Those characteristics are not the self-conscious creation of regional patriotism, or the result of imitation of older by younger, or greater by lesser, writers. They are inescapable; western life and space generate them; they are what the faithful mirror shows. When I wrote *The Big Rock Candy Mountain* I was ignorant of almost everything except what I myself had lived, and I had no context for that. By the time I wrote *Wolf Willow,* a dozen years later, and dealt with some of the same experience from another stance, I began to realize that my Bo Mason was a character with relatives throughout western fiction. I could see in him resemblance to Ole Rölvaag's Per Hansa, to Mari Sandoz's Old Jules, to A. B. Guthrie's Boone Caudill, even to the hard-jawed and invulnerable heroes of the myth. But I had not been copying other writers. I had been trying to paint a portrait of my father, and it happened that my father, an observed and particular individual, was also a type—a very western type.

Nothing suggests the separateness of western experience so clearly as the response to it of critics nourished in the Europe-oriented, politicized, sophisticated, and anti-heroic tradition of between-the-wars and postwar New York. Edmund Wilson, commenting on Hollywood writers, thought of them as wreathed in sunshine and bougainvillea, "spelling cat for the unlettered"; or as sentimental toughs, the boys in the back room; or as easterners of talent (Scott

Fitzgerald was his prime example) lost to significant achievement and drowning in the La Brea tar pits.

Leslie Fiedler, an exponent of the *Partisan Review* subculture, came west to teach in Missoula in the 1950s and discovered "the Montana face"—strong, grave, silent, bland, untroubled by thought, the face of a man playing a role invented for him two centuries earlier and a continent-and-ocean away by a French romantic philosopher.

Bernard Malamud, making a similar pilgrimage to teach at Oregon State University in Corvallis, found the life of that little college town intolerable, and retreated from it to write it up in the novel *A New Life*. His Gogolian antihero S. Levin, a Jewish intellectual, heir to a thousand years of caution, deviousness, spiritual subtlety, and airless city living, was never at home in Corvallis. The faculty he was thrown among were suspiciously open, overfriendly, overhearty, outdoorish. Instead of a commerce in abstract ideas, Levin found among his colleagues a devotion to the art of fly-fishing that simply bewildered him. Grown men!

If he had waited to write his novel until Norman Maclean had written the stories of *A River Runs through It,* Malamud would have discovered that fly-fishing is not simply an art but a religion, a code of conduct and language, a way of telling the real from the phony. And if Ivan Doig had written before Leslie Fiedler shook up Missoula by the ears, Fiedler would have had another view of the Montana face. It looks different, depending on whether you encounter it as a bizarre cultural artifact on a Montana railroad platform, or whether you see it as young Ivan Doig saw the face of his dependable, skilled, likable, rootless sheepherder father. Whether, that is, you see it from outside the culture, or from inside.

In spite of the testimony of Fiedler and Malamud, if I were advising a documentary filmmaker where he might get the most quintessential West in a fifty-six-minute can, I would steer him away from broken-down rodeo riders, away from the towns of the energy boom, away from the cities, and send him to just such a little city as Missoula or Corvallis, some settlement that has managed against difficulty to make itself into a place and is likely to remain one. It wouldn't hurt at all if this little city had a university in it to keep it in touch with its cultural origins and conscious of its changing cultural present. It would do no harm if an occasional Leslie Fiedler came through to stir up its provincialism and set it to some self-questioning. It wouldn't hurt if some native-born writer, some Doig or Hugo or Maclean or Welch or Kittredge or Raymond Carver, were around to serve as culture hero—the individual who transcends his culture without abandoning it, who leaves for a while in search of opportunity and enlargement but never forgets where he left his heart.

TIMOTHY O'SULLIVAN. *Shoshone Falls, Snake River, Idaho.* Wheeler Survey. National Archives.

INDEX

Page numbers in italic denote illustrations. Colorplate numbers are given in parentheses.

GEORGE FISKE. *Glacier Point, Yosemite, CA.*
c. 1890's. Photograph. Yosemite National
Park Research Library.

PHOTO CREDITS

The editors are grateful to the many people who contributed the illustrations for this book. We offer a
special thanks to Elizabeth Cunningham at The
Anschutz Collection; Richard Ogar at Bancroft
Library, University of California at Berkeley;
Elizabeth Holmes at Buffalo Bill Historical Center;
and Sandra Hilderbrand at The Gilcrease Museum.

Color Illustrations: Art Resource, NY: cpls. 9, 11, 13,
14, 16, 18, 22, 30, 51, 74, 104; Photo, Dean Beasom:
cpl. 98; Photo, J. Borkowski: cpl. 49; Brooklyn
Museum: cpl. 12—Dick S. Ramsay Fund, A. Augustus
Healy Fund, Frank L. Babbott Fund, Ella C.
Woodward Memorial Funds, Gift of Daniel M. Kelly,
Gift of Charles Simon, Charles Smith Memorial Fund,
Caroline Pratt Fund, Frederick Loeser Fund, Augustus
Graham School of Design Fund. Bequest of Mrs.
William T. Brewster, Gift of Mrs. W. Woodward
Phelps, Gift of Seymour Barnard, Charles Stuart Smith
Fund, Bequest of J.A.H. Bell, John B. Woodward
Memorial Fund, Bequest of Mark Finley. 76.79;
Copyright © 1984 Hubert Shuptrine: cpl. 81;
Copyright © 1984 S. Hill Corporation: cpl. 116; Photo,
Ed DeFell: cpl. 92; Photo, Melville McLean: cpl. 32;
Photo, Bill McLemore Photography: cpl. 77; Photo,
James O. Milmoe: cpls. 34, 50, 54, 70, 73, 82, 86, 87,
90, 91, 93, 94, 95, 112; Nefsky/Art Resource, NY: cpl.
44; Photo, D. O'Looney: cpl. 55; Photo, Robin
Stancliff: cpls. 2, 3, 108, 109, 111, 113; Photo, Charles
Swain: cpls. 29, 45, 53; Photo, Nick Williams: cpl. 72.

Black and white illustrations: Archive Photos: pp. 75,
196, 217; Archive Photos/American Stock: p. 184; Art
Resource, NY: pp. 54, 105; The Bettmann Archive: p.
182; eeva-inkeri: p. 376; James O. Milmoe: pp. 83, 97,
267; UPI/Bettmann: p. 270.